KT-548-448

TRAGICALLY I WAS AN ONLY TWIN –
The Complete Peter Cook

TRAGICALLY
I WAS AN ONLY TWIN

The Complete Peter Cook

━━━

EDITED BY WILLIAM COOK

arrow books

Published by Arrow Books in 2003

10

First published in the United Kingdom in 2002 by Century

Arrow Books Limited
The Random House Group Limited
20 Vauxhall Bridge Road, London SW1V 2SA

Random House Australia (Pty) Limited
20 Alfred Street, Milsons Point, Sydney,
New South Wales 2061, Australia

Random House New Zealand Limited
18 Poland Road, Glenfield
Auckland 10, New Zealand

Random House South Africa (Pty) Limited
Endulini, 5A Jubilee Road, Parktown 2193, South Africa

The Random House Group Limited Reg. No. 954009

www.randomhouse.co.uk

A CIP catalogue record for this book
is available from the British Library

Papers used by Random House are natural, recyclable
products made from wood grown in sustainable forests.
The manufacturing processes conform to the environmental
regulations of the country of origin.

ISBN 0 09 944325 2

Typeset in Garamond by MATS, Southend-on-Sea, Essex
Printed and bound in Great Britain by
Cox & Wyman Ltd, Reading, Berkshire

Contents

Acknowledgements

Grateful thanks to the following institutions, which first staged, broadcast, recorded or published much of this material: broadcasters and producers – ATV, the BBC, Channel 4, Hat Trick Productions, ITV, LBC and Talkback; record companies – Atlantic, BBC Worldwide, Capitol, Castle Classic, Decca, EMI, Essex Music, Funny Business, Island, Laughing Stock, Parlophone, Polydor, Pye Cube, Speaking Volumes, Springtime, Transatlantic and Virgin Records; publishers – Methuen, Mandarin, Penguin, Samuel French, Souvenir Press and Virgin Books; periodicals – the *Daily Mail*, the *Evening Standard*, *Golf World*, *Private Eye*, the *Sheffield & North Derbyshire Spectator*, the *Sunday People*, the *Sunday Times*, *TV Times* and *Vox*.

Grateful thanks, too, to the following individuals, who helped to write or perform this material: Clive Anderson, Rowan Atkinson, Peter Bellwood, Alan Bennett, John Bird, Clive Bull, Michael Burrell, John Cleese, Barry Fantoni, Fenella Fielding, Peter Fincham, John Fortune, Sheila Hancock, Richard Ingrams, Ludovic Kennedy, John Lloyd, Rory McGrath, Bernard McKenna, Jonathan Miller, Chris Morris and Dan Patterson; Timothy Birdsall, Dudley Moore, John Wells and Kenneth Williams.

Grateful thanks for their help in compiling this collection to the following institutions: the BBC, the British Library, the Cambridge Footlights, the Associated Newspapers reference library, *Golf World*, the *Literary Review*, Martine Avenue Productions Inc, the Press Association, *Private Eye* and Radley College.

And grateful thanks, too, for all their invaluable help, to all of the following individuals: Julian Alexander, Mark Booth, Leo Cooper, Barry Fantoni, Rena Fruchter, Bruce Hunter, Richard Ingrams,

Hilary Lowinger, Tony Money, Harry Porter, Geoffrey Strachan, Tony Rushton, Roger Wilmut, Cy Young – and Lin Cook, without whom this book never would have been published.

∿

Part of the proceeds from the sale of this book are going to support the following charities:

In memory of Peter Cook.

The Peter Cook Foundation for young adults with learning disabilities.
The Peter Cook Memorial Fund, Pembroke College, Cambridge.

In memory of Dudley Moore.
The Dudley Moore Research Fund for Progressive Supranuclear Palsy.
Music For All Seasons, taking music into facilities where people are confined.

Introduction

Not only for his friends, who were lucky enough to enjoy his strange comic genius in private, but also for his fans, who could only marvel at his virtuoso humour in public, on the stage or screen, Peter Cook was simply the funniest man they'd ever encountered. Nearly ten years after his premature death, eight years short of his old age pension, his reputation as the most talented comedian of his generation shows no sign of shrinking. 'He had funniness in the same way that beautiful people have beauty,'[1] said Stephen Fry. And whenever he was being funny, there was always something quite beautiful about Peter Cook.

Half a lifetime since his greatest triumphs, Cook's old colleagues still struggle to define the daft magic of working with him, while modern comics far too young to have enjoyed his work first time around still talk about him like an up and coming contemporary, rather than someone who became famous more than forty years ago. John Cleese called him Peter Amadeus Cook, after Mozart, another prodigy whose precocious creativity felt like the gift of an unusually cheerful god. 'Most of us would take six hours to write a good three-minute sketch,' says Cleese. 'It actually took Peter three minutes to write a three-minute sketch. I always thought he was the best of us, and the only one who came near being a genius, because genius, to me, has something to do with doing it more easily than other people.'[2]

David Dimbleby wasn't joking when he called Cook 'the funniest Englishman since Chaplin.' And Cook wasn't joking when he replied 'Well, this is no time for false modesty.'[3] But that easy genius could trip Cook up, as well as liberating him. When Cook succeeded, he succeeded big time. When he failed, he failed just as big. Cook's compulsion to create instant comedy in real time made him the world's best chat show guest, but it also made him the world's worst chat show host – as he demonstrated on his own chat show, *Where Do I Sit?*, which was cancelled after just three episodes.

Cook wasn't a natural actor. He wasn't even an outright satirist. He never wrote any plays or novels. So what was all the fuss about? Well, this book should give you a good idea. It's a collection of Cook's finest writing, from university revues via West End and Broadway shows, on to television, and into his own private world of unpublished poetry and occasional late-night radio phone-ins. Of course it's not a compendium of everything he ever did. Despite the idle image he acquired, Cook produced far more comedy than you could fit into one book. But it is a pretty comprehensive summary of the comic creations that made us laugh for more than thirty years, from the late Fifties to the early Nineties, and still make us laugh today.

Peter Cook's comic rise and fall has become the stuff of showbiz legend. How he wrote a hit West End show for Kenneth Williams while he was still an undergraduate at Cambridge University. How, fresh out of college, he became a star in *Beyond the Fringe* – the wittiest revue that Britain, or America, had ever seen. How he opened Britain's first satirical nightclub, The Establishment, importing American comic Lenny Bruce, launching Australian comic Barry Humphries, and resurrecting that Great British comic, Frankie Howerd. How he saved Britain's sharpest satirical paper, *Private Eye*. How he starred alongside Dudley Moore in three series of *Not Only But Also* – arguably the greatest sketch show ever broadcast by the BBC. How he freed British comics from a monotonous diet of trite, hand-me-down one-liners by injecting into live comedy an intelligent, imaginative parody of Anglo-Saxon attitudes that previously had been the province of the comic novel. And how, at an age when most comics are just starting out, he seemed to throw it all away, splitting up with Dudley Moore for a life of solitary drinking in front of the television.

Well, that's the legend, and like most legends, there's some truth in it. But like a lot of legends, it's hardly the whole story. True, Cook's later routines could never hope to match the frantic creativity of his twenties, when he played a leading role in Britain's funniest stage show, television series, nightclub and magazine. Yet although Cook didn't sustain his youthful vigour into middle age, he continued to create brilliant comedy – but only when he wanted to, that's all. And even though he never dominated another decade as he dominated the Sixties, it's surprising how many of the gems in this selection are from the Seventies, Eighties and even Nineties.

Cook's dark Derek & Clive duologues with Dudley Moore, recorded in the late Seventies, didn't command the same broad appeal as their earlier head-to-heads as Pete & Dud, but they still attracted a huge following, and became an anarchic landmark in British comic history. Derek & Clive's coarse, repetitive vocabulary – as revolutionary, in its own way, as the working-class naturalism of Harold Pinter's early dramas – inspired the scatological outpourings of the Alternative Comedy boom. And yet Cook's classic, timeless sketches on Channel 4's variety flagship, *Saturday Live*, in the mid-Eighties, effortlessly eclipsed the trendy, strident stand-up of the Thatcher years. His virtuoso performance, in the early Nineties, on Clive Anderson's Channel 4 chat show, as four diverse comic archetypes, oozed all the careless elegance of an entertainer at the very top of his game. And *Why Bother?* – the Radio Three series he made less than a year before his death, with Brass Eye creator Chris Morris – was one of the best things he ever did. After his twentysomething triumphs, the quantity of his comedy certainly tailed off pretty steeply, but right up until his death, the quality was still there.

Cook was a miniaturist. He was happiest when working with just a couple of characters. His speciality was a conversation of only several minutes duration. His quick-fire creativity didn't lend itself to longer, more structured genres. 'Most of my ideas are only worth about five minutes,' he admitted.[4] And if his preference was for brief monologues or duologues, it's this preference that has determined the contents of this book. It's a book to read, rather than a set of scripts to perform, and so I've kept pieces with more than two characters to a minimum. Unless you're one of those rare people who prefer reading plays to watching them, you'll find them hard to picture on the page. Some of Cook's comedy is too visual to really work in print. Other stuff is too dated. But usually, I was pleasantly surprised how comfortably Cook's humour translated from tape into type. My main problem wasn't what to include, but what to leave out.

Another pleasant problem was which versions to chose. Improvisation played a major role in many of Cook's best sketches, and his original scripts were often mere starting points for the impromptu performances that followed. Cook quickly tired of repeating work verbatim, so his most popular and frequently reprised sketches resemble variations on a theme, rather than repeat performances of one definitive version. The different demands of stage and screen also played a part. Some sketches started off onstage, were adapted for television, and then returned to the live stage, mutating en route. Cook's early performances tend to be more compact and punchy. His later performances are often far more ragged, but feature some glorious fresh asides. The written and live versions share the same relative pros and cons.

These comparisons are interesting, but only up to a point. My solution to this finitely fascinating dilemma has been completely inconsistent. I've selected some scripts and some transcripts, some early debuts and some later encores. To show how Cook's comedy changed, I've included an early and a late version of one of his most famous sketches, Interesting Facts – but that's all. This is a book for people who don't know so much about Cook's comedy, as well as those who already do, and I reckon only a truly dysfunctional Peter Cook fan would want every available version of every sketch in one volume.

Naturally, no collection of Cook's writing can recreate the special quality of his performances – but sadly, more often than not, the writing is all that's left. Neither of Cook's Cambridge Footlights shows was recorded for posterity, and although the West End shows he wrote for Kenneth Williams, *Pieces of Eight* and *One Over the Eight*, were both released as LPs, they've long since been deleted. You can still buy audio recordings of *Beyond the Fringe, Derek & Clive* and *Why Bother?* Some *Pete & Dud* and *Not Only But Also* sketches, plus some of Cook's monologues as raincoat fantasist EL Wisty, are also still for sale on cassette tape. However, if you want to actually see Cook perform, rather than just listen to him, you'll have your work cut out. Hardly any of the material in this book is generally available on DVD or VHS.

This alone is an awful shame, but even worse – far worse – most of *Not Only But Also*, Cook and Moore's comic masterpiece, was systematically destroyed by the BBC itself, as part of a routine policy of recycling old master tapes. They even threw away some of the scripts. 'Has there ever been such corporate vandalism from a company claiming to represent the best of British Broadcasting?'[5] asks Eric Idle. In 1990, twenty years after the final series, the BBC belatedly cobbled together six half-hour compilations, under the suitably apologetic title of *The Best of What's Left of Not Only But Also*, consisting partly of footage retrieved from the archives of foreign TV companies who'd bought the show from the BBC in the Sixties and fortunately treated it with more reverence than the people who'd flogged it to them. Cook and Moore selected some of these salvaged sketches for a video of the same name, but despite this partial restoration, much of the *Not Only But Also* material in this book only survived on soundtrack, and some now only exists in script form, published here for the first time.

Plenty of other stuff in this book actually works better on the printed page than it does on the small screen. When he made *Peter Cook Talks Golf Balls*, Cook had less than a year to live, but the script is sublime, and in print you can imagine him performing it in his prime, rather than the twilight of his life. Like Sixties playwright Joe Orton, who shared Cook's verbal dexterity, and his impudent delight at the inherent idiocy of language, Cook's characters specialise in saying funny things rather than doing funny things – which may be why neither of these men ever really cracked the movies. Like Orton's, Cook's writing was often far more literary than theatrical, and these idiosyncratic scripts are better reread than re-enacted. Cook was never much cop at reading other people's lines – and vice versa.

Remarkably, for a man who became notorious for rarely writing anything, quite a lot of this book was never even intended for performance – like the column he wrote for the *Daily Mail*, 'Peter

Cook's Monday Morning Feeling', or his surreal sports reports for its sister paper, London's *Evening Standard*. There's even an EL Wisty monologue in here, written for the *TV Times*, which works just as well as the ones he performed on ITV over fifteen years earlier. Cook's work for *Private Eye* became increasingly intermittent, but from 1964 to 1966 he was a key player in an inspired ensemble, alongside John Wells and Richard Ingrams. 'The Seductive Brethren', included here, was one of the pieces Cook had a main hand in – a yarn that reads not so much like swinging Sixties satire, more like *Tristram Shandy*.

If you try to think of another entertainer who shares some of Cook's unique prose style, and the parallel universe he created, the names that first spring to mind aren't those of performers, but writers. And although he's often regarded as an innovator – of Sixties Satire, Seventies Surrealism or even Eighties Alternative Comedy, Cook's comedic kindred spirits were born long before him, not soon after. True, it's hard to imagine *That Was the Week That Was*, *Monty Python's Flying Circus* or *The Comic Strip* without his influence, but Cook's own influences stretch far further back. Cook adored *The Goon Show*, Spike Milligan's delirious, demented Fifties radio serial, with Michael Bentine, Harry Secombe and Peter Sellers – who later appeared with Cook and Moore on *Not Only But Also*. At boarding school, Cook would feign illness so he could listen to Milligan's meisterwerk in the school sanatorium on Friday nights. Yet the writers whom his work most resembles aren't from the twentieth century, but the nineteenth – eminent Victorians like Edward Lear and Lewis Carroll. Cook devoured *Alice In Wonderland* as a child, and as an adult he flattered Carroll with imitation – performing Carroll's sinister nonsense poem, 'The Walrus and the Carpenter', in *Not Only But Also*, and playing the Mad Hatter in a BBC adaptation of Carroll's book, directed by Cook's old *Beyond the Fringe* partner, Jonathan Miller. He also performed Lear's poem, 'Uncle Arly', in *Not Only But Also*, with a cricket – his nonchalant nickname for critics – perched upon his nose. Indeed, the more you hear of Cook's humour, the less he seems to share with his satirical peers. 'He wasn't interested in satire at all,' says Alan Bennett. 'He was interested in being funny.'[6] Like all true artists, in any field, Cook was always far more keen on creating his own fantastic other world than in changing the workaday world around him.

Richard Ingrams categorised Cook as a conservative anarchist, but Cook's anarchy had nothing to do with overthrowing the state. He had no real quarrel with a system. 'The idea that he had an anarchic, subversive view of society is complete nonsense,' says Jonathan Miller. 'He was the most upstanding, traditional upholder of everything English and everything establishment.'[7] Cook supported worthy causes like Amnesty International, but he always recoiled from the sort of comedy that wants to bring down governments. He even felt sad for Margaret Thatcher when she left Downing Street.

Cook's comedy is curiously abstract. His characters aren't rooted in our reality, but inhabit a bizarre hinterland, where a man can spend a lifetime trying to teach worms to talk, flowers to walk, or ravens to fly underwater. Nevertheless, there is one aspect of his output that is entirely realistic. Like him, his principal alter egos, from Pete & Dud to Derek & Clive, from EL Wisty to Sir Arthur Streeb-Greebling, are typically, unapologetically English. And like all Englishmen, they're all helpless prisoners of that terribly English caste system called social class. EL Wisty is trapped in the working class, without education or opportunities, but with a wistful yearning for adventure and achievement that he can never hope to fulfil. 'I could have been a judge,' says Wisty, 'but I never had the Latin.' Conversely, Sir Arthur Streeb-Greebling is trapped in the upper class, blessed with the wealth to do whatever he wants – but not the sense to know that what he's doing is totally futile. 'I've learned from my mistakes,' says Sir Arthur, 'and I'm sure I can repeat them.'

Cook usually played down any autobiographical elements in his work. Yet there are personal echoes scattered throughout his writing which make this book a sort of accidental autobiography – albeit one that's been elaborated and distorted by an unruly imagination. Sir Arthur Streeb-Greebling is a quintessential colonial old buffer, not unkind but disconnected, buried in his own work, and alienated from his fellow man. Peter went to boarding school while his father, like his grandfather, worked in remote colonies.

Peter's father, Alec, served the British Empire with discreet distinction in Nigeria, Gibraltar, Libya and the West Indies, and was decorated by the Queen. But although Alec's lengthy absences did not diminish the lifelong fondness that endured and flourished between father and son, the immense distances that separated them during Peter's formative years weren't just geographical, but emotional. Alec did manage to see Peter briefly as a baby, but Peter's first clear memory of Alec wasn't until Peter was already seven, when Alec came back from Nigeria to the family home in Torquay after the Second World War. 'I didn't quite know who he was and I was told he was my father,' remembered Peter, a few years before Alec died. 'So we shook hands and agreed on it – he was a total stranger to me.'[8]

Peter's parents then had two daughters, Sarah and Elizabeth, but they were both significantly younger. Sarah, the elder of the two, wasn't born until the last months of the war. Peter's war began when he was a toddler, and didn't end until the year he went to boarding school. Hitler had made a father-shaped hole in the most formative years of Peter's childhood. (Cook had two daughters of his own, Lucy and Daisy, with his first wife, Wendy Snowden, whom he met at Cambridge. He subsequently married Judy Huxtable, and finally Lin Chong, becoming a stepfather to her daughter, Nina.)

Cook's comedy is littered with opaque but tantalising clues. When Sir Arthur Streeb-Greebling tells Ludovic Kennedy that his son, like him, was raised by goats, it sounds like yet another typical piece of Peter Cook tomfoolery – until you remember that the name for a female goat is Nanny. Cook's preoccupation with bees, worms, ants, and all manner of creepy crawlies appears equally random, until you reflect that in his father's absence, in the enforced matriarchy of wartime, one of his earliest male role models was the gardener. In Alec's home movies, Peter follows him around the garden, copying his spadework with a tiny toy trowel.

However the inspiration for Cook's most enduring creation was biographical, not autobiographical. His idiot savant, EL Wisty, was a character he refined throughout his adult life, but this weird park bench philosopher was initially directly based on a real, living person – Arthur Boylett, the butler at Radley College, Peter's public school. 'He was an elderly man, mostly cheerful, with a dry manner of speech,'[9] recalls Jonathan Harlow, a school friend of Peter's. Another school friend, Michael Bawtree, paints a more Dickensian picture. 'He would dress in shabby tails, grey waistcoat and tie, like a waiter in some Hungarian nightclub.'[10] Boylett was capable of wry humour. Once, he swept some breadcrumbs off the dinner table and straight into a prefect's lap. 'Well, they were your crumbs,' he said.

But Boylett's speciality was his supernatural pronouncements. He told Cook he'd seen stones move and twigs hover – that he'd sold a moving stone, and that hovering twigs might well be valuable. 'I thought I saw it move,' quickly became Cook's catchphrase, and Radley's. 'The more pathetic and simple the poor man was, the more Peter saw in him an absurdist superhero,' claims Bawtree.[11] Perhaps that was because in this caricature Cook had accidentally unearthed a hidden aspect of himself. 'I've always felt very closely identified with that sort of personality,'[12] he said, ten years later, at the very height of his fame. However successful we become, perceived Cook, there's still a bit of Boylett in all of us – bald, grey and stooping, sweeping up the crumbs from the tables of younger people, destined for better things.

When Cook went up to Cambridge, to Pembroke College, like his father, he left Boylett behind, but he took his impersonation with him, and even though his new friends had never met the subject of his impression, Cook's Boylett soon became an even bigger hit at university than he had been back at school. First at Pembroke College Smoking Concerts (whose quaint title harked back to the days when smoking was a male-only occupation), then at Footlights Smokers, and finally at *Last Laugh*, the 1959 annual Footlights revue, directed by John Bird, which launched Peter's professional show business career. Renamed Mr Grole, and finally EL Wisty, this wise fool was Cook's first small-screen success.

Boylett may have been a sleeping partner in Cook's comic apprenticeship, but there were many other willing collaborators who helped him along the way. Adrian Slade and John Fortune both wrote sketches with Cook for the Cambridge Footlights. Alan Bennett, Jonathan Miller and Dudley Moore all wrote with Cook for *Beyond the Fringe*. Cook was by far the busiest writer in this historic comic quartet. Moore reckoned Cook wrote two thirds of their celebrated script, while Bennett and Miller shared the remaining third between them – although modestly, and erroneously, Moore didn't seem to count his own immaculate musical compositions, which bound this ground-breaking show together. All the *Beyond the Fringe* sketches in this book are primarily by Cook, but comedy is a promiscuous business, and simply by performing his sketches with him, time after time, Bennett, Miller and Moore couldn't help but contribute to Cook's authorship.

It was a similar story when Cook and Moore paired up, in *Not Only But Also, Behind the Fridge* and *Derek & Clive*. As their unique comic counterpoint developed, Dudley's input increased, but even in their later series he still estimated that he only wrote around 30 per cent – less than half of Peter's contribution. However Moore's special relationship with Cook can't be measured in mere percentages. Even in the early days, when Cook did most of the writing, Moore still played a crucial part. 'Trying to collaborate, let alone compete with Peter was always incredibly difficult,' recalled Cook's *Private Eye* writing partner, John Wells. 'Any intrusion into his world sounded flat and trivial.'[13] Unlike the competitive, self-confident *Eye* scribes, Moore didn't contend with Cook – he complemented him, and this balance was what gave their partnership such poise. 'Dudley's humour is not very largely verbal,' says Bennett. 'He's much more of a clown and mugs a lot and he's a very good person to bounce off.'[14] 'It's very hard to imagine the success of the show,' adds Miller, 'without Dudley's talent as a performer.'[15]

Even when he wasn't writing, Dudley's presence liberated Peter. At last, Cook finally had a partner to write for, a more cute and fragile character – a contrast and an antidote to Cook's more aloof and condescending style. Moore's populist, sympathetic appeal opened up countless fresh comic opportunities. Comics tend to be high status, like Cook, saying things you've never thought of – or low status, like Moore, saying the things you're already thinking, but never dared to say. Like Lennon & McCartney, whom they knew, and in some respects resembled, Cook's caustic wit was balanced by Moore's softer home-spun humour. Cook, like Lennon, could be too acerbic to appease mainstream opinion, while Moore, like McCartney, was sometimes too saccharine to win critical acclaim. When Cook decided to write the script for *Bedazzled* on his own, rather than with Moore, the result was stunning, but slightly cold and strangely stilted. On the other hand, after his first two blockbusters, Moore was unable to keep on landing the leading roles that his personable dramatic skills deserved, and most of his later films are probably best forgotten, as indeed they often are. Yet as long as Cook and Moore stayed together, audiences had someone astute and sharp to marvel at, and someone warm and homely to relate to. 'There was a sort of sweet, proletarian cuddlesome quality about Dudley,' says Miller, 'and then a lot of this strange, lunatic patrician obsession on the part of Peter.'[16] In Cook and Moore's comedy, the proletarian and the patrician collided. In a decade where old class barriers were being rapidly demolished, it was a partnership that captured the spirit of its changing times.

'If there is a class divide in Britain,' declares Joe McGrath, who produced and directed the first series of *Not Only But Also*, 'they straddle it.'[17] Cook was middle-class and privately educated. Moore was working-class and state-educated. A piano prodigy with a club foot, he'd won an organ scholarship to Oxford University, but ostensibly, Oxbridge was all they had in common. Even physically, they were poles apart. Cook was over six foot, Moore was barely five. Yet despite these differences, or maybe even because of them, when they were together they behaved like brothers.

'It was an extraordinary friendship those two men had,' explains Barry Humphries. 'It was impossible to get a word in. They were constantly – not just on camera, but all the time – improvising.'[18] Yet as well as a meeting of like minds, this extraterrestrial friendship was a personality clash, too. There's a strong streak of malice in most great comedy, and there was certainly a potent sadomasochistic side to Cook and Moore's teamwork. This undercurrent helped to give their intimate alliance its momentum, but eventually it tore it apart. As long as this theatre of cruelty was safely confined to the stage, Cook's ritual humiliation of Moore made for uncomfortable yet riveting viewing, but inevitably, Cook's unremitting baiting affected him in the end. Ironically, *Not Only But Also* was originally earmarked as a star vehicle for Moore, with Cook merely cast as Moore's main guest. It was Moore who made Cook an equal partner, and gave him star billing, even reversing the title of the show from *Not Only Dudley Moore But Peter Cook* to *Not Only Peter Cook But Dudley Moore*.

When their smash-hit American stage show, *Good Evening*, finally closed in 1975, Dudley decided to stay in America, with his new American wife, Tuesday Weld, and try to conquer Hollywood alone. He succeeded, albeit briefly, starring opposite Bo Derek in *10* and Liza Minnelli in *Arthur*, and becoming, for a while, one of America's biggest movie stars. Cook returned to London, and a quieter life of comparative inactivity and obscurity. Moore occasionally came back to Blighty, teaming up with Cook on three *Derek & Clive* LPs, and one last, dreadful, movie – *The Hound of the Baskervilles*, which Kenneth Williams, its co star, called 'a hotchpotch of rubbish', and which Barry Took described as one of the worst films ever made. However their partnership was effectively finished by Moore's decision to make his home in the USA.

Moore's crucial role in Cook's creative process can best be measured by the slowdown of Cook's output after their boyish partnership fell apart. From Laurel & Hardy to Galton & Simpson (Hancock and Steptoe) or Clement & La Frenais (*The Likely Lads* and *Porridge*) an awful lot of the greatest comedy has been written or performed in tandem, and although Cook wrote some great comedy after he and Moore went their separate ways, he wrote it far less frequently.

Opinions differ as to whether Cook resented Moore's Hollywood success. Some friends said no. Others said it was inevitable. 'He must have been jealous,' concurred Dudley. 'He never said a word about any of my films – never even said he'd seen

PETER COOK

them.'[19] In fact, Peter had told Dudley he liked *Arthur 2*, but not
Arthur – a particularly backhanded compliment, if not a deliberate
insult. *Arthur* was a big hit, *Arthur 2* wasn't, and whatever the
relative merits of each movie, Dudley's role was pretty much the
same in both of them. To be fair to Peter, the drunken anti-hero
that Dudley created bore more than a passing resemblance to his
partner. When a fan collared the duo in a restaurant, and asked
Moore what had inspired his character in *Arthur*, Cook simply
pointed at himself, and Moore realised he was right.

Whatever he really felt about Moore's success, at the very least
Cook must have been exasperated by the invidious comparisons in
the press. Whenever he was asked about Dudley's triumph, Peter
was usually charming, and sometimes he cracked a joke, but
inevitably these ripostes were more prominently reported than his
more affectionate tributes – and inevitably, these jokes looked far
more harsh in print. And Dudley wasn't above firing back the odd
public rebuttal from the other side of the pond. 'I hadn't thought
of this relationship as an extraordinary marriage,'[20] said Dudley but
as in many marriages, it was the more antagonistic party who was
hit hardest by the divorce. 'I had no idea that I was so cruel to the
little bugger,'[21] Cook told John Wells.

In Cook's later, more tender years, this aggressive streak tailed
away, and this helped him repair his friendship with Dudley. Lin
told Dudley that Peter had mellowed, and their friendship
resumed, on a more conciliatory basis. It was bound to take some
time for Dudley to overcome his old suspicion and establish a new
sense of trust, but sadly, for both men, time was rapidly running
out. Dudley outlived Peter by seven years, but his last few years
were plagued by illness. 'I adored Dudley,'[22] said Cook, in his last-
ever interview, and although that affection wasn't always apparent,
it was utterly sincere. They died an ocean apart, but at least they
parted on good terms.

However, apart from the odd chat show or benefit gig, Cook and
Moore never worked together again, and Cook never sought
another partnership in which he could recreate the chemistry
they'd shared, although plenty of other people worked with him on
his less and less frequent yet still enthralling flights of fancy. Yet the

vast reservoir of Cook's humour never ran dry. Bernard McKenna helped him write the award winning *Peter Cook & Co*, for ITV. John Lloyd, Rory McGrath and Peter Fincham all collaborated on *A Life In Pieces*, Sir Arthur Streeb-Greebling's tangential ruminations on the Twelve Days of Christmas, for BBC2. Chris Morris didn't just put the sublimely pompous questions in Sir Arthur's radio series, *Why Bother?* He also assembled five eight-minute episodes from eight hours of tape. And like a latterday Boylett, small-hours radio presenter Clive Bull played an unwitting role in the cycle of Cook's creativity, as Cook telephoned Bull's nocturnal talk show, masquerading as a maudlin Norwegian fisherman called Sven. Cook's career had come full circle. Thirty years after his comic advent, performing illicit routines to entertain his schoolmates, he'd returned to cracking private jokes for his own amusement and the benefit of a few friends.

Well, almost – but not quite. It's tempting to see Cook's career as a standard rise and fall, but the facts aren't quite as tidy as all that. Cook's early work was incredibly surefooted for one so young – fluent, self-assured and wonderfully, life-enhancingly funny. And his output was prolific. Yet much of this early material was inevitably fairly superficial – ideal for a short sketch. His later work was often more sustained, and although it was more hit-or-miss, the hits have a comi-tragic depth that his early crowd-pleasers sometimes lack. 'The sensationalism of the surface has gone,' argues John Bird. 'The word which comes to mind is maturity.'[23] And he's right. Cook's mature output has a remarkable melancholic realism, especially as Sir Arthur Streeb-Greebling, in those late memoirs, *A Life In Pieces* and *Why Bother?* Even as Sven, his glum Scandinavian émigré, a practical joke performed incognito, for no fee, for the benefit of a handful of insomniacs, Cook seemed to be playing a living character, rather than looking for easy laughs. 'There is no striving for effect,' adds Bird, 'no whiff of marketing.'[24] But Cook didn't just excel in the short-wave wilderness of local radio. Bird singles out Cook's TV interviews with Clive Anderson, broadcast less than two years before his death, for special praise. 'There is in the invention and the performance of these late pieces a sense of complete command. He knows these characters from the inside and through experience, yet this supposedly is the work of a disappointed drunk who gave up the promise of a golden talent.'[25]

In the early Eighties, Cook became increasingly reclusive. He famously turned down an invitation from David Frost to dine with Prince Andrew and Sarah Ferguson, by quipping that he'd be busy watching television that night. He acquired an encyclopedic knowledge of virtually every conceivable programme – however banal or obscure – but sport, politics and old black-and-white movies were his favourites. He enjoyed frequent trips abroad, to go golfing, or to be somebody's guest of honour at some festival, or simply to go on holiday, but otherwise he rarely ventured far beyond the confines of his Hampstead home. One of the many projects that never quite materialised was a documentary called *Peter Cook's London*, solely about the short stretch of pavement between his newsagent and his front door. He loved to bet, and he'd bet on almost anything – and even when the stakes were small, he'd go to quite ridiculous lengths to win. He supported Tottenham Hotspur, but he often backed the opposition, to give himself a consolation prize if Spurs lost. Then he'd be happy either way. In *Who's Who*, he listed his recreations as gambling, gossip and golf – in that order. Cook's self-imposed absence from the public eye is usually reported in solemn, sombre terms, but though his lifestyle surely had its ups and downs, it actually sounds like rather good fun. After all, it was hardly as if he had to work for a living. 'I suppose I have some regrets,' he would quip, 'but I can't remember what they are.'

Indeed, whether you or I think his retreat from public life sounds heavenly, or hellish, or – probably – a bit of both, is beside the point. Peter Cook had no responsibilities to his paying public. His family? Yes. His friends? Maybe. But his fans? Hardly. What he did was his business. And if, during the second half of his life, he decided to do a fraction of the work he could have done, well that was his business too. After all, he'd already achieved more in his youth than most folk manage in a lifetime. If he chose to spend his middle age in a state of semi-retirement, then that was up to him. He could have died terribly young, like Timothy Birdsall, the gifted cartoonist with whom he first performed his famous 'Not An Asp' sketch, for Footlights, in 1959, killed by leukemia, just four years later, at twenty-six. He could have packed it in at twenty-one, and joined the Foreign Office, like his father. He could have carried on, and carried on, and lost his flair for being funny. He did none of these things. And if his lifestyle hastened his demise, then that's his affair, not ours. The people who knew him are thankful for the friendship he gave them. People like me who never knew him should be thankful for the fun he gave us, even though its main charm is that it reads like something he did merely to amuse himself. Significantly one of the working titles for the auto-biography he never wrote was *Retired and Emotional.*

But that's what always happens when someone like Peter Cook does something really remarkable. The rest of us can't bear the idea that it might just be a one-off. We want them to do it again and again. Perhaps we don't want our heroes to retire, because that reminds us that their lives are finite? And if our heroes' lives are finite, where does that leave the rest of us? As the journalist Christopher Hitchens observed, 'the number of vivid and active years in any given life are depressingly and remarkably few.'[26] Maybe Cook was simply smart enough to realise he could have more fun in his inactive years playing instead of working. 'To the end of his life,' remarked Michael Palin, 'he remained the funniest man in the room.'[27] And whether that room was a television studio or his own living room was a minor detail about which he became increasingly indifferent.

'One thinks of one of the stock characters in an old-fashioned Western,' wrote Alan Bennett. 'The doctor who's always found in the saloon and whose allegiance is never quite plain. Seldom sober, he is cleverer than most of the people he associates with, spending his time playing cards with the baddies but taking no sides. Still, when the chips are down, and slightly to his own surprise, he does the right thing. But there is never any suggestion that, having risen to the occasion, he is going to mend his ways in any permanent fashion. He goes on much as ever down the path to self-des-truction, knowing that redemption is not for him – and it is this that redeems him.'[28]

'I've just met the funniest man in England,' John Bird told his fellow student, Eleanor Bron, after his first encounter with Cook. Billy Connolly went even further. 'Peter was the funniest man in the world,' he told Eric Idle. Cook's comic gift was a public blessing. It could also be a private curse. 'It was almost an affliction,' says Bird. 'At least my mind can take a rest from that. I can and do turn it off when I go home and you felt that somehow Peter never did and never could.'[29] 'The weight's off my shoulders now,' said Peter Ustinov, formerly the world's funniest man, after seeing Cook perform. 'The accolade, for what it's worth, belongs to him. It's a vast relief.'[30]

Private Eye soon spotted that a talent for perpetual hilarity could quickly become a poisoned chalice, in an uncannily prophetic comic strip that depicted a thinly disguised Cook as a bright young satirist called Jonathan Crake. 'Young Jonathan Crake shows early talent for raising laughs in School Play,' ran *The Eye*'s accompanying commentary. 'At Cambridge his gay, witty little pieces in all the mags have the chaps in fits. Sparkling revue, *Short Back & Sides*, mentions Prime Minister. Crake acclaimed as biting young satirist of our time. Instantly besieged by press, TV men seeking views on Monarchy, Mr Gaitskell, Common Market. Stage, TV, film offers pour in. Featured in five glossies simultaneously. Opens satirical nightclub in Fulham. Strain becomes terrific. Cannot open his mouth without everyone collapsing at brilliant satirical comment. Moral – humour is a serious business.' Ironically, this perceptive and prescient cartoon was drawn by Willie Rushton, who performed at The Establishment, appeared on *Not Only But Also*, and once even stood in for Dudley Moore in *Beyond the Fringe*. Rushton's cartoon concludes with Crake copying out old jokes from back issues of *Punch*. Of course Cook never would have ended up like Crake, but there's some truth in the portrait of a man imprisoned by his Midas touch.

Unlike most comics, Cook didn't ration his comedy, hoarding it for commercial gain, to be auctioned to the highest bidder. Rare, for any performer, he really was just as funny offstage. Most of the folk who knew him well can recall informal, improvised riffs and rants which were even funnier than the scripted pieces he performed in public. 'This flow of uncontrollably inventive stuff came out of him,' says Jonathan Miller, recalling the first time he met Cook, over lunch, to form *Beyond the Fringe*. 'It was impossible to compete with him. You couldn't actually participate. There was no room for one to get in. One simply had to be an audience.'[31]

For Cook, laughter perhaps was a shield – a device to deflect attention, not invite it. Some of those who knew him longest confess surprise, even a sense of bafflement, at how very fond they grew of him, without ever really getting close to him at all. 'One felt sometimes,' says Barry Humphries, 'that Peter was not going to stop being funny for a minute in case you got a little bit too close to him.'[32] 'When he was not being funny,' adds Michael Bawtree, 'he was surprisingly awkward.'[33] In 1967, at the peak of his powers, Cook told Bawtree he was seeing a psychiatrist. Bawtree asked him why. 'I have been talking in other people's voices for so long that, when I don't, I have a terrible sense of emptiness,' replied Cook. 'I don't know who I am.'[34]

Cook's comedy was never a megaphone for his opinions or his personality. It was far more elusive than that. The more you read or hear or see of it, the less you sense you know. But this distance gave his sense of fun a purity that set it apart from the here today gone tomorrow topicality of conventional satire. His wit was a state of mind. It was simply the way he was. And it was completely different from anything that had come before. 'He expresses an aspect of the human condition which no Englishman had ever really explored before,' wrote Auberon Waugh. 'The philosopher king who has decided that wisdom reduces all philosophy to its elements of the absurd.'[35]

This book's title is Cook's own, one of many unrealised projects that include *The Burberry Apes*, *The False Passport Office* and *Dr Jekyll & Mrs Hyde* – his screenplay about Queen Victoria's Gynaecologist, inspired by Richard Ingrams, whose grandfather performed that regal role. 'Pulsars are small and immensely heavy,' runs one of his unused one-liners, 'and remind me strangely of my first wife.' 'There are limitations to the human mind,' runs another, 'as this series will prove.' This book proves there were few limits to Cook's incredible sense of humour. In fact, the only real limit was the amount he could be bothered to write down. 'I have never attempted to achieve my potential,' he declared, defiantly, in his last television interview. 'What could be worse than to achieve one's potential so early in life?'[36]

But Cook did achieve his potential. He achieved it twice. Once when he was young, full of casual self-confidence – and again when he was older, on a smaller scale, with more difficulty, but also with a sombre subtlety that lingers even longer in the mind's eye. This book charts both achievements, but above all it's a book to laugh at, not admire. 'He didn't crave being taken seriously or being clever, although he was desperately clever,' says Mel Smith, who appeared with him at the Nether Wallop Arts Festival, as a couple of portly synchronised swimming lesbians, in bathing costumes and rubber hats. 'He craved laughter.'[37] And not just his own. Unlike quite a lot of comedians, Cook actually enjoyed watching other comics – even those, especially those, like Rory Bremner, Julian Clary or Harry Enfield, who were younger than him, more fashionable than him, and replacing him in fame's spotlight. Cook didn't seem to care. He loved to laugh. He loved making other people laugh. And if this book makes you laugh, then, like Peter Cook, it will have achieved its full potential. Now read on.

Chapter One
Before the Fringe

'Even at school, Peter had a greater capacity for making people laugh than anyone I have ever met,'[1] recalls Cook's school friend, Michael Bawtree. Yet even in the springtime of his life, Peter Cook was just as happy making his friends laugh in private as he was making his fans laugh in public, and many of Cook's funniest school performances never even made it onto the relatively private platform of the Radley school stage. 'Every trivial incident was a source of mirth,' remembers Bawtree. 'Occasionally, we would chip with our own additions to the theme, and Peter would enjoy that too, building on them, improving them, turning them inside out, as he did his own.'[2] 'He had a tremendous ear, and caught at once distinctive speech patterns and vocabulary,' confirms another school friend, Jonathan Harlow. 'He could spin a whole fantastic web of absurdity from the merest thread of an idea or phrase.'[3] But it was a fair while before these absurdist fantasies found a forum beyond the privacy of Cook's own social circle.

Meanwhile, Cook steadily matured into a fine young comic actor. The school magazine, *The Radleian*, ignored his dramatic debut, as a Socialist duchess in *Stuck In A Lift*, but praised the 'gusto' of his Doll Common in Ben Jonson's *The Alchemist*, and adored his 'wonderful display of virtuosity' as Don Adriano de Armado in Shakespeare's *Love's Labours Lost*. Finally, in 1955, his penultimate year at Radley, Cook started staging his own revues, playing a dung beetle, demonstrating a fascination for insects that would last throughout his life, and audaciously lampooning the BBC bigwigs who'd been invited along to cast a critical eye over Radley's amateur dramatics.

Cook was equally busy as a writer, earning the princely fee of four guineas for a published contribution to *Punch*. However several of his other compositions were rather more serious affairs. 'Bric-a-Brac', which won Radley's Medrington short story trophy, was an atmospheric spine-chiller about a young woman babysitting for a sinister couple who run a junk shop. Cook also tried his hand at science fiction. 'I wrote a terrible play about Martians landing in a suburban part of England,' he recalled, a quarter of a century later. 'I can't remember what happened, except that the Martians behaved more normally than the people in suburbia.'[4] A more po-faced effort was his distinctly fascistic tract advocating the sterilisation of the 'unintelligent working class'. 'People say I've got more reactionary in my old age,' observed Cook. 'In fact, I've moved to the left from my very solid Nazi position at the age of sixteen.'[5]

Yet Cook's most ambitious and successful schoolboy creation wasn't remotely Nazi in its sentiments. Remarkably, *Black & White Blues* was a full length musical, with words by Cook and music by his fellow prefect Michael Bawtree. Written entirely in rhyming couplets, it wasn't performed by the pupils, but by puppets, all made and operated by the school's Marionette Society. The plot concerned an evangelical jazz musician called Mr Slump, who travels to darkest Africa to cure the natives of their cannibalism. Cook produced the show, provided the voice for Mr Slump, and even carved some of the marionettes. 'It really was quite appalling,'[6] recollected Cook in 1980, but his production was such a hit that the society cut a disc of the show in a proper recording studio, and sold several hundred 78rpm records around the school. 'A great success,' proclaimed *The Radleian*, in a warmly complimentary review.

Cook left Radley in 1956, and would have done National Service, had he not fortuitously failed the entrance test. 'I had been allergic to feathers and I had grown out of it, but it was still on my medical record,' he explained. 'They asked me if I would sneeze if I was in a barrack room full of feather pillows – an unlikely situation, I thought – but I said, truthfully, "yes," because everybody sneezes at some time or another, and so I was unsuitable.'[7]

While his school friends sneezed in their barrack rooms, Cook spent a year in France and Germany. The official purpose of this sabbatical was to polish his French and German, in preparation for his Modern Languages degree at Cambridge, but it also provided Cook with the inspiration for his seminal Establishment club. 'I went to these awful satirical nightclubs. I thought they were terribly bad. I spoke reasonably good French and German, and I thought the humour was very juvenile.'[8] Yet it made him wonder why there was nothing similar in London. 'For a long time my major fear was that somebody would do the obvious and start it before me.'[9] It can't have been that obvious, because nobody did, and five years later he opened London's first satirical nightclub. The British Army's loss was British Comedy's gain.

In 1957, Cook went up to Pembroke College. He appeared in Pembroke's own plays and smokers, but it wasn't until 1958 that he dared to approach the famous Cambridge Footlights. The Footlights president, Adrian Slade, persuaded Cook to reprise his impression of Mr Boylett, the Radley butler, at a Footlights smoker, and by 1959 Cook had become an integral member of the Footlights team. Together with John Bird, he successfully campaigned to open up Footlights to female performers, bringing in Eleanor Bron, with whom he continued to perform, off and on, throughout his career.

Cook's big break was the 1959 annual Footlights revue, *Last Laugh*, directed by John Bird. Set in a nuclear bunker, Bird's show was a self-conscious left-wing revolt against the cheerful but complacent house style of previous Footlights revues. Booed and badly reviewed, the unfinished first night lasted four and a half hours. Wisely, Bird trimmed the show before the second night, and this slimmed-down version won a rave review from Alistair Cooke, of *Letter From America* fame, in *The (Manchester) Guardian*. 'The whole show is acted with never a fumbling line or gesture,' wrote Cooke. 'If the West End does not soon hear of John Bird, Patrick Gowers, Geoff Pattie and Peter Cook, the West End is an ass.' Geoffrey Pattie was bound for Westminster, not the West End, as a minister under Margaret Thatcher, but Alistair Cooke was at least a quarter right. Shaftesbury Avenue would hear of Peter Cook soon enough.

Cook contributed eight sketches (three written with Adrian Slade) many of which had already raised the roof in Pembroke revues. Although sufficiently irreverent to fit *Last Laugh*'s anti-establishment theme, their satire was much less heavy-handed, and went down far better than *Last Laugh*'s other, more polemical pieces. Bird subsequently had the good grace to confess that Cook's sketches were the only ones that were actually funny.

Cook already had an agent, Donald Langdon, who'd signed him up after seeing his smash hit Pembroke show, *The Jolly Good Show Involving (To A Considerable Extent) Music With Some Richly Comic Interspersions By The Merry Pembroke Players (Theatrical People) And Some Women Too (Two) Revue*. One of those two women was Eleanor Bron. Langdon brought along Michael Codron, who'd already taken a previous Cambridge revue, Bamber Gascoigne's *Share My Lettuce*, into London's West End. Codron had booked Kenneth Williams to star in his next West End show, and he realised straight away that Cook's Boylett was a perfect fit for Williams' stage persona. Incredibly, he commissioned Cook to write Williams' show.

That show was *Pieces of Eight*, which Peter wrote at his family home during the summer holidays. The script was mainly based on Cook's own Footlights sketches, which had been rejected by the BBC. However there was some new material, including a sketch suggested by Williams himself, about a xenophobe in a continental restaurant, and several sketches by an obscure playwright called Harold Pinter. 'I was very cross at the time because royalties were awarded on the amount of time your contributions took up,' said Cook. 'Harold Pinter's contributions took up an immense amount of time because he'd written all these pauses into his sketches.'[10]

Pieces of Eight opened at Oxford's New Theatre (where Bird's material from *Last Laugh*, retitled *Here Is the News*, had flopped in a previous professional production) and, bolstered by good local reviews, advanced via Liverpool's Royal Court and Brighton's Theatre Royal to London's Apollo Theatre, where it ran for 429 performances. Seems the West End wasn't an ass, after all. Cook returned to Cambridge on a retainer of £100 per week.

Cook's final Cambridge show was *Pop Goes Mrs Jessop*, his farewell revue for Footlights – of which he was now President – which clashed horribly with his final exams. Despite some frantic last-minute cramming, Cook's Finals were merely a qualified success – he only managed a Lower Second. But *Pop Goes Mrs Jessop* was an unqualified triumph – even better than *Pieces of Eight*. Of the twenty-nine sketches, there were only six Cook didn't have a hand in, and just seven joint compositions, several of which were written with the show's director, John Wood, now better known as John Fortune. The rest were Cook's alone. *Pop Goes Mrs Jessop* wasn't politically earnest, like Bird's *Last Laugh*, but it still had a disrespectful bite. Tellingly, one of Peter's few political pieces sent up the Campaign for Nuclear Disarmament, satirising left-wing politics, rather than the Right.

Meanwhile, the success of *Pieces of Eight* had prompted a commission for a sequel – *One Over the Eight*, with Sheila Hancock (who'd been in the ill-fated *Here Is the News*) replacing Fenella Fielding opposite Kenneth Williams. Jonathan Miller criticised the 'tinselly dance routines, a-fidget with glow paint and fishnet' that Williams' producers wrapped around Cook's scripts, like gaudy foil around bitter chocolate. 'The bony outlines of Peter's contributions were softened by their gay commercial setting,'[11] complained Miller, but Cook was always actually rather fond of dancing girls in fishnets. 'I found nothing wrong with it,' said Cook. 'I loved that revue. It was old-fashioned revue, which was eventually killed off by *Beyond the Fringe*.'[12]

BLACK & WHITE BLUES
(Radley, 1956)

Take the tiger for example,
For all he wants to do
Is to seize his chance
And make a pounce
On you and chew a sample.

Oh Lord deliver us
From animals carnivorous.
Oh Lord protect us,
Let them not select us.

The python can't be beaten,
He has the strength of ten,
If he gets irate
He'll strangulate
Three men and then he'll eat them.

Oh Lord deliver us
From animals carnivorous.
Oh Lord protect us,
Let them not select us.

Now take the case of the cheetah,
Who feels no sense of shame
As he lies and waits
For time and place
To maim a dame and eat her.

Oh Lord deliver us
From animals carnivorous.
Oh Lord protect us,
Let them not select us.

Now the scorpion keeps on trying,
His method is so slick.
He can seldom fail
To flick his tail,
So quick, one prick, you're dying.

Oh Lord deliver us
From animals carnivorous.
Now we're enlightened
We're far more frightened.

GUILTY PARTY
(*Last Laugh*, Cambridge Arts Theatre, 1959)

(A police Constable and a police Inspector are in a police station. There is a knock at the door.)

INSPECTOR: See who that is, will you Constable?

CONSTABLE: It's a Mr Prone, Inspector.

(*Enter Mr Prone*)

PRONE: Mr James Prone, Inspector, of Hawkchurch. I'm sorry to disturb you at this hour.

INSPECTOR: Not at all. Won't you come in? What can we do for you?

PRONE: I'd just like you to ask me a few questions.

INSPECTOR: Questions? What about? There's nothing wrong, is there?

PRONE: It's purely a matter of routine, Inspector. There's no need for you to feel alarmed, but you are in fact investigating a murder.

CONSTABLE: Murder? But this is horrible!

PRONE: Yes, Constable. Murder is an ugly thing. That is why I should be extremely grateful if you would help me bring the culprit to bear by asking me one or two simple questions.

INSPECTOR: But I don't understand, Mr Prone. What kind of questions?

PRONE: Like 'Did I know Mrs Tallow well?'

INSPECTOR: Only slightly. You used to play bridge together, but you don't mean to say . . .

CONSTABLE: Is she? She's not! She can't be! She isn't?

PRONE: I'm afraid so. She was found stabbed this morning at 11.31 between the third and the fourth rib.

CONSTABLE: Poor Annie! Why did it have to be her? She never hurt a soul!

INSPECTOR. There, there Constable. You mustn't upset yourself. You must excuse my Constable, Mr Prone. You see, he was much closer to her than I was. But I still don't see what this horrible thing has got to do with you.

PRONE: Where was I this morning between eleven and twelve?

INSPECTOR: You were . . . you were . . . now look here Prone, you're not suggesting . . .

PRONE: I'm not suggesting anything, Inspector. I only want you to get the facts. Now, where was I this morning?

INSPECTOR: I expect you were in the garden – gardening the beds.

PRONE: And did anybody see me gardening?

INSPECTOR: How the devil should I know? Now see here Prone, I don't like your tone.

PRONE: I'm only trying to do your job, Inspector. It isn't always a very pleasant one.

INSPECTOR: I'm sorry. I'm sorry about that. It's just that you got me on the raw. Of course we'll do all we can to help you.

PRONE: And now the Constable would like to ask me a few questions.

CONSTABLE: I . . . I . . . Oh dear, I don't know what to say.

INSPECTOR: Can't you see the Constable's overwrought? He's not himself.

PRONE: Let me see your shoe, Constable. Just as I thought. This speck of gravel is identical to the gravel in Mrs Tallow's drive. You were there this morning, weren't you? Come clean now, Constable.

CONSTABLE: Oh, what's the use? You're too clever for me.

INSPECTOR: Is this true, Constable? Why didn't you tell me?

CONSTABLE: I thought you'd be angry.

PRONE: And what were you doing there?

INSPECTOR: Look here, Mr Prone – you're not implying that the Constable is in some way implicated in this affair?

PRONE: I am implying that at 11.15 precisely, he looked in through the large bay window and saw the murder done – correct, Constable?

CONSTABLE: I'm sorry, Inspector. I couldn't help it.

PRONE: Yes, Constable. I'm afraid the game's up. You looked through that window and saw me stab Mrs Tallow.

CONSTABLE: Yes, yes. I confess.

PRONE: In that case I'm afraid you have no alternative but to arrest me for wilful murder, and of course to caution me.

INSPECTOR: But this is absurd, Mr Prone. We can't possibly arrest you on such tenuous evidence as that. There's no proof.

PRONE: The Constable saw me do it.

INSPECTOR: I don't see what that's got to do with it. He's not a reliable witness. He'd soon break down under skilful cross examination.

PRONE: My fingerprints are all over the murder weapon.

INSPECTOR: But this is all purely circumstantial evidence. Besides, we haven't found it.

PRONE: Look in my pocket.

INSPECTOR: I haven't a search warrant. No, no. I tell you, Mr Prone, we haven't got enough to go on. For instance, what motive did you have?

PRONE: Money. She left me all she had. It's no use, Inspector. You must arrest me.

INSPECTOR: Are you threatening me, Prone? I warn you, I have influential friends in the force.

PRONE: Constable, take me into custody.

INSPECTOR: You'll never get away with this.

PRONE: I'm coming quietly, Inspector. You always get your man in the end.

INSPECTOR: Alright, you devil, Prone. You win. But let us have one last drink before you go. Won't you join us?

PRONE: Not while I'm on duty, thank you. Wait, what were those white crystals you put in those glasses? Give them to me!

INSPECTOR: Too late, Prone. We'll never live to run you in. You see, that was cyanide we drank.

(*The Inspector dies*)

CONSTABLE: Oh no, Mr Prone – you'll never hang.

(*The Constable dies*)

PRONE: Damn, damn, damn. I've slipped through their fingers again. I should never have allowed them that last drink. I thought it was the perfect crime, but like all murderers, I made that one fatal mistake.

(First performed by Peter Cook, David Johnson and Ray Mitchell)

MR GROLE
(*Last Laugh*, Cambridge Arts Theatre, 1959)

(Mr Grole, played by Peter Cook, is sitting in a railway compartment, with a cardboard box upon his knees. Mr Smith, played by Timothy Birdsall, is sat opposite him, reading *The Times*.)

GROLE: I've got a viper in this box, you know.

SMITH: Really? Good gracious me!

GROLE: Oh, yes. It's not an asp.

SMITH: Oh good.

GROLE: It looks rather like an asp, but it's not one. Oh, no – I wouldn't have an asp.

SMITH: I suppose not.

GROLE: Some people can't tell the difference between an asp and a viper. More fool them, I say.

SMITH: Yes.

GROLE: Cleopatra had an asp, but I haven't.

SMITH: I'm glad of that.

GROLE: I don't want one, either. I'd rather have a viper, myself.

SMITH: That's alright then.

GROLE: Not that they're cheaper to run. If anything, the viper is more voracious than the asp. My viper eats like a horse.

SMITH: Like a horse, eh?

GROLE: Oh, yes – I'd like a horse. I've nothing against horses. I could do with a horse. Mind you, you'd never get it into this box.

SMITH: It would be difficult.

GROLE: Oh, no – it's not a horse box. You'd never cram a horse into this little box. A viper, yes – but a horse, no.

SMITH: I realise that.

GROLE: It's just about right for a viper, this box – or an asp. It's no good for a fish. I'd never put a fish in here. You'd get the water seeping through in no time. It's only cardboard, you see. It's not waterproof.

SMITH: I see.

GROLE: I wish it were – but it isn't, so there it is. Oh no, they haven't waterproofed cardboard yet. Or if they have, they haven't told me. Or if they've told me, I've forgotten – one of the two. Oh no, there's no fish in this box. I haven't got a toad in here, if that's what you're thinking. You won't catch me with a toad. I can't abide toads. Vipers devour toads, I'm glad to say. Serpents hear through their jaws, you know. It's the bone structure that does it. Oh yes, good gracious, yes – there's no doubt that it's the bone structure.

SMITH: Yes, I suppose it would be.

GROLE: I haven't got a bee in here. I don't know why you should think I've got a bee. There's no bee in here, thank you. You'd hear it buzzing if there was. I'll put the box to your ear. Then you'll soon know if there's a bee in there or not. Here, have a listen.

SMITH: No thanks, I quite believe you.

GROLE: No fangs? There's no fangs on a bee, if that's what you mean. I've never seen a bee with fangs. Vipers have fangs. They're very fangy creatures, and so are asps.

SMITH: I said no thanks, not fangs.

GROLE: Oh, not fangs. Oh no, not fangs. Bees never have fangs. You'll find they sting, but they never bite. Serpents bite. Don't run away with the idea that serpents sting. Serpents bite and bees sting. Oh yes, that's the way to tell the difference between a bee and a serpent.

BALANCE OF TRADE
(*Pieces of Eight*, Apollo Theatre, London, 1959)

A: Good morning. I wonder if you could help me. I bought this shirt from you two days ago.

KENNETH: Why, so you did, sir. I remember you well. A sleeveless Gazytex, wasn't it – with the built-in deodorant.

A: That's right.

KENNETH: And what can I do for you now sir?

A: Well, I'm afraid it seems to be coming apart a bit at the sleeve.

KENNETH: Aha, just as I thought! Could I see it, sir? Yes indeed, this sleeve is very much the worse for wear – and not only the sleeve, sir. You notice the whole fabric of the shirt is rotten.

(*Kenneth tears the shirt apart.*)

KENNETH: One pull and the whole thing falls to pieces.

A: Yes, it does seem a bit weak.

KENNETH: You're so right, sir. You're so right. That's the great weakness of our shirts, their great weakness.

A: Is it?

KENNETH: Oh, yes. The main trouble with your shirt is that it's ill made, shoddy. You have every right to complain.

A: I'm glad you agree.

KENNETH: Oh, I know a bad shirt when I see one. We've had a lot of complaints about our shirts recently – every one of them justified. If I'm not much mistaken here comes another one now. I served this gentleman yesterday. Good morning sir.

B: Now look here, I bought this wretched shirt from you yesterday.

KENNETH: You did indeed, sir. You did indeed, and now you've found it wanting, I'll be bound.

B: Yes, well it does seem to be giving way at the seams.

KENNETH: That's just what this gentleman was saying about his shirt. Might I see yours a moment, please sir?

(*Kenneth tears the shirt apart.*)

KENNETH: There you are, just the same trouble, shoddy workman-ship, poor material – they all add up to a fifth-rate shirt.

B: You certainly couldn't get much worse than that.

KENNETH: Now that's where you're wrong, sir. We have in stock at the moment a wide selection of goods infinitely inferior to yours. I'd like to warn you against this one, for example.

A: I must say, it's very good of you to be so frank with us.

KENNETH: Looks very smart, doesn't it? Nice texture, pretty pattern – looks very handsome in the packet. There's just one thing, though – no back.

B: I say, that's a bit off.

KENNETH: A very big bit, if you ask me. Here's another one to avoid if you can – Arthur's patent drip-dry Scrofulin. It's very hard-wearing. In fact, nobody's managed to wear one for more than an hour. It gives you a most unpleasant rash. And here's one of our most notorious products. It's made of non-iron Spyrex. That means there's no iron in it, and it is absolutely guaranteed to shrink – very rapidly, too. I remember last week ten of our customers were strangled in a thunderstorm.

A: Good God! But why are you telling us all this?

KENNETH: We always like to be completely honest with our clients. And besides, you must understand there is a perfectly good reason for the wretched quality of our product.

B: I don't see how there could be.

KENNETH: You see, we employ a lot of very old men in the factory.

A: Oh, I see – a kind of charity.

KENNETH: That's the way we look at it. Of course, a lot of them are very decrepit, so what with that, the poor lighting and the long hours that they have to work, small wonder our shirts are substandard. We don't pay them much, either. I expect that has something to do with it, too.

B: Do you mean to say you make old men do all the work, in these frightful conditions?

KENNETH: Oh, no. We have old women, too. They're cheaper still. But let's get back to your shirts. I expect you'd both like your money back?

B: I certainly would.

A: That goes for me.

KENNETH: Quite right, sirs – quite right. If I was in your position, I'd do the same.

A: I'm glad you're being reasonable about it.

KENNETH: But there's just one difficulty. Our firm never refunds money. It's our strictest rule.

B: But this is ridiculous.

KENNETH: On the contrary, sir – there's a very good reason for it.

A & B: Oh?

KENNETH: Namely our excessive lust for profits – and that explains our prices, too. Despite the wretched quality of our shirts, I think you'll find them a good deal dearer than most.

A: But that's dishonest.

KENNETH: Well, look at it our way, sir. You lose, but on the other hand, we gain. That's the balance.

B: Seems rather a poor balance to me.

A: But this is absurd. Surely the least you can do is to refund our money.

KENNETH: No, sir. I think you'll find I can do even less than that. However, our firm is always glad to replace defective goods.

A: You mean you'll exchange these shirts for us?

KENNETH: Certainly, sir.

B: Well, that's alright, then.

KENNETH: Now, let me see – those shirts, sir. Yours is in the blue, is it – and yours the red? That's right. Now, let me see. Yes, that's the ticket. I suggest you take this one and you have this one.

(*Kenneth swaps the two shirts.*)

A: But that's ridiculous. You're just swapping them over.

KENNETH: Precisely, sir – precisely.

B: But they're both torn to shreds.

KENNETH: Exactly, sir. I think it's a very fair swap – no advantage, one way or the other.

A: Do you mean to say you're not prepared to give us new shirts?

KENNETH: Yes, sir. It's the profits I'm thinking of.

B: I don't care who you're thinking of. This is the most despicable business I've ever come across. You deserve to be locked up.

KENNETH: Oh yes, sir. You're so right.

A: You ought to be ashamed of yourself. I've never known such outrageous behaviour. Your firm, sir, is a disgrace to the country.

KENNETH: Oh yes, sir – I do so agree. Chez Arthur the customer's always right.

SNAIL REFORM

(*Pieces of Eight*, Apollo Theatre, London, 1959)

(The plush office of Mr Oates, aka Kenneth Williams, president of the SPSR – Society for the Prohibition of Snail Racing. Miss Rigby is the glamorous secretary. On the wall is a framed notice saying 'Worm or snail do no offence' – William Shakespeare.)

OATES: Take a letter would you please Miss Rigby. 'Dear Mr Frobisher, with reference to yours of the 15th inst, I have pleasure in informing you that the annual yearly subscription to SPSR has been fixed at six guineas for overseas members like yourself. This entitles you to the full use of the clubroom and the bathing facilities. As you will doubtless realise, our organisation depends entirely on voluntary donations, etc, etc.' Give him the usual stuff. You know better than I do.

RIGBY: Yes, Mr Oates.

(*The telephone rings.*)

OATES: SPSR? Oh, it's you, Wislow. How did the demonstration go? Did you? . . . Aha . . . Well done, Wislow, well done. Keep it up. Goodbye. Campaign's going well, Miss Rigby. Ten women fainted during the march and three policemen were injured in the crush. We should make the nationals with that.

(*Enter Miss Blake, another glamorous secretary.*)

BLAKE: There's a Lady Tranter outside to see you, sir.

OATES: Show her in, Miss Blake. Lady Tranter, how very good of you to come. Won't you sit down? You got my letter?

TRANTER: Yes, I'm always interested to hear of worthwhile

charities. As you know, I have a little money put away, and it seems such a pity to leave it to lie idle.

OATES: You're most kind.

TRANTER: But before we actually decide on a sum, I wonder if you could perhaps let me know a little bit more about your wonderful society, whatever it is . . .

OATES: The SPSR.

TRANTER: The SPSR. For instance, what do those initials stand for?

OATES: The SPSR is the abbreviated name for the Society for the Prohibition of Snail Racing.

TRANTER: Oh, yes. How silly of me. And what – you must forgive me, I'm really very ignorant – what exactly do you do?

OATES: Well, that's a very broad question, Lady Tranter, but I think it would be fair to say that the main objective of the SPSR is the prohibition of snail racing of any kind in this country. We seek to bring pressure to bear on the Government to legislate against this unholy sport. We would like to make snail racing illegal.

TRANTER: What wonderful work you must be doing. I remember once when I was a gel, I was taken to see one of those races. It was terrible. I could hardly bear to watch, and I never dared take off my dark glasses.

OATES: It's a cruel, ugly sight, and the effect it could have on a young child's mind is incalculable, and quite apart from the cruelty to the snails, there's the suffering caused by the inevitable gambling fever that surrounds the sport. I've seen a widow's pension change hands at the turn of a snail.

TRANTER: I never realised.

OATES: And of course the betting leads to corruption. Races are rigged, snails are drugged, and it's very difficult to check on this – a blood test is usually fatal. The snail's a frail beast, Lady Tranter – a frail beast. And as you know, the snail is a slow mover – sluggish, you might call him.

TRANTER: Extremely sluggish.

OATES: The slug, on the other hand, is a speedy creature by comparison. Well, there have been cases of unscrupulous owners attaching lightweight aluminium shells to their slugs, and racing them as snails – makes you think, doesn't it?

TRANTER: The things people will do for money.

(*Telephone rings.*)

OATES: Hello? What's that you say? Clandestine snail racing in Norwich? I see. Inadequate stabling? Snails continually under the whip over the last six inches? Thank you very much indeed, sir. That's just the sort of thing we want to hear about. We'll be sending down our camera team by helicopter. Try and keep them racing if you can. Miss Rigby, alert team seven. Proceed at once to the Nack & Noggin, Norwich. A very nasty case, your Ladyship – snails more dead than alive at the post.

TRANTER: How anyone could be so cruel to helpless animals. They should be shot.

OATES: Of course there are people who would try to tell us the snail likes it – enjoys the race, they say. But I can soon put paid to that little theory. Have a look at this. They're high-speed action photographs which have been taken during actual races. Look at the expressions on those snails' faces and then try to tell me they're enjoying it.

TRANTER: Poor little creatures. Oh, look at that one.

OATES: Not a pretty sight, is it? It is our duty to sweep this shame from off the country's face, but for this we need money.

TRANTER: Of course, but there's just one thing I'm not sure about. I mean, is there much snail racing going on nowadays? I mean, I don't seem to have heard of any – around us, at least.

OATES: Exactly. I'm proud to say that our society has almost entirely succeeded in stamping it out. In fact, I think it would be fair to say that most of the snail racing that does occur nowadays is organised by us.

TRANTER: Do you mean that you actually organise snail racing?

OATES: Most certainly – under scientific conditions, of course. The snails are weighed every three inches.

TRANTER: But I don't understand. I thought you were against snail racing.

OATES: We are. We are. That's why we organise these demon- strations. Only by showing the general public the whole horror of this disgusting sport can we educate them to abolish it. We charge a nominal entrance fee, of course, and they can see snail racing of the most diabolical nature, and I think we're winning the battle for people's minds. People have been so revolted by our displays that public opinion is gradually turning against the sport.

TRANTER: What truly great work you must be doing. I shall be only too glad to give a little something towards it. And perhaps you could let me have a ticket for one of your shows?

OATES: Of course, Lady Tranter. Now, if you'd like . . .

(*Miss Rigby and Miss Blake rush in, waving telegrams.*)

RIGBY: It's passed, Mr Oates! It's passed!

OATES: What's passed?

BLAKE: The Bill. It's through – third reading, by seven votes.

RIGBY: We've won! We've won!

TRANTER: Calm yourself, dear gel. What have you won?

BLAKE: Snail racing, the House of Commons.

RIGBY: They've made it illegal! Snail racing illegal! I'm so happy!

TRANTER: But how marvellous! Congratulations, Mr Oates! Wonderful news! What a triumph for you!

OATES: Triumph? Bloody hell! Where do you think I'm going to get another job like this one?

IF ONLY
(*Pieces of Eight*, Apollo Theatre, London, 1959)

(*Fenella is listening to the wireless.*)

WIRELESS: The death has occurred at his home in Venice of Sir Frederick Snain, the well-known libertine.

FENELLA: Oh dear.

WIRELESS: He was 107.

FENELLA: Poor old fellow. In Venice, too!

WIRELESS: And now, tomorrow's weather.

FENELLA: Already? I can't cope with it.

WIRELESS: Over most parts of England and Wales it will be fine and sunny, with temperatures in the seventies.

FENELLA: It's a sad world.

WIRELESS: Further outlook, continuing fine, warm and sunny.

FENELLA: This hot weather will be the death of fat old people who live at the top of hills.

WIRELESS: And now morning music on gramophone records.

FENELLA: I can't bear to think of them all struggling up the slope.

(*Enter Kenneth, he switches off the wireless.*)

KENNETH: Music, music, all the time! Have you nothing better to do than listen to the wireless?

FENELLA: Not that I can remember. And what have you been doing with yourself?

KENNETH: I've just wandered down to the pillar box.

FENELLA: That's nice.

KENNETH: I like to go down there and look at the collection every now and then. It makes a gay splash with the blue uniforms.

FENELLA: And the ceremony.

KENNETH: And the ceremony.

FENELLA: It's a busy life. Cup of tea, dear?

KENNETH: That would be nice, I suppose.

FENELLA: There's nothing nicer than a good cup of tea – in this house.

KENNETH: I wish I'd had the opportunities that other men have had.

FENELLA: You haven't had the opportunities.

KENNETH: If only I had been born in Shropshire. I could have set up business there.

FENELLA: There's plenty of rich men in Shropshire. You never got the breaks.

KENNETH: I often think I might have done better if I'd kept off the milk. Jack kept off the milk and he's doing alright.

FENELLA: It's the milk that's kept you back. You'd have been a force in the land without the milk. It's all pasteurised these days.

KENNETH: And bottled.

FENELLA: And frozen.

KENNETH: And thinned. I wish I'd given it a miss.

FENELLA: Luck's been against us.

KENNETH: If I'd had wings I might have got about a bit more.

FENELLA: Wings would have helped you to see the world. Still, we've done what we could. It's a busy life. In the morning, there's your teeth. Right away, there's your teeth to see to.

KENNETH: Then there's the laces. After the teeth I set about the laces, threading them through as best I may, and then the actual tying, gathering the two threads together in a knot – it all takes time.

FENELLA: And then there's always the garden to sit in. There's plenty to be done. It's been a rich life in its way.

KENNETH: If only I'd been born with more flesh on me I'd have got on better. I might have got that job as The Fattest Man In The World.

FENELLA: You nearly got it as it was. All you lacked was the build.

KENNETH: I hadn't the necessary flesh. The people like to see great mounds of the stuff, all quivering. That's what held me back. I lacked the flesh.

FENELLA: You were the thinnest Fattest Man In The World in the world, but you were well liked.

KENNETH: If only I'd had the flesh.

FENELLA: Fate was against you.

KENNETH: And there's my name. If only I'd changed my name I'd have made a name for myself. A good name might have made up for the missing pounds. That's show business. You need a glamorous name. If only I'd been called something like, like Arthur Grangeleigh. Can't you see it up in lights? 'Come and see Arthur Grangeleigh, The Fattest Man In The World'! I'd have got to the top if I'd had a name like that. If only I was called Arthur Grangeleigh.

FENELLA: You are called Arthur Grangeleigh.

KENNETH: If only I hadn't been called Arthur Grangeleigh.

FENELLA: That's what held you back.

ORNITHOLOGY
(*Pop Goes Mrs Jessop*, Cambridge Arts Theatre, 1960)

(An ornithologist is throwing bread to the ducks from a paper bag. A passer by comes up and watches him.)

ORNITHOLOGIST: Ducks, that's what they are – nothing more or less. That's what they are. Ducks, just ordinary feathered ducks. I'm feeding the ducks.

PASSER BY: Yes, I see.

ORNITHOLOGIST: They're ducks, alright. I've trained them, you know.

PASSER BY: Really?

ORNITHOLOGIST: Oh yes, I've trained these ducks. Every one of these ducks is highly trained. They're highly trained ducks you're looking at.

PASSER BY: What have you trained them to do?

ORNITHOLOGIST: Eat. I've trained them all to eat. Look, there's one of them doing it now. Marvellous, isn't it? All I have to do is to throw a bit of bread into the water, clap my hands, and my trained ducks will eat it, just like that – quite an achievement, really.

PASSER BY: Yes, I suppose it is.

ORNITHOLOGIST: Of course, I'm not trying to say that duck training is a dangerous sport. I mean, the risks involved probably aren't as great as those in lion taming. The duck is far less formidable than the lion. Of course, if you had a great flock of ducks all pecking at you, it might be quite nasty. But really, it's more a question of skill than physical courage with ducks.

PASSER BY: And you're responsible for all these ducks here?

ORNITHOLOGIST: Yes I am responsible, I suppose. Not in any official capacity – I'm not appointed by the Government. In fact, I don't think there is any real national policy as regards ducks.

PASSER BY: I see.

ORNITHOLOGIST: I do it all for love, you see – for love of ducks.

PASSER BY: Tell me, are they very hard to train?

ORNITHOLOGIST: Well, you've got to have patience, of course –
endless patience, you need. I started this lot off on tiny crumbs,
and then gradually worked up to the bigger lumps. I even had
one of them eating crusts last week – actual crusts.

PASSER BY: That is good.

ORNITHOLOGIST: Yes, I'm very proud of that. I can't think of any
other trainer who's persuaded them to eat crusts. I've trained
them to eat from my hand, too – actually pecking the bread out
of my hand.

PASSER BY: Really?

ORNITHOLOGIST: Of course, I should mention there's one duck
that will never eat out of your hand. That's your Swedish duck.
See him over there with the while tail feathers? That's your
Swedish duck. I've tried everything – shouting, ringing bells,
mating dances, the lot. But he won't come near me.

PASSER BY: How very strange.

ORNITHOLOGIST: Of course, I dare say if I covered my hand in
moss and lay stock still for hours on end, I dare say he might
sneak up and have a bite, but I'm not prepared to make that sort
of concession to a duck. I don't mind treating them as equals,
but I refuse to degrade myself.

PASSER BY: Quite right.

ORNITHOLOGIST: I will not be dominated by them.

PASSER BY: Well, I think you've done wonders.

ORNITHOLOGIST: Yes, it's quite a triumph. Not like winning the
war, but quite a triumph. I mean, these ducks are completely
under my control – eating's become second nature to them now.

PASSER BY: Wonderful. Tell me, have you any more plans for
them? Are you going to teach them any more tricks?

ORNITHOLOGIST: Oh, yes. Goodness me, there's lots to be done
with them yet. The possibilities are endless with ducks.

PASSER BY: What's your next step going to be?

ORNITHOLOGIST: Well, I was thinking, perhaps it's a bit too
ambitious, but I was thinking of trying to get them up in the air
– training them to fly.

THE BALLAD OF SIR FREDERICK SNAIN
(*Pop Goes Mrs Jessop*, Cambridge Arts Theatre, 1960)

This is the story of a man,
A man by the name of Snain,
An ordinary man,
An Englishman
But one who rapidly became
A legend in his time.
We can all learn from Snain.

Fred Snain was born in Hertfordshire
And there he went to school,
Where at an early age he learnt
Life's most important rule:
Do as you would be done by none
And never pay a fool.
In order to be kind says Snain
You must always be cruel.

Fred Snain, Fred Snain, Fred Snain, Fred Snain,
The Greatest Name in Hertfordshire.

Even as a child Fred Snain was always an example to his fellows,
He was always willing to stretch out a helping hand for his helping.

He robs the rich to help Fred Snain,
He robs the poor to help Fred Snain,
He robs them all to help Fred Snain,
And then he robs them once again.

Frederick Snain, Frederick Snain, Frederick Snain, Frederick
Snain,
The Greatest Name in Hertfordshire.

Fred Snain believes in compromise,
In British give and take.

This is his basic principle
That earthquakes wouldn't shake.
You must have heard the fine remark
That he is prone to make:
Provided that the others give
Fred Snain's prepared to take.

Frederick Snain, Frederick Snain, Frederick Snain, Frederick
Snain.
The Greatest Name in Hertfordshire.

Fred Snain was a pioneer of racial tolerance
Irrespective of race,
Colour,
Creed,
Sex,
Religion.
He regards them all as part of the great brotherhood of man.

He robs the black, he robs the white,
All men are equal in his sight
And now they've made Fred Snain a Knight
For doing what he knows is right.

Sir Frederick Snain, Sir Frederick Snain,
Greed is his creed and personal gain.
The children of England all worship the name
Of Hertfordshire's outlaw, Frederick Snain.

ORDINARY MAN
(*Pop Goes Mrs Jessop*, Cambridge Arts Theatre, 1960)

I'm an ordinary man
With an ordinary wife,
Ordinary folk

That live an ordinary life
In an ordinary house
In an ordinary street
Where the people that you meet
Are ordinary.

I do an ordinary job
In an ordinary way
Working ordinary hours
For ordinary pay
In an ordinary part
Of a little factory
And the blokes that work with me
Are ordinary.

Some people think our life is dull,
The same thing day and night.
Some people think we must be bored
And by Gawd
They're right.

INTERESTING FACTS
(*Pop Goes Mrs Jessop*, Cambridge Arts Theatre, 1960)

A classic Cook sketch which Peter continued to reprise and adapt for the rest of his career. He first performed it at a Pembroke College revue in 1959, and subsequently hired it out to Kenneth Williams for Williams' West End revue, One Over The Eight, *in 1961. A later version is on* Best Of The Balls, Laughing Stock's *compilation of Secret Policemen's Balls, those fund raising performances for Amnesty International, where it was one of the highlights of the first* Secret Policeman's Ball, *in 1979. That time, John Cleese played Peter's foil, an irate City Gent previously played by Peter Bellwood and Michael Burrell. Burrell also performed* Ornithology *with Cook in* Pop Goes Mrs Jessop *and subsequently became a prolific professional actor. Bellwood performed with Cook's Establishment Club in America before becoming a successful scriptwriter, and returned the compliment when he cast Cook as Best Man at his wedding.*

PETER COOK: Good evening.

CITY GENT: Oh, good evening.

PETER COOK: I'm extremely interested in all facets of human life, including you. Tell me you are a mariner.

CITY GENT: No, I'm afraid I'm not. I'm an architect.

PETER COOK: Oh, I see. I only mentioned that you might be a mariner so that I could lead the conversation round to an interesting fact I've accumulated. It pertains to the cod fish. That's an ocean-dwelling creature.

CITY GENT: Yes, I've heard of the cod.

PETER COOK: Yes, it's quite an interesting fact, that. The codfish relies almost solely for protection on blending with the natural seaweeds amongst which it lives.

CITY GENT: Goodness me.

PETER COOK: It is its sole protection, whereas the sole relies almost entirely on hanging about behind shoals of cod. That's quite an interesting fact, isn't it?

CITY GENT: Yes. Yes, it is.

PETER COOK: But not as interesting in my opinion as another fact I've come across.

CITY GENT: Oh?

PETER COOK: It's about the eagle. It's quite interesting that the eagle has an estimated wingspan of eighteen feet, whereas its two feet span three feet, which is double the length of its tail feather and over four times the width of its beak alone. That's quite an interesting statistic, isn't it?

CITY GENT: Fancy that – the eagle. I never knew.

PETER COOK: I doubt if the eagle does either. It's quite interesting to think that if all the Chinamen in the world linked hands they'd girdle the earth three times.

CITY GENT: Three time, eh? That's amazing.

PETER COOK: I wouldn't call it amazing. I'm not amazed by it. I just take an intelligent interest in it. Of course, I've not bothered to check up at all. I've just taken it on trust. I've not got time to go round organising Chinamen to link their hands, and the practical difficulties are immense. You'd have to have rafts over the sea. Anyway, I shouldn't think they'd agree to do it. But it's quite interesting as a fact.

CITY GENT: Yes. Yes, I suppose it is.

PETER COOK: The grasshopper is an interesting creature. It has a disproportionate leaping ability. It's the powerful hind legs that cause it. You can seem them hopping over grassy terrain. That's why it's called a grasshopper. But it is its leaping ability that interests me. Do you know that if the giraffe had the same leaping ability, pound for pound, he'd be able to jump onto the moon and Britain would be first in the space race?

CITY GENT: Yes, well I'm trying to read this article.

PETER COOK: I'm very interested in the grasshopper and its leaping ability. I haven't got an unhealthy interest in it, mind you. I'm not obsessed by it. I haven't got an unhealthy sexual interest in the grasshopper. At least I've never had any sexual activity with a grasshopper. Or if I have, nobody saw me. And if they did see me it's their look out.

CITY GENT: Well, thank you very much, but I think I've heard enough of your interesting facts.

PETER COOK: Heard enough?

CITY GENT: Yes. I must confess to being a trifle bored by some of them.

PETER COOK: Bored? That's rather interesting.

SECOND FLOOD

(*Pop Goes Mrs Jessop*, Cambridge Arts Theatre, 1960)

MARY: Goodness me! I've never known such rain! I'm soaked through!

CHARLES: Raining it is.

MARY: It's absolutely pelting down, Charles – really quite frightening.

CHARLES: Frightening? My dear Mary, what can you mean? Rain is completely harmless. It's beneficial. There's nothing to be frightened of with rain.

MARY: It's coming down so hard, Charles.

CHARLES: Without it, the crops would wither and we should all starve. It can't hurt you, rain. It's not powerful enough to stun you. No, no – rain is man's best friend.

MARY: Well, you just have a look at it.

CHARLES: Of course, my dear – if it will reassure you. Ah, yes – you're quite right. There is a bit of rain coming down, just ordinary rain, a shower of rain – nothing to worry about.

MARY: It is raining heavily though, isn't it?

CHARLES: Yes, this is what meteorologists would call heavy rain. It is a heavy shower of rain, let me put it like that – a heavy rain shower.

MARY: A very heavy shower.

CHARLES: No, no, no – not very heavy. You couldn't call this very heavy if you'd seen some of the showers we had out in Nigeria. You wouldn't call this heavy. No, this is light rain compared with tropical rain. This is nothing at all.

MARY: I don't like the look of it.

CHARLES: Nobody likes the look of rain, my dear. Rain is never beautiful, but there's nothing we can do about it. The earth is heavier than the clouds, the clouds pass over the earth and so the rain is pulled down. It can't help it. It's gravity. Gravity pulls it down. It's all proved. That's all that's happening now.

MARY: It looks to me as if it's rising.

CHARLES: Nonsense, my dear. Rain never rises – rain falls. Hot air rises – never rain.

MARY: I mean the water level is rising.

CHARLES: Yes, of course it is. That's nothing to worry about. It's only natural. The rain comes down and the ground rises to meet it. The rain comes down, settles on the ground and accumulates. Of course it's rising. It's when rain comes down and the water level starts falling that we shall need to worry. That'll mean that the garden has caved in or something. I must say it is rising quite fast – most impressive sight. Oh look, there's a bowler hat floating by. Come and look, Mary – a bowler hat.

MARY: Charles, there's a pair of ears underneath it!

CHARLES: Why, so there is. Must have . . . You sit down, my dear . . . Must have blown off in the wind – there's quite a wind. Not a gale, just a heavy wind.

MARY: Charles, I'm getting rather worried, water rising all round the house. Don't you think we ought to ring somebody up?

CHARLES: But it's just a shower, Mary – heavy shower. A passing shower, and it happens to be passing us. It is only natural that the water should rise. I mean, in the tropics I've seen . . . Still, if it'll put your mind at rest, I'll give the police a ring – just for your sake. Hello, hello? What do you mean, glug, glug, glug?

MARY: What do they say?

CHARLES: They're rather busy, my dear – but there's no need to worry. This rain will soon stop. Rain like this never lasts. It's not like the tropics.

MARY: It sounds to me as if it's getting harder, Charles.

CHARLES: That's a good sign, my dear. It's just the calm before the . . . No, I mean the storm before the calm. You remember the old saying in the Bible – the storm before the calm.

MARY: The Bible, Charles! Of course, the Bible!

CHARLES: That's right. It's a biblical saying. Jehoshaphat said it on Galgaresh.

MARY: But the Bible, it's all in the Bible! Man's wickedness and the waters came down and the whole land was flooded. Remember?

CHARLES: Of course I remember, but this is just a shower – a heavy shower . . . very heavy. There's no comparison at all. Besides, we haven't done anything wicked. We're married. There's nothing.

MARY: It's not just us, Charles. It's the whole world he punished, the whole world – flooded it all.

CHARLES: Yes, but surely . . . I mean, He's done it once. He wouldn't use the same method again – surely not.

MARY: Charles, there's water seeping through the floorboards.

CHARLES: Rubbish, my dear. It couldn't have got this far. What an idea! It's probably mice spitting, or something.

MARY: Charles, Charles! We're all going to drown, just like that man with the pamphlets said.

CHARLES: Nonsense, my dear. For goodness sake calm yourself. It's just a shower, a heavy shower – like we had in the tropics. Another flood? Ha Ha! It's still coming up a bit, but that's only natural. Mary, just for your sake and to be on the safe side, I think I'll go up into the attic – and I wonder if you'd dive out of the window and swim up the hill to Dawkins. See if you can get hold of 800 cubits of cedar wood.

WHA HAE
(*Pop Goes Mrs Jessop*, Cambridge Arts Theatre, 1960)

When the heather is in bloom
All purple on the brae
Then I hie me to the toon
For I long to get away
From the coughing of the sheep
And the monarch of the glen
And hie me doon to Glasgie toon
To get sick drunk again.

Cos when I'm sick drunk in Glasgie
On a Tuesday afternoon
Then the whole darn toon belongs to me.

When I vomit in the gutter
You can hear the people mutter
He's a credit to Balmoral and the Kirk.
When I'm drunk on Sauchiehall
And I get into a brawl
How the lassies laugh to see me draw me dirk.

From Kilmarnock to Glengoran
I am knowen by me sporran
Cos it always reeks of whisky and of gin.
Cos it only takes a drappie

To keep this chappie happy
And I find it verra hard to keep it in.

Oh I'm stupid and I'm boring
But when you get me roaring
I feel as if I was a bairn again.
I can feel the toon a whirling
And I hear the pipes a skirling
And a moment later have to pull the chain.

We won at Bannockburren
Cos a boozer couldn't learen
Exactly how to sound the new retreat.
And we would have won Culloden
If we'd been a bit more sodden
Or at least we could have drunk to our defeat.

BLETCHLEY FIRST CLASS
(*Pop Goes Mrs Jessop*, Cambridge Arts Theatre, 1960)

(*A railway ticket office. Written with John Fortune.*)

PETER COOK: First class to Bletchley, please. How much is that?

TICKET OFFICER: Bletchley first class? That'll be four pounds, nine shillings and eightpence, please sir.

PETER COOK: Alright, I'll give you ninepence.

TICKET OFFICER: I'm sorry, sir. I don't quite understand.

PETER COOK: Ninepence. I'm offering you ninepence. Take it or leave it.

TICKET OFFICER: I'm sorry, sir. The fare is four pounds, nine shillings and eightpence to Bletchley.

PETER COOK: Alright, alright. I see your point. You've got a job of work to do. I'll go up a bit. A shilling! How's that? A shilling!

TICKET OFFICER: I'm sorry, sir. It's a fixed charge. We don't make any reductions.

PETER COOK: Good, good. I like you. You're doing a good job. I like to see that. That's the way to make the railways pay. Good. Alright, one and eight – my final offer.

TICKET OFFICER: Look sir, I'm a busy man – and there's people waiting behind you.

PETER COOK: Yes, yes – I see them. All come down for a haggle. Nothing like a good haggle. I've been out East, you know. Seen the buzzard and the hashish, snakes jumping, the lot.

TICKET OFFICER: Yes, well I'm sorry sir. You'll either have to pay or leave. Four pounds, nine shillings and eightpence it is.

PETER COOK: But it's the haggling they like. Won't sell you a thing unless you haggle. Look at this watch! What do you think I paid for that?

TICKET OFFICER: Would you mind moving on, please?

PETER COOK: Ten pounds, he wanted. I said 'Agu bansika!' I speak the language. 'Agu bansika,' I said. No, no, no. Beat him down to fourpence.

TICKET OFFICER: Will you please . . .

PETER COOK: Tell you what. I like you. You're a bright boy. You know your job. I tell you what – I'll give you two and six if you'll let me ride in the engine as well. Two and six for a first class ticket to Bletchley and a ride on the engine. How's that?

TICKET OFFICER: It's a fixed charge, fixed by law. Now, if you don't move away I shall have to call the station master.

PETER COOK: Good. You do that. I like you railway people. I'd like to meet him, and I'll go up to three bob.

(*The Ticket Officer picks up the telephone and dials.*)

TICKET OFFICER: Hello? Station master? There's a gentleman here being unpleasant. I wonder if you'd deal with him. Thank you.

PETER COOK: Well done. Very impressive. Now why don't you come down a bit? Knock a shilling off.

STATION MASTER: Now then, what seems to be the trouble?

TICKET INSPECTOR: This gentleman refuses to pay his far or move out of the way.

STATION MASTER: Now sir, I'd be very grateful if you'd kindly step this way.

PETER COOK: No, you can't catch me like that. I came here for a bargain, and I'm not moving until I've got it.

STATION MASTER: Now sir, look at it our way – this is railway property, and technically you're constituting a nuisance. If you don't move, I shall be forced to fine you.

PETER COOK: Fine me, eh? How much?

STATION MASTER: The maximum penalty for this sort of offence is ten pounds.

PETER COOK: Ten pounds? Alright – give you ninepence.

OH YES
(*Pop Goes Mrs Jessop*, Cambridge Arts Theatre, 1960)

Curiously, this monologue appears in the script that was sent in advance to the office of the Lord Chamberlain for approval – a legal requirement until the Theatres Act of 1968 – but not in the programme for the show. A last minute omission or a mere printing error? Either way, it's worn far better than several scripts which appear in both places. The Lord Chamberlain is conventionally regarded as a bad thing, but he did have his uses. Not only has the theatre arguably become far less ingenuous and subtle since his role as official censor was abolished, but his insistence on vetting every theatrical script before it was performed has preserved Cook's Footlights and West End revues for a grateful nation. They now reside in London's British Library, in the hushed, academic silence of the manuscripts department.

Now you're a primitive people, you're a backward folk, and I want to make one thing quite clear from the start. I am not a god. It's an easy mistake to make. I've made it myself on occasions, caught a glimpse of myself in the mirror and fell down worshipping. Now this evening I want to talk to you about a very sinful thing, a thing which I want to warn you all against most strongly. Brother Martin has got a lot of them hidden away in that sack there. They're a very dangerous weapon, what we in the West call guns. They're very dangerous and lethal, much more dangerous than your primitive old bows and arrows. You can shoot people down from hundreds of yards and nobody will ever know who's done it, and I want to warn you most strongly never to use them against one another. After this talk, you'll be able to come up to Brother Martin here and exchange your worthless old gold and jewellery and get a chance to exercise the virtue of restraint. Now Brother Martin is just nipping off to have a quick sin. He'll be back in a minute, as repentant as can be, telling you in his own words just how he could have avoided it. After that, there'll be another collection. Now, I noticed on the last time round that some of you looked a little peevish. This is another sin – greed – and here's a heaven-sent chance to avoid it. Brother Martin will in fact be circulating with one of these new guns to show you. Now next week I'm going to talk to you about another sinful thing you won't have come across yet – drugs. Women I see you have already.

THE LOST ART OF CONVERSATION
(*One Over the Eight*, Duke of York's Theatre, London, 1961)

A: So I said to him, the trouble these days with all these tinned foods and, er . . .

B: And, er, canned peas . . .

A: And television and, er . . . the trouble with all this, er, free health . . .

B: And, er, electric Hoovers . . .

A: And fish fingers and things . . .

A: Do you find you get little bits of filth under your finger nails?

B: Er . . .

A: The trouble with all these, er, do-it-yourself gramophones . . .

B: And, er, cinemas . . .

A: Yes, er, the trouble is that people . . .

B: Er, young people . . .

A: Yes, young people seem to have lost . . .

B: Yes, lost . . .

A: Lost, young people seem to have lost the, er . . .

B: The art . . .

A: Yes, the art – they seem to have lost the art . . .

B: Yes, lost . . .

A: Lost the art of, er . . .

B: Er . . .

A: Conversation.

THE EPHEMERAL TRIANGLE

(*One Over the Eight*, Duke of York's Theatre, London, 1961)

(*Kenneth Williams rushes into a shop selling musical instruments.*)

KEN: It's a disgrace! Let me in! Where is he? Ah, there you are! It was you, wasn't it? It was you who sold me this triangle?

MAN: Yes, sir – that's right.

KEN: Three pounds I paid for it. Three pounds for this load of old rubbish. It's not worth twopence. I have never come across such shoddy, ill-made muck in all my life. It is disgusting, sir – disgusting.

MAN: Yes sir.

KEN: There I was at the end of the opening chorus, the musical climax of the entire number, the whole audience on tenterhooks, waiting for a clear, bell-like melody, and what do they get? A rotten little ping and the bloody thing falls apart. It's a disgrace, I tell you – a disgrace.

MAN: I agree, sir – but in a way, it was your own fault.

KEN: My own fault?

MAN: Yes, sir. You would insist on buying a British-made triangle – the so-called Eternal.

KEN: Of course I insisted on it. British triangles lead the world.

MAN: Yes sir, but we do find they tend to fall to pieces.

KEN: Are you suggesting that anybody else can make triangles better than us?

MAN: Yes, sir. In fact, I would recommend this one to you.

KEN: Let's have a look at it.

MAN: That is the Ewige triangle, sir – very strong.

KEN: Made in Germany, I see.

MAN: That's right, sir.

KEN: A dirty old lump of jerry-built scrap iron. Listen, there's no tone to it, no tone to it at all. Made by Herr Krupp, I suppose. He's melted down his tanks and tuned them into triangles – makes you sick.

MAN: What about this one, then?

KEN: What's it called?

MAN: That's the new Nippon.

KEN: First the Boches and now the Japs! Look at this rubbish! There's no strength to it. It's just been blown together. One pull and it falls apart.

(*It doesn't.*)

MAN: It seems strong enough to me.

KEN: It's the wrong shape. Did you ever see such an appalling ugly twisted shape?

MAN: It's exactly the same shape as the Eternal, sir.

KEN: I might have known. Stolen it, have they? Stolen the British design? That's what happens. You think of an idea, and as soon as your back is turned, some dirty Ju Jitsu monger sneaks off his junk in bamboo slippers, and before you can say Jack Robinson, he's selling it back to you. Half our Union Jacks are made in Tokyo.

MAN: I dare say, sir – but . . .

KEN: You should be ashamed of yourself, young man. You're nothing better than a war criminal. How dare you? How dare you keep this pornographic rubbish on the same counter as the Eternal? Get it off! Get it off! There we are. Beautiful, isn't it? The Eternal triangle, made in England – what a beautiful bit of work, built by craftsmen in the Cotswolds out of real Sussex ore. It's a work of art.

MAN: It did fall to pieces in your hands, sir.

KEN: Of course it fell to pieces in my hands. It's designed to fall to pieces. All British triangles are designed to fall to pieces. It's the oldest rule in music. A triangle should be played once, and once only. If you had any manners you'd know that.

MAN: I had no idea.

KEN: It's like food. You don't go on eating the same food again and again, do you? Or do you?

MAN: No.

KEN: The British triangle is like a butterfly – ephemeral, here today, gone tomorrow, a thing of beauty bringing light and joy into the lives of thousands. I don't want any of your vulgar long-lasting foreign filth. Give me an Eternal, the gentleman's triangle.

MAN: But I thought you came in here to complain.

KEN: Nonsense. Here's my £3. There was a feeble laugh when it fell apart.

MAN: Well, you can't do better than the British if you want it to fall apart.

KEN: Let me see – this doesn't fall apart at all.

MAN: I'm sorry, sir. You've got a dud.

KEN: How dare you!

CHEZ MALCOLM

(One Over the Eight, Duke of York's Theatre, London, 1961)

(Kenneth Williams is a hairdresser. His Customer is sitting in a hairdresser's chair, wearing a long gown.)

KENNETH: Now, sir – what is it to be?

CUSTOMER: Just a haircut, please.

KENNETH: Yes, sir – but what style did you have in mind?

CUSTOMER: Oh, you know – the usual thing.

KENNETH: The usual thing?

CUSTOMER: Yes, I'd like a bit off here and there.

KENNETH: You'd like a bit off? You'd like a bit off?

CUSTOMER: Yes, just a trim.

KENNETH: Well, let me tell you, sir – you don't come into my little boutique to have a bit off. You come in here to have it styled. I'm an artiste de cheveux. I'm a poet, a poet of the hair. Now, what style?

CUSTOMER: I don't know. What styles are there?

KENNETH: There's the Regency, you see – the style called Regency Buck. The Windsor, that's lovely – or of course you can always fall back on your Marcel.

CUSTOMER: On my what?

KENNETH: Your Marcel – that is your short bang style. For you, sir, I'd suggest a Marcel and a Vibrorub.

CUSTOMER: I don't need any rubbing, thank you.

KENNETH: I beg your pardon – you do, sir. You scalp is dead. I've never seen such a dead scalp. Dandruff isn't in it. It's more like coral. Your hair's falling out all over the place. Look at it. Look at it! If I was you, I'd have a Marcel, a Vibrorub and a blow wave.

CUSTOMER: I don't want any of this modern continental rubbish.

KENNETH: Modern continental? I did my first blow wave in 1908 – 1908, long before the continentals.

CUSTOMER: It looks rather Italianate to me.

KENNETH: Italianate? My blow wave is as British as roast beef.

CUSTOMER: It's just that all this Marcel business sounded rather effeminate.

KENNETH: Effeminate? Poof! You call that effeminate? Poof I say to that. I have boxers in here, all-in wrestlers. I've had them all in this chair. Bishops, great burly men, they all come in here for a wave and a tint.

CUSTOMER: I had no idea.

KENNETH: There's nothing effeminate about good grooming. Henry VIII wore a hair net in bed. You wouldn't call him effeminate, would you? There was a man come in here last week, had a manicure, blue rinse and a cold perm, went out again and knocked down three violent drunks.

CUSTOMER: Knocked them down?

KENNETH: Three violent drunks – knocked them down flat. He was driving at the time, but it goes to show.

CUSTOMER: But are you sure I'm not going to look rather chi chi?

KENNETH: Chi chi? You know what I say to that, if anyone says that to me? Poof, I say. Poof, poof, I say to them.

CUSTOMER: In my line of business, I simply can't afford to look in any way outlandish or effeminate.

KENNETH: There's nothing effeminate about my customers. Remember old Jack Schmelling, the boxer? He used to come in here in the old days. Remember him?

CUSTOMER: The heavyweight champion?

KENNETH: That's right. Old Jack Schmelling. You wouldn't call him effeminate, would you? Poof, I say. He never went near a woman, never touched a woman in his life. There was nothing effeminate about Jack.

CUSTOMER: Are you sure that . . .

KENNETH: Used to come in here between bouts, old Jack did – used to come in here for a short bang between bouts. Wouldn't go into the ring without a short bang. In he'd come, drenched in Chanel.

CUSTOMER: In Chanel?

KENNETH: Chanel from head to foot. Give me a bang, Malcolm, he used to say. Snip, snip, snip – and off to the fight in a flurry of talcum powder.

CUSTOMER: He wore talcum powder?

KENNETH: Covered in it, he was.

CUSTOMER: How disgusting.

KENNETH: It was the only way he could sell the ringside seats. Used to sweat like a pig, old Schmelling did. Give me more talcum, Malcolm, he used to shout. More talc, Malc. You could hardly see him for powder.

CUSTOMER: Let me out of here! It's a disgrace! Talcum powder, Chanel – I won't sit in the same chair.

KENNETH: But what about your Marcel and your Blow Wave?

CUSTOMER: I wouldn't let you touch my hair. Blow your Marcel. I'm not going out of here looking like a woman.

(*Customer removes his gown and exits, wearing a kilt.*)

Chapter Two
Beyond the Fringe

The show that killed off old-fashioned revue, started the Sixties satire boom, and which transformed Peter Cook from a wunderkind into an international superstar, could scarcely have had a less radical beginning. It originated in that highly respectable bastion of high culture, the Edinburgh International Festival of Music & Drama.

Since it began, in 1947, the annual Edinburgh International Festival had become increasingly upstaged by an unofficial fringe of shows – performed by uninvited artistes, alongside the official festival, but outside its control. Many of these informal performances were late-night revues, staged by troupes like Footlights or The Oxford Revue. These ad hoc entertainments were conspicuous by their absence from the smarter International Festival – until 1959, when the Festival's Artistic Director, Roger Ponsonby, decided to beat these Fringe upstarts at their own game, and stage his own revue.

In 1959 Ponsonby booked the musical duo (Michael) Flanders & (Donald) Swann, whose witty songs, though intelligent and erudite, were pretty typical of the unchanging and unchallenging world of traditional revue. In 1960 he wanted to book Louis Armstrong. When that fell through, his assistant, John Bassett, suggested a revue featuring the best Oxbridge comics of the last five years. But which comics should they cast? Bassett recommended a jobbing pianist called Dudley Moore, who'd been in Bassett's jazz band at Oxford. Moore recommended Alan Bennett, a postgraduate medievalist at Oxford, whose spoof sermons had been a big hit on the 1959 Edinburgh Fringe. Now they needed a pair from Cambridge. Bassett recommended Jonathan Miller, a doctor at a London hospital who'd shone in two Footlights revues a few years before, which had both transferred to London. And Miller recommended the star of the latest Footlights show, a chap called Peter Cook.

'Don't jeopardise your career by working with these three amateurs,' advised Cook's agent, Donald Langdon. With his own show already running in the West End, Cook was the only professional comic of this quartet, and the only one with his own agent. Thankfully, Cook ignored Langdon's advice, and agreed to do the show. Bennett, Miller and Moore signed up for what they all thought would be just a brief summer sabbatical, at £100 each. As befitted his client's professional status, Langdon negotiated Cook a fee of £110 – which, after Langdon's 10 per cent had been deducted, left Cook with £99. 'The meek shall inherit the earth,' recollected Dudley, a decade later.

Beyond the Fringe opened at Edinburgh's Lyceum Theatre in August 1960. The title was Ponsonby's idea. He wanted to imply this show was beyond the capabilities of anyone on The Fringe, but precious few people ever got the joke. The cast didn't like his title, but none of them could think of anything better, and it was actually quite catchy, despite (or maybe even because of) the fact that nobody knew what it meant. There were no stars in the cast – Cook, despite his West End success, was not yet a well-known name – and the advance publicity was scant. On the first night, the Lyceum was less than one-third full, but the show still brought the house down. 'You knew you were in the presence of something extraordinary,' says Michael Billington, the theatre critic of the

Guardian, who was there that night, as an Oxford undergraduate. 'You came out feeling physically slightly ill, because to laugh for that length of time is exhausting. And it was a shock, a slap in the face, to all of us, because we'd seen nothing like this before.'[1] Old revue had ossified, into a cliché. Even when the sketches were original, like Peter's *Pieces of Eight*, they were presented like theatrical in-jokes. 'It absolutely cut through all the showbiz rubbish,' agreed John Wells. 'What we saw was four people of our own age slipping in and out of funny voices in the way we all liked to think we did in everyday life, being effortlessly funny.'[2]

Within days, the Lyceum was full far beyond capacity, with punters queuing for returns. The broadsheet reviews were positive but restrained, and it took a junior critic from the *Daily Mail* to give the show an outright rave. 'Behind this unpromising title lies what I believe can be described as the funniest, most intelligent and most original revue to be staged in Britain for a very long time,' wrote Peter Lewis, who subsequently became a scriptwriter for the BBC satire show, *That Was the Week That Was.* 'If this show comes to London I doubt if revue will ever be the same again.' Lewis was right.

Over twice as long, but with the same minimal costumes and staging which, as much as its actual content, distinguished it from traditional revue, *Beyond the Fringe* played Cambridge and Brighton, to limber up for its West End run. The Cambridge preview went well – making a big impression on a twenty-one-year-old student called John Cleese – but the Brighton run was a stinker. 'The seats were going up like pistol shots throughout the performance,' recollected Alan Bennett. 'Come the curtain, there were scarcely more people in the audience than there were on the stage.'[3] The same show that had charmed liberal Edinburgh shocked conservative Sussex, and despite their Festive success they were only offered a short run at the tiny Fortune Theatre, to fill in for six weeks before a Bernard Cribbins revue.

It didn't matter. The show's London triumph eclipsed its Edinburgh success. *Beyond the Fringe* opened in the West End in May 1961, to ecstatic reviews. 'Satirical revue in this country has been, until now, basically cowardly,' wrote Bernard Levin in the

PETER COOK

Daily Express. 'First, it has picked on the easy targets. Second, however hard it hit the targets (and it rarely hit them at all . . .) it left its audience alone, to leave the theatre as fat and complacent as it came in. This sorry tale went on for so long that some of us began to despair of the form itself. We believed that satirical revue was impossible in this country.' *Beyond the Fringe* had changed Levin's mind. This satire was 'real, barbed, deeply planted and aimed at things and people that need it. But this is still not all.' Its ultimate target was the audience. 'It is they who feel the final punch, the last twist of the knife.'

In the *Observer*, Kenneth Tynan contrasted it with those old-fashioned revues, so beloved by Peter Cook, which *Beyond the Fringe* had rendered instantly obsolete. 'It has no slick coffee bar scenery, no glib one-line blackouts, no twirling dancers in tight trousers, no sad ballets for fisherwomen clad in fishnet stockings,' he wrote. 'Future historians may well thank me for providing them with a full account of the moment when English comedy took its first decisive step into the second half of the twentieth century.'

They hadn't set out to shock, particularly not Cook, who had no complaints about a status quo that had rewarded him so handsomely, despite his friendly mockery of its customs. Yet despite Cook's intrinsic conformity, there was something seismic about his wit, whether he wanted to shock, or not. 'When we were first writing *Beyond the Fringe*, Peter resisted anything which might seem to be offensive to the audience,' explains Jonathan Miller. 'In some odd way, however, some of the things that he did and said as a performer were much more upsetting than those things where we explicitly set out to be satirical.'[4] Cook's impersonation of Harold Macmillan, the first time anyone could remember seeing a prime minister mimicked on stage, was a perfect case in point. 'I don't think he wrote it out of any sense of indignation,' says Miller. 'I think he found him rather adorable, really.'[5]

In October 1962, the show transferred to Broadway, where President Kennedy came to see it, as Queen Elizabeth had in London, after the cast, incredibly, had refused to perform it at the White House. JFK was rather busy handling the Cuban Missile Crisis and averting World War Three, but he came anyway. *Beyond*

43

the Fringe ran until 1964, even surviving the departure of Jonathan Miller, who was replaced by Paxton Whitehead, while a London version, with a different cast, ran until 1966. So what made it so special?

'*Beyond the Fringe*, like rock and roll, was perceived as something fresh and new and dangerous,' explains Michael Palin. 'It was shocking and thrilling, but it was done with such skill and intelligence that it could not easily be shot down, dismissed or shrugged off.'[6] And if these sketches seem relatively conventional today, that's because they changed the comic landscape so completely. 'Nothing was sacred,' recalls Eric Idle. 'Not the Queen, not the Army, not the schools, not the Church, not the City, not Advertising, not the Prime Minister, not the late War, not even the impending nuclear holocaust we were all sure was coming.'[7]

The only person who wasn't thrilled was Kenneth Williams, the star of Cook's relatively old-fashioned revue, *One Over the Eight*. Williams felt Cook had fobbed him off with 'mediocre material', but it was his acting, not Cook's writing, which was behind the times. The piece Williams was most reluctant to perform was 'One Leg Too Few', Cook's sketch about a one-legged man auditioning for the role of Tarzan, which Cook included in the Broadway version of *Beyond the Fringe*, and which subsequently became one of his most famous and successful sketches. There was nothing wrong with these sketches – Cook had performed them plenty of times himself, at Cambridge – but performed by anyone else, they were like cover versions, imperfect imitations of the real thing. *Beyond the Fringe* proved to London and New York what everyone at Cambridge already knew – that when Cook was performing his own work, there was nothing funnier in all the world. Cook's comedy had emerged fully formed – not a pimply work in progress, but the complete, adult article. 'I may have done some other things as good but I am sure none better,' he reflected, a quarter of a century later. 'I haven't matured, progressed, grown, become deeper, wiser, or funnier. But then, I never thought I would.'[8]

∿

SITTING ON THE BENCH
(Fortune Theatre, London, 1961)

One of Cook's most famous sketches which, like 'Interesting Facts', he revived, in different versions, throughout his career – particularly in 'Good Evening', the American version of 'Behind The Fridge', which he performed with Dudley from 1972 to 1974. This monologue, like all of Cook's best work, varied with virtually every performance – not only from year to year, but often from night to night. As in his best work with Dudley, Peter improvised around a solid base of preprepared material – each performance building on the variations of the night before. Hence, although two consecutive performances wouldn't be all that different, a performance near the end of a long run would often differ dramatically from one at the beginning. 'Peter could tap a flow of mad verbal inventiveness that nothing could stem,' marveled Alan Bennett. 'I had the spot in the show immediately following Peter's monologue, which was scheduled to last five minutes or so but would often last for fifteen, when I would be handed an audience so weak from laughter I could do nothing with them'.[9]

Yes, I could have been a judge but I never had the Latin, never had the Latin for the judging. I just never had sufficient of it to get through the rigorous judging exams. They're noted for their rigour. People came staggering out saying 'My God, what a rigorous exam' – and so I became a miner instead. A coal miner. I managed to get through the mining exams – they're not very rigorous. They only ask one question. They say 'Who are you?', and I got 75% for that.

Of course, it's quite interesting work, getting hold of lumps of coal all day. It's quite interesting, because the coal was made in a very unusual way. You see God blew all the trees down. He didn't say 'Let's have some coal,' as he could have done – he had all the right contacts. No, he got this great wind going you see, and blew down all the trees, then over a period of three million years he changed it into coal – gradually, over a period of three million years so it wasn't noticeable to the average passer by. It was all part of the scheme, but people at the time did not see it that way. People under the trees did not say 'Hurrah, coal in three million years.' No, they said 'Oh dear, oh dear, trees falling on us – that's the last thing we want.' And of course their wish was granted.

I am very interested in the universe – I am specialising in the universe and all that surrounds it. I am studying Nesbitt's book – The Universe & All That Surrounds It, an Introduction. He tackles the subject boldly, goes through from the beginning of time right through to the present day, which according to Nesbitt is October 31, 1940. And he says the earth is spinning into the sun and we will all be burnt to death. But he ends the book on a note of hope. He says 'I hope this will not happen.' But there's not a lot of interest in this down the mine.

The trouble with it is the people. I am not saying that you get a load of riff-raff down the mine. I am not saying that. I am just saying we had a load of riff-raff down my mine – very boring conversationalists, extremely boring. All they talk about is what goes on in the mine – extremely boring. If you were searching for a word to describe the conversation, boring would spring to your lips. If ever you want to hear things like 'Hello, I've found a bit of coal.' 'Have you really?' 'Yes, no doubt about it, this black substance is coal all right.' 'Jolly good, the very thing we're looking for.' It's not enough to keep the mind alive, is it?

Whoops. Did you notice I suddenly went 'Whoops'? It's an impediment I got from being down the mine. Because one day I was walking along in the dark when I came across the body of a dead pit pony. 'Whoops.' And that's another reason why I couldn't be a judge, because I might have been up there all regal, sentencing away. 'I sentence you to – whoops.' And you see, the trouble is under English law that would have to stand. So all in all I'd rather have been a judge than a miner.

And what is more, being a miner, as soon as you are too old and tired and sick and stupid to do the job properly, you have to go. Well, the very opposite applies with the judges. So all in all I'd rather have been a judge than a miner. Because I've always been after the trappings of great luxury, you see. I really, really have. But all I've got hold of are the trappings of great poverty. I've got hold of the wrong load of trappings, and a rotten load of trappings they are too, ones I could have very well done without.

BLACK EQUALS WHITE
(Fortune Theatre, London, 1961)

COOK: Mr Akiboto Mbizu, the leader of the Pan African Folklore Party, is in London this week for the African Constitutional Conference. Now Mr Mbizu, what hopes do you hold out for a successful conclusion to the conference?

MILLER: There can be no successful conclusion at this conference until the fundamental rights of man are realised by the British government. One man, one vote – that is the law of God which all must obey, including God. One man, one vote – that is essential, especially for the nine million black idiots who vote for me.

COOK: Mr Mbizu, how do you view the imprisonment of your colleague, Mr Bandara Boko?

MILLER: The imprisonment of Mr Bandara Boko is a most immoral, disgusting and illegal act, and definitely not cricket. It is an outrageous and despicable act and I am in favour of it, as it lets me get on with a little bit of agitating on my own.

COOK: Mr Mbizu, do you in any way condone the violent methods used by your party to further their ends?

MILLER: By violent methods I presume you are referring to the isolated and sporadic outbreaks of entire communities being wiped out?

COOK: Yes I did have that in mind.

MILLER: Well all I can say to that is mote and beam.

COOK: I beg your pardon?

MILLER: Mote and beam.

COOK: What was that?

MILLER: Mote and beam! Wipe out the mote from your own eye, rich Britain, before you start messing around with our beams. Everywhere the black man is misrepresented. For example recently I went in London to see this play Fings Aint What They Used To Be, and in this play there was a black man who was leaning around all over the place doing nothing, implying that all black men are layabouts.

COOK: Surely Mr Mbizu you might as well say that the same play implied that all white people were pimps or prostitutes.

MILLER: Well that is fair comment. There can be no progress until you Englishmen stop looking down your noses at us Africans.

COOK: (*in a looking down his nose sort of a way*) Yes I think I see what you mean.

MILLER: Black equals white. No taxation without representation. Black equals white.

COOK: Mr Mbizu, one thing rather puzzles me about you, and that is your hair is extremely straight and your complexion seems to be white in colour.

MILLER: That is perfectly true. I have recently undergone an operation to straighten my hair and also to remove the pigmentation from my skin.

COOK: Doesn't this rather fly in the face of your principles?

MILLER: Not at all. I feel I can represent the interests of my people best by speaking to the white man on his own ground. Besides, it is the only way in which I can get lodgings.

THE SADDER AND WISER BEAVER
(Fortune Theatre, London, 1961)

'The Beaver' was the slightly sycophantic nickname of Lord Beverbrook, a Canadian, born in 1879, who came to Britain in 1910, already a wealthy businessman, and became a Unionist MP the same year. His finest hour was as minister responsible for aircraft production during the Battle of Britain, but he was most famous as the owner of the Daily Express and the Evening Standard and the founder of the Sunday Express. Both of his Express titles, in particular, were populist and pro empire, and their success and verve inevitably attracted prestigious contributors, like the historian AJP Taylor, who were rather more liberal and/or highbrow than the newspapers they wrote for. All ancient history now of course, but if you substitute Beaverbrook for Murdoch, Cook's sketch reads like it was written yesterday.

BENNETT: And you're still working for Beaverbrook?

COOK: Well yes, I'm still working for the Beaver, if work's the right word. Don't get me wrong, Alan, I haven't changed, working on the paper hasn't altered my outlook. You and I in the old days always used to think alike on most things. Well, it's just the same now – you name any issue and I'll agree with you on it. Just because my name's at the top of the column you mustn't think I have any connection with it. Just that I wrote it and they printed it – it's a very tenuous sort of connection in any case. I mean, I like Mountbatten – I think he does a wonderful job of work, and if ever I have to write anything on him, every now and then I am forced to write something, I always ring him up afterwards and apologise, or get my secretary to. You've met the wife, got a lovely little house now down in East Grinstead, two little kids, you've got to fight for it. We go for holidays in Germany, drink a stein with the people. I like the people. I say join the Common Market in private – I'm quite rebellious round about midnight sometimes. I'm working on the novel, you know. One day that novel's going to come out and blast the lid off the whole filthy business – name the names, show up Fleet Street for what it really is – a really accurate novel about all those people. But if you are going to write a really accurate novel, you've got to join the people you are writing about for a while anyway. I am going through a sort of research period at the moment. There are about ten of us on the paper, young, progressive liberal people who don't believe a word we are writing, and whenever the old man has a party – a cocktail party – we all gather together down the far end of the room, and drink as much as we can – we really knock it back – we drink and drink and drink – trying to break him from within; then – quite openly, behind our hands – we snigger at him.

BENNETT: You snigger at him?

COOK: That's right! We snigger and titter at him, 'Ha ha, putting on a bit of weight in St Tropez.'

BENNETT: Well, I don't know, it doesn't seem very much to me – sniggering and tittering.

COOK: A titter here, a titter there – it all adds up – you'd be surprised.

BENNETT: Well, take me – I'm no saint, but I turned down five thousand pounds a year with an advertising agency because I didn't want to make that sort of money.

COOK: Yes, I think that is wonderful of you, Alan, really wonderful

– in a way I wish I could be like you. But we don't all come into fifty thousand pounds at the age of twenty-one.

THE END OF THE WORLD
(Fortune Theatre, London, 1961)

MILLER: How will it be this end of which you have spoken, Brother Enim?

ALL: Yes, how will it be?

COOK: Well, it will be as twere a mighty rending in the sky, and the mountains will sink, and the valleys will rise and great will be the tumult thereof.

MILLER: Will the vale of the temple be rent in twain?

COOK: It will be rent in twain about two minutes before we see the manifest flying beast head in the sky.

BENNETT: And will there be a mighty wind?

COOK: Certainly there will be a mighty wind, if the word of God is anything to go by.

MOORE: And will this wind be so mighty as to lay low the mountains of the earth?

COOK: No. It will not be quite as mighty as that. That is why we have come up on the mountain, you stupid nit – to be safe from it.

MILLER: All right then – when will it be?

ALL: Ah, when will it be?

COOK: In about thirty seconds' time, according to the ancient pyramidic scrolls.

MILLER: Shall we compose ourselves then?

COOK: Good plan. Prepare for the end of the world. Fifteen seconds!

MOORE: Here, have you got the picnic basket?

BENNETT: Yes.

COOK: Five, four, three, two, one, zero!

ALL: Now is the end, perish the world!

COOK: It was GMT, wasn't it?

MILLER: Yes.

COOK: Well, it's not quite the conflagration we'd been banking on. Never mind, lad, same time tomorrow, we must get a winner one day.

TVPM
(John Golden Theatre, New York, 1962)

Peter Cook's parody of the Prime Minister caused quite a stir forty years ago, especially when Harold Macmillan came to see Cook impersonate him on the West End stage. 'When I've a spare evening,' improvised Peter, as Macmillan, 'there's nothing I like better than to wander over to a theatre and sit there listening to a group of sappy, urgent, vibrant young satirists, with a stupid great grin spread all over my silly old face.' Apart from this savage ad lib, by today's standards it seems pretty mild, but at the time it was considered terribly daring and rather shocking, and set the standard for Britain's short-lived but lively satire boom. 'My impersonation of Macmillan was in fact extremely affectionate,' explained Cook, twenty years later. 'I was a great Macmillan fan. He did have this somewhat ludicrous manner, but merely because it was the first time for some years that a living Prime Minister had been impersonated on the stage, a great deal of weight was attached to it.'[10]

Good evening. I have recently been travelling round the world, on your behalf, and at your expense, visiting some of the chaps with whom I hope to be shaping your future. I went first to Germany, and there I spoke with the German Foreign Minister, Herr . . . Herr and there and we exchanged many frank words in our respective languages, so precious little came of that in the way of understanding. I would, however, emphasise that the little that did come of it was indeed truly precious. I then went on to America, and there I had talks with the young, vigorous President of that great country, and danced with his very lovely lady wife. We talked of many things, including Great Britain's position in the world as some kind of honest broker. I agreed with him when he said that no nation could be more honest, and he agreed with me when I chaffed him and said that no nation could be broker. This type of genial, statesmanlike banter often went on late into the night. Our talks ranged over a wide variety of subjects, including that of the Skybolt Missile programme. And after a great deal of good-natured give and take I decided on behalf of Great Britain to accept Polaris in place of the Skybolt. This is a good solution because, as far as I can see, the Polaris starts where the Skybolt left off – in the sea.

I was privileged to see some actual photographs of this weapon. The President was kind enough to show me actual photographs of this missile, beautiful photographs taken by Karsh of Ottawa. A very handsome weapon – we shall be very proud to have them. The photographs, that is. We don't get the missile until around 1970. In the meantime, we shall just have to keep our fingers crossed, sit very quietly, and try not to alienate anyone. This is not to say that we do not have our own Nuclear Striking Force. We do. We have the Blue Steel, a very effective missile, as it has a range of 150 miles, which means we can just about get Paris. And by God we will.

While I was abroad, I was very moved to receive letters from people in acute distress all over the country. And one in particular from an old age pensioner in Fife is indelibly printed on my memory. Let me read it to you. It reads 'Dear Prime Minister, I am an old age pensioner in Fife, living on a fixed income of some two pounds, seven shillings a week. This is not enough. What do you of the Conservative Party propose to do about it?' (*tears up letter*) Well, let me say right away, Mrs McFarlane, as one Scottish old age pensioner to another, be of good cheer. There are many people in this country today who are far worse off than yourself. And it is the policy of the Conservative Party to see that this position is maintained.

The young and vigorous President to whom Cook referred was John F. Kennedy, and his very lovely lady wife was Jackie Kennedy. Macmillan did indeed visit Kennedy, but Cook went one better. 'When we were in New York, playing on Broadway, I think he may have seen something of Jackie Kennedy,' revealed Alan Bennett. 'Certainly, when the President and his wife (at her urging) came to see Beyond the Fringe *I have a vision of the presidential party in the Green Room having drinks in the interval, with Mrs Kennedy absently stroking Peter's hand as they chatted.'*[11]

PETER COOK

THE GREAT TRAIN ROBBERY
(John Golden Theatre, New York, 1964)

There was really nothing remotely great about the so-called Great Train Robbery of 1963, in which a gang held up the Royal Mail train en route from Glasgow to London, but several of these train robbers became tabloid folk heroes of sorts, including Buster Edwards, who was played by Phil Collins in the 1988 movie, Buster. *The driver was hit over the head with an iron bar – he later died – but the robbery nevertheless acquired a more glamorous cachet than it deserves, probably because of the vast amount of cash stolen (actually £2,631,684 – not £3million, as Bennett says below, but still a fortune in 1963, maybe as much as ten times its real value today) and possibly because these were old notes, withdrawn from circulation, and about to be destroyed. Cook sidestepped the tabloids' fascination with lovable villains, and used this crime as a springboard for his own separate, satirical fantasy. Yet the real robbery was back in the news a year later, when another of the robbers, Ronnie Biggs, escaped from Wandsworth Prison and ended up in Brazil.*

BENNETT: The great train robbery of over three million pounds continues to baffle the British Police.

COOK: Good evening.

BENNETT: However, we have here with us in the studio this evening . . .

COOK: Good evening.

BENNETT: Sir Arthur Gappy, the First Deputy Head of New Scotland Yard, and I'm going to ask him a few questions about the train robbery.

COOK: Good evening.

BENNETT: Good evening, Sir Arthur. I'm going to ask you a few questions about the train robbery.

COOK: Good – the very thing we are investigating. In fact I would like to make one thing quite clear at the very outset and that is, when you speak of a train robbery, this involved no loss of train, merely what I like to call, the contents of the train, which were pilfered. We haven't lost a train since 1946, I believe it was – the year of the great snows when we mislaid a small one. Trains are very bulky and cumbersome, making them extremely difficult to lose as compared with a small jewel for example or a small pearl, which could easily fall off a lady's neck and disappear into the tall grass – whereas a huge train with steam coming out is very . . .

BENNETT: I think you have made that point rather well, Sir Arthur. Who do you think may have perpetrated this awful crime?

COOK: Well, we believe this to be the work of thieves, and I'll tell you why. The whole pattern is very reminiscent of past robberies where we have found thieves to have been involved. The tell-tale loss of property – that's one of the signs we look for, the snatching away of the money substances – it all points to thieves.

BENNETT: So you feel that thieves are responsible?

COOK: Good heavens no! I feel that thieves are totally irresponsible. They're a ghastly group of people, snatching away your money, stealing from you . . .

BENNETT: I appreciate that, Sir Arthur, but . . .

COOK: You may appreciate it, but I don't. I'm sorry I can't agree with you. If you appreciate having your money snatched away from you I will have to consider you some sort of odd fish . . .

BENNETT: You misunderstand me, Sir Arthur, but who in your opinion is behind the criminals?

COOK: Well, we are – considerably. Months, days, even seconds . . .

BENNETT: No, I mean, who do you think is the organising genius behind the crime?

COOK: Of course now, you're asking me who is the organising genius behind the crime.

BENNETT: You are a man of very acute perception, Sir Arthur.

COOK: Well let me say this. We think it's a mindermast.

BENNETT: A mindermast?

COOK: Yes, a mindermast.

BENNETT: What exactly is a mindermast?

COOK: Well a mindermast is the code word we use at Scotland Yard to describe a mastermind. We don't like to use the word mastermind as that depresses the men to think they're up against that, so we call it a mindermast in a futile endeavour to deceive ourselves.

BENNETT: I see.

COOK: But we are using the wonderful equipment known as Identikit – do you know about that?

BENNETT: Yes, I believe it's when you piece together the face of the criminal.

COOK: Not entirely, no – it's when you piece together the appearance of the face of the criminal. Unfortunately we're not able to piece together the face of the criminal – I wish we could. Once you have captured the criminal's face the other parts of the criminal's body are not too far behind, being situated immediately below the criminal's face ... Anyway, through this wonderful equipment of Identikit, we have pieced together a remarkable likeness to the Archbishop of Canterbury.

BENNETT: So his Grace is your number one suspect?

COOK: Let me put it this way. His Grace is the man we are currently beating the living daylights out of down at the Yard.

BENNETT: And he is still your number one suspect?

COOK: No, I'm happy to say that the Archbishop, God Bless him, no longer resembles the picture we built up. A change I think for the better. He thinks for the worse – a difference of opinion.

BENNETT: I see. I believe I'm right in saying that some of the stolen money has been recovered?

COOK: Yes, that's right.

BENNETT: And what is being done with this?

COOK: We're spending it as quickly as we can. It's a short life, but a merry one down at the Yard. Goodnight.

ONE LEG TOO FEW
(John Golden Theatre, New York, 1964)

Probably Cook's most famous sketch, about a one legged man auditioning for the role of Tarzan, 'One Leg Too Few' first surfaced in a Pembroke College revue in 1960, reappeared later that year in the Footlights revue, Pop Goes Mrs Jessop, *and was farmed out to Kenneth Williams for his 1961 West End revue,* One Over The Eight. *However in the version included here, Dudley took on the role of the one legged Tarzan, and his indefatigably eager playing style provided the perfect contrast to Peter's portrait of English reserve, thus turning a good sketch into a great one. A year later, Cook and Moore did it for The Queen, in ITV's* Royal Gala Show, *and in 1973, they took it back to New York in their two man stage show,* Good Evening *(aka Behind The Fridge). Unfortunately, it ended up in* The Hound of The Baskervilles, *their disastrous Sherlock Holmes parody, but thankfully this disastrous movie wasn't its last resting place. They performed it together for American Comic Relief in 1987, and finally for an Amnesty International fundraiser, 'The Secret Policeman's Biggest Ball' back in London, in 1989.*

COOK: Miss Rigby! Stella, my love! Would you send in the next auditioner, please, Mr Spiggott, I believe it is.

(*Enter MOORE, hopping on one leg.*)

Mr Spiggott, I believe?

MOORE: Yes – Spiggott by name, Spiggott by nature.

(*MOORE follows COOK around the room.*)

COOK: Yes . . . there's no need to follow me, Mr Spiggott. Please be stood. Now, Mr Spiggott, you are, I believe, auditioning for the part of Tarzan.

MOORE: Right.

COOK: Now, Mr Spiggott, I couldn't help noticing almost at once that you are a one-legged person.

MOORE: You noticed that?

COOK: I noticed that, Mr Spiggott. When you have been in the business as long as I have you get to notice these little things almost instinctively. Now, Mr Spiggott, you, a one-legged man, are applying for the role of Tarzan – a role which traditionally involves the use of a two-legged actor.

MOORE: Correct.

COOK: And yet, you, a unidexter, are applying for the role.

MOORE: Right.

COOK: A role for which two legs would seem to be the minimum requirement.

MOORE: Very true.

COOK: Well, Mr Spiggott, need I point out to you where your

deficiency lies as regards landing the role?

MOORE: Yes, I think you ought to.

COOK: Need I say with overmuch emphasis that it is in the leg division that you are deficient.

MOORE: The leg division?

COOK: Yes, the leg division, Mr Spiggott. You are deficient in it – to the tune of one. Your right leg I like. I like your right leg – a lovely leg for the role. That's what I said when I saw it come in. I said 'A lovely leg for the role.' I've got nothing against your right leg. The trouble is – neither have you. You fall down on your left.

MOORE: You mean it's inadequate?

COOK: Yes, it's inadequate, Mr Spiggott. And to my mind, the British public is just not ready for the sight of a one-legged ape man swinging through the jungly tendrils.

MOORE: I see.

COOK: However, don't despair. After all, you score over a man with no legs at all. Should a legless man come in here demanding the role, I should have no hesitation in saying, 'Get out, run away.'

MOORE: So there's still a chance?

COOK: There is still a very good chance. If we get no two-legged character actors in here within the next two months, there is still a very good chance that you'll land this vital role. Failing two-legged actors, you, a unidexter, are just the sort of person we shall be attempting to contact telephonicly.

MOORE: Well . . . thank you very much.

COOK: So my advice is, to hop on a bus, go home, and sit by your telephone, in the hope that we will be getting in touch with you. I'm really sorry I can't be more definite, but as you realise, it's really a two-legged man we're after. Good morning, Mr Spiggott.

(*Exit MOORE, hopping.*)

Chapter Three
EL Wisty

Peter's American excursion was an extraordinary achievement for a young man in his mid-twenties. As well as starring in *Beyond the Fringe*, he even found time to open a thriving New York branch of The Establishment Club. Yet by the time Cook returned to London, in 1964, Britain's brief satire boom had gone bust. The Establishment had folded, *Private Eye*'s circulation had tumbled from 80,000 to 20,000, and *That Was the Week That Was* had been axed by the BBC, so as not to upset any politicians during the 1964 General Election. Satire was suddenly last year's thing, and so – temporarily – was Peter Cook. 'I came back expecting to be enormously well known, and of course nobody knew me from Adam,' he admitted.[1] Ironically, while he looked around for work, *Beyond the Fringe* was still running in the West End – without him. Peter had wanted the show to close when he went to America, to stop it from 'dribbling away'. Rather, the reverse had happened.

Cook kept himself busy by reviving *Private Eye*, the only survivor of the Sixties satirical explosion, and his one lasting legacy – but it was still a pretty sharp comedown for a young comedian who'd starred in the hottest show in London and New York, had opened London and New York's trendiest nightclubs, and been feted by the Queen of England, the Prime Minister of Great Britain, and the President of the United States. What's more, most of Cook's Establishment and *Beyond the Fringe* colleagues had now been snapped up by television. Jonathan Miller was presenting the BBC's highbrow arts series, *Monitor*, while Alan Bennett, John Bird, Eleanor Bron and John Fortune were all appearing on *Not So Much a Programme, More a Way of Life*, supporting David Frost, who'd been transformed from Cook's Footlights fan into Britain's brightest new TV star, by his slick, accomplished stewardship of TW3 – the hip topical series Peter had inspired, but played virtually no part in.

Cook's unlikely saviour from this televisual wilderness was a Canadian broadcaster called Bernard Braden. They'd met a few years before, when Cook was still at Cambridge, during a decidedly establishment 'do' in honour of the Duke of Bedford, at his stately home, Woburn – where Cook was performing some Footlights sketches. Braden was now fronting a light hearted blend of consumer and current affairs called *On the Braden Beat*. A humorist himself, Braden invited Cook to revive Mr Grole, for a four-week trial on his ATV series.

Braden's offer was relatively modest compared with Cook's American excesses, but Cook worked hard. Every Wednesday, he improvised alone as Grole, whom he'd now renamed EL Wisty. Cook tape-recorded the results, then distilled the highlights into a compact monologue, to be filmed on Thursday for a Saturday transmission. Wisty was a hit, and Cook's four weeks turned into twenty, spawning a wonderful LP and even a highly successful series of radio and telly commercials for Watneys Ale. Although they were soon overshadowed by his partnership with Dudley Moore, these surreal, semi-detached soliloquies remain among Cook's finest – and funniest – work. The programme's tight production schedule (and Cook's last-minute preparation) left him little time to learn his lines, leaving him reliant on the autocue. This short cut became a bad habit, which subsequently hampered some of his less static future roles, but for EL Wisty it was almost an asset. Wisty stared unsmiling (and apparently unblinking) straight into the camera from start to finish, and the result was hypnotic.

'He is a completely lost creature,' said Peter, describing his alter ego a few years later. 'He never works, never moves, has no background and suspects everybody is peering at him and trying to get his secrets out of him.'[2] Over the decade since he'd first evolved, what had started off as a fairly straightforward impersonation of Mr Boylett the school butler had gradually become a comic self-portrait, a twilit version of himself. 'I'm terrified I shall become some kind of Wisty figure,' he admitted.[3] However by far the best summary of EL Wisty's personality is the manifesto that Cook wrote in 1965 for the World Domination League, which Wisty had formed the year before with his friend Spotty Muldoon:

1 Total domination of the world by 1964.
2 Domination of the astral spheres quite soon too.
3 The finding of lovely ladies for Spotty Muldoon within the foreseeable future.
4 GETTING A NUCLEAR ARM to deter with.
5 The bodily removal from this planet of CP Snow and Alan Freeman and their replacement with fine TREES.
6 Stopping the GOVERNMENT peering up the pipes at us and listening to ALL WE SAY.
7 Training BEES for uses against Foreign Powers and so on.
8 Elimination of spindly insects and encouragement of lovely little newts who dance about and are happy.
9 EL Wisty for GOD.

∿

THE WORLD DOMINATION LEAGUE
(*On the Braden Beat*, ITV, 1964)

If there's one thing I can't bear, it's when hundreds of old men come creeping in through the window in the middle of the night and throw all manner of garbage all over me. I can't bear that. I think that's unbearable – ghastly old men, with great pails of garbage, throwing it all over me. I don't think it should be allowed. I think there should be a place for those people to go. And I don't think it should be my room. I'd vote for any party that would say 'I won't allow people to throw garbage all over me.' But none of the parties seem to be particularly interested. That's why I formed the World Domination League. It's a wonderful league, the World Domination League. The aims, as published in the manifesto, are total domination of the world by 1958. That's what we're planning to do. We've had to revise it. We're hoping to bring a new manifesto out with a more realistic target. How we aim to go about it is as follows. We shall move about into people's rooms and say 'Excuse me, we are the World Domination League. May we dominate you?' Then, if they say 'Get out,' of course we give up. Well, you have to give up if you're told to get out.

There's been some wonderful dominators in history, you know. Attila was one. He was a wonderful dominator, Attila the Nun. He was an amazing dominator. He had a Gothic horde, and he used to move about entire countries and strangle people completely to death. And then, when everybody woke up, they'd see a little note pinned to their chest, saying 'You've been dominated. Ha, ha. Attila the Nun.'

Hitler was a very peculiar person, wasn't he? He was another dominator, you know, Hitler. And he was a wonderful ballroom dancer. Not many people know that. He was a wonderful little dancer. He used to waltz around with a number eight on his back. The only trouble was, he was very short, and people used to shout out to him when he was dancing, and say 'Wie kurz du bist – how short you are.' And this of course enraged Hitler. He flew into a tantrum, and he gave up ballroom dancing, and took up wholesale raping and pillaging instead. Of course, Mrs Hitler was a charming woman, wasn't she. Mrs Hitler, a lovely woman. She's still alive, you know. I saw her down the Edgware Road only the other day. She'd just popped into the chemist's to buy something, and I saw her sign the cheque. 'Mrs Hitler.' So I knew it was she. I tried to go up and talk to her, but she slipped away into the crowd. I was hoping she'd be able to come to the next meeting of the World Domination League. Not many people do.

I've had a new manifesto printed, which should boost our programme a bit. There's a picture of me on the cover with the words I Will Dominate You at the top of it. It's a very compelling picture and I think there's a good chance of me doing a bit of dominating soon. I've had some wonderful ideas for getting the dominating going. I've got some extremely subtle advertising slogans that should get the public behind us. Things like 'vote for EL Wisty and lovely nude ladies will come and dance with you.' It's a complete lie, of course, but you can't afford to be too scrupulous if you're going to dominate the world. Then there's another good one, which says 'if you don't vote for EL Wisty, horrible black spiders with hairy legs will creep into your room in the middle of the night and bite your ears off.' That should get the women's vote. If there is one thing they can't bear it's black spiders grabbing hold of them in the night.

Another way I'm going to get people's votes is to start shouting off about all the filth on television. As far as I'm concerned I could do with a great deal more of it. All the same I formed an EL Wisty Clean Up TV campaign, pointing out some of the suggestive things that get on the air. The first thing I say they should ban is that Invisible Man show. Have you seen it? It's absolutely disgusting. It's all about this man who's turned invisible because he fell into a vat of HLBO5. That was an experimental magic ingredient in a detergent. Anyway, poor devil falls in this rubbish and he turns invisible, and the programme is all about his amazing adventures. As he's invisible, the only way you can tell where he is is if he's smoking. You can see his cigarette moving about in the air. Or else you can see a telephone waving about the place. It's all very ingenious, but the thing that amazes me is that he does it all in the nude. You don't actually see him of course because he's invisible but you can easily tell he's got nothing on because otherwise you'd see his clothes. Sometimes he dresses up in bandages, poor devil, and dark glasses, and you can see his outline, but you never see any trousers or jackets moving about the place, so it stands to reason he's wandering about the place with nothing on. A ghastly invisible nudist, there for everyone to see – or, rather, not to see. And, for all we know, there may be millions of other invisible nudists in the other programmes. I might be able to use them in the World Domination League. It'd be a very good slogan. 'Vote for EL Wisty or else invisible nudists will come along and smash you round the face.'

ROYALTY
(*On the Braden Beat*, ITV, 1964)

I've always wanted to be a member of the royal family. I've always wanted to be part of the royal family because there are great advantages to being royal. If you're royal, whatever you do is very interesting. Whatever you do, people are very interested in it. Even if you do something very boring, people are still very interested in it. If a royal person does something extremely boring, people say, 'Oh, isn't it interesting that he's doing something extremely boring.' If I do something extremely boring, people say, 'Oh, how extremely boring', it's not so good. You never get newspaper cuttings about me, you never see headlines saying, 'E L Wisty was looking radiant, as he got off the 17A bus, from Hounslow.' You don't see pictures saying, 'E L Wisty was looking tense but dignified as he entered the municipal baths.' You don't get that sort of treatment.

Another wonderful thing about being royal is that people get interested in what you're interested in. That's how the corgis have caught on, you see. Everybody loves a corgi because the royal people are connected with them. I think newts have had a very hard time. If I was a royal person I think I would patronise the newts. They're lovely little creatures, newts, you know. They are not as cuddly as corgis, of course. You don't nestle up to a newt as you would to a corgi, but they're lovely things. I'd have whole packs of royal newts wandering about the palace gardens and I'd be seen with them the whole time, and I'd create a special post called Royal Master of the Newts – The Lord High Newter, and he'd have to walk about with a golden stick, you see, tapping the ground continuously and saying, 'Newtarty, newtarty, let the world bring forth newts in abundance,' and then I think we'd see an end to the corgis and a beginning of the newts.

Of course, there are disadvantages to being royal. Everybody has to come in backwards you see. That's a disadvantage. They have to come in and go out backwards if they're in the royal presence. That's why you only see royalty dancing with royalty. They can't dance with ordinary people unless they're back-to-back with them. And that's never really caught on, that sort of thing.

Of course, if you're royal, it's wonderful to be able to tell royal jokes, that's very wonderful. You always get a good laugh if you tell a royal joke. I'd tell lots of royal jokes if I was royal. For example, if somebody gave me a wonderful silver newt container, a newt casket, I'd say, 'Thank you very much indeed for this wonderful gift of a newt casket. I hope it's not going to be a bloody newtsense.' All of England would be chuckling if I said that. That's the point of royalty, to make people a tiny bit happier in this drab life.

We've all got royal blood in our veins, you know. It's the best place for it in my view. We've all got a little bit of royal blood in our veins, we're all in line for the succession, and if nineteen million, four hundred thousand, two hundred and eight people die, I'll be king tomorrow. It's not very likely but it's a nice thought and helps keep you going.

THE TADPOLE EXPERT
(*On the Braden Beat*, ITV, 1964)

I've always wanted to be an expert on tadpoles, I've always fancied being a tadpole expert. It's a wonderful life if you become an experty tadpoleous, as they are known in the trade. You get invited out to all the smart parties and social gatherings. When smart people are making out their lists for the dinner parties, they say, 'Now, who can we have to make up the ten? A tadpole expert would be very nice. He could sit next to Lady Sonia.' And at all the smart functions people come up to you and say, 'I hear you're a tadpole expert. Tell me, what are tadpoles really like?' And lovely ladies invite you back to their flat and say, 'You know I'm longing to hear about your tadpoles. Hang on a minute while I slip into a gossamer trench coat.'

I've tried over the years to become a tadpole expert. I studied the tadpole and attempted to learn everything about them. There isn't very much to learn actually. The main thing to learn is that there are two kinds of tadpoles. There's the ones that turn into the frogs and the ones that turn into the toads. I call them the toadpole and the frogpole. Now the only way to distinguish between the two is that the toadpole tends to turn into a toad, whereas the frogpole will tend to turn into a frog. But there's no way that I've found of predicting this.

Of course, tadpoles are lovely little creatures, aren't they? They're so good-natured, and they have such lovely little smiles. It's very hard to see their little smiles actually, because they're black all over, and they have little black mouths and the inside of their mouths are black as well, so when they smile, it's just a little black blob. You can't really tell when they're smiling.

They make lovely pets you know, the tadpole – very faithful. The only trouble is as soon as you get to know them properly and they start doing tricks and things, and they can answer to their name, they turn into horrible toads and frogs. I can't abide toads and frogs – horrible slimy creatures that go around eating flies and laying their slime all over the place. Such a pity when you think of the lovely little tadpoles wiggling about in the jar.

I used to keep tadpoles in a jar, by my bedside when I was studying to be a tadpole expert – lovely little things, squiggling about. That was until I had the tragedy – I had a terrible tragedy. I had three lovely little tadpoles in my jar – Deirdre, Margaret and Beryl. Lovely little things, and I switched the light out last thing at night, and I must have had a very violent dream about gossamer trench coats or something. When I woke up in the morning, there they were. Strewn all over my pillow. All dried up like three little raisins. I tried to revive them, by throwing water all over them, but it was too late. They just went into soggy little raisins – horrible soggy little black raisins. Tragic business. Deirdre was just getting her first legs too. But I suppose it was all for the best. They would only have turned into ghastly old toads and frogs in the end and left me. It's rather a thankless life being a tadpole expert.

ARE YOU SPOTTY?
(*On the Braden Beat*, ITV, 1964)

I was looking through the newspaper the other day, and I saw a little advertisement that was very rude – a very rude little advertisement. It said 'Are you spotty?' There was a nasty man pointing his finger out at you and saying 'Are you spotty?' I don't think people should be allowed to say 'Are you spotty?' – just like that. You don't buy a newspaper to have people say 'Are you spotty?' to you. I mean if you are spotty, you know you're spotty. You don't want people telling you you're spotty, or asking if you're spotty. And if you're not spotty, why should people imply you're spotty, by saying 'Are you spotty?' I don't think people should be allowed to say 'Are you spotty?' just like that.

I've got a very spotty friend. He's called Arthur Muldoon. He's covered in spots. He's got spots all over him. He's a very spotty person. People call him Spotty Muldoon because of his spots. He wasn't christened Spotty of course, he was christened Arthur, but people call him Spotty and when he goes out for a walk people come up to him in the street and say 'Hello, aren't you a spotty one then?'

Of course, it gets Arthur down, being so spotty. And he saw an advertisement which said 'Are you spotty? Are you very spotty? Are you unbelievably spotty? Tick in the right box, and enclose five shillings.' Well, poor old Arthur didn't know what he was so he came round to me and asked which he was – spotty, very spotty or unbelievably spotty. And I told him he was somewhere between very spotty and unbelievably spotty. So he wrote in saying he was almost unbelievably spotty. He wrote in saying 'I am almost unbelievably spotty. I enclose five shillings.' And he got a letter back saying 'Bad luck.' That's all he had out of them.

I saw an advertisement the other day for the secret of life. It said 'The secret of life can be yours for twenty-five shillings. Send to Secret of Life Institute, Willesden.' So I wrote away, seemed a good bargain, secret of life, twenty-five shillings. And I got a letter back saying, 'If you think you can get the secret of life for twenty-five shillings, you don't deserve to have it. Send fifty shillings for the secret of life.' So I sent fifty shillings along and got no reply so I went along to the place, the Institute. And there was a little man there and he said the secret of life people have gone out of business but would you be interested in dynamic strength through your glands – Gandhi's wonderful secret in tablet form at last. I asked him then if it would be any good for spots. And they said 'Well, Gandhi never had any trouble with that at all.' So I bought some for Arthur Muldoon and gave them to him. I don't know if they've done any good, I've not seen much of him recently. Pity about those secret of life people going out of business – I could do with the secret of life.

CP SNOW
(*On the Braden Beat*, ITV, 1964)

I tried to get round to see CP Snow yesterday. I went round to the House of Lords with a few suggestions. I had a wonderful idea for CP. I call him CP. It's a peculiar name isn't it? CP Snow. Sounds horrible, CP Snow – it sounds as if he's dripping, and covered in moss and slime and things. CP Snow. So I went round to attempt to see him, because I had this wonderful idea for an aircraft that would go at a million miles an hour. Not just six hundred and seventy-five miles an hour, but a million miles an hour, and it would only cost one penny a year to run. It's a wonderful idea. I hadn't really developed it beyond that. It's just in the idea stage at the moment.

But I attempted to see CP. I said 'I'd like to see Lord Snow, about modernising Britain.' And they said 'You can't do that. He's too busy getting his ceremonial robes on to see anybody about doing that.' I said 'I've got a wonderful idea for C P Snow.' And they said 'Who hasn't? Get out.' Well, I wasn't going to hang around and just be insulted. So I went home.

Of course, CP Snow is the one who is trying to get all the automation going. Trying to get machines in to do everything that we're doing. He's very fond of machines. He wants machines to be doing everything. And this shall give everybody else a lot of leisure, you see. And if everybody has a lot of leisure, they'll be forced to read his ghastly old books. He's written lots of books about adultery in corridors and walnuts and things. And he thinks if we all have a great deal of leisure we'll get round to reading the ghastly things. He'd like to see machines all over the place you see, spying on what we're doing. Some people think C P Snow is a machine. Have you every looked at him? He moves in a very jerky fashion, and he's got very small hands and a very big head. I think he's some kind of robot. Possibly he's an electrical robot, because you've never seen anybody touch him with wet hands. It's always a sign of an electrical robot.

But very soon, you see, all the machines will be wandering around on spindly legs, great metal spindly legs. We'll all be living in little metal boxes and the machines will pass by and awful antennae will come in through the window and they'll check up whether you're reading the CP Snow novel. And then they'll all start breeding amongst themselves, the machines, and going out to the cinemas with each other and sitting and whispering in the dark and holding their metallic tentacles together. It's a horrible idea. I can't bear the ideas of machines doing everything. I tried to ring up CP Snow about it. I couldn't bear the idea. I rang up the Ministry of Technology. I said I can't bear the idea of these machines and this voice said 'This is a recording, record your message to the machine now. It will be passed on to CP Snow.' So I didn't say anything. You won't catch me talking to a bloody old machine.

PEACE THROUGH NUDISM
(*On the Braden Beat*, ITV, 1964)

I was very disappointed not to be called to Number Ten Downing Street. I'd been expecting a call, but none came through at all. Most upsetting. I was Shadow Minister of Nudism. It's a wonderful post, designed to promote nudism throughout the world and with it peace. Peace and nudism go hand in hand, you see. War and nudism do not mix. You've never had a war, ever, started by a nudist. There's no nudist ever has started a war. And that is why nudism is such an important thing to get over.

There's been some wonderful nudists about, you know. Khrushchev, he was a nudist, and that's why he had to go, because the anti-nudist faction in the Kremlin got at him. Khrushchev used to wander about the Kremlin with nothing on, wearing only a little chain of daisies, humming Tchaikovsky all the time. Just round about midnight – a lovely sight, a little chubby man with nothing on wandering around with the daisies dangling round his neck. And Mr Mikoyan was an anti-nudist, you see, and saw Khrushchev disappearing around the corner, so he called the Presidium and they got rid of him. It's a great shame. Of course Kosygin and Brezhnev, they're anti-nudist and never take their clothes off at all. They're appalling people. They take their bath with their clothes on.

If I did become Minister of Nudism, I'd be allowed to be on television every evening round about nine thirty. I'd come on and say 'Good evening – this is the Minister of Nudism. Take off your clothes and begin to dance about.' And everybody in the world would start dancing about with nothing on, and if you didn't, special inspectors would come round and tear your clothes off and fine you a thousand pounds for every article of clothes you're wearing.

I wish I could get into the government. I've been trying for a very long time, you know. I tried during the war. I had quite a lot of influence during the war, although I wasn't in the government. A lot of my policies were adopted. I used to write to Winston Churchill and tell him what was going on. Right at the beginning of the war, I said 'The people to get are the Boches – beat the Germans and the war's over.' And I said 'The man behind the Germans is Adolf Hitler. Once you kill Hitler, you're laughing.' And eventually, after about six years, he took my advice.

At the end of the war I didn't get much credit for it. The idea of beating the Germans was all mine, but at the end you didn't see me waving from the balconies. You didn't see me driving in golden coaches, through the cheering crowds, but I would like to have had some recognition. I've written a little poem about international nudism. It's a lovely little poem. It's:

> If all the world were nudists
> If all the world were bare
> Every one would live in peace
> No war would they declare.
> If every one went dancing
> Around with nothing on
> Everybody would be happy
> As a person I know called John.

I don't actually know anybody called John. I just put that in for the rhyme. It's poet's licence. I hope very much that they will call me to Downing Street but I've been standing by for years now and nobody has.

O'ER HILL AND DALE
(*On the Braden Beat*, ITV, 1964)

Once upon a time there was a man of between thirty and eighty-two years old. He used to get up in the morning and have a small breakfast, and after breakfast he put on a coat and he'd go wandering round, for several hours, through the trees and through the shrubs, and when he'd wandered round for several hours he'd wander back again, to where he'd wandered from. And he'd have a bit of lunch and then he'd go out and start wandering about again.

PETER COOK

Wander, wander, wander. He'd go wandering o'er the hill and o'er the dale. That's where poets wander, is o'er the hill and dale. Other people wander over hill and dale. But not the poets they go o'er, o'er they go, they think it sounds better.

Anyway, when he's wandered o'er the hill and o'er the dale, he comes back again for a bit of tea. And then he settles down for the evening, until he falls asleep. It's not much of a life is it? I can't see how anyone can bear to go on with it. It's such a mouldy time we all have. I've been looking at my diary. it's the most boring document I've ever seen in my life. I hadn't realised what a boring life I've been living until I read my diary. It's unbelievably boring. It's probably the most boring book in the world. It should be given to school children as an examination subject. If you listened to it you would believe it. Listen to this: 'Monday, got up, went for a walk, had lunch, went to lavatory, came out again, wrote up diary.' And then the next day, it reads 'Got up, went out, came in, went to bed.' Didn't even go to the lavatory. Next day: 'Got up, wandered round to see Spotty Muldoon. He wasn't in. Wandered back. Went to bed.' It's not what you'd call exciting reading, is it?

I think it's about time I started doing a few interesting things. It's time I found something out like the secret of eternal life, the meaning of the universe, or how to get hold of women or something. I've got the feeling that I must do something important and amazing very soon. Perhaps if I grabbed hold of somebody in the government and threw them into the sea. I must do something with my life, something that I'll be remembered for when I'm gone. Perhaps if I got hold of some bees and trained them to fly up people's noses that might do some good. I could release them in the House of Commons and every year people would burn effigies of me on E L Wisty night and dance round a beehive.

There must be something memorable that I can do before I die and leave this mortal coil on which we strut and fret our vulgar ways, as Shakespeare put it, God bless him. Anyway, I decided to go out and do something, so if you read of CP Snow exploding in his bath, you'll know it's my work.

A BEE LIFE
(*On the Braden Beat*, ITV, 1964)

God bless you all. I want to talk to you all about bees. They're
lovely little creatures, bees, with little round furry smiling faces and
lovely cuddly little bodies, and they fly about the place in such a
cheerful way. Not like the horrid old wasp, who goes glistening
through the air, with his horrible hard shining body all covered in
stings. The bee is all furry and friendly. Did you know that bees
have a terrible time in life, because what they have to do is go round
to every flower they can lay their hands on and poke their noses
right into it and suck out as much nectar as they can get? Then they
wipe their noses onto their legs, and go back to the hive with this
tiny bit of honey on their legs. They're not allowed to eat it
themselves. It all has to be stored in the hive, and very gradually
they build up enough honey for the winter. It takes thousands and
thousands of bee hours to get it all together. And then when all the
honey is in and all the flowers have died, a horrible old man in a
veil comes along and steals it all away. The beekeeper takes all their
honey away. Isn't that dreadful?

And do you know that none of the lady bees are allowed to
have children? They're not allowed to have love affairs and
babies. Only one lady bee is allowed to have love affairs, and
that's the queen bee. It's a dreadful situation. All the other lady
bees have to sit around twiddling their legs all day, while the fat
old queen bee has all the love affairs. She's a beastly fat old thing,
the queen bee. I shouldn't think many of the men bees really
fancy her, but they're forced to go up to her and kiss her and
everything. It's a dreadful life. Imagine what it would be like if it
happened to us people. If only the Queen was allowed to have
children. That's why all the bees look the same. They've all got
the same mother.

Of course the worst thing about being a bee is your sting. Bees
have got a sting in their bottom, which God gave them to use
against their enemies in moments of peril. The only trouble is that
if they ever use their sting, they die. As soon as the bee uses its sting,
it dies. It's an absolutely useless sting. I suppose God means them

to use it on the deterrent principle – something which they must never use, but that will deter the enemy. I'd rather not have a sting in my bottom at all if it will kill me if I use it. I don't know why we weren't made like that. We could have been given special guns, which we could deter people with, but as soon as they used them they'd fire in both directions, backwards and forwards, so you'd shoot yourself at the same time. That would put an end to all this violence in the streets. I wonder if bees know they're going to die if they use their stings.

Poor old bees, they have a rotten time in life. I made a little rhyme about it actually. It's called Ode to the Bee, a lovely little rhyme.

If a lovely little bee should come and sting you on the knee,
Don't shout out resentfully – remember he will die.
So when you see a little bee, flying o'er the land and sea
Don't shriek out in jealousy – he's worse off than you or I.

THE MAN WHO INVENTED THE WHEEL
(*On the Braden Beat*, ITV, 1964)

During the last few weeks I've been trying to think of something absolutely original and devastating. I've been trying to lay my hands on some idea that'll revolutionise the world in some way – something like fire, or the wheel. Of course, it's no good thinking of those two because they've already been invented, but something along those lines. It's a very good thing to do, you know. I mean, look at the man who thought of fire. He could have made an absolute fortune. As soon as he thought of it he should have patented it, and every time anybody lit a fire they'd have had to pay him a royalty. But being a rather primitive person he didn't think of that.

The same thing happened to the bloke who thought of the wheel. Actually, nobody really knows who was the first person to invent the wheel. It's all shrouded in mystery. Apparently, in primeval times, there were these two primitive people, who were both working on inventions in their caves. They were called Drodbar and Gorbly – two extremely primitive people. Then one day Drodbar came out with a great smile all over his hairy face, and he said 'Guess what? I've just invented the bandanbladderstiddle. It's absolutely brilliant. Brilliant!' And so Gorbly came out, and said 'Hello Drodbar. I hear you've invented the bandan-bladderstiddle. Congratulations. Er, what exactly is it?' And Drodbar said 'It's a wonderful device that will revolutionise the world. It's very simple. It's just a round thing that's easy to push along. that's all.' And then Gorbly went white, and said in a strangled voice 'It hasn't by any chance got spokes in it, has it?' 'Yes it has, as a matter of fact,' said Drodbar. 'How the devil did you know?' And Gorbly said 'That's not a bandanbladderstiddle, you stupid idiot. That's a wheel, and I invented it first. How dare you steal my idea?' And a great fight broke out between them, and if the man who invented fire hadn't come along and threatened to set light to them both, they might have killed each other.

Anyway, there was a great dispute, and all the hairy old Neanderthals met together at Stonehenge – a lovely place – to decide who really thought of it first. And eventually, after days and days of argument, they come to the conclusion that although it seemed likely that Drodbar thought of his bandanbladderstiddle before Gorbly thought of his wheel, nevertheless they were going to give the credit to Gorbly because he thought of a much better name for it.

I think they were right, actually. I mean, think of going into a garage and asking them to put a bit more air into your bandanbladderstiddle. Still, you can't help feeling sorry for poor old Drodbar, you know. He went into a great depression and went round mumbling and moaning about his wretched old bandanbladderstiddle. Eventually, he was run down by the world's first pterodactyl-drawn chariot – a terrible end. I know lots of people who've thought of things just a little too late. Poor old Spotty Muldoon. He thought of splitting the atom the other day. If only he could have had the idea about thirty years ago. He'd have made a bloody fortune.

FOOD FOR THOUGHT
(*On the Braden Beat*, ITV, 1964)

I've been reading a very interesting book recently. It's called *The Universe and All That Surrounds It* by T J Bleendreeble. It's an extremely good book about it. It's about seventy pages long, so it's fairly comprehensive about the whole thing and it's fairly interesting. Bleendreeble specialises in the universe. He doesn't branch out much beyond that. But he's quite interested in this limited field. I found out quite a lot from him.

Do you know for example, that if all the Chinamen in the world linked hands, they'd girdle the Earth, three times? They would. They'd go round three times – girdle, girdle, girdle. It's an amazing fact, isn't it? Of course there's no real way of checking up on it. You couldn't very well persuade all the Chinamen in the world to link hands simultaneously and girdle the Earth. You couldn't very well say 'Excuse me Mr Wang. Meet Mr Wong. Link hands, would you, and girdle the Earth.' Of course, you'd have to build rafts to get them across the sea, so the whole thing's perfectly impractical. You just have to take these facts on trust.

I've been finding out quite a lot of interesting facts in the last few weeks from Bleendreeble. Did you know, for example, you've got three miles of tubing inside you? There's over three miles of horrible old intestine wound up inside us, and every time we eat, the food has to travel three miles along the awful stringy intestines before it can get to your stomach. Imagine the poor old bits of potato, fighting their way through the miles and miles and miles of thin tubing before they get to their destination. It must take hours to get there. Of course, this means that none of the food we eat is ever really fresh. It never is, no matter what it's like when you put it in your mouth. It's always stale by the time it reaches your stomach. And that's the reason why most people feel so ill all the time.

I must say I can't bear the thought of all the food I eat, struggling along for miles and miles in the dark, getting staler and staler every moment. I can't see why we couldn't have one simple tube that would go straight to the stomach without any of the detours. If you just put the food into our mouths, it would drop directly down onto the stomach. I suppose the only trouble is that it might bounce back. At least if you ate a great big heavy mouthful it might drop down and land on the rubbery lining of the tummy and jump right out again. It'll be dreadful sitting at dinner parties with all the food jumping out of everybody's mouth all the time. People would have to have special little nets to catch the food, so they could get it when it bounced back. Perhaps there's something to be said for the intestines after all. I should read a bit of Bleendreeble if you're interested in your insides.

SPINDLY LEGS
(*On the Braden Beat*, ITV, 1964)

I would like to say a special hello to all of you out there with spindly legs. My message to you this evening is – don't worry about your spindly legs. Lots of people have had spindly legs in the past and got to the top. Look at Mahatma Gandhi. He was a very spindly person, Mahatma Gandhi – very spindly indeed. He was known as El Spindleroso. The spindly one, people called him. People used to shout out at him as he wandered by in his white nightie. 'Hello, spindly one.' And 'Goodness me, what spindly legs you've got!' But Gandhi just smiled and went and sat on the railway lines and became leader of all India, and took his country away from us, the rotten creature. Cheer up, spindly people. There's no reason why your legs should hold you back. If Gandhi can do it, so can you.

The spindliest person I know is Marjorie Grindle. She's called Grindle the spindle. She looks just like a horrible old stick insect. She's very fed up with being so spindly, Marjorie. She keeps moaning about it and saying 'If only I wasn't so spindly, I could get a job as a fat lady in a circus.' She's always moaning and grumbling, and so people keep saying to her 'Look at it this way Marjorie – however spindly you are, there's always somebody even spindlier than you that you should be worrying about. You may be very spindly, but somewhere in the world there's somebody spindlier than you are.'

That's what people always say when there's something the matter with you. They say 'You may be badly off, but think of all the suffering in the world. You may have got a nasty dose of flu, but think of all the people in India who are dying of starvation.' They always say that to comfort you. I think that's a fat lot of bloody use that is. If you've got flu, you feel miserable. It's no good being told that somebody in India is even worse off than you are. That's no comfort at all. It just makes you feel miserable about the person in India as well.

Somewhere in the world, there must be somebody who is worse off than everybody else. I'd like to meet him. I think it will be a very good idea to have a competition to see who is the person in the world who is worse off and more miserable than everybody else. All the people who've got a grumble should be invited to come to Wembley Stadium and mount the rostrum and tell everybody what their trouble is. Spotty Muldoon could come along. He could say 'Ladies and gentlemen, I have got awful spots, which come up all over my face whenever I eat spinach. I am worse off than everybody in the world.' Then somebody else should come to the platform and say 'Rubbish, Muldoon. Your spots are nothing compared to my ghastly rheumaticky pains behind the knees. I'm far worse off than you are, Spotty.' Then another person would come and say 'Rheumaticky pains in the knee? My eye! That's nothing! I've got rheumaticky pains all over my body, and what's more, my wife's just been eaten by a shark.'

Then finally, after days and days of miserable people moaning on about their diseases and worries, there'd be a vote, and somebody would be elected Worst Off Person in the World – spottier than Spotty Muldoon, spindlier than Marjorie Grindle, more miserable than Patrick Gordon Walker. He'd be elected Super Misery and every week he'd appear on television and tell us how wretched he was and show us his diseases, I think it might cheer people up a bit in this cold weather.

MAN'S BEST FRIEND
(*On the Braden Beat*, ITV, 1964)

The trouble with dogs is they always know what you're thinking. They've got horrible clairvoyant minds that can see deep into yours. And they can always tell when you're frightened of them, which is always. Whenever I'm walking along the street and I see a dog, I try to pretend that I'm an extremely courageous person. I try to look completely unconcerned and nonchalant. Sometimes I hum a confident little song to put them off. I hum 'If you think I'm afraid of you, you better have another think or two. I'm not afraid, good gracious no, you're wasting your time round here, off you go.' But the dog can always see through that and he starts sidling up to me very slowly. So I try walking a bit faster, but without appearing to hurry or looking back. And I can feel the beastly dog, creeping up on me – nearer and nearer and nearer. And then, as soon as I look back and see where it is, it rushes up to me and starts sniffing around my ankles for no reason at all, and baring its horrible yellow teeth.

The trouble is, you can never hit them or anything. If a dog starts biting you, you can't kick it up the throat like it deserves. People always say 'Oh dear, poor little dog, he was only trying to be friendly. That's the way he tries to be friendly, sniffing at your ankles and biting you, you cruel, wicked man.' So you have to be very gentle with it and say 'Good dog, good dog, come along now. Stop it, there's a nice chap. Good dog, there's a nice fellow.' Nice fellow my old boots.

I think it's very dull of everybody having dogs as pets when there's so many other animals about with nicer natures. There's a friend of mine, George Spindler, he had a bee for a pet – a lovely little creature, the bee. This was a female of the species called Beryl, and he used to take it out for walks in the street. He had a very thin, light lead made out of cotton, tied to her back right leg, and Beryl used to fly ahead of him, about three foot in front of him. He used to have his hand out there you see. He held the cotton very delicately and the bee went on. They made a lovely picture together on twilight evenings.

PETER COOK

The tragedy was that one evening he's just taken his bee out into the garden, so she could do her business, before retiring, and Beryl was buzzing about on her lead looking for a likely spot, when suddenly a beastly great bat came up and ate her. Ghastly occurrence. Poor old George was left with a bat on the end of his lead. He couldn't get rid of it. In the end he had to drive out to Barnstaple and abandon it. If you see a bat with a piece of cotton hanging from its mouth, that'll probably be George Spindler's. I must say I wish I could lay my hands on something to keep the dogs off. Perhaps a giant horned toad might do the trick. I must find something soon.

THE EL WISTY FESTIVAL OF ARTS
(On the Braden Beat, ITV, 1964)

I've always been keenly interested in the arts and all that pertain unto them. I think it would be extremely timely and advisable to have a festival, called the EL Wisty Festival of the Arts, Literature & Nudism. I'm sure I'll be able to organise something of an amazingly successful nature. I've got some very good ideas for the drama section in particular. One of the highlights of the festival will be a new play by an extremely exciting author of the new school, called *EL Wisty Meets the Amazing Nude Women.* It would star EL Wisty in the title role. It's a play that I wrote a few years ago, and I think it's just the sort of thing to revive ordinary people's interest in the theatre.

It's an amazingly effective piece of drama. It's the story of this man who is sitting on a bench when the curtain rises. He sits there for a time while the audience settle themselves and undo their sweets and then suddenly after about ten minutes of his sitting there, he starts to speak and says 'Good evening everybody, and welcome to the show. Amazing things will soon be seen, as you will maybe know. In ancient days, when dinosaurs roamed nightly o'er the land, there was a man called Wisty who ran a small dance band. That man is I, and though you cry "Good Lord, can this be so?" I

79

tell you now, and pledge my vow. After all, well, I ought to know.'

And then at this crucial moment in the drama when I have just revealed that I am over a million years old, an amazing development occurs. As I am speaking, five hundred nude women come creeping in through the scenery behind me and say in unison 'Hello Mr Wisty, we are the wandering nudies, and we've heard that you are an amazingly attractive and dynamic personality of the very kind that we are anxious to dance with. And for this reason we have wandered over many miles of treacherous terrain to be with you, and bring you strange delights.' And then E L Wisty, who is of course myself, gets off the bench and begins to dance about with them in a curiously sensuous and individual style. And after about an hour of this the curtain goes down, and there's an interval of about fifteen minutes during which refreshments will be available in the foyer.

Then up goes the curtain again, and the dancing continues in an even more lively fashion than before for a few more hours. Then a huge tank full of water is lowered onto the stage and ladders are placed up against it, and one by one all the nude ladies climb up the ladders and dive into the water, and when all five hundred are safely in, thrashing about inside the tank, I lower an enormous great lid on the top of it – completely air-tight, so they can't get out – and then I walk forward to the front of the stage, lit in a green spotlight, and say in an amazingly effective way 'Ladies and gentlemen, the nude ladies are trapped, there is no way out for them, let that be a warning unto ye.' And the curtain falls to amazingly thunderous applause. I think people would flock to see something like that.

EL WISTY IN THE AFTERLIFE
(*Holiday Startime*, ITV, 1970)

Good evening ladies and gentlemen. This is EL Wisty speaking, and I have a very important announcement to make, perhaps the most important announcement of my life. I am dead. I died several weeks ago and you're watching a telerecording. This telerecording was made shortly before my death – otherwise this broadcast would not be possible. As this is a jolly, fun-filled family programme, I do not wish to depress you by dwelling on the morbid details. Suffice it to say that I am no longer with you and that I have passed on to pastures new.

During my life I have attempted many things, including knitting, painting silver fir cones and dominating the world. Perhaps I have not been totally successful. I doubt if my silver fir cones will be auctioned at Sotheby's. I have a feeling that my finely ribbed woollen nighties that I gave to Aunt Madge for Christmas will not be acclaimed by the critics. But in one ambition I have achieved complete success – namely, the total domination of the world. Every action you take, every word you say, is a direct result of my uncanny powers. Why did you kick the cat last Tuesday? The answer – is me. Why is the country plunged in industrial chaos? The answer is me. Why did I kick the bucket a few weeks ago? The answer – is you. Now that I have dominated you completely, now that the world is in my grasp, it seems a fitting time to go. I know that some of you watching now will be muttering things to each other like 'that old twit never had any power over me. I didn't kick the cat last Tuesday because of him.' But you're wrong. There are uncanny forces in me that can make you do anything and if you happen to be jumping to your feet saying 'what a load of rubbish, let's switch to the BBC!' it is because I have willed it.

Many men have tried to dominate the world – Genghis Khan, Attila the Hun, Eloise Hitler, as he was before the operation – but they all went about it in such an obvious way, starting wars, killing people, shouting. ITV asked me to appear live on this programme, but I said 'I'd rather appear dead.' So here I am. Or rather, here I'm not. But how can you tell what is 'live' or what is recorded? In fact, how do you tell what the bloody hell is going on anywhere? If you would like to know the answer to any of these questions, write to me, care of God, Cloud, Heaven W1 BXC. Please enclose a stamped addressed envelope.

FROM BEYOND THE VEIL
(Mermaid Theatre, London, 1977)

Good morning. You all seem to be very worried about how easy it would be for a terrorist to manufacture an atomic bomb. Even the *Daily Express* knows how to do it. There's really no cause for alarm. Up here we all have atomic bombs. It's one of the first things we get on arrival. We file a request for our personal deterrent, and it's delivered by the council. You have a choice of colours. Mine is rather an alluring blue. I live down the street from Mr & Mrs Hitler. They have a nice little red one, and he's very proud of it. Whenever I go round to tea, the first thing he says is always 'Do have a look at my little red device.' He polishes it a lot and puts it on the pillow by him when he goes to sleep. The only snag about them is their tendency to go off. It makes an awful noise and kills everybody again, which means a lot more paperwork when we get back. It's usually the newcomers who are to blame. The last accident was caused by the Big Bopper. He had it on his piano when he was playing Chantilly Lace for the Beethovens. It toppled off when he sang 'You Know What I Like.' But he's been very good since then. My main worry these days is Pope John. He likes to play Frisbee with his, but luckily Houdini, his partner, is very good at catching. The nice thing about everybody having one, there's no reason for envy. We don't have all that awful keeping up with the Joneses, which causes you so many difficulties. I'd be terribly cross if Napoleon had one and I didn't – he's got a red one as well, by the way. As I say, the only minor nuisance is when they go off. But cheer up, you soon get used to dying. It's like riding a bicycle. Once you've learned, you never forget how to do it. Good morning.

DO YOU KNOW YOU ARE A TV SET?
(*TV Times*, 1980)

Written to promote ITV's Peter Cook & Co *(see Chapter Ten) this article proved Wisty worked just as well in print. And like the previous two sketches in this section, which both date from one off performances in the Seventies, it also proved that Wisty had lost none of his powers, even over fifteen years after his string of monologues in* On The Braden Beat.

This is EL Wisty speaking. I knew you were going to start reading this article at this very moment. What's more I can predict exactly when you'll finish it. That's the wonderful thing about possessing paranormal powers – it enables me to know what everyone in the world is going to do at any given time.

Stop it, Mr Brigginshawe. Your dog didn't mean to whip your Dubonnet off the table with its tail, and beating him won't get the stain out of the carpet. That's right, pour some salt on it – no, not the dog, the carpet.

Sometimes I despair of the human race. Talking of the human race, did you know that each and every one of us has psychic powers? It's just that very few people know how to develop their innate potential. All of us at one time or another have had a sense of déjà vu, a feeling that this has happened before, that this has happened before, that this has happened before. You probably got it when you read that last sentence.

What I and other psychics have in common is a sense of avant vu – the ability to see things before they happen. How can I develop this power? I hear you ask. Well, Marmite helps and so does thermal underwear, but the real key for precognition lies in the 98% of your brain that remains unused.

Most of use 1% of our brain to get out of bed in the morning, have breakfast, go to work, have lunch, get home, eat a meal and switch on the telly. We use the other 1% to switch it off and go to bed again. The secret is to let your mind go completely blank and allow the unused 98% to take over. This may take a while but remember, Rome wasn't burnt in a day.

One method is to imagine that your mind is a television set that has been switched off, with the plug carefully removed from the wall. The screen is entirely blank. Now pretend that three of the fingers on your left hand are a plug and push them into a cushion, which represents the socket. Your mind will remain blank until you switch on. Keeping your three fingers pressed into the cushion, use your right hand to push the ON button. I usually pretend that the ON button is my nose. Just apply gentle pressure and wait for the picture to appear.

It is best to try this experiment in the privacy of your own home. People tend to look askance at you if you walk round holding your nose and plunging your fingers into their cushions.

If no picture comes after an hour, try gently wiggling your nose from side to side, but be careful not to hold your nose in too strong a grip as this can inhibit breathing and death is the last thing we wish to achieve. Sooner or later, by a strange process still to be understood by scientists, the unused 98% of your brain will be reactivated and start receiving pictures. At first they may only be in black and white and without sound. If the pictures are at all blurred or fuzzy, try sticking your leg out of the window or, better still, climb up on the roof and wave a foot about. Remember at no time should you remove your fingers from the cushion or your nose as this will cause an immediate psychic power failure.

After a little practice you will be able to tune in almost automatically and the whole process will become as easy as falling off a log – or a roof for that matter. When, like me, you reach a really advanced state of psychic consciousness you won't even have to switch on your nose or plunge your fingers into the cushion. Psychic intuition will become automatic.

I didn't have to ask Beryl Reid, John Cleese, Rowan Atkinson, Terry Jones, Paula Wilcox or Robert Longden to be guests on my programme on Sunday. They're all paranormal people themselves and arrived instinctively at London Weekend by astral projection. None of them trust the underground system, and they prefer to beam themselves in by mind control.

There's one disadvantage in being so psychic. Although most performers on television have no idea of what the audience is thinking, all of us on the programme will be fully aware of what is going through every viewer's mind. We will be watching your every movement and lack of it. Please don't let this inhibit you. If you hadn't been told, you wouldn't have known. If you feel like undressing in front of the fireplace, don't let the thought that John

Cleese and Beryl Reid are looking in put you off: they're both grown men.

In the same way as you will have switched us on, we will be tuned into you. Let me assure you that none of us are government agents and we will not report any of your activities to the police or the Inland Revenue.

The only time we will not be able to follow your activities during the programme is in the commercial break, so if you are at all self-conscious this is a good time to go to the toilet or pick your nose. I wouldn't recommend making love during the commercial break as most modern couples like to spend well over two minutes on this important aspect of life.

All right, Mr Brigginshawe, have it your own way, but don't blame me when she runs off with the greengrocer. In the meantime, on behalf of all my paranormal guests, I'd just like to say how much we look forward to seeing you on Sunday.

Chapter Four
Not Only But Also

While EL Wisty was dominating ITV, in *On the Braden Beat*, the BBC offered Dudley Moore his own one-off special. What he did with it was his business. Still more familiar – and more confident – as a musician than as a comedian, modest Dudley sensibly sent for his old *Beyond the Fringe* buddy, Peter Cook. In fact, Cook was merely one of several guests, including John Lennon, who'd agreed to perform a couple of poems from his recently published book, *In His Own Write*. The book's full title was *In His Own Write and Draw* – it was illustrated with Lennon's drawings – and its slightly sinister nonsense rhymes weren't a million miles away from Cook's own experimental excursions into verse.

Lennon was already a big fan of Cook and Moore. 'I dig what they're doing,' he said. Booking one of the Beatles was a huge coup for what was barely more than a broadcast pilot, but despite his stage success, Dudley was relatively unknown on TV. To sidestep the absurdity of a star vehicle featuring a guest who was infinitely more famous than the vehicle's own star, the show's title was changed, from *The Dudley Moore Show* to *Not Only But Also*, as in

Not Only Dudley Moore but also John Lennon, Peter Cook & Co.

Not only Dudley but also Peter could easily have been upstaged by Lennon, who claimed, just a few weeks later, with some fleeting justification, that The Beatles had become more popular than Jesus Christ. However, as well as appearing in the programme, Peter was also booked to write some sketches. And the two he wrote were a couple of the funniest sketches ever seen on TV. In one, Peter, as Sir Arthur Streeb-Greebling, tells Dudley how he's wasted his life trying to teach ravens to fly underwater – creating the classic template for all of Peter's patrician archetypes to come. In the other, Peter and Dudley metamorphose for the first time into their working-class alter egos, Pete & Dud – two idiotic, self-deluded losers from Dudley's hopelessly unexotic home town, Dagenham (a drab London suburb, stranded in between Essex and the East End), who've somehow convinced themselves that they're being constantly pestered by beautiful female film stars. And it was this unique mix of the surreal with kitchen sink drama that really brought the house down.

Inexplicably, this comic masterclass had fallen flat in rehearsal, but once they were in costume, in front of a live audience, their creations came alive. Dressed in their trademark flat caps and raincoats, which were to become as iconic as Laurel & Hardy's bowler hats, Pete & Dud raised the roof. When Dudley corpsed disgracefully, struggling to keep a straight face during Peter's deliberately disruptive ad libs, everyone laughed even louder. The BBC's Head of Light Entertainment was unimpressed by such slapdash standards, but the Controller of BBC2 wasn't bothered. He commissioned an entire series. Peter was overjoyed. It was just like being back at university, he said, but with bigger grants. Subsequent guests included Ronnie Barker, Barry Humphries, Spike Milligan, Peter Sellers and Eric Sykes, but Cook was now part of the main title. *Not Only Dudley Moore But Peter Cook* became *Not Only Dudley Moore And Peter Cook*, and finally *Not Only Peter Cook And Dudley Moore*.

The production schedules were tight – five days writing, two days filming and just a few days rehearsals for each episode – but Peter always wrote right up to the wire. 'We were always late on deadlines,' he admitted. 'We always had enough material for the show, but practically inevitably we'd change it. We'd become dissatisfied with the stuff we'd written, and do something at the last minute.'[1] Yet these last-minute rewrites gave the show a fresh, theatrical feel. The recordings were 'as live', in front of several hundred spectators, who responded like paying punters at a public performance, rather than a studio audience. There was no canned laughter. There was no need.

The series was a critical hit, praised by highbrow (*The Times*), middlebrow (*Mail*) and lowbrow (*Sun*) press alike. The Guild of Television Producers and Directors voted them comedians of the year. A second series followed a year later, Dick Clement replacing Joe McGrath as producer director. Clement later went on to form a classic comic partnership of his own, co-writing *The Likely Lads*, *Porridge* and *Auf Wiedersehen Pet* with Ian La Frenais.

This second series was even more warmly received than the first, but the lure of the movies meant it was several years before they made another. In 1968, TV mogul Lew Grade enticed them onto ATV, the channel that had made *On the Braden Beat*, with an offer they couldn't refuse – but like so many of ITV's big-money transfers, *Goodbye Again* couldn't quite recapture the low-budget magic of *Not Only But Also*. This time, the press reaction was tepid.

The third BBC series suffered from being made at short notice, but judged against any yardstick, it still qualifies as a classic. Tragically, only some of the prerecorded film footage survived the BBC's wanton tape destruction (ironically, ITV's inferior *Goodbye Again* fared far better), but at least we still have the scripts of series three and two (the scripts of series one have vanished).

By now, Dudley was taking a more active role in the writing. 'I tend to flutter off very quickly, and improvise, and ignore illogicalities,' explained Peter. 'I'd rather get through a whole sketch quickly, and then come back and deal with whatever is wrong. Dudley began, when we had an idea, to examine what was logically incorrect, right at the beginning.'[2] Dudley's logical corrections helped to organise Peter's imagination, giving his stream of consciousness some integral order, and a sense of plot progression. Apart from a couple of Australian specials, there was no more *Not Only But Also*, but the benefits of Dudley's logic bore fruit in their Seventies stage show, *Behind the Fridge*, whose sketches have a much stronger structure, allowing Peter to sustain his instinctive creativity for longer. But sadly, what should have been only the end of the beginning of their partnership was actually already the beginning of the end.

∿

TRAMPONUNS
(BBC2, 1965)

(*Peter Cook is dressed as a nun.*)

DUDLEY: Last week we took our cameras to the convent of the Order of Saint Beryl in Norwich. We've brought along the Mother Superior, Fiona of Quarls, to answer a few questions on the Order of Saint Beryl, which is a very unique Order, as you'll gather.

PETER: Good evening.

DUDLEY: Mother Superior, or may I call you mother?

PETER: I think that would be inappropriate. I think Madam. Call me Madam.

DUDLEY: Right, Madam. I wonder if you would mind telling us in what respect the Order of Saint Beryl differs from other orders of nuns.

PETER: Well, the Order of Saint Beryl differs in this respect, young man. We are a leaping order. We do a great deal of leaping in the air, as part of our everyday routine. Leaping here, leaping there, leaping, leaping everywhere.

DUDLEY: And I wonder, could you tell us how this leaping actually originated?

PETER: Well, it all began in the fourteenth or fifteenth century. It had its origins there, you know. When Saint Beryl, who was the daughter of Saint Vitus, the well-known dancer, she lived in Norwich, you see, in a very strict order of nuns, who were forbidden to take any life, human or animal. Now, around Norwich there were these ghastly snakes which infested the area – vipers, adders and that sort of thing, who used to attack the nuns, and bite them to death. And so the nuns arrived at this compromise of leaping over the snakey substances. Should a snake appear, up the nuns would go, leaping all the time. A great deal of leaping went on and so the famous leaping nuns of Norwich came into being.

DUDLEY: I see, and what in fact is the order of the day for the Order of Saint Beryl?

PETER: Well, we're early risers. We get up at four o'clock in the morning, then go back to bed again at five, when we realise we've got up too early. Then up again at six for the early morning leap. That's quite a small leap, usually about six inches. Then we have a light leaping breakfast – a hard-boiled fish or something like that, to settle on the stomach, and then the morning leaping begins in earnest. You know, quite a lot of heavy leaping goes on. Then there's lunch, afternoon leaping, evening leaping and finally vespers and bandaging.

DUDLEY: I don't understand. Bandaging?

PETER: Bandaging for those nuns who have leapt unsuccessfully.

DUDLEY: I see. Do you leap at all yourself, Madam?

PETER: Well I love to leap, as indeed, who doesn't?

DUDLEY: I don't particularly.

PETER: Really? Well, I really love to leap. I used to be a great leaper in the old days. In fact, I achieved the leaping record for the convent – a hundred foot, vertically. Amazing really. Unfortunately I landed in a lawnmower, which rather curtailed my leaping facilities, and since then I've been sticking to about a quarter of an inch leaping, which isn't very exciting, but it keeps one in practice.

DUDLEY: Yes, I see. Who actually instructs the nuns in their leaping?

PETER: Well we're very fortunate indeed in having a wonderful trainer. Sister Domination, who's just come over from Dijon actually, at a record fee. She was transferred from Dijon. She is a wonderful creature She really knows how to leap and she's

training the nuns in the all the modern techniques, including the
trampoline of course.

DUDLEY: That's wonderful. Well, thank you very much, Mother
Superior.

FACTS OF LIFE
(BBC2, 1966)

(*Peter is sitting in a smart domestic drawing room. Enter Dudley, as a schoolboy.*)

PETER: Is that you, Roger?

DUDLEY: Yes, father.

PETER: There's a pot of tea in here for you, if you'd like some.

DUDLEY: That's very kind of you Sir, but I've just come in from
rugger and I'm a bit grubby. I think I ought to go and have a
shower first, Sir.

PETER: Well pour me a cup, there's a good chap, would you?

DUDLEY: Certainly Sir. Yes of course.

PETER: Thank you. How was school today?

DUDLEY: Oh, much as usual, thank you Sir, but I caught someone
having a crafty smoke behind the wooden buildings. Had to give
him rather a ticking off. Such a filthy habit you know Sir.

PETER: It's a filthy habit, Roger.

DUDLEY: There we are, Sir. Now if you'll excuse me.

PETER: Roger?

DUDLEY: Yes Sir?

Sit down. Roger, your mother and I were having a bit of a chat the
other day and she thought it might be a good idea if I was to have
a bit of a chat with you.

DUDLEY: A bit of a chat, Sir?

PETER: A bit of a chat, yes, Roger. Just a bit of a chat.

DUDLEY: What about, Sir?

PETER: Well, there's nothing to be worried about, Roger. It's just
that, well, to be perfectly frank, how old are you?

DUDLEY: Well, to be perfectly frank, Sir, I'm coming up to eighteen.

PETER: Just coming up to eighteen?

DUDLEY: Well, on the verge.

PETER: On the verge of eighteen. Yes, well, I thought it might be a good idea to have a bit of a chat now, because I remember from my own experience that it was when I was just, you know, coming up to eighteen . . .

DUDLEY: On the verge.

PETER: On the verge of it, that I first began to take a serious interest in the, in the opposite, the opposite number. Now I don't know, Roger, if you know anything about the method whereby you came to be brought about?

DUDLEY: Well Sir, some of the boys at school say very filthy things about it, Sir.

PETER: This is what I was worried about, and this is why I thought I'd have a bit of a chat, and explain absolutely frankly and openly the method whereby you and everybody in this world came to be. Roger, in order for you to be brought about, it was necessary for your mother and I to do something. In particular, it was necessary for your mother to sit on a chair. To sit on a chair, which I had recently vacated and which was still warm from my body. And then something very mysterious, rather wonderful and beautiful happened, and sure enough, four years later, you were born. There was nothing unhealthy about this, Roger. There's nothing unnatural. It's a beautiful thing in the right hands, and there's no need to think less of your mother because of it. She had to do it, she did it, and here you are.

DUDLEY: I must say it's very kind of you to tell me. One thing, actually, slightly alarms me. I was sitting in this very chair yesterday, Sir, and I vacated it, and the cat sat on it while it was still warm. And should we have it destroyed?

PETER: It's a lovely chair, Roger.

DUDLEY: The cat, Sir.

PETER: Destroyed? Oh no, Roger, you don't understand. This thing of which I speak can only happen between two people who are married, and you're not married.

DUDLEY: Not yet anyway, Sir.

PETER: Not to the cat, in any case. Well, Roger, now you have this knowledge about chairs and warmth, I hope you'll use it wisely. And take no notice of your school friends, or what Uncle Bertie may say.

DUDLEY: Dirty Uncle Bertie they call him at school, Sir.

PETER: Dirty Uncle Bertie and they're right, Roger. Your Uncle Bertie is a dirty, dirty man. He's been living with us now for forty years, and it does seem a day too much. You know, if it hadn't been for your mother, Roger, I don't know where we'd have been. She's the only person who can really cope with Uncle Bertie. She's the only one who can really deal with him. I don't know if you realise this, Roger, but your mother even has to sleep in the same bed as Uncle Bertie, to prevent him getting up to anything in the night. If only there were more people like your mother, Roger.

DUDLEY: Well, I'm very pleased that you have told me this, Sir, because, as I say, I'm very glad that I don't have to believe all those filthy things that the boys at school say. And only yesterday Uncle Bertie said to me . . .

PETER: Take no notice of Uncle Bertie, Roger. He's a sick, sick man and we should feel sorry for him.

DUDLEY: Well, I'll try, Sir. I wonder if I should take a cup of tea up to mother.

PETER: I wouldn't do that, Roger. She's upstairs at the moment, coping with Uncle Bertie.

DUDLEY: Poor Uncle Bertie.

PETER: Poor Uncle Bertie.

FATHER & SON
(BBC2, 1966)

(*Dudley plays a working-class father. Peter plays his middle-class son.*)

DUDLEY: Is that you, Brian?

PETER: Yes father.

DUDLEY: What time of night do you call this, then?

PETER: It's four o'clock in the morning, father.

DUDLEY: I'll four o'clock in the morning you, my boy. I've been sitting here since half past eleven wondering what's happened to you. I've been sitting here, eating my heart out. I have to get up in two hours' time.

PETER: I know, father.

DUDLEY: I have to get up at half past six. Where have you been?

PETER: Father, I'm twenty-eight years old. Surely I'm old enough to go where I like, with whom I like, at what time I like. I was out with friends.

DUDLEY: Friends? Friends? I call 'em fiends. They're nothing but a pack of whoers.

PETER: The word is whore, father.

DUDLEY: You've become a regular little rolling stone ever since you opened that stupid little shop of yours.

PETER: There's nothing stupid about the boutique, father. It happens to cater for modern trends which you may be a little out of touch with, that's all.

DUDLEY: Well, I thank the lord I've lost contact with painted ties, kinky boots and PVC underwear. What sort of a bloody job is that then, eh? Well, wash my mouth out with soap and water. What I'd like to know is, what's wrong with the drains then, eh? I've been down the drains all my life. My father before me, he's been down the drains, and my grandfather before me, been down the drains. The whole family's been down the drains for centuries. I suppose you're too big down the drains, aren't you?

PETER: Father, the mere fact that our entire family tree grew in the drains is no reason why I should spend my life in a sewer.

DUDLEY: If your mother was alive today, she'd have something to say about it. Oh, Rosie, Rosie, why did you leave me, my darling, to cope with such an ungrateful son?

PETER: Don't drag mother into it, please.

DUDLEY: I can scarcely drag your poor mother into it when she's five foot underground can I? How did we spawn this fop? You're all la di da, ain't ya? You're too clever clever for your own father now, ain't ya? Yes, of course you're too good for the drains. I forgot. You're a bloody Marquis, aren't you? Oh, wash my mouth out with soap. Look here my boy, I tell you – the drains are too good for you. That's what it is. I've seen better things than you floating down the drains.

PETER: Father, I don't know why you go on about the drains. You know perfectly well you retired at thirty-one and you haven't been down there since.

DUDLEY: I'll haven't been down there since you, my boy. Now then, Rosie, Rosie my darling. Do you see what a popinjay we have for a son? What a strutting peacock? Did I fight in the war to hear you abuse me in such a way? Eh, did I?

PETER: I've no idea, father. If indeed you did fight in the war.

DUDLEY: If indeed I did fight? I'll if indeed I did fight you my boy. What's this then, eh? Tell me what this is! Tell me what that is, then! Go on?

PETER: That's your navel father.

DUDLEY: Really? That's funny. I thought I contracted that on Dunkirk, on the beach. Crawling on my hands and knees to preserve you, eh?

PETER: Father, if that's a war wound, I think you'll find I've got a similar one under my shirt.

DUDLEY: I don't want to see under your shirt. You disgust me. I've been a verger at St Thomas's, Beacontree for forty-five years, and I've never seen you in that place. I've never seen you within two yards of its portal.

PETER: Father, I can't help being an agnostic. I wish I had faith like you.

DUDLEY: I'll I wish I had faith like you you, my boy. Now then, you come in at all hours of the morning, smelling of honey and flowers and reading your poncy magazines, and mixing your Bloody Marys. I've got a good mind to give you a good hiding. I've got a good mind to take my belt off to you.

PETER: I wouldn't do that, father. Your trousers will fall down.

DUDLEY: Very funny. Very amusing. Very witty. Oh yes. I wouldn't have had that sort of cheek from you when you were a little boy. You were such a lovely little boy. My golden-haired beauty, you were. Your mother and I, we used to go along the cliffs at Westcliff, and she used to be on one side and I used to be on the other, holding your little warm wet hands. And you used to see a ship on the horizon. You used to say 'Daddy, what's that?' I used to say 'It's a ship.' You never ask me that anymore, do you? You don't have to ask me anything. Do you, eh? Fancy pants. All you need to do is go strutting down the Kings Road every Saturday afternoon, showing off to your fiends. Every word you say is a stab in the back. Every gesture, every look you make is a thorn in my side.

PETER: Father, there's no need for you to come down the Kings Road too. I could do perfectly well without you.

DUDLEY: I'll perfectly well without you my boy. Rosie, did we in our moment of joy, spawn this werewolf, this Beelzebub?

PETER: I don't know why you keep looking upwards when you mention mother. You know perfectly well she's living in Frinton with a sailor.

DUDLEY: That's a terrible thing to say. That's a bloody terrible thing to say. Soap and water. Do you think my wife would have left me? Do you think your mother would have left me? She loved me as I loved her. Good lord! Do you think your mother would have gone off to live with some dirty matelot in Frinton? She worshipped the ground I walked on.

PETER: She liked the ground, but she didn't care for you, father.

DUDLEY: I'll didn't care for you you, my boy. Now then, she's gone up there to the great sewer in the sky, the biggest drain of them all. All you can do is make this place into a sin cellar. Here, you're nothing but a whoer. Get out of my house. Go on. Get out of my house.

PETER: Father, it's not your house. It's my house.

DUDLEY: Oh, pardon me for living. Pardon me for having two strong sturdy legs to stand on. I'll get out of your house then, and never darken your doorstep again.

PETER: I'm going to bed, father. Why don't you have a Sydrax?

DUDLEY: Oh, Rosie, Rosie my darling, my doll, my sweetheart. Where did we go wrong? Where did we go wrong?

THE PSYCHIATRIST
(BBC2, 1966)

(Peter is a psychiatrist, Dudley is his patient.)

PETER: Hello Roger.
DUDLEY: Hello Doctor Braintree.
PETER: Hello. Come in.
DUDLEY: I'm so sorry I'm late.
PETER: That's quite all right. How are you?
DUDLEY: I'm very well, thank you.
PETER: Would you like to sit down, or would you prefer to lie?
DUDLEY: I'll sit, thanks.
PETER: Right, well sit right down. Now tell me, how are you in yourself?
DUDLEY: Well, I'm really feeling rather in the pink.
PETER: This is terrific.
DUDLEY: Yes, it's funny really. You know, if anybody had told me that talking to psychiatrists would have helped me at all I'd have laughed in their faces, but I can honestly say that our little chats together have really been of tremendous benefit to me.
PETER: I'm so glad Roger. Of course, a lot of people are instinctively very suspicious of psychiatry, and possibly, you know, with reason. But it can help at times.
DUDLEY: Well, I really think it can, because I've got so much more self-confidence now, and I'm much less self-conscious in the company of the opposite sex, which I wasn't, as you know.
PETER: You're less inhibited, are you?
DUDLEY: Oh, I should say.
PETER: Good. This is terrific.
DUDLEY: And the wonderful thing is really, about it all – well, I'm in love.
PETER: This is wonderful news, Roger. You're in love. With a woman?
DUDLEY: Yes.
PETER: So much the better. That's terrific.
DUDLEY: It's so wonderful to be in love. I can't tell you the

absolute joy I have.

PETER: Well, love is a wonderful thing. I've been there myself. It's a wonderful thing.

DUDLEY: I mean this girl, this creature, this goddess, she's so . . . it's so right – everything is so wonderful.

PETER: Yes. You really click together?

DUDLEY: Yes. Oh, it's so marvellous. But the only trouble is that apart from this wonderful light-hearted love that I have, I seem to be saddled with this tremendous burning sense of guilt.

PETER: You have guilt as well as love. Well this is unfortunate, Roger. You know, sex is the most natural, healthy thing in the world. There's no reason at all to have any guilt about it. I mean, why would you have guilt about sex? It's a lovely, beautiful thing, Roger.

DUDLEY: Well it's not really as simple as that. You know, it's rather difficult to explain. I don't really know where to start.

PETER: Well, begin at the beginning. That's always the best place. What's the girl's name?

DUDLEY: Stephanie.

PETER: Stephanie. That's a lovely name, isn't it? Well, my wife's name, in fact, isn't it?

DUDLEY: Yes, it's Stephanie.

PETER: Yes, it's Stephanie.

DUDLEY: No, it's Stephanie.

PETER: Yes, it's Stephanie, Roger.

DUDLEY: Yes, it's Stephanie. It's your wife, Stephanie.

PETER: Oh, you're in love with my wife, Stephanie?

DUDLEY: Yes.

PETER: Well this is a perfectly understandable thing, Roger. She's a very attractive woman. I married her myself. I don't see why you should feel upset about that.

DUDLEY: But she's in love with me.

PETER: Well this again is perfectly understandable, Roger. I mean, you're a perfectly attractive human being, as I've told you over the last few weeks. There's nothing repulsive about you, is there? There's no reason why a highly sexed woman, such as Stephanie, shouldn't fall in love with you. And I must explain to you,

Roger, that I'm a very busy man. I have many, many patients to see. I see rather less of my wife perhaps than I should, and I think it's very understandable that she should seek some sort of companionship outside the marriage. I don't think that's unreasonable at all.

DUDLEY: But she's not seeking anything outside marriage, Doctor Braintree, and nor am I. We want to get married.

PETER: Well this again, I think, is perfectly understandable. After all, you're two young people in love, you want to manifest your love feelings, within the confines of a bourgeois society, through marriage. I think this is very appropriate.

DUDLEY: The awful thing is, you see, I should feel so grateful to you for what you've done for me, and all I can feel is this burning jealousy. I can't bear the thought of you touching her.

PETER: Well of course you can't. I can understand that. One is tremendously possessive about someone one loves. One is tremendously possessive. It would be unhealthy not to have this jealousy reaction, Roger.

DUDLEY: But don't you see? I hate you for it!

PETER: Of course you hate me, Roger.

DUDLEY: I hate you for being so near her.

PETER: Yes, of course you hate me, Roger. You love to hate the one who loves the one you hate to love to love. This is a very old rule, Roger. There's nothing to feel ashamed about. It's absolutely reasonable.

DUDLEY: Don't you understand? I want to kill you!

PETER: Of course you want to kill me, because by killing me, Roger, you eradicate the one you hate. This is a perfectly natural reaction, Roger.

DUDLEY: You're so reasonable aren't you?

PETER: Yes, I am.

DUDLEY: You understand it all so much. You're so logical.

PETER: Yes, I am. It's my job, Roger.

DUDLEY: I'm going to have to kill you now!

PETER: Ah, Roger, this is a little inconvenient because I have another patient at six thirty, and then somebody else at seven, after that. I wonder if you could make it some time next week?

Can you make it early in the week, say?

DUDLEY: When? When do you think?

PETER: How are you fixed on Wednesday morning? Say at nine thirty? Would that be convenient?

DUDLEY: Yes, that's perfect.

PETER: Right. Well, if you could pop along at nine thirty and kill me then.

DUDLEY: Once again, Doctor Braintree, I'm amazed, you know, really. I'm so grateful to you for, you know, showing me the way.

PETER: It's what I'm here for, Roger.

DUDLEY: Thank you so much.

PETER: Thank you. And with a bit of luck, this should be the last time you need to visit me.

RAVENS
(BBC2, 1965)

(Dudley Moore is interviewing Peter Cook, aka Sir Arthur Streeb-Greebling.)

DUDLEY: We are very pleased to have in the studio tonight one of the very few people in the world, if not the only person in the world, who has spent the major part of his life under water attempting to teach ravens to fly.

SIR ARTHUR STREEB-GREEBLING: Good evening.

DUDLEY: Good evening. We're very pleased to welcome to the studio Sir Arthur Greeb-Streebling.

SIR ARTHUR STREEB-GREEBLING: Streeb-Greebling.

DUDLEY: I beg your pardon.

SIR ARTHUR STREEB-GREEBLING: You're confusing me with Sir Arthur Greeb-Streebling. Good evening.

DUDLEY: Yes. Good evening. Thank you very much.

SIR ARTHUR STREEB-GREEBLING: And good Greebling.

DUDLEY: Good Greebling indeed.

SIR ARTHUR STREEB-GREEBLING: Hello fans.

DUDLEY: Shut up, Sir Arthur.

SIR ARTHUR STREEB-GREEBLING: Good evening.

DUDLEY: Good evening. Sir Arthur, could you tell us what first led you to this way of life, teaching ravens to fly underwater?

SIR ARTHUR STREEB-GREEBLING: Well, it's always very difficult to say what prompts anybody to do anything, let alone getting underwater and teaching ravens to fly. But I think it probably all dates back to a very early age, when I was quite a young fellow. My mother, Lady Beryl Streeb-Greebling, you know, the wonderful dancer – a hundred and seven tomorrow and still dancing – she came up to me in the conservatory – I was pruning some walnuts – and she said 'Arthur' – I wasn't Sir Arthur in those days – she said 'Arthur, if you don't get underwater and start teaching ravens to fly, I'll smash your stupid face off,' and I think it was this that sort of first started my interest in the whole business of getting them underwater.

DUDLEY: How old were you then?

SIR ARTHUR STREEB-GREEBLING: I was forty-seven. I'd just majored in O Level in Forestry – I got through that – and I was looking about for something to do.

DUDLEY: Yes. Where did you strat your work?

SIR ARTHUR STREEB-GREEBLING: I think it can be said of me that I have never, ever strated my work. That is one thing I have never done. I can lay my hand on my heart, or indeed anybody else's heart, and say I have never strated my work, never strated at all. I think what you probably want to know is when I started my work. You've misread completely the question.

DUDLEY: Yes, I'm awfully sorry. I did make an error. Where did you start your work?

SIR ARTHUR STREEB-GREEBLING: Where did I start it? Well, I started almost immediately. My mother had given me this hint. She's a powerful woman, Lady Beryl. She can break a swan's wing with a blow of her nose. Incredible creature.

DUDLEY: Sir Arthur, is it difficult to get ravens to fly underwater?

SIR ARTHUR STREEB-GREEBLING: Well, I think the word difficult is an awfully good one here. Yes, it is. It's well nigh impossible. The trouble is, you see, God, in his infinite wisdom and mercy, designed these creatures to fly in the air, rather than through the watery substances of the deep. Hence they experience enormous difficulty, as you said, difficulty, in beating their tiny wings against the water. It's a disastrous experience for them.

DUDLEY: How do you manage to breathe?

SIR ARTHUR STREEB-GREEBLING: Through the mouth and the nose – the usual method, in fact. God gave us these orifices to breathe through and who am I to condemn him? I think you can't breathe through anything else. If you start breathing through your ears, you can't hear yourself speak for the rush to your ears, you can't hear yourself speak. Nose and mouth is what I use, and I trust you do.

DUDLEY: Yes, I most certainly do of course, but what I was meaning was how do you manage to breathe underwater?

SIR ARTHUR STREEB-GREEBLING: Well that's completely impossible. Nobody can breathe underwater. That's what makes it so difficult. I have to keep bobbing to the surface every thirty seconds. Makes it impossible to conduct a sustained training programme on the ravens. And they're no better. They can't even be taught to hold their beaks – horrible little animals. There they are, sitting on my wrist. I say 'Fly! Fly, you devils!' And they inhale a face full of water.

DUDLEY: I suppose they drown, do they?

SIR ARTHUR STREEB-GREEBLING: It's curtains, yes. They drown. Little black feathery figure topples off my wrist, spirals very slowly down to a watery grave. We're knee-deep in feathers off that part of the coast.

DUDLEY: Sir Arthur, have you ever managed to get a raven to fly underwater?

SIR ARTHUR STREEB-GREEBLING: No. I have never managed to get one to fly underwater. Not at all – not a single success in the whole forty years of training.

DUDLEY: Sounds rather a miserable failure then, your whole life, really, I suppose.

SIR ARTHUR STREEB-GREEBLING: My life has been a miserable failure, yes.

DUDLEY: How old are you, if that's not a personal question?

SIR ARTHUR STREEB-GREEBLING: It is a personal question, but I am eighty-three. Remarkably well preserved because of the water, of course, on the face.

DUDLEY: Well I would say then that your life probably has been a bit of a shambles.

SIR ARTHUR STREEB-GREEBLING: It's a bit late in life, you see, to turn to anything else. I've often thought of taking something else up, you know – a bit more commercial. But it's very difficult when you go round to a firm and they say 'what were you doing before this?' And you say 'well, I was hovering about ten foot underwater, attempting unsuccessfully to get ravens to fly.' They tend to look down their noses at you.

DUDLEY: What a miserable thing.

SIR ARTHUR STREEB-GREEBLING: A miserable thing indeed.

DUDLEY: Well, thank you very much indeed, Sir Arthur, for telling us your absolute tale of woe. Thank you very much for coming along.

SIR ARTHUR STREEB-GREEBLING: Thank you and good evening.

WORMS
(BBC2, 1970)

DUDLEY: Hello, I'm standing in the laboratory of Sir Arthur Greeb-Streebling . . .

SIR ARTHUR STREEB-GREEBLING: Streeb-Greebling.

DUDLEY: . . . who is perhaps the world's leading authority on worms. Sir Arthur, you are a worm expert?

SIR ARTHUR STREEB-GREEBLING: Er, hold on – that's rather a tricky one to start with. Could you phrase it again?

DUDLEY: Sir Arthur, are you an expert on worms?

SIR ARTHUR STREEB-GREEBLING: That's still an awfully difficult one to start with. Couldn't you ease me into it? Couldn't you ask me who played inside left for Portugal in 1908?

DUDLEY: Who played inside left for Portugal in 1908?

SIR ARTHUR STREEB-GREEBLING: God almighty – inside left. Not altogether sure. Can you give me a clue? Was it a worm?

DUDLEY: No.

SIR ARTHUR STREEB-GREEBLING: Then I'm completely stuck. All I really know about is worms.

DUDLEY: Could I ask you about worms?

SIR ARTHUR STREEB-GREEBLING: Ah, now you're talking. That's much more like it. That football question rather confused me. Fire ahead.

DUDLEY: What, Sir Arthur, can we learn from the worm?

SIR ARTHUR STREEB-GREEBLING: Well, I've been studying the worm for thirty odd years – thirty very odd years indeed – and I think the main thing I've learnt about worms is that they are very uncommunicative, self-effacing creatures.

DUDLEY: Is it possible, in fact, for a worm to communicate?

SIR ARTHUR STREEB-GREEBLING: Well, let me put it this way. In all my many years of intensive study of the worm, I've never known a worm to speak to me. I don't know why. Perhaps it's something I've said, or possibly something I've left unsaid.

DUDLEY: But can they hear?

SIR ARTHUR STREEB-GREEBLING: Oh yes, but don't feel inhibited. My worms have seen it all. They are unshockable. Feel free to say anything you like.

DUDLEY: What led you into this somewhat specialised field of wormology?

SIR ARTHUR STREEB-GREEBLING: I think it was my father who was responsible, both for me, and my interest in worms. He, in fact, was the discoverer of the world's longest worm.

DUDLEY: How long was that?

SIR ARTHUR STREEB-GREEBLING: Approximately three thousand miles. He came across it in the Andes, and spent five years tracing it back to its source in the Azores.

DUDLEY: There has been some doubt expressed about the authenticity of this claim. Wasn't it Professor Hans Gauleiter who suggested that your father had sighted the head of one worm in the Andes and the tail of another worm in the Azores?

SIR ARTHUR STREEB-GREEBLING: Well, Gauleiter was of course prejudiced against my father, who was at the time romantically involved with Frau Gauleiter, the Professor's wife. She shared my father's interest in enormous worms.

DUDLEY: I wonder if I could have a look at some of the worms you have here in captivity?

SIR ARTHUR STREEB-GREEBLING: I very much doubt it. You see, worms spend most of their life underground. I've got a couple in here, but they haven't been out for years. If you like, we could sit down here with a thermos and some sandwiches, but it might be years before we sighted one.

DUDLEY: But I believe you have some slides of worms in action.

SIR ARTHUR STREEB-GREEBLING: No. I have some slides of worms in Acton, where I do most of my research. These are characteristic studies of the varying moods of worms in North London.

(*Sir Arthur shows Dudley some pictures of worms.*)

SIR ARTHUR STREEB-GREEBLING: Here we see a worm in repose, and one can see from this study why the worm has inspired the artist throughout the ages.

DUDLEY: There is certainly a kind of classical simplicity about the line.

SIR ARTHUR STREEB-GREEBLING: A tremendously relaxed quality. But in startling contrast, let me show you another side of the worm's nature. This is an enraged worm, under conditions of great stress.

DUDLEY: There seems to be no real difference in its expression. How do you know it was under stress?

SIR ARTHUR STREEB-GREEBLING: I was shouting at it, saying 'You stupid worm! Move along there, worm!' And other inflammatory phrases. But as you've noticed, the worm keeps its feelings well under control. In this respect, they are superior to the human race.

DUDLEY: How do worms reproduce?

SIR ARTHUR STREEB-GREEBLING: I mean, worms aren't in the habit of having a great deal to eat and drink, staggering upstairs, getting into bed and taking all their clothes off and muttering 'I love you' and 'was it alright for you, darling?' The worm has a more earthy approach.

DUDLEY: How do they go about it?

SIR ARTHUR STREEB-GREEBLING: Slowly but surely. I don't know whether you've ever been underground for any length of time, but take it from me – it's dark, damp and visibility is nil. Not an ideal setting for romance. Just let me show you a male and a female worm in a prenuptial mating display.

DUDLEY: How do you tell the difference between the male and the female?

SIR ARTHUR STREEB-GREEBLING: Well, men wear trousers, whereas women have long hair and things out here.

DUDLEY: I meant in worms.

SIR ARTHUR STREEB-GREEBLING: Well, the answer is you can't, and nor can they. It's rather a hit-or-miss affair. The worm tunnels along, hoping he'll hit a miss, and if he doesn't, it's apologies all round and the worm turns in considerable embarrassment. Here is a worm on the turn. Notice the slight blush.

DUDLEY: It must also be difficult to distinguish one end of the worm from the other.

SIR ARTHUR STREEB-GREEBLING: It is a bit of a toss up. Heads or tails, there's nothing in it. And this leads to the worm's worst dilemma, trapped in a narrow tunnel of its own making, approached on either side by two rampant worms in a state of sexual arousal.

DUDLEY: What does the worm do in these circumstances?

SIR ARTHUR STREEB-GREEBLING: Either the worm decides to face the music and take the consequences, or else, as is more usual, it makes a suicidal leap for the surface, where of course it's a sitting duck for any bird.

DUDLEY: May I ask what your plans are for the future?

SIR ARTHUR STREEB-GREEBLING: Well, I've written a book, *Helga the Worm Cub*. I've got 4000 copies in the conservatory. It's the story of a kindly old man who finds a wounded worm and nurses it back to health. It would make a terrific film. I saw myself as the man and either Virginia McKenna or Brigitte Bardot as my wife. Bardot in particular looks as if she could have a soft spot for a worm.

DUDLEY: Has there been any interest in the subject?

SIR ARTHUR STREEB-GREEBLING: Not from the major companies. I think it may be more of an underground project. I've sent off some slow-motion footage of worms asleep to Andy Warhol and I think it might trigger him off.

DUDLEY: Good luck with the film, Sir Arthur.

SIR ARTHUR STREEB-GREEBLING: It's called *Helga the Worm*, not Sir Arthur.

DUDLEY: Thank you Sir Arthur, *Helga the Worm*, not Sir Arthur.

SIR ARTHUR STREEB-GREEBLING: By the way, there's just one thing. For a sort of exciting finish to the programme, would you like to see one of my worms leap through a flaming hoop?

DUDLEY: Yes, indeed I would.

SIR ARTHUR STREEB-GREEBLING: So would I, but they won't. Damn things don't even try.

DUDLEY: What a disappointment. And that's all we have time for, though I'm sure we could go on talking about this fascinating subject all night.

SIR ARTHUR STREEB-GREEBLING: No we couldn't. You've sucked me dry. I've nothing else to say.

DUDLEY: Well, anyway, thank you, Sir Arthur.

FLOWERS
(BBC2, 1970)

(*Dudley is in the greenhouse of Syon House, a stately home in West London, with Peter, aka SIR ARTHUR STREEB-GREEBLING.*)

DUDLEY: I am talking once again to Sir Arthur Streeb-Greebling.

SIR ARTHUR STREEB-GREEBLING: Streeb-Greebling.

DUDLEY: That's what I said.

SIR ARTHUR STREEB-GREEBLING: I know. You were absolutely correct.

DUDLEY: How long have you been interested in flowers?

SIR ARTHUR STREEB-GREEBLING: From very early days. I was

found under a gooseberry bush, and I've been caught up in flora ever since.

DUDLEY: I must say, you have a marvellous collection.

SIR ARTHUR STREEB-GREEBLING: Must you really?

DUDLEY: Yes, it's down in the script.

SIR ARTHUR STREEB-GREEBLING: This where I keep my hydrangeas, a few low drangers – over there, my prize specimens, the Queens Park drangers.

DUDLEY: I wonder if we could see your dwarf chrysanthemums?

SIR ARTHUR STREEB-GREEBLING: Depends on your eyesight. We can have a look. They are tiny, aren't they?

DUDLEY: Some of your experiments, Sir Arthur, have aroused controversy in botanical circles.

SIR ARTHUR STREEB-GREEBLING: Yes, they have. But let us remember that they sneered at Isaac Newton when an apple fell on his head, and he invented gravity. They laughed at Archimedes when he got into the bath, and one can understand why. The innovator is always a figure of ridicule.

DUDLEY: You feel you're ahead of your time?

SIR ARTHUR STREEB-GREEBLING: Yes. I was the first man to try and get lime juice out of roses, but of course my main passion is in the field of what I call flora ambulanda – teaching flowers to walk.

DUDLEY: Have you had any success?

SIR ARTHUR STREEB-GREEBLING: Of a marginal nature. No actual walking yet, but quite a deal of creeping and climbing. I've got a few begonias outside, and have been trying to drive them up the wall, but they're very uncooperative.

DUDLEY: Why do you have this urge to get flowers on the move?

SIR ARTHUR STREEB-GREEBLING: I suppose it's pity, really – a deep feeling of compassion for a poor little flower, rooted in the ground, being eaten by slugs and unable to move. To my mind, there's nothing more tragic than the sight of an innocent dahlia being approached by a greedy slug.

DUDLEY: Isn't there a danger if you do succeed that you might wake up one morning and find that all your flowers have walked next door?

SIR ARTHUR STREEB-GREEBLING: Yes, but I think flowers deserve their freedom. You see, their romantic life is terribly inhibited. Pollination is a very poor substitute for sex.

DUDLEY: How do flowers multiply?

SIR ARTHUR STREEB-GREEBLING: In a very boring way, poor loves. They just stand around and wait for a bee to poke his head into their petals.

DUDLEY: What does the bee do?

SIR ARTHUR STREEB-GREEBLING: While he's rooting round for the nectar, he tends to get a bit of pollen stuck on his hairy legs, so he flies off and rubs it in the face of his next victim.

DUDLEY: A kind of involuntary promiscuity.

SIR ARTHUR STREEB-GREEBLING: Exactly. How would you like to spend all your life waist-deep in compost, waiting for a bee to land on your nose?

DUDLEY: Not exactly the bee's knees in romance.

SIR ARTHUR STREEB-GREEBLING: That's precisely what it is.

DUDLEY: I gather you have a theory that flowers can be made to talk.

SIR ARTHUR STREEB-GREEBLING: Yes, I'm sure they can, and I do everything to encourage them.

DUDLEY: With any success?

SIR ARTHUR STREEB-GREEBLING: I thought I heard a delphinium say 'Tea's ready, Arthur,' but it could have been my wife. So far, my only demonstrable success has been in the field of mime. I've got a very bright community of tulips. They're very well trained.

DUDLEY: I'd love to see them.

SIR ARTHUR STREEB-GREEBLING: So you shall.

(*They Exit.*)

Chapter Five
Pete & Dud

Not Only But Also spawned several celebrated comic characters, but none of them captured the popular imagination quite like Pete & Dud. And yet if *On the Braden Beat* had been on the BBC, rather than on ITV, Cook and Moore's most durable creation might never have evolved.

When Peter Cook was commissioned to write two two-handed sketches for *The Dudley Moore Show*, his natural inclination was to showcase his best characters, but EL Wisty was far too self-absorbed to respond to conventional questioning. And in any case, Cook's autistic alter ego was already working for the other side. Cook's solution was to put Wisty in a double act, with a Wistyesque sidekick, and so Pete & Dud were born. 'As far as I'm concerned, Pete is a slightly more active extension of EL Wisty,' explained Cook. 'Pete is the informed idiot, and Dud is the uninformed idiot. They're both idiots, but Pete is always slightly superior. In fact, he knows nothing either. They discuss the same lofty subjects as EL Wisty.'[1] But although Wisty provided the initial impetus, Pete & Dud quickly acquired lives – and lifestyles – of their own. Wisty was an unearthly misfit, imprisoned in his own unreal netherworld. Pete & Dud talked bizarre nonsense, but they lived in the real world. You'd see people like Pete & Dud in the pub or on the bus every day of the week.

This realistic setting gave Pete & Dud a more solid and enduring appeal than any of Peter Cook's previous characters, and the root of this new realism was undoubtedly Dudley Moore. Moore's main talent, in this context, was as a naturalistic actor, and this casual naturalism liberated Cook's imagination. Cook was always ready to explore strange new worlds, but for viewers with less explosive minds, it could be disorientating. Moore's eye for everyday detail gave the world of Pete & Dud a reassuring normality that had been conspicuously absent from Cook's work so far. Now, Cook's giddy conceptual leaps were balanced by Moore's realistic Dagenham memories, which littered their scripts like autobiographical footnotes.

Not that they had scripts as such. 'We had a lot of headings,' said Cook. 'We'd rehearsed a lot, and we roughly knew what we were going to say, but not word for word. It came across as if we were improvising it, which was not strictly true, but we had a lot of latitude.'[2] In fact, Cook had far more latitude than Moore. They'd create the initial script much as Cook created his Wisty monologues, by improvising into a tape recorder, and then distilling the written transcript. Yet while Dudley committed this shooting script to memory, by copying it out in longhand, Peter relied on prompt-cards to navigate his way through his own imagination. Peter's reluctance to learn his lines by rote did nothing to dispel that detached and rather distant air from which his acting always suffered – the faraway look of someone transfixed by an extraordinary vision. However, grounded by Moore's more down-to-earth acting, Pete & Dud's mix of improvisation and recitation proved a winning combination. Cook's freeform style gave their duologues a sense of spontaneity and danger, while Moore's discipline and focus held them together.

Of course, Cook & Moore's mainstream fans didn't give a damn about the mechanics of this new genre. Viewers saw only two brilliant young men sending up the boring old men they saw propping up the bar down at the local. The generation gap had never been wider, but Pete & Dud bridged this gap, just as they bridged the class divide. Dud was pretty close to the working class archetypes of Moore's childhood home, but Pete was a world away from Cook's upper-middle-class upbringing. For a comedian who made very few claims for his versatility as an actor, it was actually a fairly faithful portrait of a character from a completely different social class. In 1965, the same year as their TV debut, Pete & Dud played the Royal Variety Performance, at the London Palladium, in front of their old *Beyond the Fringe* fan, the Queen, stealing the show from more established names like Peter Sellers and Spike Milligan. During its first hectic decade, Cook's comedy had come as far as it could travel.

∿

FILM STARS
(*Not Only But Also*, BBC2, 1965)

DUD: Alright Pete then, are you?

PETE: Not too bad, you know. Not too bad.

DUD: Cheers.

PETE: Cheers.

(*They both sup their pints.*)

DUD: What you been doing lately then?

PETE: Well quiet, pretty quiet, not been up to much. Had a spot of the usual trouble the other day.

DUD: Oh, did you? What happened then?

PETE: Spot of the usual trouble. Well, I come home about half past eleven – we'd been having a couple of drinks, remember? I come home about half past eleven, you know, feeling a bit tired, so you know, I thought I'd go to bed, you know, take me clothes off and so on, you know.

DUD: Well, don't you take your clothes off before you go to bed?

PETE: No, I made that mistake this time. I got it the wrong round.

Anyway, I got into bed, settled down. I was reading *The Swiss Family Robinson.*

DUD: It's good, innit?

PETE: It's a lovely book Dud. It's a lovely book. And I got up to about page 483, second paragraph when suddenly 'bring bring, bring bring.'

DUD: What's that?

PETE: That's a phone going 'bring bring.' So I picked up the phone, and you know who it was?

DUD: Who?

PETE: Bloody Betty Grable. Calling transatlantic. Bloody Betty Grable. I said 'Look Betty, what do you think you're doing, calling me up at half past eleven at night?' She said 'It's half past two in the afternoon over here.' I said 'I don't care what bloody time it is. There's no need to wake me up.' She said 'Peter, Peter, get on a plane. Come dance with me. Be mine tonight.'

DUD: I thought it was the middle of the afternoon.

PETE: Yeah, well what she probably meant was 'Be mine tonight, tomorrow afternoon our time.' Anyway, 'Be mine tonight' she said. I said 'Look, Betty – we've had our laughs, we've had our fun, but it's all over.' I said 'Stop pestering me! Get back to Harry James and his trumpet!'

DUD: Yeah.

PETE: 'Stop pestering me,' I said. I slammed the phone down and said 'Stop pestering me.'

DUD: Shouldn't you have said 'Stop pestering me' before you slammed the phone down?

PETE: I should have, yes.

DUD: Well, it's funny you should say that because a couple of nights ago – you remember we had a couple of drinks?

PETE: I remember that, yeah.

DUD: I come home, you know, I was going to bed – felt a bit tired, was having a nightcap.

PETE: Yeah, course you were.

DUD: And I was just dropping off nicely, and all a sudden I heard this hollering in the kitchen.

PETE: Hollering?

DUD: And screaming and banging on the door, you know. I thought I must have left the gas on. So I go down here, I fling open the door. You never guess – it's bloody Anna Magnani, up to her knees in rice, screaming at me. 'Amore me por favor!'

PETE: Italian.

DUD: Italian, yeah. She was covered in muck. She grabbed hold of me. She pulled me all over the floor. She had one of them see-through blouses on.

PETE: All damp, showing everything through it.

DUD: We rolled all over the floor, I picked her up, I said 'Get out of here! Get out of here, you Italian . . . thing.'

PETE: You Italian thing?

DUD: Yeah.

PETE: Good thing to call her.

DUD: Yeah. I said 'Don't you come here, mess up my rice again, mate.'

PETE: I should hope not. I had the same bloody trouble about two nights ago. I come in, about half past eleven at night. We'd been having a couple of drinks, I remember. I come in, I get into bed, you see, feeling quite sleepy. I could feel the lids of me eyes beginning to droop, you see – a bit of the droop in the eyes. I was just about to drop off when suddenly – tap, tap, tap at the bloody window pane. I looked out. You know who it was?

DUD: Who?

PETE: Bloody Greta Garbo. Bloody Greta Garbo, stark naked, save for a shortie nightie, hanging on to the window sill, and I could see her knuckles all white, saying 'Peter, Peter.' You know how these bloody Swedes go on. I said 'Get out of it!' Bloody Greta Garbo. She wouldn't go, she wouldn't go, I had to smash her down with a broomstick – poke her off the window sill. She fell down onto the pavement with a great crash.

DUD: She just had a nightie on, is that all?

PETE: That's all she had on Dud.

DUD: See-through?

PETE: A see-through shortie nightie, nothing else – except for her dark glasses, of course. Dreadful business.

DUD: Well it's funny you should say that.

PETE: Yeah, it's funny I should say that.

DUD: Yeah, four nights ago, I come home – you know, we'd been having a couple of drinks. I come home, I come through the door, and – sniff, sniff, I went, you know. Funny smell, I thought. Smells like wood burning.

PETE: Probably burning wood, Dud.

DUD: What's that?

PETE: Burning Wood? That's a perfume worn by sensual, earthy women.

DUD: Oh, funny you should say that, because I come in the bathroom – sniff – it's a bit stronger here, you know. That's funny. I come in the bedroom – sniff – it's getting ridiculous, this smell! And so I get into bed, you know, turn the covers back – it's a bit warm in bed. I thought that's funny, you know, being warm, like, and I get into bed, I put out the light, and I'm just getting off to kip, when suddenly I feel a hand on my cheek.

PETE: Which cheek was that Dud? Come on! Which cheek was it?

DUD: It was the left upper. I thought, you know, funny. I turned on the light – bloody hand, scarlet fingernails.

PETE: Yeah? Who was it?

DUD: You'll never guess. Bloody Jane Russell.

PETE: Jane Russell?

DUD: Jane Russell, in bed with me – stark naked. 'Jane!' I said. 'Get out of here!' I said 'You may be mean, moody and magnificent, but as far as I'm concerned, it's all over.' I took her out the bed, I threw her down the stairs, I threw her bra and her gauze panties after her – I threw them down there – and her silk green scarf. 'Get out of here! Get out of here, you hussy!' I said. I threw her fag holder, I threw it down the stairs after her. I threw a bucket of water over her. I said 'Get out of here, you hussy!' I said 'Don't come in my bed again, mate – it's disgusting' Terrible. I was shocked to the quick.

PETE: You're quite right. You've got to do something about these bloody women who pester you all the bloody time.

DUD: Don't they go on?

PETE: They go on and on.

DUD: Yeah. What you doing tonight then?

PETE: Well, I thought we might go to the pictures.

AT THE ART GALLERY
(*Not Only But Also*, BBC2, 1965)

DUD: Pete! Pete! Peter! Oh look, there you are.

PETE: I'm looking at 'The Passing Out of the Money Lenders'.

DUD: I don't care about that. I've been looking for you for the last half hour. We said we'd rendezvous in front of the Flemish Masters.

PETE: No we didn't, Dud, we never said anything of the sort.

DUD: When I last saw you, you were in the Bruegel, weren't you?

PETE: That's right. I said I'd whip through the Abstracts, go through the El Greco, up the Van Dyke and I'd see you in front of the bloody Rubens.

DUD: I said I was going to go round the Velasquez, through the Abstracts, up the Impressionists and meet you in front of the Flemish Masters.

PETE: No you didn't, Dud. It doesn't matter anyway.

DUD: Here, have a sandwich. My feet are killing me.

PETE: What's that got to do with the sandwich?

DUD: Nothing, I just said it afterwards, that's all.

PETE: Well you shouldn't say things like that together, it could confuse a stupid person.

DUD: Y'know, Pete, I reckon there's a lot of rubbish in this gallery here.

PETE: Not only rubbish, Dud, there's a lot of muck about. I've been looking all over the place for something good.

DUD: I've been looking for that lovely green gypsy lady. You know, the one with . . .

PETE: The one with the lovely shiny skin.

DUD: Where is she? Nowhere.

PETE: Nowhere.

DUD: So I went up to the commissionaire. I said 'Here.' I got him by the lapel. I said 'Here . . .'

PETE: 'Here.'

DUD: I said, 'Here . . .'

PETE: You didn't spit sandwich at him, did you?

DUD: Sorry Pete. Sorry about that. I said, 'Where's that bloody Chinese flying horse, then?'

PETE: What did he say?

DUD: He said, 'Get out.' So I had to run up the Impressionists for half an hour and hide out. But what I can't understand frankly, Peter, is that there's not a Vernon Ward gallery in here.

PETE: There's not a duck in the building, there's no Peter Scott, there's no Vernon Ward. Not a duck to be seen.

DUD: Nothing. The marvellous thing about Vernon Ward is that of course he's been doing ducks all his life.

PETE: Well, he's done more ducks than you've had hot breakfasts, Dud. If he's done anything he's done ducks.

DUD: He's done ducks in all positions.

PETE: Yeah.

DUD: Ducks in the morning, ducks in the evening, ducks in the summer time. What's that song?

Dud & Pete (*sing*): Ducks in the morning, Ducks in the evening, Ducks in the summertime.

DUD: Thought I recognised it.

PETE: The thing what makes you know that Vernon Ward is a good painter is if you look at his ducks, you see the eyes follow you round the room.

DUD: You noticed that?

PETE: Yeah, when you see sixteen of his ducks, you see thirty-two little eyes following you round the room.

DUD: No, you only see sixteen because they're flying sideways and you can't see the other eye on the other side. He never does a frontal duck.

PETE: No, but you get the impression, Dud, that the other eye is craning round the beak to look at you, don't you? That's a sign of a good painting, Dud. If the eyes follow you round the room, it's a good painting. If they don't, it isn't.

DUD: It's funny you say that, Pete, 'cause I was in the bathroom the other day.

PETE: Course you were, I remember that.

DUD: Course I was, Pete, and I had the feeling of somebody in the room with me. I thought – funny – you know, and I didn't see no one come in and I thought – funny. And I felt these eyes burning in the back of my head.

PETE: Funny.

DUD: So I whip round like a flash and I see the bloody Laughing Cavalier up there, having a giggle. I felt embarrassed, you know.

PETE: Of course you would, Dud.

DUD: So I went out of the bathroom and I went to Mrs Connolly's across the road and asked if I could use her toilet.

PETE: Of course – you feel a bit daft with someone looking at the back of you.

DUD: She's all right, though, 'cause she's only got a bowl of pansies in her toilet.

PETE: A real bowl of pansies or a painting, Dud?

DUD: A real painting.

PETE: Oh that's all right then. I tell you what's even worse, Dud, than the Laughing Cavalier.

DUD: What's that?

PETE: Can you think of anything worse?

DUD: No.

PETE: There is something worse than a Laughing Cavalier, what my Auntie Muriel has. She has the bloody Mona Lisa in her toilet.

DUD: That's dreadful.

PETE: That awful po-faced look about her, looking so superior, you know, peering down at you. She looks as if she'd never been to the lav in her life.

DUD: I mean that's the thing about the Laughing Cavalier, at least he has a giggle. He doesn't sit there all prissy.

PETE: No.

DUD: That's dreadful.

PETE: Have you been down the Rubens?

DUD: No.

PETE: You haven't seen the Rubens?

DUD: No.

PETE: There's one over there.

DUD: Is there?

PETE: Yeah, he does all the fat ladies with nothing on. Great big fat ladies, naked except for a tiny little wisp of gauze that always lands on the appropriate place, if you know what I mean. Always the wind blows a little bit of gauze over you know where, Dud.

DUD: Course, it must be a million to one chance, Pete, that the gauze lands in the right place at the right time, you know.

PETE: Course it is.

DUD: I bet there's thousands of paintings that we're not allowed to see where the gauze hasn't landed in the right place – it's on their nose or something.

PETE: But I suppose if the gauze landed on the wrong place, Dud, – you know, landed on the nose or the elbow or somewhere unimportant, what Rubens did was put down his painting and go off to have lunch or something.

DUD: Or have a good look. Course you don't get gauze floating around in the air these days, do you?

PETE: No, not like in the Renaissance time. There was always gauze in the air in those days.

DUD: Course, similarly, you don't get those lovely little Botticelli cherubs.

PETE: They died out, of course – they hunted them down for their silken skin, you know.

DUD: No they didn't, they couldn't kill them, Pete, 'cause they were immortal.

PETE: No they weren't, they shot them through with arrows through their tiny little bellies and then their skin was turned into underwear for rich ladies and courtesans.

DUD: I reckon they went up to heaven like the angels.

PETE: No they didn't.

DUD: Course there's no call for angels now, is there?

PETE: No, you don't see much of them these days, do you? Mrs Wisbey saw one actually the other day in the garden. She saw this angel. Actually it turned out to be a burglar. She went down on her knees praying to it and he was in the kitchen whipping away her silver.

DUD: Awful business.

PETE: Terrible. Have you seen that bloody Leonardo Da Vinci cartoon?

DUD: Well, of course, you know, Pete, people's sense of humour must have changed over the years.

PETE: Yes of course it has, that why it's not funny any more.

DUD: I bet, when that Da Vinci cartoon first come out, I bet people were killing themselves. I bet old Da Vinci had an accident when he drew it.

PETE: Well, it's difficult to see the joke, just that lady sitting there with the children round her. It's not much of a joke as far as I'm concerned, Dud.

DUD: Well apart from that, Pete, it's a different culture. It's Italian, you see.

PETE: It's Italianate.

DUD: We don't understand it. For instance, *The Mousetrap* did terribly in Pakistan.

PETE: Another thing we've wasted public money on is that bloody Cézanne – 'Grandes Baigneuses'. Have you see that load of rubbish?

DUD: No.

PETE: It's over there. There it is – those fat, nude ladies with their bottoms towards you. That's 'Les Grandes Baigneuses'. You know what that means, don't you?

DUD: No what does it mean?

PETE: 'Big Bathers'.

DUD: Is that all?

PETE: That's all. 'Big Bathers' – £500,000 quid we paid for that. Those nude women come out of our pocket, Dud.

DUD: Well you could get the real nude ladies over here for that price. My Aunt Dolly would have done it for nothing.

PETE: She does anything for nothing, doesn't she? Dirty old cow.

DUD: And you can't tell whether it's a good painting or not, either, 'cause you can't see their eyes – whether they follow you round the room.

PETE: No, the sign of a good painting when its people's backs towards you is if the bottoms follow you round the room.

DUD: If it's a good painting the bottoms will follow you round the room.

PETE: Right.

DUD: Shall I test it, then?

PETE: Are they moving, Dud?

DUD: I reckon they are, Pete.

PETE: No those bottoms aren't following you around the room, your eyes are following the bottoms around the room.

DUD: The same thing, isn't it?

PETE: Course it isn't. There's a good deal of difference between being followed by a bottom and you following a bottom.

DUD: You come here, then, and see what I see.

PETE: I don't see anything at all – just a load of bottoms extremely stationary.

DUD: Well, you go that way and I'll go this way and you see if your bottoms move the same as mine.

PETE: That's difficult for the bottoms, if we go in different directions.

DUD: Well, they can divide up amongst themselves.

PETE: See what happens.

DUD: Mine are moving, Pete.

PETE: My bottoms haven't budged yet.

DUD: Mine are going berserk.

PETE: Mine haven't moved at all. You've got a fevered imagination. You coming?

DUD: No, I'll hang on a bit.

PETE: All right. See you in the Pissarro.

ON THE BUS
(*Not Only But Also*, BBC2, 1965)

PETE: Right, Dud?

DUD: Right, Pete. Let's go and sit up the front, eh?

PETE: No, mustn't sit up the front, Dud, that's the least safe part of the bus. You ought to sit at the back, like you do in an aeroplane, that's where you're safe.

DUD: Why, what's wrong with the front?

PETE: Well, see, if there's a fatality, if the bus is involved in a fatal accident of any kind, it's the people up the front who get killed first, and the people up the back who get killed last.

DUD: Well, you get killed all the same though, don't you?

PETE: Yeah, well you get killed about two seconds later, you see, and in those last two seconds of your life you might suddenly start to believe in God, or you'd be able to make out your will or something like that.

DUD: Oh I see, yeah.

PETE: That's why I always sit at the back.

DUD: Yeah. Course you know, I always look forward to these Saturday afternoon outings on a bus. I reckon these roustabout tickets are a real bargain.

PETE: The Red Rover roustabout ticket, it's fantastic value, Dud. For six and eight you have available 695,000 miles of British roadway – an unsurpassed view of the British countryside, and all the loveliness thereof. Course, the only trouble is you're not allowed off the bus.

DUD: Well it wouldn't be so bad if they had facilities on the bus.

PETE: Yeah, as they don't have facilities most people have to get off after a couple of days. They can't stand it any longer.

DUD: You remember that clapped-out bus on the waste ground, behind the Green Lane Junior School?

PETE: Behind the wooden buildings?

DUD: That's right. Well, I thought, looks very nice, could make a little home out of that, and I went up there one night with a couple of blankets, and I went in and stayed there – it was a bit nippy, you know. I thought it's all right, but it's got no facilities.

PETE: Yeah, so I suppose you had to nip off down the public. Well, they used to build facilities on the buses, you know, but all the people stayed on them, for years and years, they wouldn't get off 'em. In fact, my Auntie Muriel, she bought some second-hand facilities from the buses. She claims they're ex-army but they're not – you can see London Bus Company written all over them.

Lovely work. I like to get on a bus because you meet a wonderful class of people.

DUD: A wonderful class of people.

PETE: A wonderful opportunity to mingle with all types of people. Did I ever tell you about that tempestuous affair I had on the 82B?

DUD: They've stopped that route now, haven't they?

PETE: As a direct result of the incident I'm about to relate. I used to go on the 82B, as you know, and one day I got on it and sat down, in this seat here – well not this actual seat – but one in a similar position.

DUD: Course you did, Pete.

PETE: And I got on, the bell rang; I paid me fare, went on a couple of stops, the bus stopped, nobody got off and nobody got on. The bus went on, another stop, nobody got off, nobody got on. Went on another stop, nobody got off and nobody got on. Another stop, nobody got off, and nobody got on.

DUD: How long does this go on for, Pete?

PETE: About five stops, Dud. It was a fairy uneventful journey until the incident. I won't bore you with the details.

DUD: You already have, Pete.

PETE: I'm trying to fill you in on the background. Suddenly we come to this stop under the overhanging elm what overhangs the road, just down by Farley Road. You know, it has a strange atmosphere about it.

DUD: Strangely romantic atmosphere about it, Pete.

PETE: Well anyway, the bus drew to a halt, and onto the platform steps this uncannily beautiful woman with incredibly sensuous looks about her. She had sensuality written all over her face.

DUD: Did she really?

PETE: Well not literally, no – she just oozed sensuality.

DUD: I know – bit sweaty.

PETE: I sometimes wish, you know, that women would have 'sensuality' or something actually written over their face – 'sensuality' or 'frigidity'.

DUD: Yeah, you'd know where you were then, wouldn't you?

PETE: You wouldn't waste your money.

DUD: What would you have if you had something written on your face, Pete?

PETE: I think I'd have 'dynamic lust' on my face.

DUD: I'd have 'insatiable passion'.

PETE: Anyway, this bird got on the platform, delicious-looking girl, and I could see immediately what she was after.

DUD: Yeah? What was she after, Pete?

PETE: Getting on the bus first of all, and secondly, she was filled with this crazy passion for me, you know. You could see it – she gave me this fleeting glance.

DUD: Like that, Pete?

PETE: Yeah, very similar to the glance which you've just perpetrated, Dud. And she gave me this glance and immediately climbed upstairs. So I thought – funny, going upstairs, it's obvious what she wants, me being downstairs and her going upstairs – funny. You can see what she's on. So I thought I'd play it very cool and stay downstairs. Sure enough, four stops later she comes down without even looking at me, got right off the bus and walked away.

DUD: What happened?

PETE: Well I stayed on – I thought I'm not going to give in to this sort of blatant blandishment, and I went on four stops and got off at Gribley Street, and I never saw her again.

DUD: You guessed her little game. Here, did I tell you about that bird, Joan Harold, about fourteen years ago?

PETE: Joan Harold – Spring of 1948.

DUD: That's right, right to the day.

PETE: Incredibly sensuous.

DUD: Yeah, moist lips, loosely parted, flaring negroid nostrils.

PETE: Amazing gypsy laugh.

DUD: That's right. Anyway you know she used to get the 5.45, 25B. Course she used to come out at 5.45 and I used to leave work about five, nowhere near where she was. So what I used to do, I used to get a 62A up Chadwell Heath, then I used to get the 514 trolley down to the Merry Fiddlers, then I used to have to run across that hill down by the railway bridge, over that field where the turnips were, over by the dye works, then I used to leap over

the privet hedge, and hurl myself onto the 25B as it came round
Hog Hill. There wasn't a bus stop there but it used to have to
slow down because it was a very dangerous curve. I used to lie
down in the middle of the road sometimes if it was going too
fast. I used to leap on to the platform and spend about twenty
minutes trying to get my breath back. Course I never spoke to
her. Actually, once she got off and I got off in front and I said –
'Ere' – I thought I'd tease her a bit – coax her – and I said 'Chase
me', and I started running off, but I was halfway across
Lymington Gardens before I realised she hadn't budged an inch.

PETE: That's no good, Dud. Play it cool. It's no good saying 'Chase
me' and being that blatant. You got to play it extremely cool if
you want to go out with women.

DUD: Well, I did go out with her once. I took her up West Ham
speedway, and do you know, I gave her two cups of tea, a box of
Pontefract cakes and a ham sandwich – nothing.

PETE: Nothing?

DUD: Nothing.

PETE: How much did you spend on her?

DUD: About seven and three.

PETE: Seven and three and nothing? You must be a bloody fool. It's
no good treating them like that, giving them Pontefract cakes. I
tell you what to do. Treat them extremely rough. You know I
used to go up Gants Hill in 1953. Model aeroplane racing. Well
I was standing down the bottom of Strawberry Lane . . .

DUD: What did you used to race?

PETE: I used to race a blue Spitfire. Elastic powered. I was waiting
for the 91A which takes you to the top of Gants Hill.

DUD: They've discontinued that route now, haven't they?

PETE: Yeah, due to the incident which I'm now about to relate. I
was waiting by the stop with my Spitfire under my arm, and
suddenly this fantastic bird come up to me, stood by me. She was
an incredibly sensuous-looking creature with all the fire of Egypt
plunging out of her peekaboo blouse, lightly covered with a see-
through shirt.

DUD: And a teasing sweater.

PETE: She had a figure-hugging sweater on, and a duffel coat over the lot of it, and galoshes, and anyway she obviously delved deep into the works of Sartre.

DUD: Obviously spent a couple of years in view of the Seine with some randy poet.

PETE: She'd obviously done that sort of thing, and I could see immediately what she was after. It stands to reason. I'm standing by the bus stop, she comes up, stood to reason. She come to me and she was offering it on a plate.

DUD: Was she really?

PETE: Not literally, Dud. I sometimes wish they would. She said, 'Excuse me, does the 83B go up to Gants Hill?' You know what I said? I said, 'Maybe it does, maybe it doesn't, what business is it of yours, fat face?' That's the way to treat 'em – rough.

DUD: I don't know how you do it, Pete.

PETE: Oh it's quite easy. I just say the words.

DUD: What happened anyway?

PETE: I said, 'Get out of my life, I never wish to see you again, slatternly woman.'

DUD: What did she do?

PETE: She took my advice – I never seen her again. That's the way – tell them what to do, they'll do it. If you say 'I never want to see you again', chances are you never will. Do you see those couple of birds up there? Which one do you fancy?

DUD: I fancy the one on the aisle.

PETE: The thin one? She could be yours tonight – in a matter of moments, if you play your cards right. Play it extremely cool. If I was you, Dud, if you fancy her – she's quite thin isn't she – go up to her and say something ironic and sophisticated, you know, like, 'Hello Fatty' – ironic. 'Hello Fatty, come home with me and make love to me.'

DUD: Shall I do that then, Pete?

PETE: Yeah. Go on up and see what happens.

DUD: Alright.

(*Dud walks up the bus to the girl.*)

DUD: Hello, fat face, come and make love to me tonight.

(*She slaps his face. Dud returns to his seat.*)

PETE: What happened then?

DUD: Well I said, 'Hello fat face, come and make love to me tonight' and she slapped my face.

PETE: Yeah. You see what she's wanting, don't you? Stands to reason. You're well away.

RELIGION
(*Not Only But Also*, BBC2, 1965)

PETE: I was reading the Bible the other day, you know.

DUD: It's good, isn't it?

PETE: It's a very good book, Dud. It's beautifully done, it's beautifully bound, it's beautifully put together. I was reading the chapter about Ishmael begat Remus and Remus begat Isobar and Isobar begat this other bloke.

DUD: They were certainly begetting.

PETE: Yeah. Everyone begat each other.

DUD: Sort of, sort of historical document thing.

PETE: Like, you know, who gave birth to who and that.

DUD: Like at Somerset House, isn't it?

PETE: George Meacham began Daphne Meacham, Daphne Meacham begat Fred Taylor, and so on.

DUD: Course you can trace it all back to Adam and Eve.

PETE: The first two.

DUD: Yes, they were the first two. But what I don't understand, Pete, is how two people produced so many millions of different colour, kith, race and creed.

PETE: You mean how did Adam and Eve have all these children of myriad hues?

DUD: Yeah.

PETE: Well, the point of that, Dud, is that Genesis isn't true in the literal sense. It's an allergy. Genesis is an allergy of La Condition Humaine. It's about the whole lot of the human race. Adam and Eve aren't just Adam and Eve. They're the whole human race personified. Do you believe in God, actually?

DUD: I tell you Pete, when I'm in a tight spot I say to myself, 'God please help me out, if You're there. If You do help me out, I'll believe in You and thank You very much. I'll know You're there for future reference.'

PETE: Yeah, I have a similar attitude. Whenever I feel ill, you know, I get a dose of the flu or something, I say a little prayer. I say, 'Dear God in heaven, if You're there, heed my prayer. If You're not there, don't take any notice. But if You are, make me better by Tuesday at twelve o'clock and I'll know You've done it, and I promise to be good for ever more and believe in You.' Of course the trouble is, when you get better you don't know whether it's because God's done it or whether you would have got better in any case. There's no real way of telling what He's up to or even where He is.

DUD: No, you can't tell, can you really.

PETE: I often wish He'd manifest himself a bit more, you know, in the sky.

DUD: Yeah, it'd be nice if every now and again He parted the clouds and in a golden burst of sunshine gave you a wave. 'Hello down there, you can believe in me.'

PETE: I asked the Reverend Stephens about this, and he said, 'Much as God would like to keep manifesting Himself, He daren't, you see, because it debases the currency.' He can't go round all the football matches and fetes and everything, so He limits himself to once in a million years if we're lucky.

DUD: Well, you've got to be careful about over-exposure. Course you know, actually, Pete, I wish I'd never been told about God at all 'cause it means we can't get away with nothing, doesn't it? I mean you've been told about Him, you know He's there or you think He's there, and you can't really mess about then, can you?

PETE: You can't.

DUD: No, and what about the people who haven't been told about God?

PETE: Well, I asked the Reverend Stephens this, and he said that if you haven't been told about God, Dud, you're laughing. If you don't know good from evil then you're away. You can do anything you bloody well like. There's these people in New

Guinea, for example. They wander about with nothing on and they commit adultery, steal, and covet their neighbour's wife, which everyone wants to do. As there are no vicars about, to tell them everything, they can't be got at, so they go up to heaven whatever they do. This means all these nig-nogs are getting up to heaven, and perfectly decent blokes like you and me, who have never even committed adultery, we can't get up there – we're being kept out by these Guineans.

DUD: You see in that case, Pete, it'd be a crime to tell people about God.

PETE: I've never told anyone about God.

DUD: I haven't told anyone. I haven't mentioned it to a soul, Pete.

PETE: St Paul's got a bloody lot to answer for.

DUD: He started it didn't he – all those letters he wrote.

PETE: To the Ephiscans.

DUD: You know, 'Dear Ephiscans, Stop enjoying yourselves, God's about the place. Signed Paul.'

PETE: You can just imagine it, can't you? There's a nice Ephiscan family settling down to a good breakfast of fried mussels and hot coffee and just sitting there. It's a lovely day outside and they're thinking of taking the children out for a picnic by the sea and everything's happy and the sun's coming through the trees, birds are chirping away.

DUD: The distant cry of happy children, and clouds scudding across the sky.

PETE: In fact, an idyllic scene is what you'd call it – an idyllic scene. When suddenly into the midst of it all – tap, tap, on the bloody door. You know who it is?

DUD: No.

PETE: It's a messenger bearing a letter from Paul.

DUD: Dad runs to the door to open it, thinking it may be good news.

PETE: Perhaps Grandfather's died and left them the vineyards.

DUD: They open it up and what do they discover?

PETE: 'Dear George and Deirdre and Family, Stop having a good time, resign yourself to not having a picnic, cover yourself with ashes and start flaying yourselves, until further notice, Signed Paul.'

Dud: A dreadful sort of letter to get, isn't it?

Pete: Terrible.

Dud: Course, you know, actually I'm fascinated by those religions which say you come back in a different form.

Pete: Reincarnation.

Dud: Reincarnation.

Pete: Yeah. Buddhists believe in that, coming back as a different creature of some kind or other.

Dud: What would you come back as?

Pete: Well, I think if I had a choice, I'd probably come back as a royal corgi and go sniffing about the Palace, you know.

Dud: That's very good, actually – improve your situation.

Pete: Course you could come back as something terrible, couldn't you?

Dud: Well, suppose you came back as a humble mayfly.

Pete: Well, of course you'd only live for six hours, wouldn't you? They have a very futile life, them mayflies, they only live six hours. As soon as they're born, they're worried about old age. By the time they're three hours old they're really middle-aged, they can't run for buses like they used to. They got grey hairs all over their legs, and in another three hours they're gaga and they die.

Dud: Terrible business.

Pete: You know Mr Thomas.

Dud: Yeah.

Pete: Next door.

Dud: Yeah.

Pete: He's a Buddhist.

Dud: He's not.

Pete: Yeah, he's a Buddhist.

Dud: Is he really?

Pete: Yeah, he's a Buddhist. He's got this bluebottle in the bathroom. He thinks it's Keats. He thinks it's the poet Keats reincarnated, so he keeps going into the bathroom, takes it in marshmallows and marmalade. The bluebottle's getting very fat – terrible great thing. He puts out bits of paper, hoping he'll complete some poems. He's just got a lot of bluebottle droppings so far. He still frames them, though.

DUD: They'd probably mean something to another bluebottle.

PETE: Well, true bluebottles would understand it wouldn't they?

DUD: Course actually I'd like to come back as a sparrow so I could see down ladies' blouses.

PETE: There wouldn't be much point in that, Dud. If you came back as a sparrow, you wouldn't want to look down ladies' blouses.

DUD: No, you'd just want to look down sparrows' blouses.

PETE: You'd be interested in them – as a sparrow. If I had my choice I'd like to come back as Grace Kelly.

DUD: Why's that?

PETE: I've always wanted to know what she looks like in the bath. I've always been fascinated by her glacial beauty.

DUD: Course, actually, you know, Pete, in the end, it's a bit of a toss up as to which religion is right, isn't it? You can't actually know which religion is right.

PETE: No, you can't tell. There are millions of religions. It might be Buddhism – it might be Christianity.

DUD: You don't know what to go for, do you, actually?

PETE: No, you might be a perfectly good Buddhist all your life, get up to heaven and there will be the Reverend Stephens saying, 'Get out – ha, ha, ha, Buddhism is wrong. We're right! Buddha off!'

DUD: Alternatively you might be a very good Christian, Church of England, behave yourself very nicely, get up there and there's Buddha.

PETE: Laughing all over his face and sends you back as a worm.

DUD: I think the best thing is to remain a prognostic.

PETE: An agnostic.

DUD: Do you think God's been listening while we've been talking?

PETE: Well, if He exists, He's been listening because He's omnipresent. He's heard every word we've said.

DUD: Oh, we'd better look religious, then.

PETE: It's no good just looking religious Dud, He can see through that. You have to be religious. What do you really believe in?

DUD: I believe in having a good time – food and kip and Joan Whittaker and that.

PETE: That's not religion, Dud. That's Hedonism. You're a Heddist.

DUD: No, I'm a Duddist. That's what I call it.

AT THE ZOO
(*Not Only But Also*, BBC2, 1966)

DUD: Nice and warm in here, isn't it, Pete?

PETE: Nothing like a nice warm reptile house.

DUD: Nothing like a nice warm reptile house.

PETE: Have you seen those geckos over there?

DUD: Geckos, what are they?

PETE: A gecko, Dud, is a lizard what has sucking pads on its feet.

DUD: So it can hang on glass.

PETE: It can if it likes. It can hang on anything it fancies. It has a wonderful life, except, of course, it has to eat flies. Did you know that?

DUD: No I didn't.

PETE: Oh yes, it has to eat flies, 'cause, as you know, God created it, like he did everything else in his almighty wisdom, and all the animals have to eat each other to keep the population down. And geckos got lumbered with flies. It's all right when it's born. Its mother gives it some flies, all mashed up, daintily garnished with a daisy on top of it, so it can't tell what it's eating. But as soon as it learns to speak, Dud, and communicate, it says to its mother, 'Excuse me, what's this I'm eating?' and she has to reply 'Flies.'

DUD: 'Darling'.

PETE: Of course. She says, 'Flies, darling, and they're very good for you.' But that's why the gecko doesn't live very long, because he can't bear eating the stuff.

DUD: Eating flies, I couldn't bear that. I wouldn't like to be a gecko. I'd like to be a poisonous snake, – get a real feeling of power with all them fangs.

PETE: Well you've got prominent teeth already, haven't you?

DUD: I could sharpen 'em up and put a bit of cyanide in 'em and go round and, you know, sort of put my teeth into people's arms and kill 'em.

PETE: What sort of a poisonous snake would you be? Would you be an asp?

DUD: No, I'd like to be a viper.

PETE: That's the same thing as an asp but an asp's bigger, Dud.

DUD: Is it?

PETE: Asp was a word invented by Shakespeare during the thirteenth century to denote a viper, 'cause, as you know, Shakespeare was a wonderful writer.

DUD: Knockout.

PETE: And he was doing this wonderful verse play about Cleopatra – how she got wrapped up in the carpet. Shakespeare had been writing this couplet to describe the scene when the snake comes rustling up her undies and begins to start biting into her busty substances. And he'd almost finished this magnificent verse couplet, you see, but the only thing is he only had one syllable left to describe the snake, and 'viper' was too long for the snake so he invented the word 'asp', and a very good word it is too.

DUD: Wonderful. I suppose it was a sort of Shakespearian abbreviation for 'A Stinging Personality'.

PETE: ASP. Yes, I suppose that's the reason.

DUD: Here, I don't reckon it was an asp what stung Cleopatra in the chest, I bet it was a bra constrictor.

PETE: What do you mean? It was an asp.

DUD: No, a bra constrictor, Pete – boa constrictor, it's a joke, Pete.

PETE: Oh, it was a joke, was it? Oh. It was very bad taste. You shouldn't make jokes about people who are dead, 'cause they can't fight back, Dud.

DUD: Sorry, Pete.

PETE: I wouldn't be a reptile at all if I had a choice. If I had a choice I'd be something lovely and cuddly and lovable. Something like those lovely humming birds, which hum with their various hues above the flowers. Those long tongues, all coiled up like watch springs. They can poke them out to forty yards long. A humming bird, Dud, can kiss at immense distances.

DUD: That means that you could stand on the Chiswick flyover and kiss someone up the Staines bypass.

PETE: Hovering four foot above the ground and humming, a wonderful opportunity. I tell you a creature I think is a very cuddly little thing, that's the chameleon – very versatile.

DUD: Versatile creature, Pete. They can take on the shape and colour of anything they like, all the hues. You remember Mr Rigby?

PETE: Yeah.

DUD: He nearly went through a wedding ceremony with one.

PETE: He would have been very happy with a chameleon. They make lovely wives.

DUD: You know, I was here last week, Pete, I don't know if I told you.

PETE: Yeah.

DUD: I saw this big sign saying 'Topical fish this way'. I thought, that's OK, see a few topical fish, a few up-to-the-minute bits of satire. You know, topical barbs about the current situation in the world today.

PETE: What did you see?

DUD: Well I go in there and it's just a lot of fish swimming about, more timeless than topical.

PETE: I tell you what you done, you gone into the tropical fish department – that's TROPICAL rather than topical, you see. What happens is that during the winter months, all through the blustery weather, sometimes some of the letters become dislodged because of the gales. And obviously the letter R had become dislodged in this way. I was talking to the keeper about it actually, and he said that very often during the winter months, his Rs blew off. During the winter months, his Rs blew off.

DUD: I think I've had enough of the reptile house. Let's go on to the wonkey house.

PETE: No, that's an M what's got blown upside down.

PETER COOK

SEX
(*Not Only But Also*, BBC2, 1966)

PETE: Come over here, will you please.

DUD: Here, you've been ferreting around in my sandwich box, haven't you?

PETE: I certainly have, and I found something not altogether connected with sandwiches. I refer of course to Blauberger's Encyclopaedia of Sexual Knowledge. How do you explain this?

DUD: I found it on the Heath, Pete, and I thought I better keep it in my sandwich tin to keep it dry until someone claimed it.

PETE: You're hiding it away, aren't you, because you're ashamed of it.

DUD: No I'm not. I just kept it there for safe keeping.

PETE: You shouldn't be ashamed of sex, Dud. It's no good hiding your sex away in a sandwich tin. Bring it out in the open.

DUD: It's a good book that, some good bits in it. Have you read any of it?

PETE: Yes, I've been through it up to page three thousand and one.

DUD: You've read the whole lot of it then, haven't you?

PETE: Yeah, it's quite good.

DUD: I like it because it tells you everything about sex from the word go.

PETE: It's wonderfully informative about the sexual mores throughout the ages, Dud.

DUD: And it tells you of human sexual endeavour from the time of Adam and Eve, Pete.

PETE: It certainly does, all the myths about it as well. Of course, Adam and Eve while they were in the Garden of Eden, they didn't have anything to do with sex to start with, you know. When they were in Paradise, they didn't have anything to do with sex 'cause they were wandering around naked but they didn't know they were naked.

DUD: I bet they did know. I mean, you'd soon know once you got caught up on the brambles.

PETE: They had no idea – they were remarkably stupid, as well as naked. They didn't know they were naked until up come a

135

serpent – as some authorities have it. Up come a serpent and said, 'Here's an apple. Lay your teeth into that.' Then they laid their teeth into the apple and the serpent said, 'You're nude, you're completely nude.'

DUD: Hello nudies! Course they dashed off into the brush and covered themselves with embarrassment, didn't they?

PETE: And mulberry leaves as well. They covered themselves altogether with this primitive clothing made of leaves, and suddenly, as soon as they became completely covered, they began to get attracted to each other, and then, of course, they tore off the mulberry leaves and it all started, the whole business.

DUD: Well, I think once you've got clothes on you're more attractive to other people. Like I think Aunt Dolly's more attractive with her clothes on than off. So Uncle Bert says, anyway.

PETE: Well, Aunt Dolly is really at her most attractive when she's completely covered in wool and has a black veil over her face and, ideally, she should be in another room from you.

DUD: Who's your sort of ideal woman, Pete?

PETE: Well, above all others I covet the elfin beauty, the gazelle slim elfin beauty, very slim, very slender, but all the same, still being endowed with a certain amount of . . .

DUD: Busty substances.

PETE: Yes, a kind of Audrey Hepburn with Anita Ekberg overtones is what I go for. What do you like?

DUD: Me? The same sort of thing. Actually I like the sort of woman who throws herself on you and tears your clothes off with rancid sensuality.

PETE: Yes, they're quite good, aren't they? I think you're referring to 'rampant sensuality'.

DUD: Either one will do. Of course, the important thing is that they tear your clothes off.

PETE: That's the chief thing. I like a good rampant woman.

DUD: I tell you a rampant woman – or rancid – or whatever your prefer. That's Veronica Pilbrow. Do you remember her?

PETE: Do I remember her? Yeah.

DUD: She was always throwing herself on Roger Braintree, never me, though.

PETE: Well Roger Braintree at school, he always knew more than anyone else. He was always boasting about things he knew.

DUD: Old clever drawers, weren't he, eh?

PETE: You remember that time he came round behind the wooden buildings and he had, what was his name, Kenny Vare with him, and he come up and told me, 'I've discovered the most disgusting word in the world. It's so filthy that no one's allowed to see it except bishops and nobody knows what it means. It's the worst word in the world.'

DUD: What was the word?

PETE: He wouldn't tell me. I had to give him half a pound of peppermints before he let it out. Do you know what it was?

DUD: No.

PETE: 'Bastard.'

DUD: What's that mean Pete?

PETE: Well he wouldn't tell me. I knew it was filthy but I didn't know how to use it. So he said the only place I could see it was down at the Town Hall in the enormous dictionary they have there – an enormous one with a whole volume to each letter. You can only get in with a medical certificate. So I went down there and sneaked in, you know, very secretively, and went up and took down from the shelf this enormous great dusty 'B' and opened it out and there was the word in all its horror – 'BASTARD'.

DUD: What was the definition, Pete?

PETE: It said, 'BASTARD – Child born out of wedlock.'

DUD: Urrgh! What's a wedlock, Pete?

PETE: A wedlock, Dud, is a horrible thing. It's a mixture of a steam engine and a padlock and some children are born out of them instead of through the normal channels and it's another one of the filthiest words in the world.

DUD: Make your hair drop out if you say it. I like looking up words in the dictionary. You know, I like going round the Valence library and going to the reference library and getting out the dictionary of unconventional English and looking up 'BLOOMERS'.

PETE: Yes, it's quite a good way of spending an afternoon.

DUD: Course I tell you what, Pete, the whole business of sex is a bit of a let-down really when you compare it with the wonderful romantic tales of a novelist who can portray sexual endeavours in so much better form, Pete.

PETE: Well, he makes it all so perfect. In the hands of a skilled novelist, sex becomes something which can never be attained in real life. Have you read Nevil Shute?

DUD: Very little.

PETE: How much of Nevil Shute have you read?

DUD: Nothing.

PETE: Yes, well Nevil Shute is a master of sensuality. He has some wonderful erotic passages, like in 'A Town Like Alice' in the hardcover version, page 81. If you go down the library, it falls open at that page. It's a description set in Australia, Dud, and there's this ash-blonde girl, Tina.

DUD: (*sings*) Tina, don't you be meaner . . .

PETE: Shut up. And she's there, standing on the runway, you see, of this aerodrome and it's very hot – Australian bush heat. It's very hot indeed and she's standing there waiting for her rugged Aussie pilot to come – bronzed Tim Bradley – and it's very hot. The cicadas are rubbing their legs together making that strange noise – very similar to that nasty noise which is coming from your mouth at this very moment. And it's very hot and she's covered in dust. The Australian dust is all over her. She's got dust on her knees, dust on her shoulders.

DUD: Dust on her bust, Pete.

PETE: Dust on her bust, as you so rightly point out, Dud. And it's very dusty and it's very hot – hot and dusty. And suddenly, out of nowhere, the clouds open. There's a tremendous clap of thunder and suddenly the mongoose is on her. The tropical rain storm is soaking through the frail poplin she is wearing and as the dress gets damper and damper, damper and damper, her wonderful frail form is outlined against the poplin. And then what does she hear but, in the distance, the distant buzzing of an approaching plane. She cups her ear to hear, like this.

DUD: She cups her perfectly proportioned up-thrusting ear, Pete.

PETE: She cups it, the plane comes down on the runway and comes to a halt and out comes the bronzed Aussie. But all the propellers are going very fast still. There's a tremendous rushing wind and it blows up against her and it blows the damp dress right up against her and reveals, for all the world to see, her perfectly defined . . .

DUD: Busty substances.

PETE: Busty substances.

DUD: What happened after that Pete?

PETE: Well, the bronzed pilot goes up to her and they walk away, and the chapter ends in three dots.

DUD: What do those three dots mean, Pete?

PETE: Well, in Shute's hands, three dots can mean anything.

DUD: How's your father, perhaps?

PETE: When Shute uses three dots it means, 'Use your own imagination. Conjure the scene up yourself.' Whenever I see three dots I feel all funny.

DUD: That's put me in the mood to go up to the Valence library and look up 'BOSOM' again.

PETE: No, it no good looking up 'BOSOM', it only says 'see BUST'.

DUD: But it's nice to read it all again.

PETE: It gives you something to do.

THE FUTILITY OF LIFE
(*Not Only But Also*, BBC2, 1970)

DUD: Tea's up, Pete.

PETE: No, thank you.

DUD: What, no tea?

PETE: Would you like me to submit a memo? No.

DUD: Oh. Have you got the collywobbles or something? You feeling a bit peaky?

PETE: No.

DUD: I thought perhaps those whelks might be clashing with the éclairs.

PETE: They are not, and if they were I would keep it to myself.

DUD: I'm not sure that you'd have the option. What's the matter?

PETE: No words can convey the merest inkling of my innermost thoughts.

DUD: On the contrary. What you've just said has conveyed to me in detail the nature of your malaise. You're feeling a bit droopy.

PETE: A bit droopy? You're the sort of person who'd have gone up to Joan of Arc as the flames licked round her vitals and said, 'Feeling one degree under? Like a nice cup of tea?'

DUD: You know what my mother would say?

PETE: No.

DUD: 'Somebody has got out of bed the wrong side this morning.'

PETE: If your mother said that to me today, I'd smash her in the teeth with the coal scuttle.

DUD: Oh, I see. You're feeling a bit temperamental. As Dr Groarke would say 'half temper, half mental.'

PETE: These glib platitudes are, if anything, exacerbating an already unbearable mood of depression.

DUD: If you're depressed, there's no point sitting around feeling sorry for yourself. That won't get the washing up done.

PETE: Dud, your uncanny grasp of domestic trivia is of negligible therapeutic value, and if you tell me to pull myself together or snap out of it, I might well do something rash.

DUD: I wouldn't say anything like that. Get a grip on yourself, look on the bright side.

Dud and Pete (*together*): Count your blessings.

DUD: Ooh, Mr Acid Drop himself. Come on, you'll feel better if you get it off your chest. You can confide in me. I mean, what am I here for?

PETE: In your fumbling way you have actually articulated the fundamental question. What are you here for? What am I here for? What is the purpose of life?

DUD: The purpose of life? Well, we are here on this earth for a brief sojourn, life is a precious gift, the more we put into it, the more we get out of it, and if on the way I can have spread a little sunshine, then my living shall not be in vain.

PETE: Thank you, Patience Strong. Have you ever thought about death? Do you realise that we each must die?

DUD: Of course we must die, but not yet. It's only half past four of a Wednesday afternoon.

PETE: No one knows when God in his Almighty Wisdom will choose to vouchsafe His precious gift of Death.

DUD: Granted. But chances are He won't be making a pounce at this time of day.

PETE: As far as I'm concerned, He can get a bloody move on.

DUD: That's morbid. Think of all the good things in life.

PETE: Like what?

DUD: Just look out the window.

(*Dud opens the curtains, then quickly closes them again.*)

DUD: Perhaps not.

PETE: I think it was rightly said, 'See Dagenham Dye Works and die.'

DUD: Yes, but think of all the happy times you've had. That's what I do when I'm feeling below par. This room is filled with joyous memories. Look at this – a certificate proving we've been up the Post Office Tower.

PETE: And why did we go up it?

DUD: Because it was there, Pete, a challenge.

PETE: A brief escape from a life consisting of cups of tea, interminable games of Ludo and the occasional visit to your Aunt Dolly.

DUD: Well, what does this remind you of?

(*Dud shows Pete a souvenir programme.*)

PETE: It reminds me of our dismal visit to the Planetarium.

DUD: That was nice, wasn't it? Seeing the sky at night during broad daylight.

PETE: And emerging into a cold wind and drizzle, buying a newspaper only to read the headline 'London Airport Disaster – thirty old ladies sucked to death in Jumbo Jet engine.'

DUD: But think of the millions of old ladies who weren't sucked to death in a jet engine, who are now happily playing snap up and down the country.

PETE: The mental image of millions of old ladies shouting 'Snap' at each other merely confirms my ideas about the futility of life.

DUD: What about that time we went to the National Gallery then?

PETE: And you spent four hours with your nose up against one of Rubens's more voluptuous nudes.

DUD: I was bewitched by the Dutch master's handling of light and shade.

PETE: With particular reference to busty substances.

DUD: My apparent concentration on this area was due to the fact that I had heard that Rubens had used these busty appurtenances to obliterate an earlier more controversial study of Clapham Common.

PETE: Did you perceive any blades of grass peeping through the opulent pink orbs?

DUD: No, but I could see the dim outline of Battersea Power Station looming up through her nether regions. I think I've got the postcard somewhere.

PETE: Yes, it's up in the bedroom amongst your art collection of *Spick and Span* and *Beautiful Britons*.

DUD: Actually, I think you borrowed it to use as a bookmark for your copy of *La Vie Parisienne*, or was it *Lilliput*, edition number 159? One or other of your nudie books.

PETE: I purchased that copy of *La Vie Parisienne* for the very interesting article on marine life by Captain Cousteau.

DUD: Strange then that it should always fall open at a page not so much connected with the sea bed as with a scantily clad adagio dancer from the Moulin Rouge.

PETE: That must have been caused by the previous owner. I'm not interested in that sort of thing.

DUD: No wonder you're depressed. It's not healthy not to be interested in ladies of the opposite sex.

PETE: Nothing is seething beneath my mackintosh save for a general feeling of despair and futility and boredom with you.

DUD: I know. I know what will perk you up. Sausages and Mash.

PETE: I'm not hungry.

DUD: No, the game, Sausages and Mash. You read a book out loud and put the word 'sausage' for every word beginning with 's' and 'mash' for every word beginning with 'm'. It's very funny. Look what happens. 'I mash go down to the sausages again, to the lonely sausage and the sausage. And all I ask is a tall sausage and a sausage to sausage her,' by John Mash.

PETE: Bloody stupid.

DUD: Bloody sausage, you mean. I mean, you mash. I mash, you mash.

PETE: What's this then? 'Sausage sausages sausage sausages on the sausage sausage. The sausages sausage sausages are sausage sausages for sausage.

DUD: Keats?

PETE: No, 'She sells sea shells on the sea shore.' We could also waste our time playing 'Fish and Chips'.

DUD: I don't know that one.

PETE: I'll give you an example. Why don't you fish off, chips chips.

DUD: I don't get that one. Fish off?

PETE: I'll give you a clue. The 'chips' in 'chip chips' stands for 'chops'.

DUD: Oh I see, so it's 'Why don't you fish off chip chops.' Oh, I sausage what you mash.

PETE: What?

DUD: I see what you mean.

Chapter Six

Private Eye

Beyond the Fringe and The Establishment made Cook the star of London and New York theatreland, while *Not Only But Also* made him a household name throughout Britain and Australia – a reputation that even his progressively mediocre film career could never quite dispel. Yet while the clubs, the theatre shows and the TV series all came and went, the one constant in his career, and indeed his life, was his magazine, *Private Eye*.

Cook always wanted to start a satirical magazine, just as he'd always wanted to start a satirical nightclub. *Private Eye* had been launched in 1961, by Peter Usborne (who provided the initial impetus), Andrew Osmond (who provided the initial money), Christopher Booker (the inaugural editor, who wrote most of the early issues) and Willie Rushton (who drew most of the cartoons, and who'd had the smart idea of starting such a journal in the first place). Richard Ingrams became increasingly involved, particularly after his theatre company, Tomorrow's Audience, went bust. He eventually replaced Booker as editor. Ingrams was subsequently joined by his old friends Paul Foot and John Wells, who'd been working respectively as a journalist on the *Glasgow Daily Record* and as a schoolmaster at Eton.

Ingrams and Rushton had boarded together at Shrewbury School, where they had transformed the school magazine, *The Salopian*, from a stuffy almanac of sports results into a subversive absurdist comic. Foot and Booker also went to Shrewsbury, and both wrote for *The Salopian*. Ingrams was reunited with Foot at Oxford University, on Usborne's humorous magazine, *Mesopotamia*, alongside Andrew Osmond and John Wells. Meanwhile, Booker went up to Cambridge, where he met a young undergraduate called Peter Cook. A few years later, Cook was Britain's first satirical superstar, and Booker turned up at his Establishment Club with the first issue of *Private Eye*.

Cook was disappointed to discover that someone had got in there first, but despite his frustration, Cook suggested that Booker use photos of public figures with satirical speech bubbles on the cover – something that Cook had seen in an American magazine. Although it was not an original idea (there are few original ideas in journalism) this device quickly became a *Private Eye* hallmark.

By 1962, *The Eye* had become one of the most talked-about journals around town. Yet its circulation was only 18,000, and Andrew Osmond, who'd stumped up the cash to start *The Eye*, reckoned they needed to sell 50,000 to make a living. Under pressure from his parents, and reluctant to fund the further investment this circulation hike required, Osmond left to join the Foreign Office – the very career Cook had originally intended to pursue. Together with his Establishment business partner, former Footlights treasurer Nicholas Luard, Cook took over.

Luard put the staff on proper wages, and gave the magazine a new masthead, which has survived until today. Cook's first act as proprietor was rather less successful – he moved *Private Eye* into The Establishment Club. At the very least, this presented severe practical problems. *The Eye*'s new office doubled as the waiters' changing room, and the only way in or out was via the stage. Anyone who didn't get out before the show began was stuck backstage until it finished. Cook held joint lunches once a week, to pool old ideas and inspire new ones. However this arranged marriage proved that *The Eye*, with its roots in Cavalier Oxford, was utterly incompatible with The Establishment, rooted in Roundhead Cambridge. '*Private Eye* was virtually edited from a pub,' revealed Wells. 'The mood was rough, bluff, philistine and beery.'[1] Unlike The Establishment. 'The Cambridge lot, on the other hand, already gave off a hum of high tech earnestness, producing precision-made satirical jokes.'[2] Thankfully, Cook quickly transferred The Eye to similarly claustrophobic but completely separate premises, a few doors away in Soho, and the circulation soon reached Osmond's target of 50,000.

However, Cook's greatest contribution to *The Eye* came a couple of years later, when he came back to Britain from the American run of *Beyond the Fringe*. Now satire was out of fashion, and so was *Private Eye*. Circulation had hit 80,000 during the Profumo scandal. Now it had shrunk to 20,000. *That Was the Week That Was* had finished, The Establishment had closed, and nobody would have been too surprised if *Private Eye* had followed suit. Ironically, Cook had considered *The Eye* the most ephemeral part of his satire empire. In fact, it was the only part of it to endure.

Cook put up £2,000, and charmed £100 contributions from many of his famous friends, such as Jane Asher, Dirk Bogarde and Bernard Braden, who became fellow shareholders. Yet Cook's input wasn't just financial. For the next few years, he was a core contributor, alongside Wells, Ingrams and Barry Fantoni. 'Although he had acquired the reputation of a savage political satirist during the satire boom, Cook's talent has always been for outrageous nonsense fantasies,' explains Ingrams. 'He would impersonate a zoo keeper attempting to recapture a very rare type of bee which had become lodged in a lady's knickers.'[3] Virtually everything in *The Eye* was written by committee, so most of the time, Cook would stride around the office, dictating in a variety of silly voices, while his colleagues tried to stop laughing for long enough to write it down. The only piece he actually wrote rather than recited was 'The Seductive Brethren', starring his most vivid *Eye* creation, Sir Basil Nardly Stoads. However Cook also played a major part in 'The Memoirs of Rhandhi P'hurr' – Rudyard Kipling meets a precessor of the Maharishi Mahesh Yogi in the pages of the *Kama Sutra*. Both epics are included here.

Cook's subsequent contributions were more indirect, but equally influential. He coined several of *The Eye*'s favourite catchphrases, like 'my lady wife, whose name for a moment escapes me,' and 'not a million miles from the truth'. He also had the idea which prompted Mrs Wilson's Diary – Wells and Ingrams' cod memoir, supposedly written by the prime minister's wife. It became *Private Eye*'s most successful series, spawning two books, and a West End play, directed by Joan Littlewood, which was subsequently broadcast on TV. With fellow *Eye* writer and artist Barry Fantoni, Cook also sent up music and sports journalism in a series of reports on a pop group called The Turds (who bore a striking resemblance to The Beatles) and Neasden FC, a useless football team.

When Ingrams was away, Cook sometimes edited *The Eye* himself, in a style that was undoubtedly far bawdier than Ingrams' – and arguably even bolder. He printed a full-frontal nude drawing by Ralph Steadman of Judge Michael Argyle, who was presiding over the *Oz* magazine obscenity trail. He named The Krays, whose dealings with Conservative peer Lord Boothby had been the subject of much pointed but anonymous innuendo in the national press. Peter made sure he was safely out of the country by the time that issue hit the street.

In 1966, *Private Eye* lost its first court case, after Lord Russell of Liverpool sued for libel, and was awarded £5,000 damages and £3,000 costs. Since *The Eye*'s income was then only about £1,300 a fortnight, this was a potentially crippling sum, so Cook organised a fundraising show at London's Prince of Wales Theatre. *Rustle of Spring* starred Cook and Moore, plus Larry Adler, Bernard Braden, John Bird, David Frost, George Melly, Spike Milligan, Bob Monkhouse, Peter Sellers, Willie Rushton and many more. Readers like John Betjeman made up the remainder. Russell got his £8,000.

Cook's appearances at *The Eye* became increasingly irregular, but he always provided moral and practical support whenever the magazine was in trouble, and continued to make occasional, inspirational contributions, both on *The Eye*'s records, and in the magazine. One of Cook's particular favourites was Gnome Mart, *Private Eye*'s perennial Christmas gift catalogue. Peter's gifts included Ice Skating Ants and Screaming Hawaiian Grass.

However Cook's role as *The Eye*'s Lord Gnome was infinitely greater than the sum of its elusive parts. 'He was the proprietor,' wrote Cook's *Eye* colleague, Auberon Waugh, 'but his powers were never fully explained, possibly never understood, certainly never exercised.'[4] Cook considered his proprietorial neutrality to be his greatest strength. 'Where else would they find someone like me, who does nothing?'[5] Yet even when he wasn't doing anything, Cook's influence on *The Eye* was immense. As Waugh explained, 'In my sixteen years on *Private Eye*, Peter's visits stand out as moments when everybody suddenly became possessed with a new energy.'[6] And despite his death, *The Eye* still possesses some of that strange energy today.

∿

THE SEDUCTIVE BRETHREN
(1964–65)

St Arnolph's Eve
Being an account of the trial, imprisonment, and untimely death of Sir Basil Nardly Stoads as recorded in the pages of the *New Stoadsman*, with a posthumous foreword by the Chief Rammer of the Seductive Brethren.

Posthumous Foreword
As Chief Rammer of the Seductive Brethren it is often my pleasure and privilege to seize hold of young women and clamber hotly all over their bodies. I am often asked, by those who want to know, what exactly the Seductive Brethren do and what they believe in: to this there is no simple answer but to say that the BODY SEIZING

OF YOUNG WOMEN is at least part and parcel of our belief would be no exaggeration.

The Function of the Rammer

In my position, or rather in my numerous positions as Chief Rammer, it is my solemn duty to uphold the traditions of the sect and deal with the thousand and one contingencies that needs must occur in an organisation of this kind; in this I am assisted by the Holy Dragger (elected annually), Sir Arthur Starborgling. Sir Arthur saw service, and indeed, a number of other things in Dieppe. Between them the Rammer and the Dragger control the discipline of the Brethren.

How Many Are There of Us

The exact number of the Brethren at any given time is always hard to calculate, but it can be safely said that a figure of two would be exact: it is our proud claim that we are far more exclusive than our religious competitors, The Exclusive Brethren, and their sinister affiliates, The Elusive Brethren.

The Origins of the Sect

As long ago as 1961 Saint Basil first discovered (or in the words of the Holy Stoadscript: came across) the mystic words in the New Testament: 'Go forth and seize young women.' This was taken by Saint Basil to be the essence of the message that God, in his infinite wisdom, was trying to get across. AND GO FORTH HE CERTAINLY HAS. In the words of the Dragger, Sir Arthur Starborgling, 'Sir Basil has certainly gone forth and seized them all right.'

After the Seizure

Once the seizing has taken place it is the sacred function of the Rammer and Dragger jointly to achieve the SPODE OF AARON. What this is can never be revealed to those outside the Brethren, but I feel that the words 'Rumba', 'Spreading' and 'Hub' might well indicate to the sophisticated reader the nature of the ceremony.

In Conclusion
In conclusion I could scarcely do better than quote the words of the
Seductive Hymn, traditionally sung, in the musical way, during the
age-old ceremony of 'Downing the Squames'.

> Seductivi ubique
> Piniculu quondam
> Grabbando praeternaturales
> Et draggando pubique
> Sed nonne cum spubo
> Penetrati semper
> Floreat Basilius !*

New Stoadsman 18 December 1964
Snow fell over parts of Stoad Hall last night as the traditional
Seductive preparations for Christmas got under way. Among the
many guests who have already arrived at the Hall are Sir Arthur
Starborgling (Chief Dragger of the Brethren), the Clintistorit of
Wintistering (Holy Relic and Keeper of the Gribling),
accompanied by his mother, the 103 year old Dowager Wintisteria,
M. Alphonse Enorme, the French Seductive Leader, and a delega-
tion from I Seductivi di Milano led by Signor Phillatio Absurdi.

Early in the day the guests were privileged to see a 'dress'
rehearsal of the special Christmas entertainment, 'Stoads of Stoad
Hall', a work that had been specially commissioned by Sir Basil for
the occasion. The author of the piece, Sir Arthur Starborgling, read
out a special prologue before the curtain was raised.

> 'Welcome, Welcome Gentles all!
> Seductive doings will be seen,
> Upon our stage great things shall fall
> Upon Sir Basil and his 'Queen'.†

---

*The Basilius referred to is believed to be none other than Sir Basil Nardy Stoads.
†This no doubt referred to the collapse of the scenery during the 'love' scene in
Act II – featuring Sir Basil and 84-year-old Queenie Simpson.

Exotic is the garb that brings
Delight to the beholder.
Amazing the devices
That strap onto the shoulder.
And so farewell, good night good day,
We trust you will enjoy the play.

The 'action' of the play begins when King Stradwallader (Sir Basil Nardly Stoads) captures the Tower of London and erects an amazing device on the battlements to bewitch the ladies of the town. One of those to be drawn into his thrall is the lovely Princess Quarldilda (84-year-old 'Queenie' Simpson) who responds to his blandishments and is persuaded to dance before the King and his barons (Sir Arthur Starborgling and the Clintistorit of Wintistering). Overcome with passion, the barons begin to manoeuvre in an astonishing fashion and the music (played on this occasion by Ambrose and his Orchestra) rises to a climax. The following scenes take place with the curtain lowered. But it is clear from the sounds which emerge and the subtle movements of the curtain itself, that the play is by no means over.

When we rejoin the case, some two hours later, a duel is in progress between the King and a Baron Farg (Sir Arthur Starborgling) while the Princess looks on in trembling anticipation of the outcome. At last, with a cry of 'Have at you, graimly varlet,' the King plunges his fighting device into the lower regions of the Baron, who hobbles from the stage in some distress and is heard crying 'I am dead.' A moment later, a country youth (Sir Arthur Starborgling) enters with quantities of silken cord and the play ends with the nuptial ceremony between the King and Princess Quarldilda (also played behind the curtains) to the strains of 'The Blue Tube Stomp'.

The performance was exceptionally well received by the small audience, who later retired to nearby chambers all of which were equipped with 'Chaises énormes'. AS, critic of the *Evening Stoad*, described the play as 'a triumph'. 'Never before', he wrote, 'have I seen such fervour, such passion, such intricate devices. The writing throughout is superb.'

Following the play, a group of 'youths' from the nearby village of Nardly (pop. 103) assisted the Seductive delegates in the 'decoration' of the Hall. This included 'straming the blages' – a complicated manoeuvre whereby the traditional 'blages' (long cotton wool objects) are strewn about the Hall with imported finery, much of it from the fine leather works of Tarragon. Drinks were then served by 87-year-old Hovis, the butler, and the lights were extinguished for the playing of curious music and the showing of Sir Basil's 'holiday slides' – these produced an immediate reaction in the hall and the traditional Christmas cries of 'Grab!' 'Probe!' and 'Grope!' filled the air. More drinks were then served by Hovis the butler and from behind a velvet curtain there emerged a quantity of electric machinery. This heralded the surprise entrance of Sir Basil who, descending the chimney, clad only in a 7 foot white nylon beard, began to distribute Seductive Favours among the guests, including crackers, which on being opened were found to contain sophisticated aphorisms and tiny accessories. Drinks were then served by Hovis the butler and the company moved off in the direction of Nardly to entertain the villagers with a collection of 'rare carols and curious glees'.

An incident then occurred outside the rectory which caused the Vicar, the Rev. Knocker Prume, hitherto thought to be a de facto Seductive, to telephone for the Nardly constabulary, PC Grabbitas. The latter on his arrival found the Rector in an unfortunate state, bemoaning the loss of his ferial vestments and thurible and muttering in an incoherent manner. When PC Grabbitas called later at Stoads Hall he was informed by Hovis the butler that Sir Basil had just left for India by Stoadicopter to distribute the 'Holy Spubes' to the poor. Alas, the unmistakable form of Sir Basil Nardly Stoads lurking an inch behind Hovis belied the butler's tale, and on learning that Rev. Prume intended to prefer charges against him he stated: 'I am first a man, and second a Seductive. It is absurd that someone in my position should be hauled into court.' He was assured by PC Grabbitas that the proceedings would not be taken till the New Year and there was no question of interfering with the Day of the Gribling (December 24th).

Sir Basil then retired for a period of 'intense reflection' in the

'Blue Room'. A statement published in the *Morning Starborgling* today states that Sir Basil is resting and that although shaken by his experiences, 'he has been able to enjoy a goose and a little stuffing.'

New Stoadsman 8 January 1965

The fact that Sir Basil Nardly Stoads is shortly to be arraigned before the justices on a charge of disturbing the Queen's peace and that of the Rev. K Prume, has cast something of a gloom over the New Year festivities at Stoad Hall. The arrival of a group of German Seductives (led by Herr Otto Kohlpardz) to celebrate the traditional Viktor Silvesterabend did little to dispel the air of melancholy which has lain heavy on the hall since the fateful night of December 20th. At the ceremony of welcome the Germans performed a special 'Garland of Bavarian Practices' for their British hosts, including the rare 'Bümsfüsli' and 'Alpenfrigerei', which lasted several hours.

As a finale Herr Kohlpardz himself gave a rendering of his own little-known epic poem 'Der Ring der Seduktiven', which tells the story of Otto, King of the Rhinedwarves, and his curious adventures among the water maidens. As Herr Kohlpardz declaimed in his ringing voice the final couplet Sir Basil Nardly Stoads was observed lying on the floor in a state of what was later described as 'mystical ennui' while Sir Arthur Starborgling appeared to have left the gathering some time previously. When Herr Kohlpardz, speaking, as he said, in German, drew Sir Basil's attention to Sir Arthur's apparent lack of enthusiasm for Teutonic culture, Sir Arthur suddenly reappeared and explained in a drowsy voice that he had been forced to retire to the 'Chamber of Contemplation' for a period of intense self examination.

When the party finally retired for the night after linking hands for the singing of the traditional 'Auld Lang Basil', an uproar broke out in Sir Arthur Starborgling's chambers. It appeared that on getting into bed, a receptacle (later stated to contain 'refuse and other offensive matter') had fallen on his head, causing acute embarrassment both to himself and his 'companions'. Herr Kohlpardz however explained that this was a Bavarian New Year's custom designed to reciprocate the hospitality of one's host. Sir

Arthur treated his guests to a cold smile and a word believed to be of foreign origin, and retired for the second time to his chambers. On this occasion however he discovered 'a large object' concealed between the sheets, and expressed the view later in a written statement that 'this had gone too far.'

The following morning curious passers by were vouchsafed a glimpse of the Seductives getting into shape for their 'Winter Sports'. Although no snow had fallen, authentic conditions had been reproduced in the Recreation Room with 'fibre-glass apparatus, large quantities of cotton wool and artificial lubricants.' After hours of rigorous exertion, spirits were stated to be high, though certain guests were later seen hobbling about in apparent pain with a variety of 'sprains and torn ligaments'. The Clintistorit of Wintistering appeared to have suffered the worst damage in the shape of a badly distorted 'limb' supported by a splint and encased in plaster of Paris. This was duly autographed and inscribed with aphorisms of a cautionary nature by the German visitors. Sir Basil then retired for a period of subdued revivification in the 'Aubergine Room', pending the preparation of his defence by his solicitors Messrs Grab, Probe, Threshing, Grab and Grope.

New Stoadsman 22 January 1965
The trial of Sir Basil Nardly Stoads opened yesterday at Nardly Magistrates Court. Sir Basil, who looked pale, is charged with 'an offence' against the person of the Rev. Knocker Prume, Vicar of Nardly and All Souls. The 'offence' is alleged to have taken place on December 20th, 1964.

Giving evidence for The Crown, PC 'Thark' Grabbitas testified that he had been summoned to the rectory on the aforesaid night. On his arrival he found the vicar distraught and trembling. At this counsel for Stoads, Mr Ephraim Grab (of Grab, Probe, Threshing, Grab and Grope) intervened submitting that the use of the word 'trembling' was open to an emotive interpretation which could discredit his client.

Summoned to the witness box, Rev. Knocker Prume stated that on the night of December 20th at about 3 p.m. he had been aroused by 'certain sounds' emanating from his garden. The vicar went on to relate how on descending to inspect the source of the 'certain sound' his ear led him through the asparagus bed to a clump of mulberry bushes where he discovered the accused with certain other persons, taking part in 'events'. Rev. K. Prume went on to relate how, on remonstrating with the participants, his vestments were seized and he was invited to joint in 'the events'. When he refused, 'an incident' took place.

Sir Basil was then asked to confirm or deny the accusation. There was a pause while a troop of small antelopes which had accompanied Sir Basil were asked to leave the court. He then read out the following prepared statement (reprinted by permission of the *Morning Starborgling*.)

'Gentlemen, ladies, and fellow Seductives. It has been said, and rightly so, that there is a time and a place for everything in the affairs of men. Was it not Winston Churchill himself, in common with Pascal, Diderot and Alphonse Enorme, who deemed that the liberty of man is a sacred flame that we can ill afford to douse? Let it not be said by those who shall come after that you, sir, (here Sir Basil flourishes the Gribling in the direction of Brigadier Thrames) that you did on this day of God and within this precinct seek to snuffle the sacred candle of liberty. For liberty is not merely a word, or a group of ants. It is a substance that permeates every fibre of a righteous man. And who am I, an humble Seductive, to question the noble whims of any one of my fibres. A million years ago today, few people would have thought that I would be standing here before you now. And yet today I am. I stand before you, gentlemen of the jury, accused of the crime of St. Arnolph. If it is a crime to give succour to a bee, then I am a criminal. If it is a crime to give honey to a newt, then it is your solemn duty to cast me forth into another place. If however, you believe, as I do, in the flame of justice and the ballsaching tediousness of the Rev. Prume and his ilk, then I am your man.'

Pronouncing judgement, Brigadier Thrames (making himself heard with difficulty) stated that he was not competent to try the case. Sir Basil would appear before the justices later this month at the Quarter Sessions. He was granted bail and carried from the court by enthusiastic supporters, amongst them Sir Arthur

Starborgling and the 84-year-old Queenie Simpson. At half past six the following morning the lights were still blazing at Stoads Hall.

New Stoadsman 5 February 1965
Sir Basil Nardly Stoads, who is shortly to appear before the High Court charged with committing 'an offence' (believed to be 'causing grievous bodily pleasure' against the person or parsons unknown, namely the Rev. Knocker Prume, Vicar of Nardly and All Stoads), arrived in London yesterday to consult a leading 'silk', thought to be the alleged Sir Quentin Bloab QC, war hero and appalling bore.

Prior to his visit to 'chambers' he called on his solicitors, Messrs Grab, Probe, Threshing, Grab & Grope and conferred for some time with the senior partner, FQ Robinson Esq, believed to be the Hero of the Dordogne and an avowed poove. The subject of the meeting was not disclosed but loud shouts of 'Where are my fees?' were to be distinguished by those not blessed with God's precious gift of deafness. Sir Basil, who emerged flushed from the meeting, told reporters that FQ Robinson had enjoyed a peaceful knight (believed to be Sir Arthur Starborgling) and that there had been 'no appreciable change in his bank balance'.

Proceeding to the Inns of Court, Sir Basil, accompanied by FQ Robinson and other interested parties, conferred for several hours with Sir Quentin Bloab. Also present were Mr George Frodds, clerk in ordinary to Sir Quentin Bloab, and Mrs Elspeth Spimble (decd.), clerk in peculiar to Mr Robinson. On emerging from the Inns, Sir Basil Nardly Stoads proceeded to an Inn to celebrate the Feast Day of the Blessed Spube in what was described in the *Morning Starborgling* as 'an unusual manner'.

New Stoadsman 19 February 1965
The trial of Sir Basil Nardly Stoads, charged with an 'offence' against the person of the Rev. Knocker Prume, opened yesterday before Justice Quarble at the Old Baillie. Opening the case for the prosecution, Mervyn Grabely Stapps QC related the events of the now famous night of December 20th. 'It will be our solemn duty,' he said, 'to show in the eyes of this court how on the aforesaid night

the accused did wittingly and with intent, harbour and procure bodily substances of a loathsome nature against the parson heretofore, namely Rev. K. Prume.'

Cross-examined by counsel, the Rev. Knocker Prume stated that whilst his religious principles were opposed to the application of unduly severe punishment which, he felt, should be reserved for the Almighty, he nonetheless expressed a desire to see the defendant 'lashed to within an inch of his life'.

Opening for the defence, Sir Quentin Bloab QC told the Jury that the very fact that he, a man of the utmost integrity and enormous income, had consented to take on the case was no small indication of the innocence of his client, Sir Basil Nudely Stopes.

Sir Basil: Nardly Stoads, your lunacy.

Bloab: That's as may be. Leave this to me, fatface. It shall be, gentlemen of the Jury, my submission that the accused, Sir Basil Nardly Stoads, did ipso volente and entirely without prejudice perform acts which in this day and age are considered to be of an 'artistic' nature and we shall witnesses to this effect. Gentlemen of the Jury, I put it to you that we are no longer living in the 20th Century. The days are long gone when the sign of an unclothed sheep would cause amazement and despair amongst the populace at large.

Quarble: Gentlemen of the Jury, you have heard both sides of this unsavoury and appalling story. It is not for me to stress the loathsome, repulsive and disgusting nature of the creature who cowers before you in the dock; it is solely my province to direct you on matters of law. If you take the view that the defendant, despite the flagrant holes in the fabric of his evidence, is in some way innocent of these heinous crimes, then it is your duty to bring in a verdict of Guilty, that is to say, Not Guilty. But, contra, should you feel, as I do, that the accused has been overwhelmingly proven to be a shameless and perverted person fit only to be locked up with others of his ilk pending Her Majesty's pleasure, then it is your solemn duty to pronounce him Guilty. Pray consider your verdict and for God's sake be quick about it.

The jury then retired; as indeed Justice Quarble should have done in 1903. As he left the court in an open Brougham, the Clintistorit of Wintistering was booed and jeered by Seductive elements in the crowd who threw matter of an 'unusual' nature in his direction.

New Stoadsman 5 March 1965

Sir Basil Nardly Stoads, leader of the Seductive Brethen, was sentenced last week to six months imprisonment by a jury of good men and true having been found guilty of indecent practices and offences against the parson, namely Rev. K. Prume. As he was being escorted to the Police van prior to his departure for HM Prison, Strangeways, Godalming, a scene took place described by bystanders as 'curious to say the least.'

It is believed that Sir Basil had to be restrained by an officer from making what was termed an 'emotional' farewell to 84-year-old Queenie Simpson, the retired Music Hall entertainer. Afterwards, his condition was stated to be 'unusual to say the least'. Later Mrs. Simpson commented: 'I do not know what I shall do with myself. He has been very close to me on many occasions over the years.' Mrs Simpson was then assisted into a special conveyance by Sir Arthur Starborgling, M. Alphonse Enorme, Signor Phillatio Absurdi and certain other persons. Said Mrs. Simpson: 'We just want to be alone.'

Today the Governor of Strangeways, Brig. (Retd.) Sir Navel Throbes, denied rumours that anything untoward had been occasioned by Sir Basil's admission into his area of responsibility. Reports had been circulating on the 'grapevine' that certain warders in the prison had been involved in 'incidents'. Residents close to the prison walls are believed to have complained about disturbances during the night hours. Mr Sibley, one of the residents, explained: 'I do not know what is going on in there, but there is certainly something afoot. I am not alone in having heard singing of a religious nature and histrionic phenomena of a type I would prefer not be describe.'

Brig. Throbes confirmed that Sir Basil had been moved from his previous cell to the Elizabeth Fry Wing. This is reserved for 'hardened offenders'. The Brigadier explained that Sir Basil, who he described as a 'most charming and cultivated person', had specially requested the move in order to devote more of his time to literary and other pursuits. The Governor added: 'He has be-witched and enchanted all those members of the Prison Staff with whom he has come in contact.'

It is believed that Sir Basil is engaged on a work entitled 'De Profundis. Prison thoughts of a Penitent Philosopher'. Extracts from the work written in Sir Basil's own hand on 'perforated lengths of paper' have been circulated amongst the prison staff. One warder described the writing as 'most inventive and sophisticated', and the Prison Chaplain, Rev. A. Framlingham Prume, said it was tragic that a man of Sir Basil's unusual gifts and sensitive characteristics should find himself in this humiliating position. 'I visit him daily and we have had many illuminating and fruitful exchanges,' he said. 'Sir Basil under my tuition has acquired a taste for handwork and has already produced many tiny replicas.'

Yesterday Sir Basil was visited by Sir Quentin Bloab, QC, the well-known silk. 'He was in high spirits and very chirpy,' quipped Sir Quentin, who left the prison holding a mustard plaster close to his right eye, which appeared puffy and swollen. 'I told him that justice was on our side and that posterity would exonerate him. I also had to attend to a trifling matter of legal expenses and litigation costs about which he was most understanding.' Sir Quentin then limped to his chauffeur-driven ambulance and was swept out of sight. Amongst other visitors were Sir Arthur Starborgling and M. Alphonse Enorme, who brought gifts, including 'items of a personal nature, literary matter and various appliances'. They were assured that these would be put to good use.

There is still no news of the Clintistorit of Wintistering, last heard of in Paris, whose astonishing volte face during the trial caused widespread dismay amongst Seductive Elements. However, members of the French Sécurité are investigating an incident which occurred last night during which a public monument depicting Virtue Feeding at the Breast of Truth was defaced and inscribed with the words 'Let the spubes commence,' and 'BNS est un vieux pouffe.' It is believed that this may have been the work of a man answering to the description of the Clintistorit.

New Stoadsman 19 March 1965

Reports that Sir Basil Nardly Stoads, leader of the Seductive Brethren, had been seen wearing an unusual swimming costume on a private beach in Uruguay in the company of an elderly 'belle', the Marchesa Robinson de Greemvil (alias 84-year-old Queenie Simpson) and Monsignor Arturo Smith (alias Sir Arthur Starborgling) were being treated with 'unqualified amusement' at Interpol Headquarters in Paris last night. The reports followed an announcement issued by a spokesman at Strangeways Prison, Godalming, to the effect that unconfirmed rumours of Sir Basil no longer being entirely within the prison's area of responsibility could not be said to be completely without foundation.

According to an 'informed source' within the grey walls of the prison, events had taken an unlikely turn shortly after prayers on Tuesday evening. It was then that several 'hardened cases', 'enlightened warders' and other persons had assembled in the Ethel Grebe Memorial Wing for a meeting of the Strangeways Society for Zen Yoga, Eurythmics and Allied Activities which Sir Basil had recently formed with the full approval of the prison authorities and under the Honorary Presidency of the Rev. A. Framlingham Prume, the prison chaplain.

Gymnastic activities and a discussion had been in progress for some time when the prison warders were alerted by cries of 'Grab! Probe! Grope!' 'Strame the blages' and 'Let the Spubes commence!' Arriving on the scene, they discovered members entwined in what was described as the Pyramid of the Seventh Enlightenment and into which, they were told, Sir Basil had disappeared some moments before, proposing as he went to give a demonstration of 'Iambic mysticism and some Confucian holds'. Satisfied by the assurances of the chaplain and the apparent goodwill of the members, many of whom were said to be in a state of mystical ecstasy, the warders had withdrawn.

Three hours later, however, they had returned to sounds of renewed clamour and found the pyramid still in situ, the prison chaplain Rev. A. Framlingham Prume performing the little-known dance of Shiva the Many-Armed Goddess about its foot. One of them, Prison Warder Athanasius Snow, insisted on the proceedings being brought to a speedy end, and despite fervent protests on the part of Rev. A. Framlingham Prume and others, the pyramid was dismantled, revealing at its base an irregular orifice described by Rev. A. Framlingham Prume as 'probably caused by a meteorite'. The Prison Governor, Brig. (Retd.) Sir Navel Throbes, intimated, however, that he was not entirely satisfied with this explanation and ordered a counting of heads, which brought to light 'a certain discrepancy', namely the incontrovertible physical absence of one member, believed to be Sir B. Nardly Stoads.

Further examination of the orifice had revealed the presence of a recently excavated underground tunnel, the earth from which had been concealed about the persons of some of the younger gymnasts. Eye-witness reports from outside the prison walls mentioned the presence of 'a sophisticated figure', wearing traditional Highland costume and answering to the description of the McDoon of McDoon, the little-known Scottish philanthropist and eccentric, who was stated to have loitered in the neighbourhood of the Dame Agatha Gramewarbling Gate for a not unconsiderable period of time. When he finally moved away, curious observers noted 'certain movements' beneath the voluminous pleats of his kilt. He had been seen to climb, with some difficulty, into a nearby helicopter, soon to dwindle into the grey skies.

Tonight the Governor denied rumours that the prison chaplain Rev. A. Framlingham Prume had been asked to relinquish his position. He had in fact been offered the absorbing and challenging post of Assistant Superintendent of the Ablutions, which he declined to accept. 'We are very sorry to lose him. The links that tied him to the prisoners were very close ones and we shall all feel a considerable wrench at his departure.' Speculation has been aroused by an insertion in the 'Agony Column' of the *Evening Starborgling* which reads: 'C. of W. Come home precious all is forgiven. B.N.S.' It is thought that the expression 'C. of W.' may possibly have some reference to the Clintistorit of Wintistering, who was last heard of three weeks ago in Metropolitan France.

New Stoadsman 1 April 1965

Three viewers rang last night to complain about the BBC's controversial programme, 'The Open Spube'. The programme, which was described as an exposé of Seductive Practices, revealed many hitherto closely guarded secrets of the sect. The Initiation Room at Stoads Hall was recreated at Studio 418b, Shepherd's Bush and Richard Dimbleby introduced actors who took the parts of leading Seductives. Viewers witnessed the 'Ceremony of the Gribling' in addition to the famed 'Straming of the Blages' and were vouchsafed a glimpse of the notorious 'Seductio ad absurdam' in which satirical Seductives poke light-hearted fun at themselves.

Controversy has inevitably sprung up as to the identity of the masked and silhouetted Seductive who blew the gaff on such Seductive code words as 'Farg' and 'Drebbidge'. From certain characteristics that were apparent even in silhouette skilled observers discerned the likely presence of the Clintistorit of Wintistering, whose notorious volte face during the recent trial of Sir Basil Nardly Stoads contributed largely to the latter's conviction. Further evidence were the words 'Basil Nardly Stoads est un vieux pouffe' which were inscribed on the anonymous speaker's armband. (The Clintistorit is known to have strong views on his leader's alleged leanings.)

Towards the end of the programme, viewers were amazed to see the re-enactment of Seductive ritual take on an unexpected turn, as the 'actors' became at one with their parts and with loud cries of 'Grab', 'Probe', and 'Grope' began to interfere with Mr. Dimbleby's clothing. The screen blacked out for a moment and viewers were shown a five-minute film of waterfalls in Scotland. A spokesman for the Seductives said later: 'This programme was a travesty of all we hold most often. We shall not hesitate to issue writs.'

Meanwhile the whereabouts of Sir Basil Nardly Stoads, who is believed to have escaped from Strangeways Prison, Godalming, last month, remain a mystery. However, a letter which arrived in the offices of the *Morning Starborgling* attached to the hind leg of a bee demonstrated that the Seductive leader may well be still 'at large'. The letter, which bore an Isle of Wight postmark, was couched in

confident tones and was inscribed on fine parchment bearing the
insignia of the Mcdoon of McDoon. (Motto: OMNES ME
IMPUNE LACESSUNT). It is reproduced below:

I AM IN GOOD
HANDS AND AM BEG-
INNING TO FEEL
MYSELF AGAIN
B.N.S.

Reporters who rushed to the remote fastness of the Glen O'Doon
(ancestral home of the McDoons of McDoon) were denied
admittance to the castle by the McDoon's personal bodyguard
Father Heinrich von Pöm, the former peace criminal who
demonstrated against the folly of Nuclear Warfare by parading
nude in the Vatican Gardens several years ago. The local
constabulary in the shape of P.C. McDoon said it was unthinkable
that the McDoon of McDoon should have been alarmed by recent
events in the area of the Whistling Hole, a local ugly spot,
traditionally the haunt of the Phantom O'Doon. Legend has it that
on moonlight nights a small bespectacled man clad only in
butterfly wings and bearing aloft an amazing device will run
screaming through the stunted mulberry tres wailing mournfully
and chanting the traditional faery verse:

'Hop come awa
Hop come awee
I'll dunk all the lassies
From here to the brae'

Recently, however, villagers have noticed a subtle change in the
wording of the verse. One witness, in the shape of a courting
couple, swear that they distinctly heard the words 'A'Grabbie and
A'Gropie', and 'Awa wi' the Spubie' as the tiny white figure was
seen dwindling into the mist.

New Stoadsman 16 April 1965

In the remote fastness of Glen O'Doon, excitement has been aroused by the arrival of Detective Superintendent (formerly PC) 'Thark' Grabbitas, who is believed to be endowed with 'special' powers' to investigate the whereabouts of the missing aristocrat, Sir Basil Nardly Stoads. Today the Superintendent was granted an interview with the McDoon himself. Thanks to the foresight and skilful manipulations of a leading Hibernian 'bugger', who succeeded in concealing a tiny listening device in the McDoon's sporran, a transcript of the interview was made available to Seductive readers in later editions of yesterday's *Evening Starborgling*.

DEPT SUPT. GRABBITAS: Good Day, McDoon !

McDOON: This is a ghastly business, Inspector. What can I do to help you in your inquiries?

GRABBITAS: As you may know, we are conducting investigations concerning the whereabouts of the escaped felon, Basil Stoads.

A METALLIC VOICE: Nardly!

GRABBITAS: I beg your pardon?

McDOON: Shut up you old fool.

GRABBITAS: Come now, that is no way to talk.

McDOON: Pray continue.

GRABBITAS: It is believed that the felon has been observed in the vicinity of your residence.

McDOON: Aha!

A METALLIC VOICE: A Grabbie and a Gropie!

McDOON: For Heaven's sale, Basil, how can I possibly delude this elderly flat-foot if you insist on wearying us with your uncalled-for observations?

GRABBITAS: I hesitate to probe into your personal areas, McDoon, but why are you talking to that suit of armour?

McDOON: Aha, Inspector, I can see that you are a man of perception and insight. It is the chain mail of my ancestor, the seventeenth McDoon. Unhappy man! Legend has it that he returned home from the chase to find his favourite struggling in the brawny arms of the Factor . . .

(Metallic laugh, faint cry of 'Awa wi' the spubie!')
McDOON: Poor soul! Flying into a violent passion, he plunged a
strabely poignard full through the lovers twain and with a most
despairing cry of 'Then die McDoon, thy gorrach shall nae more
be raised, nor heeld, tha reekie doun the glen', he fell upon them
both, doing himself a fatal mischief. Since then, his spirit can
find no rest, and is destined to haunt these halls for all eternity.
(Metallic moaning, chain mail jingles.)

But come, Inspector, the light is fading, and you must see my
gloxinias before you go . . .

*(They leave, immersed in quiet conversation. A heavy metallic crash,
then silence.)*

New Stoadsman 30 April 1965
Acting on information received, police last night swooped on Glen
O'Doon, ancestral home of the McDoon of McDoon. They were
led by Det. Insp. (formerly PC) 'Thark' Grabbitas, and arrived in
the small hours of the morning. In all, 73 policemen were admitted
to the castle. Their arrival, which had been planned as a complete
surprise, was preceded by a series of firework explosions in the sky
which spelt the words: SWOOP NOW CONSTABLES. The
McDoon, who had been studying certain documents in the privacy
of his book-lined turret, became aroused, and summoned his
bodyguard, Father Heinrich von Pöm, the former peace criminal.
Armed only with certain jewelled devices, they descended to find
Insp. Grabbitas standing at the foot of the stairs. 'The game's up,
McDoon,' he said, 'you know I'm in here.' A piece of paper was
then handed to the Inspector.

McDOON: Come off it, officer. This will never stand up in a Court
of Law.

An incident then took place, which was later described as 'curious,
but, in a historical sense, almost inevitable'.

INSPECTOR: I think I must warn you that anything you have about you may be taken down and thrown into the lavatory.

McDOON: Very well, Inspector, I'll come quietly.

Another incident then took place.

INSPECTOR: I have reason to believe that you are harbouring within these precincts the bodily shape of Sir Basil Nardly Stoads.

McDOON: Come again?

INSPECTOR: I am sick and tired of these 'incidents'. Come to the point and produce the above-mentioned felon.

FATHER HEINRICH VON PÖM: Gentlemen, if you are under the impression that Sir Basil is in the Green Room in the Southern Turret engaged in certain activities with other persons you are entirely mistaken.

McDOON: Hush, you teuton poove, ye'll gie the game awee.* Gentlemen, I have been expecting you: for legend has it that when the moon is in decline, and the grabely bat doth flicker through the orchard bush and tiny bees, each one endowed with elkin sword, shall strut and weep their frumely way, then shall a man clad all in blue with metal helmet o'er his head present himself beneath my ivied tower. That man is you . . .

INSPECTOR: Get on with it.

McDOON: Very well. Get out of here, you lop-eared flatfoot!

A distant shout was then heard from the Southern Turret, 'If you think I'm in here you are much mistaken.' This was followed by a low moan. Whistles were then blown and the men in blue thundered up the ancient staircases to the Green Room. But even as they were on the point of battering down the frail oaken door that had for centuries withstood the wreak of time, a woman's voice was heard within, reciting the following verse:

* give the game away (dialect)

'Batter ye not this ancient door,
Awa' ye breek unhallow'd men!
For puir Sir Basil is nae moore
And we'll ne'er see his like again (Repeat)
And we'll ne'er see his like again.'

On opening the door, Insp. Grabbitas discovered the physical remains of Sir Basil Nardly Stoads lying white and peaceful in a fur-lined coffin, while 84-year-old 'Queenie' Simpson, the retired music hall entertainer, attempted to administer the kiss of life. The McDoon of McDoon on entering the room immediately removed his clothes as a sign of respect, and requested all officers to do the same. Murmuring apologies for his untimely intrusion, Insp. Grabbitas led his naked force down the ancient stairs in a slow march, with truncheons reversed.

Preparations then began for a candlelit wake. The funeral will closely follow the lines laid down by Sir Basil in his famous secret document 'Seductivi Moribundi sed Allegri' (1946 Limited Edition). Messages and 'tributes' are already pouring into the offices of the *Morning Starborgling* and the *Evening Stoad* including, it is thought, a telegram from the Clintistorit of Wintistering. All night long the candles blazed at Castle O'Doon.

New Stoadsman 14 May 1965
Numerous Seductive bodies came together last week to pay their final respects to the corporeal substances and physical remains of their first leader, Sir Basil Nardly Stoads. In accordance with Sir Basil's wishes, the coffin was brought to Stoads Hall by rail, a first class sleeping car having been reserved, and the coffin being escorted by leading Seductives, amongst them Sir Arthur Starborgling, 84-year-old Queenie Simpson, the retired music hall entertainer, and the McDoon of McDoon. The latter was seen to board the train at Blairdoonie Station bearing certain parcels, said later to be the 'funeral meats' and 'unguents'.

It is not known whether Sir Basil's body was embalmed, but observers on the train spoke of 'not unfrenzied activity' and the singing of certain 'spirited dirges'. Phials, which had presumably contained unguents, were also seen to be thrown from behind closely drawn blinds as the train passed through one sequestered halt. When the party changed trains at Crewe, watching mourners commented on the 'miraculous lightness of the coffin' and the presence of a bare legged and blanket-swathed figure, thought at first to be an oriental recluse, but later identified by Sir Arthur as a 'close relative of the deceased'. The party crossed the platform in silence, punctuated only by the raucous singing of Seductive hymns, including one by Mr. (formerly Rev.) A. Framlingham Prume, which is reproduced below:

> 'O Wand of Basil, now struck down
> By Death's immortal Sting,
> How limp and pale we see thee lie
> But still the Game's the thing.
> So shall we in our nightly rounds
> And holy revels prove
> The bodying forth of thy sweet self
> With transcendental Spube.'
> (*Hymns Ancient and Bizarre* 514, Tune: Cwymquietllwi)

The lying in state began the following day in the Gladys Twicenightlie Memorial Wing at Stoads Hall. The lid of the coffin was removed, and a seraphic smile of 'almost complete fulfilment' was seen to play about the pale lips of the deceased, as mourners filed reverently over the coffin, laying a hand on the recumbent prophet as they passed, to the accompaniment of solemn music, played by Ambrose and his Teatime Five.

Mourners were particularly impressed by an 'unusual tribute' from the Clintistorit of Wintistering. This took the form of a postcard of an artistic nature (bearing a South American postmark) and inscribed on the reverse: 'Sorry to hear you are dead. See you Thursday. Je t'embrasse. Clinty.' This was taken by observers to imply a final reconciliation between Sir Basil and the Clintistorit and also to affirm the Seductive Belief in the 'Mystic Reincarnation of the Spube'.

The funeral itself took place behind closed doors in accordance with Sir Basil's dying fish. Preceded by lightly clad acolytes, closely followed by some of those that Sir Basil had loved, the coffin was seen to glide through into a silk-lined recess, after which the curtains closed behind it. Seductive rituals were then performed, mourners recited the traditional verses, many of which date back to 1963, and the lowering of the Gribling took place. The curtains were then drawn back, the coffin shown to be empty, and to the singing of the Seductive Hymn of St. Arnolph, 'Lo he is vanished', Sir Basil's ashes were scattered over 84-year-old Queenie Simpson. Seductives were then served with hot 'Memorial Spubes of Remembrance' and an unidentified amber fluid. They then dispersed, and the ancient cries of 'Grab!' 'Probe!' and 'Grope!' 'Sir Basil is dead, long live Sir Basil!' were heard to echo for what was perhaps not the last time from the ivy-mantled turrets of Stoad Hall.

THE MEMOIRS OF RHANDHI P'HURR
(1965)

Foreword

India has been described by my wife, Lady Amarinth Navel Throbes, who in a lucid moment before her timely decease, shouted 'India is a precious Ruby set in the sweating belly of the world.' These prophetic words come back to me tonight as with pen in hand I attempt to eke a meagre living by writing this worthless foreword. Who can forget the beautiful films of Sanjhit and Ted Ray? I for one. But India is fabled not only for its art, but for its beautiful women, amongst whom the name Rhandhi P'hurr must stand alone. What memories – indeed what mammaries – she brings back, this extraordinary lady. I remember my wife, Lady Amarinth Navel Throbes (prior to her timely decease), sitting in a fashionable restaurant in the middle of the Ganges remarking as a particularly beautiful member of the opposite sex passed by, 'Isn't that Rhandhi P'hurr?' 'No,' I replied. For it was not she. This, I think, illustrates the complexity of India in all its many faucets. It is with great pleasure that I conclude this foreword and hand you over to the capable pen of Sir Winthrop Fargs.

Navel Throbes (Brig. Gen. Retd.)

Preface

You will have read with as much interest as I* the boring foreword by my old friend and bridge companion Brig. Gen. (Retd.) Sir Navel Throbes – 'Naughty Navel' as he is known to his intimates, amongst whom I am proud to number myself.

India. The very name conjures up a continent. The very names conjures up a name to conjure with. The name of Rhandhi P'hurr. The very name brings back the magic of the Orient.

It was Kipling, I think, who said 'An India without Rhandhi P'hurr is as hard to imagine as a fish without marmalade.' Who am I to cross swords with Kipling? The answer: Sir Winthrop Fargs. The time: '44–'45. The place: a little known sandwich bar in Clapham. But that is another story.† But now, on with the motley. And who better to tell the tale than Rhandhi P'hurr. Go to it Rhandhi! I love you, you tantalising authoress. Your lips are the breasts of doves. Your breasts are the lips of bees . . . ‡

---

* Practically nil AS

† See 'My life as a Holy Relic' by Sir Winthrop Fargs. Typescript available from author.

‡ Here Sir Winthrop's manuscript tails away in a mass of stains and blotches. (It is not unlikely that a tse tse fly was responsible. Ed.)

Chapter One

I was born on the banks of the Ganges in the hot blustering summer of 1905 by the year of God. My father was the Indian Unknown Soldier, Raj Jhitipur Shostri. My mother, a frail woman of 108, would often speak of him in hushed tones as she accompanied herself on the Hurg. One song, in particular, comes back to me now.

Song of the Unknown Indian Soldier

All hail, Raj Jhitipur Shostri,
Who came to me like a bee in the night
His wings aflame with hair love.
He was no dove, Raj Jhitipur!
By the Ganges pool
We saw Gribbur*
And made the moon dance with our shout.
He knew what he was about,
Raj Jhitipur!
All hail, thou hairy one!

Alas my father was destined to perish at the hands of the British Raj. Early one morning as he was taking his customary fisdah, a bullet struck him in the abdomen and next of kin were informed. After he became the Unknown Indian Soldier, my mother, distraught with grief, took up residence with Capt. 'Banger' O'Knee, the very man whose bullet had killed Papa. There were those who said that there was something almost indecent about the speed with which she forgot Raj Jhitipur. Those near her timed the delay at three seconds after the feather had been placed on the mouth of my father. Brandishing an enormous gusht the Captain carried her off into a nearby tent crying 'Come on, pretty lady, a drop of brandy will soon set you right!'

(* Possibly the sun. Ed.)

Later, disturbed by low moans within, I peered, like a child (for I was one), through a narrow slit in the tent and saw the Captain and the lady from whose womb I danced in the unmistakable throes of the Congress of the Stag Beetle. My mother glimpsing my horrified face sprang to her feet breaking the Captain's gusht. O'Knee, never a placid man, gathered up the broken fragments of the gusht and hurled them in my direction. They fell with a clatter to the ground. 'From henceforth you are banished from this tent,' he cried. It was the last I was to see of the warted* Captain.

Chapter Two

After the dramatic events described in the last chapter, I left home and sought solace in the desert. I wandered aimlessly for over a year. My food was the grass, my drink the newt's spit. At last my wanderings came to an end when I fell exhausted to the ground. How long I lay there is a matter of conjecture.† When I awoke, I found myself staring into the eyes of an enormous beard. It was the beard that all India had grown to love. Yes, for it was the beard of H'hoshti F'hart, the so-called Uhuru Guru whose militant pacifism was at the time a thorn in the flesh of the Raj.

'Come my child,' he said, lowering his beard into my proffered hand, 'you must be starving.' 'Oh, Guru,' I moaned, 'you have the wisdom of the partridge, and your beard is as the beard of the bee.'

The Holy Man knelt and raised me off the ground, the muscles in his wiry body cracking and hissing with the holy g'hout. Very slowly he tottered to his wickerwork d'hosht where he gave me a bowl of sacred milk culled from the shapeless titties of a holy goat.‡

* Rhandhi P'hurr is of course referring to the warts on the Captain, blemishes which caused him to be known as 'Warty' to some of his associates.
† Probably between one second and four years. Ed.
‡ The law of God forbids all contact with the holy goat and so milk has to be extracted by trained bees. Ed.

'Drink this, my child, the bees have done their work and the milk is good.' As I drank, I noticed a bee swimming in the milk. 'There is a bee in my milk!' I cried.

'Bee that as it may,' replied the holy one with a smile, 'there is milk in your bee.' For such was the wisdom of H'hoshti F'hart, a man alike feared and respected by O'Knee and his ilk.

I was to learn much in the d'hosht of the Holy One. Rising at two in the morning he would begin to fall asleep. He called this the state of Nurj – for he said, whilst in this condition, the spirits of the dead would walk upon his beard.

'The spirits of the dead dance in my long beard and the sound of my snoring is as music in their ears,' he would tell me when he awoke.

I would often ask him what the spirits would say to him during the twenty-three hours slumber which formed no small part of his day's work. 'They say: "Sleep on, Guru. For surely as the dove swims through the water and as surely as the bee leaps over the frog, thy beard will surely lead India to victory."'

But it was not all sheep and goats milk with Guru H'hoshti F'hart. During his waking hours the holy man was in constant contact with Mahatma Gandhi. He first met the Mahatma at the award-giving ceremony for India's best-dressed man of 1923. The snappily clad Gandhi had carried the title for the sixth year in succession and the bazaars hummed with topical witticisms like 'If you want to get a head, get a Mahatma.' Gandhi took an instant non-violent dislike to the Guru and showed his contempt by striking him non-violently about the face with a fly swat. H'hoshti F'hart, whose religion forbade any form of retaliation, asked his brother, Rhashti F'hart, to fell Gandhi. This he did. No one was more surprised than the great leader to be smashed to the floor with a bottle of sacred milk. And the sudden blow caused the Mahatma to come out with one of his rare displays of irritation. 'You sonofabitch!' he cried, and attempted to strangle the Guru by clutching hold of his beard and tying it around his neck. It was at this moment that the British military police under the direction of Maj. Gen. Bugely Nargs intervened, arresting the still struggling Holy Men. Happily a busty blonde, Anita Lush, who describes herself as Gandhi's closest friend, succeeded in diverting the inexorable course of British justice by some well-timed movements. The Mahatma and H'hoshti F'hart were released and lived to fight another day.

Chapter Three

(In her last chapter, it will be remembered, Miss P'hurr recounted her first meeting with Guru H'hoshti F'hart, the famous 'Uhuru Guru' whose non-violent campaigning did so much for Indian Independence. Ed.)

The Guru would often take me on his non-violent expeditions to the railway. Here, watched by millions of his followers, he would lie in feigned slumber on the tracks, his foot mystically enclosed in his mouth in the state of sacred Grajma. On the arrival of the train, the driver, Stanley Grabes, a Lancastrian, would shout 'Get off it, you filthy old F'hart!'; whereupon the Guru would leap to his foot and skip off the line with a gay shout of 'Victoria Regina, my arse.' Alas for the Guru, one day as he lay on the track, his foot duly inserted into his mouth, he inadvertently entered into the state of Nurj* and to the horror of all was severed irreparably by the callous Grabes. I was to have the privilege of setting fire to his corpse and scattering the ashes in the Viceroy's swimming pool.

Song of the Dead Guru

O thin wizened Guru
Your beard will rise no more.
Now walking in the clouds
You see us below
Treading the earth in the moon's holy glow.

* Deep sleep

O Guru pray for me
For I am a poor gnat
Compared to the mighty elephant that is God.
O, Guru, forget the gnat not.

Here are the sayings of Guru H'hoshti F'hart as they were revealed
to R'handi P'hurr:
Place thy foot in thy mouth and thy drink* in thy navel. Then
mayest thou enter into the state of Grishnu, that is communion
with the Holy One.
Know that the state of Nurj (deep sleep) is the most blessed of all
states.
He who wishes to meet God must rub his b'hom† with honey from
the holy bee and anoint his drinj with onions.

Chapter Four

Following the timely death of the Guru I sought to banish my grief
in hard work. I applied for a job with the Sydney Darlow Genuine
Dance Troupe which was touring India at the time. As luck would
have it, there was a vacancy, caused by an outbreak of pregnancy
amongst the ladies, and I became No. 23 in the famous line-up
which at that time included such famous names as Sonia Stribling
and Lady Clementine Frobes. It was long, exhausting work, but
extremely boring. Sydney was a hard task master and indeed a hired
tusk master, as he had been placed in charge of a number of hired
tusks. These played an important part in the famed Tableau of the
Bees, a dramatic interlude which was especially popular with the
native audiences.

Dear Sydney! He was devoted to Terpsichore and her kindred
muses. The dance was his life and when at the age of 85 fate was to

* Hand? (Ed.)
† Elbow (Ed.)

strike him down with an attack of dry rot, it was as if a beacon had been extinguished from the world of theatre. I can remember him now as I stare at a photograph of him. How he used to come into our dressing room swathed in luminous tulle, accompanied by his friend and boon companion, Fred Wound, the musician and pigeon fancier. It had been whispered in the bazaars that Sydney was a grajdah* owing no doubt to his habit of wandering through the streets dressed only a gossamer jock strap, high heels and dark glasses.

But such rumours were once and for all discounted at the famous performance of the Tableau of the Bees in Simla, where Sydney, overcome perhaps by the sly goadings of the ladies about his manhood, invaded the stage, his gosht at the ready, and there and then plunged bodily into each and every member of the troupe before he was dragged away by the local constabulary, PC Sheikh Wazidah.

But I digress. It was in the autumn of 1926 that we came at last to Delhi. Delhi in those days was much as it is now, only younger, its bazaars teeming with life, its rivers awash with sacred hoshtis,† and the music of the Hizbah ever present in the perfumed air. We were engaged to perform in what was then the Capital's most intimate theatre. I refer, of course, to the Warren Hastings Playhouse, which made a name for itself as the heart of Indian political satire. The famous Indian satirist, Abu Siph, would have the audience in stiches with his brilliant imitation of Gandhi in the lavatory and his startling aside. 'Who was that voshti I saw you with last night?' 'Voshti, my foot, that was the Mahatma.'

Sometimes the satire cut too deep. I remember the critic of the *Delhi Telegraph*, Wada Rlington, leaping up from his seat at a particularly savage reference to Ramsay Macdonald, and shouting 'When are you going to get a point of view?' For a moment the satirist was nonplussed. Then with typical brilliance he hurled a spear at the unhappy critic, who collapsed into a hiph.‡

* Not altogether as other men. Ed.
† A lump of dung from the sacred cow.
‡ Possibly a heap. Ed.

Such was the atmosphere when Sydney and his ladies arrived in town. I can hardly describe the excitement of that opening night. Delhi. One had dreamed of the great brown way for so many years and here I was, little Rhandhi P'hurr, about to make my debut at the Warren Hastings. How would I be received?

It was a glittering first night. The Viceroy (Sir Herbert Strume-Garbling) and his lady (Cynthia Scruggs from Walthamstow) were there in the front row of the stalls. The Mahatma, a lone, pensive figure, clad in a beautifully cut black silk evening rag, squatted in the gods. The lights dimmed, the orchestra struck up the theme song, 'Hello, Delhi', and the giant crepe curtains rose on the Sydney Darlow troupe. An appreciative murmur ran through the audience, but was hurriedly grabbed by an attendant and shown the door. We opened as usual with the Dance of the Seven Million Slobcs. The applause was thunderous and the Viceroy was visibly moved. I could see him struggling with uniformed attendants as they attempted to replace his trousers. We followed with a gentle musical parody, 'In the tents of Abdul the Lecherous', which was equally well received. In the interval my dressing room was besieged by delighted fans and all augured well for the second, more controversial, half. Alas, triumph was to escape us by a bee's length. For in the famous Tableau of the Bees, dancing at fever pitch and with the music throbbing to a tremendous climax, one of our tiny, furry winged friends fell dead. The audience was stunned. Huge sobs rent the air and the evening was ruined. Sydney attempted to revive the tiny creature with the kiss of life. Brandy was rubbed into its chest, but all to no avail. Monsieur B, as I knew him, had breathed his last and the other bees, distraught with grief, flew out into the night never to be seen again.

It was the end of an era. Sydney never recovered from his loss. The Tableau of the Bees became meaningless without the tiny insects and had to be re-titled 'The Tableau of the Absent Bees'. For obvious reasons, it had none of the impact of its famous predecessor.

CHAPTER FIVE

The death of the Bees struck Sydney hard and it seemed that my career on the b'hordes* was about to come to an end. But happily, during the last tragic performance of the famous Darlow tableau, I had been noticed by the bead eye† of P'heta Rhorleee, the famed theatrical agent and bearded loon. After the performance, he came round and came round to see me.‡ Imagine my surprise as I sat dejectedly in my dressing room to be suddenly seized by the b'hum by the spindly fingers of this cultured and naked man. 'Miss P'hurr,' he breathed,§ 'with the proper handling and the right kind of exposure I think you can be very big, not only in Delhi, but also in the world to come.' His delicate hands were still investigating the contours of by b'hum and now he leant over me, his face working with professional skills. All at once I felt a strange weightiness in the regions that the D'hama proscribes,** and to my horror I realised that my new friend's beaded eye was lodged within.

I was most anxious not to offend so powerful a man as R'horlee, for an ill-judged remark such as: 'You've dropped your eye up my b'hum, fartface' might well have jeopardised my career. I contented myself with bending over, as if to buckle my shoe, in such a way that his jewelled device was staring directly at him. The hint was taken as indeed was the eye, and moments later we were driving down the Ganges in his superb ice-blue Y'huahgt, the Taj of T'harbrush.

It was a beautiful evening. The moon shone above and the air was filled with the cries of a myriad dying natives. The romantic strains of 'Breasts of Arabee' came gently from P'heta's Hi-Fi F'ho

---

* rostrum. Ed.

† The person in question lost one eye in the Khyber Rising, and this had been replaced with elaborate Indian beadwork by the famous firm of Eyebeads with Me.

‡ This is not a printing error. Read it again, fatface.

§ He had to, otherwise he would have died. Ed.

** Possibly the b'hum. Ed.

Fum record player. We sipped our Djinn Slings, and talked of life. Gradually he began to open out to me, his pale body gleaming in the soft moonlight, and he revealed that beneath his suave exterior he was fundamentally insecure. A second later I saw the truth of his words as he tumbled overboard, still clutching his Djinn.

I could see P'heta was in difficulties. The waters swirled above his head. I had to act fast. And so, as his body sank, I read out Hitler's famous speech from *Die Walküre* performed in the record time of one and three quarter seconds. Then, unravelling my V'hast* which was lying draped carelessly over the s'hofa,† I hurled the threads towards him. He clutched at them like a drowning man, for he was a superb mimic, hauled himself to safety and lay exhausted on the deck. 'I am dying' he murmured, 'quick, quick, the Vole.' For a moment I was nonplussed. The Vole? What could he mean? And then I remembered the early teachings of the Guru H'hoshti F'hart. The Congress of the Vole was none other than that holy state that the Mahatma had recommended to those whose hearts were heavy with the woes of life. Further unravelling my V'hast, I seized the necessary ropes and began the preliminary movements. Gradually the sodden form before me began to tremble: his eyelids flickered open and to my joy he was coming too.‡

---

* A large woollen garment, worn next to the skin.
† Possibly a piece of furniture.
‡ to? Ed.

Chapter Seven
Behind the Fridge

Apart from Derek & Clive, *Behind the Fridge* was effectively the end of Cook and Moore's professional partnership. With the sole exception of the disastrous *Hound of the Baskervilles*, they never worked together again. It was a difficult time in both their lives. Dudley was splitting up with his first wife, Suzy Kendall. Peter was also splitting up from his first wife, Wendy Snowden, the mother of his two children. With his marriage at an end, Peter began to drink heavily while he was performing this stage show in Australia, and his drinking continued during the show's American run. When this finally ended, Dudley decided to stay in America, while Peter returned to England. 'Rumours that we have split up are true,' wrote Dudley, only half joking, in the programme for the show's London run.

Peter's drinking certainly damaged some of his performances, but although he'd found it difficult to complete the script, it did remarkably little damage to his writing. True, a couple of these sketches ('Frog & Peach', 'Crime & Punishment') were merely revivals of old *Not Only But Also* sketches – but they'd never been done onstage before, and despite their success on TV, the stage was their natural home. A couple of other new sketches were far darker than anything Cook and Moore had written before, but one of them 'On Location', was also very funny, while the darkest, 'Mini Drama', though hardly a laugh a minute, crackled with sinister suspense and malice worthy of Harold Pinter at his best. Indeed Pinter's praise helped to save the sketch after the promoters of the London run wanted to cut it, to make the show a little lighter.

But *Behind the Fridge* wasn't all doom and gloom. 'Hello' was a crisp yet pertinent curtain-raiser about the superficiality of friendship, which would have graced *Beyond the Fringe*. 'Women's Rights', Pete & Dud's considered assessment of the pros and cons of feminism, was as good as anything they'd done before, and 'Gospel Truth' was funny, controversial and profound. 'Dean of University', a perceptive satire about pompous, idle academics, broadcast in BBC's TV version of the show, proved that whatever else prevented a fourth series of *Not Only But Also*, it certainly wasn't an inability to write new material.

Behind the Fridge was a critical and commercial success in Australia, aided and abetted by Australia's Broadcasting Control Board, which forbade Cook and Moore from performing live on any of Australia's TV or radio stations. This unprecedented (and unrepeated) ban was prompted by Peter and Dudley's (mild) bad language on Dave Allen's chat show, and a televised broadcast of 'Gospel Truth'. A committee of 'expert clergymen' had vetted this sketch in advance, and a couple of lines had been removed, but there were still more than 300 complaints, about a sketch which the board's chairman said contained 'the most blatantly offensive reference to homosexuality and masturbation' that he had ever seen. The resultant controversy was priceless publicity, and the tour sold out in advance. Peter and Dudley even flouted the ban, by starring in a live show for Australia's leading TV station, Channel 9. Since the show was a fundraising gala for famine relief, there was little that the beleaguered Broadcasting Control Board could do.

Back in London, later that year, the critical reaction was more muted, and unfortunately there were no obliging TV censors to generate a ticket-selling furore in the press. The first night was hardly helped by Dudley's surprise appearance on *This Is Your Life*, which scuppered the dress rehearsal. Peter got drunk, delaying the start of the show, but it was Dudley's performance that suffered. Despite this calamitous start, which put a further strain on their relationship, both onstage and off it, the show survived, but even Cook admitted that it could have been better. 'We did it rather lazily in the West End,' he said. 'We didn't work hard enough at it.'[1]

The American transfer scarcely boded any better. Peter's drinking continued, yet against all odds, the show fared far better in the States. It won a Tony award, the soundtrack won a Grammy, and after breaking various box office records on Broadway, it completed a successful American tour. 'When we took it to the States we had Alexander Cohen producing, and he made us work,' explained Peter. 'It was a much, much better show on Broadway.'[2] When Peter married Judy Huxtable, in New York, Cohen was best man. Another of Cohen's contributions was to change the show's title to *Good Evening*, one of Peter's favourite catchphrases, which was ironic, since its original title had actually been coined in New York, a decade earlier, during the American run of *Beyond the Fringe*, by an Italian waiter who'd been unable to pronounce it.

∿

DUDLEY MOORE BY PETER COOK
(Cambridge Theatre, London, 1972)

Dudley Moore was born in Dagenham in 1935, which makes him some three years older than myself; despite the use of heavy make-up and yearly visits to a Swiss clinic, this age difference is readily apparent to the perceptive observer (namely me). He was educated (and I use the word in the loosest possible sense) at a local grammar school. Having failed in his attempt to become a pole-vaulting champion, he turned his attention to music; by diligent study, or possibly bribery, he won an Organ Scholarship to Magdalen College Oxford. It was here, through mingling with his betters (not me, I was at Cambridge) that he acquired his somewhat effete upper-class accent.

At Oxford he divided his time between the serious study of his classical organ and the futile pursuit of women. It was for the latter reason that he took up jazz, his main influences being Oscar Peterson, Errol Garner and Mae West. In 1959 came his first stroke of real luck; he met me, and together with Jonathan Miller and Alan Bennett we wrote and performed *Beyond the Fringe*, which ran for four years in London and three years on Broadway.

Since returning from America in 1964, we have worked on several series of *Not Only But Also*. Out of a feeling of charity, I have also managed to secure him supporting roles with me in such films as *Bedazzled*, *Monte Carlo Or Bust* and *The Bed Sitting Room*.

Like many smallish men (Napoleon, Adolf Hitler, to name but two), Dudley has a superficial charm and warmth that deceive many. Underneath lurks a demented sadist, capable in private of unspeakable deeds. It is my personal belief that his secret ambition is to initiate World War Three. I can only hope that my unfailing modesty and tact may prevent this disaster for a few years to come.

HELLO
(Plymouth Theatre, New York, 1973)

PETER: Hello.

DUDLEY: Hello.

PETER: How are you?

DUDLEY: I'm terribly well! How are you?

PETER: I'm terribly well as well!

DUDLEY: I must say you're looking very fit.

PETER: I'm feeling pretty fit actually. Isn't it amazing – us just bumping into each other like this?

DUDLEY: Yes. I mean here of all places.

PETER: Here of all places! I mean, I haven't seen you since, er . . .

DUDLEY: Now, er . . . hold on a minute . . . er, when was it? Er . . . we, we haven't seen each other . . .

PETER: Well actually we haven't seen each other . . .

DUDLEY: We haven't seen each other . . . er . . . before.

PETER: That's right. We've never seen each other before, have we?

DUDLEY: No.

PETER: You've never seen me.

DUDLEY: And I've never seen you. What a small world!

PETER: What a small world!

DUDLEY: Last thing I expected.

PETER: Well, it must be about a million to one chance.

DUDLEY: Oh, more than that.

PETER: Do you think so?

DUDLEY: A couple of billion to one.

PETER: Couple of billion, yes. Couple of billion and a half, possibly.

DUDLEY: Yes. Probably three billion to one, the way the world is going.

PETER: Yes, they're breeding like rabbits, aren't they?

DUDLEY: Yes, indeed. Anyway, it's awfully nice to . . . um . . . er . . . see you.

PETER: Well, it's terribly nice to see you.

DUDLEY: Yes. Tell me . . . er . . . are you still doing . . . er . . . whatever you have been doing . . . that is, of course, if you ever do anything.

PETER: Oh, yes. I'm still with the old firm, you know.

DUDLEY: Oh, the old firm.

PETER: Yes, soldiering on. I've just been made a Director, in fact.

DUDLEY: Oh, congratulations.

PETER: Well, under somewhat tragic circumstances . . . er . . . I've stepped into poor old Bender's shoes. Did you know Bender?

DUDLEY: Bender. The name certainly doesn't ring a bell. Bender who?

PETER: Bender Harrison.

Peter & Dudley (*Together*): Oh ! Bender Harrison! Yes!

DUDLEY: No, I've never heard of him.

PETER: You never will now, poor chap. He died last week.

DUDLEY: God! So, poor old Bender's dead.

PETER: Completely dead, yes. Yes.

DUDLEY: I'm so sorry. I had no idea.

PETER: Nor did Bender, really. He sort of . . . er . . . keeled over at the office party. Mind you, knowing Bender the way I knew Bender, which was pretty well, I think that's the way he would have wanted to go.

DUDLEY: Yes, you knowing Bender the way you must have known Bender, I'm sure that's the way he must have wanted to go.

PETER: Yes, yes.

DUDLEY: Not much point lingering on.

PETER: No, he was 106. I tell you the one thing I really ought to know, and that is, how's your . . . er . . . if you . . . er . . . have a . . . er . . .

DUDLEY: My wife? Vera?

PETER: Yes. How is she?

DUDLEY: She's awfully well.

PETER: I'm so pleased about that.

DUDLEY: Yes, terribly well, Vera. And of course young Martin's going to school now.

PETER: Martin going to school? Good God, I had no idea! How time flies!

DUDLEY: Yes, one moment they're that high. The next moment, they're . . .

Peter & Dudley (*Together*): That high.

PETER: Good heavens! Martin at school!

DUDLEY: Yes. Tell me, how's um . . . er . . . er . . .

PETER: Roger Braintree?

DUDLEY: Yes. How's Roger Braintree?

PETER: Absolutely no idea. I've never met him. I just saw his name in the telephone book and I . . . er . . . I was rather hoping you might be able to fill me in on what Roger's up to.

DUDLEY: I . . . I . . . I can't help you there, I'm afraid.

PETER: You've no idea what Roger might be doing?

DUDLEY: No . . . Well, not apart from what you've told me.

PETER: About him being in the telephone book.

DUDLEY: Yes, yes. Mind you, that's bloody good news.

PETER: Well, I'm very pleased for Roger.

DUDLEY: Yes, tremendous. I suppose he is under B is he?

PETER: Yes he is, right under B, which is a . . . pretty bloody good place to start.

DUDLEY: What? B.R.A.I.N.T.R.E.E.?

PETER: The whole thing. Yes, he's got his whole thing in there.

DUDLEY: I'm very pleased for Roger.

PETER: Yes, I'm sorry you don't know more about what Roger might be doing in other directions.

DUDLEY: Sorry, I can't really help there. Perhaps I could give him a ring this evening and see what he's up to?

PETER: Good idea. Anyway, terribly nice . . . to see you. I . . . I really ought to be dashing back to the office . . . time waits for no man.

DUDLEY: I'd better be toddling along myself, I think.

PETER: Do remember me to . . . er . . . um . . .

DUDLEY: Vera.

PETER: Yes. You must forgive me. I'm terribly bad at names. I keep forgetting them.

DUDLEY: Quite all right.

PETER: Do remember me to . . . um . . . er . . .

DUDLEY: Vera.

PETER: That's the chap. And jolly good luck with . . . um . . . er . . . it.

DUDLEY: Yes, well, the same to you. And we must keep in touch.

PETER: Yes, absolutely. I'll give you a tinkle.

DUDLEY: Yes, or vice versa.

PETER: Yes, we must do this again.

DUDLEY: Yes. Goodbye.

PETER: Goodbye.

CRIME AND PUNISHMENT
(Plymouth Theatre, New York, 1973)

(*Dudley is a schoolmaster, in his study. There is knock at the door.*)

DUDLEY: Come in.

(*Enter Peter, as a schoolboy.*)

PETER: You sent for me, sir?

DUDLEY: Yes, I did indeed, Rawlings. Rawlings, I had a rather distressing piece of news this morning. As you know, three generations of Rawlings have brought distinction and credit to this school.

PETER: Yes, sir.

DUDLEY: Your father, your grandfather and your great grandfather have all, in their time, been head boy of the school.

PETER: Yes, sir.

DUDLEY: You yourself are in line for this privilege when Whitwell leaves the school next year and goes up to Oxford to study forestry. However, Rawlings, I was rather disappointed to hear from Mr Asprey, the physical training master, that a pair of very valuable gymnasium slippers disappeared from his stock room Tuesday last and reappeared as if by magic in your locker next to a copy of *Busty Beauties Around the World.*

PETER: Yes, sir.

DUDLEY: Well, do you have any explanation for the appearance of these gym shoes in your locker, other than the one that immediately springs to mind?

PETER: No, sir. I wanted the gym shoes, sir, and I took them.

DUDLEY: You wanted the gym shoes, Rawlings, and you took them?

PETER: Yes, sir.

DUDLEY: Good God, man! Do you realise what would happen in this world if people took exactly what they wanted? We'd be living in a sea of anarchy! The whole moral fibre of society would fall apart! You feel you're somebody unique and exempt from these basic laws of human behaviour?

PETER: No, sir.

DUDLEY: Do you feel that the ethics of a civilised society should apply to everyone except yourself?

PETER: No, sir.

DUDLEY: Are you some latter-day Hitler, Rawlings, who feels he can annex whatever he wants? Today gym shoes, tomorrow the world! It is my responsibility, Rawlings, to douse the flames of such overweening ambition, to exorcise this creeping cancer. And you will find, Rawlings, not for me the policy of appeasement. Oh, no! Like Churchill, I will fight you on the beaches, I will fight you in the air, I will repel your doodlebugs, I will snatch your Messerschmits from the sky! You may gather, Rawlings, there is only one course open to me. I must punish you very severely. I must ask you to bend over this desk and take six of the best.

PETER: Yes, sir. Could I just say one thing, sir?

DUDLEY: Well, come on, Rawlings, out with it. But I'm afraid you'll find that any plea for mercy will fall on deaf ears.

PETER: I did take the slippers, sir, and I deserve to be punished, and you're much older and wiser than I am, sir . . .

DUDLEY: Come on, Rawlings! Out with it!

PETER: I'm much bigger than you are, sir, and if you lay a finger on me I'll smash your stupid little face in.

DUDLEY: Rawlings, why didn't you tell me all this before?

PETER: Sorry, sir.

DUDLEY: Well, Rawlings, this puts a completely different complexion on the whole thing! Now, Rawlings – I'd like you to accept on behalf of the school, my private collection of *Screw Magazine*, this excellent deck of Acapulco Gold – here's ten pounds, why don't you pop up to the school nurse, present her my compliments and have her give you a deep, relaxing Swedish massage on me.

GOSPEL TRUTH
(Plymouth Theatre, New York, 1973)

(*Peter is dressed as a Shepherd, is seated. We hear sounds of sheep.*)

PETER: Stop that! Get off her! She's only young! And you! Get off! (*Enter Dudley, dressed in robes and carrying a scroll and quill pen.*)

DUDLEY: I believe you are Mr Arthur Shepherd.

PETER: That's right, Shepherd by name and shepherd by nature.

DUDLEY: Let me introduce myself. My name is Matthew.

PETER: Hello, Matthew.

DUDLEY: Hello, Arthur. You may have heard of me, and my colleagues – Mark, Luke and John?

PETER: Oh yeah, I've heard of you lot. You're celebrities. Can I touch your raiment?

DUDLEY: Certainly.

PETER: Knockout.

DUDLEY: Yes, well, we are doing an in-depth profile of Jesus, or the Messiah as you may know him.

PETER: No, I don't.

DUDLEY: You don't know him?

PETER: Well, yes I do. I know him as Jesus.

DUDLEY: Oh, fine.

PETER: Not that other thing. Which paper do you work for?

DUDLEY: The *Bethlehem Star*.

PETER: Oh, yeah. The wife and I take the *Star* actually.

DUDLEY: Oh?

PETER: I don't think much of your Racing Correspondent.

DUDLEY: Oh?

PETER: I had three shekels on that camel in the 3.15 at Galilee. It's still bloody running, that one is.

DUDLEY: I don't work on that side of the paper – I work on the more serious side. You know, reportage. And we're doing this in-depth profile of Jesus, and I gather that you were actually in on the very first moments surrounding the birth of the Holy Child.

PETER: Yes, I was. Yeah.

DUDLEY: That is marvellous. Now, what I'd like you to do, if you are willing, is to tell me what happened, in your own words.

PETER: Yes. Well it's quite simple, really. Basically, what happened was that me and the lads were abiding in the fields.

DUDLEY: (*Writing*) Abiding in the fields, yes.

PETER: Yes. Mind you, I can't abide these fields.

DUDLEY: No?

PETER: I mean, look around you. They are unabidable fields.

DUDLEY: Yeah.

PETER: I'd say these are about the most unabidable bleeding fields I've ever had to abide in.

DUDLEY: Yeah, I'll abide by that.

(*Dudley laughs at his joke – Peter is unmoved.*)

DUDLEY: No, no – my apologies, Arthur. You were abiding in the fields?

PETER: And we were watching our flocks by night.

DUDLEY: (*Writing*) Watching our flocks by night, yeah.

PETER: Yes, because that's when you have to watch them, you know. That's when they get up to all their rubbish.

DUDLEY: Yeah, yeah.

PETER: Hot summer nights, the rams go mad – especially that one over there. He's a dirty little bugger. Cut that out! Doing it in broad daylight, in front of you, a Holy Man!

DUDLEY: Ah, it's only human.

PETER: Yeah, I may be a bit old-fashioned, but I don't like to see one ram doing it to another.

DUDLEY: Oh, yes. He's an enthusiast, isn't he?

PETER: Oh, yeah. Top marks for enthusiasm, zero for accuracy.

DUDLEY: It's a bit distracting, isn't it?

PETER: Yeah, sorry about all those ramifications going on down there, though. I've got no control over them.

DUDLEY: Oh, they're only young once.

PETER: Yeah, I think I'll get my next lot from Gomorrah.

DUDLEY: Anyway, you were abiding in the fields, watching your flocks by night.

PETER: Yeah.

DUDLEY: And then what happened?

PETER: Well, much to our surprise, the Angel of the Lord flew down.

DUDLEY: Oh, now that must have been a fantastic experience.

PETER: Well, it made a break, you know – bit of a break just from abiding, him flashing down like that.

DUDLEY: Tell me, Arthur, how did you know it was the Angel of the Lord?

PETER: Oh, I'll tell you what the giveaway was, Matthew. It was this ethereal glow he was emanating. He was emanating an ethereal glow.

DUDLEY: Oh, I see.

PETER: And as soon as I saw Him emanating, I said 'Ello – Angel of the Lord.'

DUDLEY: Halo?

PETER: Er, halo, certainly, yes. Halo, and goodbye we said afterwards. He wasn't there for long. He just gave his little message, and then He was off, like a bat out of 'ell.

DUDLEY: Yeah. Wings?

PETER: Oh, wings, Matthew – I've never seen such a gorgeous pair on a man before.

DUDLEY: Yeah?

PETER: They were outstanding wings – all gossamer, shimmering there in the starlight.

DUDLEY: Oh, it must have been remarkable.

PETER: Yes, it was. I noticed it.

DUDLEY: What did He say to you, Arthur?

PETER: Well, He sort of singled me out from the other lowly shepherd folk . . .

DUDLEY: Oh, lovely.

PETER: And He said 'Unto ye a Child is born. Unto ye a Son is given.'

DUDLEY: Yes. What was your reaction?

PETER: Total shock. I mean I wasn't even married at the time. And I thought, you know, 'Blimey! What was I doing this time last year?'

DUDLEY: Yeah.

PETER: Could it be that little bird I met down the Shepherd's Delight?

DUDLEY: Yeah.

PETER: But the Angel of the Lord went on to explain that when He said Ye, he didn't mean me personal, like. He meant Ye in the sense of the whole world. Unto the whole world a Child is born. Unto the whole world a Son is given.

DUDLEY: Yes, He was using the universal Ye.

PETER: Was He? Well I wouldn't know. I'm not educated myself.

DUDLEY: Yes. That's what He was using – the universal Ye.

PETER: Yes, He was very effluent.

DUDLEY: Yes. I suppose your first reaction was to whip over there and have a peep, eh?

PETER: Well, naturally we all dashed down to the stable, but when I arrived I was in for a bit of a shock.

DUDLEY: Really? Go on.

PETER: I will. Because when He said 'Ye shall find the Child all meanly wrapped in swaddling clothes,' I thought to myself, 'Fair enough. He'll be fairly meanly wrapped. Nothing flashy, nothing gaudy.'

DUDLEY: Yes.

PETER: But when I arrived, it was diabolical. It was the meanest bit of wrapping I've ever seen. What's more, that kid was barely swaddled. I'd say, it was the worst job of wrapping and swaddling I have ever seen in my life.

DUDLEY: How very distressing.

PETER: It was alarming to behold.

DUDLEY: Now, Arthur, I want you to think back in time . . .

PETER: Well, I'll do it now, if you like.

DUDLEY: No, what I meant was, think back now – to then.

PETER: That's what I meant – think back to then, now.

DUDLEY: Right. Now then, what was the atmosphere like in the stable on this joyous, historic occasion?

PETER: The atmosphere in the stable was very, very smelly, with all these cows and goats and sheep about, you know. And they had no sense of occasion.

DUDLEY: That's a fascinating sidelight, but what I'm really after, Arthur, is – what was the atmosphere like amongst the members of the Holy family?

PETER: Oh, I see – the personal atmosphere.

DUDLEY: Yes.

PETER: Well, in one word – tense.

DUDLEY: Tense? You surprise me.

PETER: Joseph in particular. He was sitting in the corner of the stable, looking very gloomy indeed.

DUDLEY: Well he might have been feeling a bit disgruntled, not being the real father.

PETER: I think that was it. I think he felt left out of the whole thing, you know, and personally, I think this is why he done such a rotten job on the swaddling – he just couldn't be bothered to swaddle. And let's face it, there had been a lot of tittle tattle about his wife and the 'oly Ghost. I mean, rumours had been flying round Bethlehem – as indeed the 'oly Ghost must have been.

DUDLEY: Was the Holy Ghost there?

PETER: Hard to say. He's an elusive little bugger at the best of times – and I did not see Him. I was very disappointed because I felt strongly at the time He should have been there. You know, in His capacity as the Godfather.

DUDLEY: Especially after His treatment of the Virgin Mary – making Her an offer She couldn't refuse.

PETER: Well, making Her an offer She didn't even notice.

DUDLEY: I gather that later on in the evening the three wise men came by. Am I right?

PETER: Yeah, three wise men arrived. Yeah, three bloody idiots if ever I saw any. In they come, called themselves Magi (*Peter pronounces it as Maggie*).

DUDLEY: Three blokes came in and called themselves Magi?

PETER: Yeah. They peered around the stable door and said 'Hello, we're Magi.'

DUDLEY: How very embarrassing.

PETER: We didn't know where to look. And they were bearing these gifts – gold, frankincense and myrrh.

DUDLEY: That's M. E. R. H. Nice of them to bring these gifts, eh?

PETER: Well, I suppose the gold was welcome, but what's a little kid going to do with frankincense and myrrh, I ask you?

DUDLEY: Right.

PETER: I mean, myrrh's that stuff what poofs put behind their ears, isn't it?

DUDLEY: Yes.

PETER: That over-perfumed jelly stuff, but Jesus, He was so polite about it. He sat up in the manger, He adjusted His swaddling and He said 'Thank you, gentlemen, for these lovely prezzies, I hope you have a safe trip back – Merry Christmas.'

MINI DRAMA
(Plymouth Theatre, New York, 1973)

(Peter is a Scottish minicab driver. He drives up to a smart Hampstead house, gets out of his cab, and knocks on the front door.)

PETER: Your minicab, Lord Nesbitt.

(Enter Dudley.)

DUDLEY: You're late. My car's broken down and I've got to make a speech in the House of Lords in half an hour.

PETER: Right, sir. Would you like to sit in the front or make yourself comfortable in the back?

DUDLEY: I'll sit in the back. I've got a few papers I've got to read through.

PETER: Certainly. In you get, sir.

(Peter sits in the driver's seat, Dudley gets into the back.)

PETER: I see yours is about seven inches long.

DUDLEY: I beg your pardon?

PETER: I see your entry in *Who's Who* is about seven inches long. That's quite a length, you know.

DUDLEY: Oh, I see. You – you've been reading up about me, have you?

PETER: Yes, I like to keep tabs on who I've got in the back of the car.

DUDLEY: Extraordinary hobby.

PETER: Keeps the mind alive.

(Into his radio) Four Five.

RADIO: Yes, Four Five.

PETER: P.O.B. Hampstead, proceeding House of Lords.

RADIO: Roger, Four Five.

(Peter starts the car.)

DUDLEY: I'm due to make a speech in about half an hour's time, I'd be very obliged if you'd put your foot down.

PETER: Right. Might I suggest, at this time of night, we take a few back doubles – it's bloody murder in the West End.

DUDLEY: Whatever you think is the quickest.

RADIO: Apple Five, Apple Five. Have you picked up those parcels yet? Roger, Rog, but get a move on.

PETER: How'd you get our number, sir?

DUDLEY: Oh, I think one of your chappies just dropped a card in through the letterbox. My wife gave it to me.

PETER: Oh, yes, we a lot of customers that way – through the letterbox.

(*He laughs menacingly.*)

PETER: I said we get a lot of customers that way.

(*He laughs menacingly, again.*)

DUDLEY: Did I say something funny?

PETER: No, sir. It's just that you have to have a laugh to stay alive in this miserable job. I wonder if we could try something, sir? A little party game that might amuse you. Knock knock.

DUDLEY: Pardon?

PETER: It's a little game, sir. I say 'Knock knock' and you say 'Who's there?'

DUDLEY: Who's there?

PETER: That's it. That's very good. Shall we try it? I think it will amuse you.

DUDLEY: (*Half-heartedly*) Oh, yes. By all means.

PETER: Knock knock.

DUDLEY: Er, who's there?

PETER: Sam and Janet.

DUDLEY: Er, yes – that's very good. Jolly good.

PETER: No, it's not good at all, sir. I say 'Sam and Janet' and you say 'Sam and Janet who?' Then I come back with the killer line. Shall we try again? 'Knock knock.' 'Who's there?' 'Sam and Janet.' 'Sam and Janet who?' from you. Then it's my line. I think the end result will tickle you.

DUDLEY: Undoubtedly.

PETER: Knock knock.

DUDLEY: Er, who's there?

PETER: Sam and Janet.

DUDLEY: Sam . . .

TOGETHER: Sam and Janet Who?

PETER: (*sings, to the tune of 'Some Enchanted Evening'*) Sam and Janet evening. (*Laughs*) Sam and Janet evening . . .

DUDLEY: What do I say now?

PETER: You don't say anything, sir. That's it. That's the wee joke.

DUDLEY: Oh, yes, yes. That's awfully good.

RADIO: Apple Five. Apple Five. Look, how many times have I got to tell you, to pick up the four brown paper parcels and dump them in a canal.

PETER: It must be quite nice to be in the House of Lords, you know, and make a speech now and then. Get reported in the Press. Get invited on Television. It must be very nice to be famous.

DUDLEY: Well, I wouldn't say I was famous, you know.

PETER: But you're well known, aren't you, sir?

DUDLEY: Yes. Yes, I'm well known. I'll grant you that.

PETER: It's all a matter of luck really, isn't it? Where you're born, who your parents were. I was found in a dustbin in Glasgow. I never knew my parents.

DUDLEY: I'm very sorry.

RADIO: First call. Blind Beggar Pub. Whitechapel.

PETER: (*into his radio*) Four Five.

RADIO: Second call. Blind Beggar Pub. Whitechapel.

PETER: Four Five.

RADIO: Assistance. Blind Beggar Pub!

PETER: Four bloody Five here.

RADIO: Roger, Four Five.

PETER: Dropping Westminster in about ten minutes. I could be in Whitechapel in twenty.

RADIO: Roger, Four Five. Pick up torso and drop on Wimbledon Common.

PETER: Is that cash, or account?

RADIO: Cash. The money's in a brown paper envelope.

PETER: Roger, Rog.

DUDLEY: Did I . . . did I hear that chap say 'torso'?

PETER: Yes, that's right, sir. Torso. Old Tony Torso. He's one of our regulars.

DUDLEY: God, what a bloody stupid name.

PETER: What, torso? Not really. You'd be surprised at the number of torsos floating around these days. Tony runs a very successful little Italian restaurant on the A6.

RADIO: Apple Five. Apple Five. Look, it doesn't matter which canal. Just dump the bloody parcels.

DUDLEY: Would you mind turning that thing off. I find it rather distracting.

PETER: What, the radiophone? By all means. I've got the torso job after this – so I'm laughing. Would you mind if I put on a cassette?

DUDLEY: Whatever you like.

PETER: A little music, to while away the time as we drive through the fog.

(*Peter puts on grim, discordant music.*)

PETER: Interesting piece, actually.

(*Peter turns on the windscreen wipers.*)

PETER: Written by a young Russian. Tragic life. He committed suicide at the age of thirty. He was never recognised by the critics. This music sort of reflects the despair and despondency of his life. I identify with it strongly. It conjures up a mood for me.

DUDLEY: It's bloody gloomy.

PETER: Yes. Well, life can be very gloomy, can't it, sir?

(*Peter takes a gun out of glove compartment.*)

DUDLEY: Good God man, what are you doing with a gun in your glove compartment?

PETER: What am I doing with a gun? I'm not doing anything with it – at the moment. But these days you never know who you're going to get in the back, eh? (*Laughs*) That's rather good, isn't it? You never know who you'll get in the back. Do you get it, sir?

DUDLEY: No, I don't get it.

PETER: Oh, you'll get it in time. It'll come to you in a sudden blinding flash.

(*A sudden flash from oncoming headlights. Peter swerves.*)

DUDLEY: For God's sake, man, look where you're going!

PETER: Bloody Nuns. Shouldn't be allowed on the road. Talking of guns, sir – which we were – didn't I read somewhere that you're on that commission investigating the rise in violent crimes?

DUDLEY: Er, yes. Yes, I am. Why?

PETER: What do you put it down to, sir? I mean, what is it in Society that produces a Lee Harvey Oswald, or that Bremer bloke who tried to gun down Wallace?

DUDLEY: Well, I think these chaps had one thing in common.

PETER: They had one thing in common, did they, sir?

DUDLEY: Yes. They were all loners.

PETER: Loners. Take me, for example. I've no family – women have always laughed at me. I've just drifted from job to job. You could call me a loner, if you like.

DUDLEY: (*Laughs uncomfortably*) No, you're not a loner, not in this sort of a job. I mean, you must meet lots of interesting people. Take me, for example . . .

PETER: Bullshit.

DUDLEY: I wasn't suggesting . . .

PETER: I don't like people.

DUDLEY: There's no obligation . . .

PETER: People don't like me.

DUDLEY: Of course they like you. My dear chap – you're a very likeable chap. You've a marvellous sense of humour. I mean, I love that joke of yours. (*Sings*) Sam and Janet evening . . .

PETER: You don't really like me.

DUDLEY: I do. I know this is terribly sudden, but I'm absolutely enchanted by you.

(*Dudley touches Peter on the shoulder.*)

PETER: Don't touch me, sir.

(*Dudley quickly withdraws his hand.*)

PETER: You know my theory why people go round assassinating famous people?

DUDLEY: No. I'd be interested to hear it.

PETER: It's their only chance in life of getting some sort of recognition.

DUDLEY: But violence will get us nowhere.

PETER: Do you not think so, sir? What about Lee Harvey Oswald? He was a nobody, a nonentity. Nobody had heard of him, and then . . . Boom Boom!

DUDLEY: Who's there?

PETER: Lee Harvey Oswald is a household word.

DUDLEY: Oh, very good. I like that one.

PETER: I mean, what chance have I got of going down in History? You won't find many minicab drivers with their obituary in the *Times*.

DUDLEY: I have contacts on the *Times*. There'll be a letter in the post tomorrow.

PETER: But Lee Harvey Oswald – Lee Harvey Oswald. That's a name to be reckoned with.

(*Peter stops the car, gets out and opens Dudley's door. Peter is still holding his gun.*)

PETER: Get out, sir.

(*Dudley gets out.*)

DUDLEY: For God's sake, let's be reasonable!

PETER: I've got a job to do, sir.

DUDLEY: For God's sake, don't do anything rash!

PETER: This is it, sir.

DUDLEY: I'm a rich man. Take my money.

(*Dudley pulls out his wallet.*)

DUDLEY: Here. For God's sake, anything!

PETER: Just two pounds.

DUDLEY: Look, don't toy with me. Take it all!

(*Dudley drops to his knees and covers his head.*)

DUDLEY: Don't do it! Please don't do it!

PETER: We're here, sir – at the House of Lords.

(*Dudley looks up.*)

DUDLEY: So we are.

PETER: Your final destination.

(*Dudley gets up.*)

DUDLEY: Oh, er . . . I'm sorry . . . I slipped getting out of the car – my legs aren't what they were . . .

PETER: Accidents will happen.

DUDLEY: I know it sounds very stupid – I thought you were going to shoot me.

PETER: To shoot you, sir?

DUDLEY: Yes.

PETER: To shoot you? It never crossed my mind, sir. You're not famous enough.

DUDLEY: Of course not.

PETER: I mean, Page Two, Column Three – who needs that? It's the front page we're after, isn't it?

DUDLEY: Yes, of course.

PETER: Cheerio then, sir. Goodbye. Pip pip.

(*Exit Dudley, Peter gets back into the cab.*)

PETER: Four Five.

RADIO: Four Five.

PETER: Proceeding torso job.

VOICE: Roger, Four Five.

PETER: Roger, Rog.

FROG & PEACH
(Plymouth Theatre, New York, 1973)

DUDLEY: Good evening. I am talking this evening to Sir Arthur Greeb-Streebling . . .

PETER: Oh no you're not – not at all. You're talking to Sir Arthur Streeb-Greebling. You're confusing me with Sir Arthur Greeb-Streebling. The T is silent, as in Fox. Good evening.

DUDLEY: I'm sorry. I'd like to ask Sir Arthur, actually, about his rather unique restaurant – The Frog & Peach.

PETER: This seems like the ideal opportunity, what with me being here and you being there. The ideal opportunity – seize it!

DUDLEY: If you would tell us something about the Frog & Peach, Sir Arthur? How did the idea come to you?

PETER: Yes, well, the idea for the Frog & Peach came to me in the bath. A great number of things come to me in the bath – mainly mosquitoes, various forms of water snakes – but on this occasion, a rather stunning and unique idea. I suddenly thought, where can a young couple go, with not too much money, feeling a bit hungry, a bit peckish, want something to eat – where can they go? Where can they go and get a really big frog and a damn fine peach? Where can they go? And the answer came there none. And it was on this premise that I founded the Frog & Peach.

DUDLEY: On these premises?

PETER: On these precise premises, yes.

DUDLEY: How long ago did you start this venture?

PETER: Tricky to say – certainly within living memory. It was shortly after World War Two. Do you remember that? Absolutely ghastly business – I was against the whole thing.

DUDLEY: I think we all were.

PETER: Yes, well, I wrote a letter.

DUDLEY: Getting back to the Frog & Peach, how has business been?

PETER: Let me answer that in two parts. Business hasn't been and there hasn't been any business. These last thirty-five years have been a rather lean time for us here at the old F & P.

DUDLEY: But don't you feel that you're at a slight disadvantage, being stuck out here in the middle of a bog in the heart of the Yorkshire Moors?

PETER: I think the word disadvantage is awfully well chosen here. Yes, that is what we're at. We're at a disadvantage, stuck out here in the middle of a bog in the heart of the Yorkshire Moors. But I thought, rightly or wrongly – possibly both – that the people of this country were crying out for a restaurant without a parking problem. And here in the middle of a bog in the heart of the Yorkshire Moors, there is no problem parking the car. A little difficulty extricating it – but parking is sheer joy.

DUDLEY: Don't you also feel that you're at a disadvantage with regard to your menu?

PETER: Yes, this has been a terrible disadvantage to us. Have you seen it?

DUDLEY: Very briefly.

PETER: That's the only way to see it. I mean, the choice is so limited. You only have two dishes to choose from. Now what are they? Blast! I should know this by heart after thirty-five years. Oh, yes, first there is Frog à la Pêche. Frog à la Pêche is basically a large frog, brought to your table, covering in boiling Cointreau, with a peach stuck in its mouth. It is one of the most disgusting sights I have ever seen. The only alternative to Frog à la Pêche is even worse – Pêche à la Frog. In this case, a peach is brought to your table by the waiter, again covered in boiling Cointreau.

DUDLEY: The waiter?

PETER: Very often. Very often the waiter is covered in boiling Cointreau, but the policy here is to aim the Cointreau at the peach. The peach is then sliced down the middle to reveal – Oh, God! – about 300 squiggling, black tadpoles. It is the most disgusting sight I have ever seen in my life! It's enough to put you off your food – which is a damn good thing, considering what the food is like.

DUDLEY: Who does the cooking?

PETER: My wife. My wife does all the cooking, and luckily, she does all the eating as well. She's not a well woman.

DUDLEY: She's not a well woman?

PETER: She is not a well woman, and she very much resents having to go down the well every morning to feed the frogs. She dislikes it intensely. We have to lower her screaming on a rope. Frogs don't like it either.

DUDLEY: How did you meet your wife?

PETER: I met Morag under somewhat unusual circumstances. It was during World War Two – you remember that thing I tried to stop? She blew in through the window on a piece of shrapnel, became embedded in the sofa. One thing led to her mother, and we were married in the hour. Her mother is a very powerful woman. She can break a swan's wing with a blow of her nose. Kids love it at parties.

DUDLEY: Getting back to the Frog and Peach . . .

PETER: By all means.

DUDLEY: The whole venture of the Frog and Peach sounds a bit disastrous.

PETER: I don't think I'd use the word disastrous here. I think the word catastrophe is closer to the mark. The whole venture of the Frog and Peach has been a total failure and huge catastrophe.

PETER COOK

DUDLEY: Do you think you've learned from your mistakes?
PETER: Oh, yes, I've learned from my mistakes and I'm sure I could repeat them exactly.
DUDLEY: Thank you, Sir Arthur Greeb-Streebling.
PETER: Streeb-Greebling.

Chapter Eight
Derek and Clive

Derek & Clive were an X-rated version of Pete & Dud, and none of Peter Cook's comedy divides audiences quite like the three notorious albums that this foulmouthed pair produced. The first, and by far the best, of these was *Derek & Clive (Live)* – originally entitled *Derek & Clive (Dead)* – which originated in a series of largely improvised New York recording sessions, initiated by Peter to alleviate the boredom of the long Broadway run of *Good Evening*. Partly recorded in two Manhattan recording studios, with only a few sound technicians for company, and partly in a Greenwich Village club, before a small audience of invited friends, these scatological sketches were never intended for public consumption. Indeed, Cook and Moore had done something similar a decade earlier, during the New York run of *Beyond the Fringe*, recording *The Dead Sea Tapes*, their comic equivalent of *The Dead Sea Scrolls* – a series of frank reminiscences by various acquaintances of Jesus Christ, which somehow never made it into the Authorised Version of The Bible.

However, this time bootleg copies began to circulate among

Cook and Moore's more well connected fans, including three of the world's biggest rock bands – The Rolling Stones, Led Zeppelin and The Who. Within a few years, private collectors were publicly hawking Derek & Clive bootlegs via small ads in the back of *Private Eye*. Everyone else appeared to be making money out of Derek & Clive apart from Cook and Moore. It seemed daft (and increasingly futile) not to climb aboard the bandwagon they'd started. Nearly three years after Derek & Clive's first informal recording session, Island Records finally released *Derek & Clive (Live)*.

Incredibly, this obscure cult record was a big hit on both sides of the Atlantic. In Britain, it sold 50,000 copies in the first few weeks, and twice that number overall. It eventually became Cook and Moore's biggest-selling LP – outselling more well mannered and painstaking produced albums like *The Clean Tapes* (billed as the very best of) and *The World of Pete & Dud*.

A couple of the live sketches on the record were actually new versions of old favourites. 'Blind' had been performed in New York a decade earlier, in the American premises of Peter's Establishment Club. 'Bo Duddley' was from the second series of *Not Only But Also*. It's not included here, since the star of this sketch is Dudley's piano – but thankfully anyone with a video player and a few quid to spare can still see it, since it's one of the relatively few sketches from that series which survived the BBC's destructive cull, and was later rereleased by the BBC on a commercial VHS.

Their first (and again, their funniest) Derek & Clive sketch, in which Clive tells Derek about the worst job he ever had, removing lobsters from Jayne Mansfield's backside, was a fantasy Peter had been batting about, in various impromptu forms, for the benefit of his *Private Eye* colleagues, for an entire decade. Indeed its inspiration – a newspaper report about how Ms Mansfield was shipwrecked on a Bahamian island dressed only in her bikini – dated back to 1962. However only Cook could have transformed such a bog standard showbiz yarn into something so hilarious and bizarre. 'I think the idea of retrieving lobsters from Jayne Mansfield's arsehole as a job is about as funny an idea as I've ever heard in my life,'[1] declared Mel Smith. Dudley's hasty response, about his worst job, picking up Winston Churchill's bogeys, wasn't quite so amusing or inventive – not a lot is – but then again, he hadn't had ten years practice. And if the rest of the LP didn't quite scale the dizzy heights of Clive's lobster-retrieving exploits, several passages certainly came pretty close. 'These obsessive dialogues, of a transcendental lewdness, mostly improvised, one surmised, under the influence of various popular stimulants, are amongst the funniest of Cook and Moore's virtuoso turns,'[2] claims Barry Humphries.

Not everyone agreed. Anyone who disapproves of swearing is highly unlikely to like Derek & Clive, and the same goes for anyone who feels at all uncomfortable listening to graphic fantasies about violence or explicit jokes about sexual intercourse. Even some of Cook's friends and fans, who weren't remotely uptight about sex or swearing, felt this profane stream of semi-consciousness was a breach of taste too far. Indeed, it's perfectly possible to admire virtually everything else Peter Cook ever did, and still dislike Derek & Clive intensely. However if you've ever marvelled at the infinite capacity of British blokes of a certain class (Derek & Clive are toilet cleaners) to use the words fuck and cunt as punctuation rather than vocabulary, then Derek & Clive (Live) is irresistible. Comedy, like pornography, is a bastard art form that can bypass the brain and head straight for the baser senses. A laugh, like an erection, is largely involuntary. Consequently, you can disapprove of Derek & Clive and simultaneously enjoy them.

The second and third albums, Come Again and Ad Nauseam, were a lot less enjoyable. They're also a lot harder to defend. The first album's coarse but amiable charm lay in its underground beginnings. Cook and Moore made these recordings for their own amusement, and listening to them still feels almost like eavesdropping. This feeling was enhanced by the record's eccentric evolution. The bootleg success of Derek & Clive (Live) preceded its mainstream release. Conversely, Come Again and Ad Nauseam were straightforward commercial records made for straightforward commercial gain, though neither of them matched the commercial success of their best-selling pirate predecessor.

Come Again was recorded in a single day, and it shows. Cook and

Moore's best work dovetailed improvised and pre-prepared material. In *Not Only But Also*, Dudley prepared while Peter improvised. On *Derek & Clive (Live)* it was the other way around. *On Come Again*, neither of them had done much preparation, and it's painfully apparent. There are a few fleeting moments of iconoclastic inspiration, one of which, 'Joan Crawford', is included here – but apart from that sketch, the best thing on this album was the sleeve notes, also reprinted below. These notes and that sketch both belong on a better album. Fast and loose comedy is rarely off the cuff.

Peter and Dudley prepared only one sketch for the third album, *Ad Nauseam*, and again, this pre-prepared sketch, 'Horse Racing', was one of the best. In fact, *Ad Nauseam* is both better and worse than *Come Again*. Worse, since its malevolence is, if anything, even more virulent. Better, since there are actually several successful sketches this time around. One of these was 'The Critics', which satirised those snobs who adored the use of 'bad' language by highbrow playwrights like Harold Pinter, but abhorred its use by popular entertainers like Cook and Moore. It's a fair point, but the most unpleasant thing about *Ad Nauseam* wasn't its language but its attitude. *Derek & Clive (Live)* was like a foulmouthed but friendly drunkard. *Ad Nauseam*, like *Come Again*, was like a furious, foulmouthed drunkard spoiling for a fight. Nevertheless, *Ad Nauseam* did carry a unique disclaimer. As Cook pointed out, anybody who buys a record that comes complete with its own sick bag can hardly say they weren't warned.

Ad Nauseam was recorded in two days, twice as long as *Come Again*, which perhaps accounts for its slightly superior quality. However, on the second day Derek & Clive had the added distraction of an attendant film crew, invited in by Peter without Dudley's advance knowledge or consent. The result of this bizarre experiment was *Derek & Clive Get the Horn*, a full-length feature film whose style and content make it one of the most unintentionally depressing movies ever made. As a documentary record of a brilliant partnership on the brink of complete collapse, it has a certain morbid fascination, but whatever its biographical value, it's devoid of all but the sickest laughs. Finally released fifteen years later, on video, it was initially denied a certificate by the British Board of Film Censors, which was certainly a relief for Dudley, and perhaps even for Peter too. 'The point of this comic exercise is to be as offensive as possible and to break every taboo the performers can think of, however outrageous,' wrote the Board's James Ferman, in a letter to the producers. 'Cutting would be pointless although we believe that the sequence about Jesus Christ and the sexuality of the lower half of his body is probably blasphemous in the legal sense of the term. If this is so then this brief scene would have to be cut. The offensive references to the Pope and the Holocaust, are not, in our view, illegal, though they will certainly prove deeply offensive to some people.'

The studio had been booked for three days, but Dudley failed to show up on the third day. 'He probably wanted to shock people and he did – there's no doubt he shocked me and that was, it seemed, his main source of pleasure,' reflected Dudley. 'It just became an arena for us to throw mud at each other.'[3] Cook and Moore had always grappled with big themes, like fine art, philosophy or religion. Now, with those themes all spent, they were reduced to grappling with each other.

Initially, Peter defended the album, and even the film, but eventually he came round to Dudley's point of view. 'We were scraping the bottom of several barrels,' he admitted in 1993, the year of the film's belated video release. 'It's only when I saw it all through again that I realised what a bully I was.'[4] 'He used to shock the shit out of me,' said Dudley. 'He had a genius for obscenity. I never succeeded in shocking him, though I used to try all right. I could never match him for speed, for one thing. And I usually had to fall back on filthy tales of family life. He was mounting an endless assault on the humour button. He wouldn't stop until he got a laugh. Never mind how much dross there was, he had to come up with a jewel.'[5] And in the end, that's probably the best possible summary of Derek & Clive – the good bits, the bad bits, and the downright ugly. Dudley's right. There's an awful lot of dross in it – but in the midst of it all, there are some shocking, shitty jewels.

∿

PETER COOK

ALIAS DEREK AND CLIVE
(*Sheffield & North Derbyshire Spectator*, 1976)

Sometime late in 1973 Dudley Moore and I booked a recording studio for a late night ad lib session after performing what seemed like the millionth performance of *Good Evening* in New York. I never believe performers who maintain that constant repetition of the same material is not enormously tedious. Once I have got through the tension and excitement of the first night and the brief period of elation or despair that comes from reading the critical reaction, acting becomes just another job. The one redeeming factor about our show was that we had written it and therefore felt quite entitled to mess about with it to a certain extent; but there is a limit to how much one can alter a show, which in our case opened to very flattering reviews. We both felt that we really ought to offer up at least a fair approximation of what had been described in the press. I suppose we felt restrained by the Trade Descriptions Act. We had to produce the advertised goods. Moments of pleasure came when something technical went wrong. Lights would go out, teapots shatter for no good reason . . . at times like these we felt perfectly free to improvise and guiltlessly enjoy ourselves with no text to follow.

This brings me to why we went to Electric Lady Studios, armed with several bottles of wine, just to see what happened if we talked with no prior ideas into two microphones. We had no preconceived attitudes or intentions. What emerged, on the whole was a shower of filth, with no socially redeeming or artistic value. We heard it back the next day and found it to be funny, but on the other hand we had no idea what to do with it. What we did was very practical, i.e. nothing. A few weeks later we decided to try out the same sort of rambling filth on a small audience. We did and they laughed. This time we did something; we sent a whole bunch of unedited tapes to a long-time friend of mine, Christopher Blackwell, head of Island records. He and his good lady also laughed and wondered what the hell to do with them.

The whole matter lapsed. Dudley and I went on tour round the States and forgot about the tapes in our relentless pursuit of dollars.

209

Christopher played them to various people in pop circles, most of whom laughed. On our tour we began to meet a number of Rock groups such as The Rolling Stones, The Who, Led Zeppelin etc, who all had 'pirate' copies of the tapes. They too found them funny. I got the cynical thought that if rock groups found something funny then probably people who like rock groups would find it funny too. Suddenly the thought of making money out of a few hours 'work' began to appeal. We left it all until we got back to Britain and, down at Island records, listened back to the two separate sessions, one without an audience, one with. To myself, Dudley and Christopher they still sounded very funny, and jointly (pardon the pun) we thought why not put them out as an LP?

All of us had certain fears. Dudley and I because we thought it might destroy our 'cuddly' family image and Christopher for legal reasons and the possibility that his normal distributors EMI would not distribute the record. In this he was right, but at the moment of writing we are number 12 in the LP charts, the highest to my knowledge that a comedy LP has ever reached. Smith's and Boots have lent their traditional support in banning the record from their shops, thus ensuring it some kind of notoriety, depriving themselves and their shareholders of income and increasing sales at other outlets.

In the few weeks that the album has been cut we have done a great deal of interviews. On the whole the music papers have been very favourable to the album, with its resolute single entendres. The only bad reaction we had is from the impermeable Upper Class (such as Emma Soames of the *Evening Standard*), who came out with lines such as 'How could two such witty satirists such as you RESORT to material such as this?' We have a simple reply. It's not resorting, it's just a part of us that has always been there and what's the harm in putting it out?

Over the course of the interviews we have gradually put together a composite of what Derek & Clive are: they are probably both mechanics, strongly Tory, like a drink, are embarrassed by women, like football and the whole world's gone [fucking] mad. Life ended for them with the Big Bopper. They don't like poufs or having to pay taxes when the country goes down the toilet. They've never heard of the *Tatler* but would prefer it to the *Socialist Worker*. On the other hand the *Socialist Worker* offered 'readies' instead of a cheque from the *Tatler* they'd probably settle for the untaxable cash. There are a lot of Derek and Clives about.

THE WORST JOB I EVER HAD
(*Derek & Clive (Live)*, 1976)

CLIVE: I'll tell you the worst job I ever had.

DEREK: What was that?

CLIVE: The worst job I ever had was with Jayne Mansfield. She's a fantastic bird – big tits, huge bum, and everything like that – but I had the terrible job of retrieving lobsters from her bum.

DEREK: Really? Bloody hell! That must have been a task.

CLIVE: It's quite a task because she had a big bum and they were big lobsters.

DEREK: I remember. She had a huge bum.

CLIVE: Well she had one, and presumably in the afterlife she still has one. Well I used to have to go round, of an evening, when Jayne was sleeping, or sort of comatose like, you know, just lying there. And I had to retrieve these lobsters from her arsehole.

DEREK: Yeah, well I remember she had a lot of trouble with lobsters up her arsehole, didn't she? Basically, she suffered from what was known in the medical trade as lobsters up the arsehole.

CLIVE: Well, this is what is said scientifically, you know. Lobsters up the bum – this was the scientific term for it. But in general terms, it was known as Lobstericimus Bumbecissimus. And it was my job every evening to go around to Jayne, who was a sweet girl – sweet, charming, shy, mysterious girl – and get these fucking lobsters out of her arsehole, which was so tricky, because she was a very sensitive woman. I used to go around there every evening, and these lobsters – you know, she used to go out bathing in Malibu. Which is worse, she used to go out bathing. And up went the lobsters. Boing! Straight up her arsehole.

DEREK: Well, I think she brought it on herself really, didn't she?

CLIVE: Not so much brought them on herself so much as encouraged them, by the flagrant display that she got up to.

DEREK: Well, I think she was a dirty tart.

CLIVE: No, no. Be fair. Be fair. You can call her a dirty cow, but let's face it – a lot of lobsters fancied her bum.

DEREK: Let's face it – I think it was a fifty-fifty arrangement.

CLIVE: The lobsters didn't say 'we have the upper hand.' Jayne didn't say 'we have the upper hand.'

DEREK: There was no feeling of domination.

CLIVE: No, it was a fifty-fifty thing.

DEREK: I think the lobsters got quite a nip out of it, and I think Jayne got a lot out of it.

CLIVE: Yeah, but it was my job to retrieve the lobsters from her bum after the event.

DEREK: What event?

CLIVE: Post hocta prompt.

DEREK: Post what?

CLIVE: Post hocta prompt.

DEREK: Oh yeah.

CLIVE: That's what it is in Latin.

DEREK: What?

CLIVE: Getting lobsters out of people's bums.

DEREK: Oh, post hocta prompt.

CLIVE: But she was a sweet girl and I wouldn't knock her.

DEREK: Well I gather you wouldn't, no.

CLIVE: No, I gather I wouldn't. But I tell you one thing Tony Newley said to me.

DEREK: What was that?

CLIVE: Who are you?

DEREK: Yeah? Just like that?

CLIVE: Just like that. And I thought that made Tony Newley a wonderful human being.

THIS BLOKE CAME UP TO ME
(*Derek & Clive (Live)*, 1976)

DEREK: I tell you the other day some bloke came up to me.

CLIVE: What? Tony Newley?

DEREK: No, no. I don't know who it was. And he said 'you cunt.' I said 'what?' He said 'you cunt.'

CLIVE: Yeah. And you replied 'you fucking cunt.'

DEREK: Well, not straight away. I said 'you cunt,' I said.

CLIVE: What did he come back with?

DEREK: He come back, he said 'you fucking cunt.'

CLIVE: You're joking. You said 'you fucking cunt'?

DEREK: Yeah, he said 'd'you call me a cunt, you fucking cunt?' I said 'you fucking cunt.'

CLIVE: I should hope so. You fucking cunt.

DEREK: I said 'you fucking cunt.' I said 'you fucking come here and call me a fucking cunt.'

CLIVE: I should say so.

DEREK: I said 'you cunt.' I said 'you fucking cunt.' I said 'who are you fucking calling cunt, cunt?'

CLIVE: Yeah? What did he say, cunt?

DEREK: He said 'you fucking cunt.'

CLIVE: You fucking cunt. Who are you to say to him that he was a fucking cunt?

DEREK: What do you fucking think? I was fucking defending my fucking self, wasn't I?

CLIVE: Well, no. He came up to you and called you a cunt. That's fair enough. He said 'you fucking cunt' and you said back to him 'you fucking fucking cunt.' Well, what do you expect him to say back apart from 'you fucking stupid fucking cunt?'

DEREK: Well, I don't expect nothing, do I?

CLIVE: No.

DEREK: But the cunt came back with 'you fucking cunt, cunt.'

CLIVE: Oh Christ.

DEREK: I said 'you cunt.' I said 'you calling me a fucking cunt?' I said 'you fucking cunt.'

CLIVE: Jesus Christ.

DEREK: I said 'you fucking cunt.' I said it like that.

CLIVE: You said it like that, did you? To him? Or was he gone by then?

DEREK: No, he fucking hit me.

CLIVE: He hit you, did he?

DEREK: Yeah, the fucking cunt.

CLIVE: Killed you dead, did he?

DEREK: He fucking hit me.

CLIVE: Yeah, well you can't blame him, can you?

DEREK: I said 'you rotter.' And he went off.

CLIVE: Did he?

DEREK: And he said 'you cunt' again.

CLIVE: Well, that's the only way to deal with them, isn't it?

DEREK: Yeah, well I showed him, didn't I?

CLIVE: Yeah, well you had to, didn't you? You had to stand up for what you stood for, didn't you? I mean, the only time I remember a similar occasion was I was at Spurs, Tottenham Hotspurs. I was watching a game against Arsenal. And this bloke came up to me and said 'hello.'

DEREK: Oh no.

CLIVE: And I thought 'Christ!' This bloke comes up to me. He says 'hello.'

DEREK: Provocative fucker.

CLIVE: Fucking provocative. I said 'what d'you mean – hello?' And d'you know what he came back with? He said 'I just meant "hello."' I says 'I can suss you out for a start. Here, get this in the bollocks for a start.' So I kicked him right in the balls, he fell to the floor. As he fell to the floor he said 'urgh.' I said 'don't you "urgh" me, mate.'

DEREK: Yeah. Like he comes in with 'hello' and then goes out with 'urgh.'

CLIVE: Yeah. I said 'don't you "urgh" me mate', and I kicked his fucking teeth in. But he went 'argh' and I said 'fucking hell.'

DEREK: This is fucking too much.

CLIVE: 'Don't you fucking "argh" me.' And I really kicked his ear in, you know. I bunged him right in the ear with the left boot. And do you know, he still had the audacity to come out with

'I'm dying.' Well, what could I say to that? I just walked away. I left the situation. I wasn't going to be put upon in that way.

DEREK: You weren't going to be dictated to, were you?

CLIVE: Well, no. Why should I be dictated to by some cunt who says 'urgh'?

DEREK: Yeah. Preceded with 'hello.'

CLIVE: 'Hello' was the worst thing. That was what got me going.

DEREK: Fucking cunt. What a cunt.

CLIVE: What a cunt, eh?

BLIND
(Derek & Clive (Live) 1976)

PETER: Ladies and gentlemen, all of us know, or at least realise, how terrible it must be to be blind. Deprived of sight, unable to read. This is perhaps the greatest loss to the blind person. I am blind, but I am able to read thanks to a wonderful new system known as broil. I'm sorry – I'll just feel that again.

COME AGAIN – SLEEVE NOTES
(1977)

Derek & Clive (Live) was the first genuinely philosophical album to sell more than 50 million copies. Inevitably superstardom brought problems to these two young men, whose only ambition was to run a quiet toilet. At first they invested their newfound wealth wisely. Derek installed high-class Swiss musical toilet rolls that went 'cuckoo' when pulled. Not to be outdone, Clive erected quadraphonic cisterns that played Wagner when flushed. The Gents at the British Trade Centre became the talk of New York. The Beautiful People flocked to 'The Ultimate Kazi'. As Clive put it so aptly, 'all the big nobs hang out here.' Peter Cook and Dudley Moore, who first discovered them in 1973, put a great deal of pressure on them to embark on a world tour. Staggering sums of money were offered. Derek and Clive resisted, although Derek did accept a commission to design a 'Nazi Kazi' for the National Front in Lewisham. They were also subjected to enormous pressure from fans and groupies. On one celebrated occasion in 1977 Clive was attacked by an 85-year-old woman who wanted him to sign his name on her thigh with Dayglo. Luckily his bodyguard Bruce Beame was on hand and calmed the hysterical woman by shoving her headfirst down a lavatory. 'That's when the fan really hit the shit,' was Clive's wry comment. Derek, always a sensitive soul, developed strange phobias. He locked himself in the toilet for weeks on end watching re-runs of *Emmerdale Farm*. He also had a morbid fear of germs and insisted on boiling his Peugeot before going for a drive. He also wanted to boil Clive, who rightly insisted that his mate should see a psychiatrist. Completely swathed in Bronco, Derek went to see Dr Fritz Leprechaun on Fifth Avenue. The consultation was a failure and the eminent doctor was found parboiled in his own fish tank. Cook and Moore finally persuaded the pair to do a six week tour of North Korea, where they have a huge cult following. Unfortunately, one of the huge cults followed them back to their hotel and beat the shit out of them. Clive then turned to the twilight world of drugs. It seemed harmless at first. Just the occasional snort of Harpic, but this escalated and he soon reached the stage that he couldn't reach the stage without massive injections of Fairy Snow and Jeyes Fluid. In October of 1977 they got on what they thought was a Laker flight to Washington and found themselves in Amsterdam. This album was recorded immediately after their arrival. Despite their personal problems, their inherent wisdom and decency shine through once again. Will they ever work together again? Can they resolve their artistic differences? Has stardom claimed two more victims? We may never know. Derek collapsed after the recording and Clive was last seen at a crematorium asking to be burnt alive and have his ashes scattered over Gracie Fields.

PETER COOK

JOAN CRAWFORD
(Derek & Clive – Come Again, 1977)

CLIVE: I had this work permit to be a window cleaner cum plumber, and I was down this house in Beverly Hills. You been there?

DEREK: No.

CLIVE: Just close to Beverly Sills, the opera singer.

DEREK: Yeah, right.

CLIVE: And got this window-cleaning job. Just went in a big house, you know, walked in there, a big fucking poof nigger butler.

DEREK: Yeah, right fucking cunt.

CLIVE: Fucking cunt, he said 'come this way, sir.' You know how they fucking speak. Can't even speak fucking English. So I said 'alright, where's the window, cunt?' He said 'you just walked through it.' He was quite right. There was fucking glass all up my fucking body. Anyway, I said 'well, I can't clean it because I broke it.' And he said 'there are other windows in this house.' So I was just cleaning the window. I've got all of the fluids out, you know. And I look round, and I saw somebody lying on a bed. I thought 'that's a fucking familiar face.' And it was Joan Crawford.

DEREK: Gawd. Fucking hell.

CLIVE: JC, as she was known to her friends.

DEREK: Right.

CLIVE: And I'm cleaning the window, and this fucking wind blew up, tropical storm invaded the bedroom, and I was swept away by this huge gust of wind, straight up her fucking cunt.

DEREK: Oh, no.

CLIVE: Yeah. I went straight through the nylon underwear, tore through the diaphragm she was wearing, and then there was no exit. One end was rubber, and up the other end, the biggest fucking disaster area I've ever fucking seen.

DEREK: Really?

CLIVE: Fuck me. You've heard of the Bermuda Triangle?

DEREK: Yeah.

CLIVE: Well this was worse. Up Joan Crawford's cunt there are fucking fleets of ships, light aircraft.

DEREK: Hamburger stands.

CLIVE: Hamburger stands, but no fucking hamburgers. Just the fucking stands. The only single of piece of entertainment is one disco.

DEREK: They've got a disco in there?

CLIVE: They've got a disco there.

DEREK: Lovely.

CLIVE: In a cruise ship, one of those cruising ships, you know. And they've got a pool there. They've got a pool in there, and there's no water up Joan Crawford at all, so they've filled it full of shit. They have this fucking pool full of shit, and they go up there, have a bathe in the shit, and then go down the disco all covered in turds.

DEREK: Well, you know I had a terrible experience with Joan.

CLIVE: What, Crawfie?

DEREK: Yeah, Crawfie.

CLIVE: The Queen Mother's nanny?

DEREK: Yeah. After you'd told me about Joan's cunt, of course I was very curious and I thought 'well, I've got to go and have a look at this, mate.' I went up there and frankly, I was appalled.

CLIVE: What, by the state of her cunt?

DEREK: The people up there, wandering about, lost. It was pathetic. Anyway, to cut a long story short, I got a bit lost myself, you know. And of course, her arsehole was completely blocked with Spanish revolutionaries.

CLIVE: Are they still there?

DEREK: Still there.

CLIVE: That's the fucking trouble, because they can't speak a word of fucking Belgian.

DEREK: And I thought 'well fuck this for a lark. I'm going to go North.'

CLIVE: Did you get up to her tits? They're frozen over. Worst time of the year.

DEREK: Well, I thought to myself 'I'll make my way through the gall bladder, and then tickle her larynx, or something round there, and she can sick me up.' I went into the gall bladder, I stepped through, I fucking fell. Of course, she'd had it fucking removed.

CLIVE: What? Her gall bladder?

DEREK: Her gall bladder wasn't there!

CLIVE: Well, there's no fucking signs on her saying her gall bladder's removed. Fucking hell. There should be a fucking sign up there 'danger – no fucking gall bladder.' Fucking hell.

DEREK: Anyway, to cut a long story short, I got in the stomach, I got in a rather dodgy way – I got in by osmosis. And I went in there, I kicked up a fucking storm in there. I ran around all the walls, kicking the shit out of them, Anyway, I stuck a pencil up her epiglottis, and in a fucking trice I came flying up with all this Chinese takeaway food that she'd just had.

CLIVE: Oh, shit.

DEREK: No, sick.

CLIVE: Sorry.

DEREK: And I come flying out and fuck me, out of the frying pan into the fire, I landed straight in the fucking toilet, because she was leaning over the toilet.

CLIVE: That's fucking Hollywood, innit?

HORSE RACING
(*Derek & Clive – Ad Nauseam*, 1979)

DUDLEY: Good afternoon and welcome to racing at Newmarket. They're about to go into the stalls for the three thirty, so over to you, Peter.

PETER: Thank you. Yes, the seven runners for this Durex handicap over six furlongs just begin to load up. That's The Poof, very much on his toes, and beautifully turned out. He really looked a picture in the paddock. Just coming into our picture is Vagina. Vagina's one of the fillies in the race. She's very good speed. The overnight rain will have helped her. She likes it a bit soft underfoot. That's The Wanker, going into the stalls. A steady performer, The Wanker, but he tends to be a bit one-paced. Just going in is Buttocks. Buttocks, a big colt, blinkered for the first time. And there's our favourite, The Prick. I think he would have preferred slightly firmer going. And just going in is the outsider of the field, the seven-year-old Arsehole. Arsehole by Shit out of Bumhole. He's been tailed off on his last three outings – rather disappointing horse, this. And one of the last to go in is Big Tits, who's carrying the top weight. Steady performer, but I think that ten-pound penalty will be a little too much for her this afternoon. She's safely in. Oh dear, The Prick is rearing up. He tends to get excited – a very excitable horse. I remember he had to be withdrawn at Lingfield. Yes, they're going to put the hood on him. They're very good, the handlers here at Newmarket. And now a late show of betting.

DUDLEY: Thank you, Peter. The Prick has hardened half a point to eleven to eight, Vagina is threes, The Poof and Buttocks both nine to two, there's been some late money for Big Tits, who's coming to join The Wanker on eight to one, and Arsehole is sixty-six to one.

PETER: As expected, Arsehole is the sixty-six to one complete outsider. And they're all in, they're under starter's orders, and they're off! Big Tits got a flyer and is the first to show. Arsehole was slowly away, and as they settle down, it's Big Tits from Vagina with The Prick tucked in behind these two, then comes the blinkered Buttocks, being pressed by The Poof, going steadily behind these five is The Wanker, and trailing the field Arsehole. And as they start to climb the hill, it's Vagina, who just shows clear of Buttocks, The Prick is close up third, nothing between these three, Big Tits is hanging slightly to the left, tucked in behind is The Poof, still trailing the field is Arsehole, there is The Poof again, making a challenge, with Arsehole under pressure, but finding nothing. And as they race to the line, it's Vagina being pressed by The Prick, with The Poof making rapid progress, trying to squeeze in between Buttocks and the rail. The Prick and Vagina, nothing between these two. And The Wanker's coming with a late run, The Wanker is coming with a late run, and Big Tits has dropped out of it altogether. And with a hundred yards to go, it's The Prick and Vagina drawing clear, The Prick and Vagina, it must be a photo, I can't separate them, but I think The Poof takes third from The Wanker and still to finish is the tiring Arsehole. Well, one hell of a race. The Prick may just have got up in the last strides, but I wouldn't like to put my money on it.

DUDLEY: And now it's back to Topless Darts at Roehampton.

THE CRITICS
(Derek & Clive – Ad Nauseam, 1979)

PETER: What one has to wonder is why artists of the calibre of Cook and Moore should resort to material which basically could be done by . . .

DUDLEY: By me.

PETER: By you, yes. I mean, I don't know if you saw the play the other night on television, *No Man's Land* by Harold Pinter. Now, Pinter uses these words, these, I suppose to the general public shocking words, but he uses them to effect.

DUDLEY: Yes, to punctuate.

PETER: He punctuates his dialogue, and when he uses the word 'arsehole,' it means something.

DUDLEY: Exactly.

PETER: And prick.

DUDLEY: Yes.

PETER: And cunt.

DUDLEY: Yes.

PETER: Take on this sort of metaphysical punctuation.

DUDLEY: They become almost sounds.

PETER: Which I find absolutely delightful. Especially Gielgud and Richardson, who are so absolutely terrific.

DUDLEY: Yes, I mean arsehole in Richardson's mouth, it comes out as . . .

PETER: Pure gold.

DUDLEY: Pure gold.

PETER: But when Cook and Moore, I mean – it's not the same. I mean, prick in the hands of Pinter is, as you say, a punctuation point.

DUDLEY: An epithet.

PETER: A marvellous moment, the end of an extremely witty line, whereas a prick or a cunt in the hands of Cook and Moore, it's just a gratuitous prick or cunt.

DUDLEY: One feels it's being abused in some way.

PETER: It is being abused, and I myself, I cannot see why in the civilised world it is necessary for people with a certain amount of understanding, who've been to university, to use the word prick or fuck or cunt. I mean, I never have the slightest urge to use the word fuck. Do you? Do you ever say fuck?

DUDLEY: I never say fuck.

PETER: No, I mean why the fuck should I say fuck. I've got no reason for saying fuck.

DUDLEY: Exactly. I'd rather say carpet than fuck.

PETER: There's no fucking reason to say fuck.

DUDLEY: Exactly. Who the fuck cares about fuck?

PETER: It's absolutely fucking stupid to say fuck.

DUDLEY: Exactly.

PETER: What could be more stupid than going round the whole time and saying fuck and cunt and prick and arsehole, tit and bum and shit? It's stupid. I mean, I'm not going to go 'fucking hell, shit, tit, bum, arsehole,' because I don't need to.

DUDLEY: Of course you're not going to.

PETER: What is the point? What is the point of saying 'fuck, shit, tit, bum, arsehole, cunt, arsehole, tit, tit, tit, cut your tits off, fuck, tit, bum, shit.' No, there is absolutely no point in saying 'fuck, tit, shit, bum, arsehole, cunt, prick, fuck, cock, penis, cunt, shit, fuck, prick, cunt, arsehole, tit, bumhole, shit, arsehole, bum, tit, bumhole, cunt, shit.' There is absolutely no point whatsoever. There is no point whatsoever in using these stupid words for shock effect.

DUDLEY: Arsehole, bum, orifice, cunt, shove it up your arse, bum, cunt, arse. Who the fuck wants to say shit arse cunt, tear your tits off, stuff your bollocks up your arse?

PETER: And there I'm afraid we have to leave our critics' forum. I will be here, together with Sir George Makepiece – Sir George Makepiece and I will be here again for critics' choice at the same time next Sunday at six o'clock.

DUDLEY: Put your foreskin over your head, fart up your bum.

PETER: I mean, when I want to say fuck, I don't want to say radiator.

DUDLEY: I don't want to say all of that?

PETER: I don't want to say radiator.

DUDLEY: Do I want to say all of the things that I've just said?

PETER: Do you want to say radiator?

DUDLEY: No I fucking don't. I do not want to say all of the things that I have just fucking said.

Chapter Nine
Monday Morning Feeling

Peter Cook had the perfect qualifications for a national newspaper columnist. He knew lots of famous people, but wasn't at all in awe of them. He had a healthy disrespect for self-important celebrities, but he was amused by them, all the same. He wasn't afraid to speak his mind – about himself, or other people. But you could never predict what he'd say about anything – and maybe until he'd said it, nor could he. He had opinions, but he wasn't opinionated, and he understood the difference. He was candid and irreverent, and he had a columnist's knack of spotting an incongruous connection between two completely separate events or issues, linking a supposedly serious news item to something trivial or absurd. In 1977, the *Daily Mail* signed him up to write his own page every Monday, called 'Peter Cook's Monday Morning Feeling'. From the very first column, it felt like the natural thing for him to do. Columnists need things to write about. They don't need scoops, but they need stories. Most of them depend, at least in part, on scavenging other people's stories, from other papers. Journeymen columnists just regurgitate them, but like a journalistic silkworm,

Cook transformed the tales he devoured.

A lot of columnists, you can't help feeling, don't really feel like journalists. They'd rather be novelists. They feel the other papers, even the other bits of their own papers, are a bit beneath them. Not Peter Cook. You wouldn't call Cook a journalist, but he was far more of a journalist than a novelist. Cook loved newspapers, and he consumed them with the same compulsion that he smoked his sixty cigarettes a day. He read every paper, every day, 'starting with the *Sun*.' And he always stuck up for *Private Eye*, even though some of his celebrity friends despised it.

Cook's addictive appetite for newsprint gave him a vast fund of stories, from editorials in serious broadsheets via front-page splashes in national tabloids to bizarre fillers buried in back issues of obscure specialist magazines. 'His jokes, like John Bird's were fuelled by an immense amount of reading,' confirmed his *Private Eye* writing partner John Wells. 'He read all the newspapers and political weeklies and, unlike John Bird, allowed his researches to carry him into *Rubberwear News*, the *Budgerigar Fancier* and *Frilly Knickers*. He took a particular delight in misprints, subeditors' clichés and Fleet Street journalese.'[1]

Sadly, Peter terminated this column on his fortieth birthday, after less than a year on the job. This was a shame, since the best columns tend to improve with age, and with its combination of personal revelations and impertinent jokes about public figures, 'Monday Morning Feeling' found its feet virtually straight away. Of course, there were a few duds, as there always are in every column, but at its best it bears comparison with Auberon Waugh's brilliant diary in *Private Eye*. Waugh's diary filled two books, but it ran for fourteen years. If Cook's 'Monday Morning Feeling' had run for half that time, it might have made an entire volume, rather than a single chapter.

∿

This column is here on a strictly trial basis for four weeks. If it disappears as suddenly and mysteriously as it has arrived, there will be three possible explanations:

That it has been found to be insufferably tedious by all and sundry;

That I have found the job too time consuming and ill rewarded;

(and most likely) That there has been a massive walkout by other writers on the paper to protest against the 'unfair competition' of the sustained brilliance of my contributions.

There are already signs of this. I telephoned the Features Editor asking him to select a photograph of me looking 'Byronic'. He claims that it was a bad line and thought he'd heard me say 'moronic'.

CAN ENOCH SAVE US FROM THE GIANT BLANCMANGE?

Maureen Colquhoun, MP, thinks the Labour Party should sometimes listen to Enoch Powell.[1] What about the Tories? Winston Churchill (very junior), MP, dismisses him as 'a fading politician'. His better-known grandfather made the same mistake of ignoring Mr Powell's prophecies. In 1948, armed with maps and statistics, young Enoch carefully explained the grand strategy to his leader. As soon as he had left the room, Churchill rang up his research department and inquired: 'Who was that young madman who has been telling me how many divisions I'll need to reconquer India?'

But Mr Powell was not a 'madman': he was, and is, a clairvoyant. Twenty-five years before the event he, and only he, foresaw that Indira Gandhi[2] (then a lissom, seemingly innocent 31 year old country girl) would one day establish a quasi dictatorship. If Mr Powell predicts that London will be attacked by a giant blancmange in 1990, I will immediately prepare myself for the event. And what about India? Is it now too late? I pray not.

What a stirring sight it would be – Brigadier Powell in full hunting pink, Corporal Bernard Levin[3] at his side, leading his cavalry in triumph through the plains of Nepal and on to capture Delhi. Democracy restored at a stroke. A hopeless dream? Perhaps – but think of the movie rights.

BELT UP, GERTRUDE!

I am puzzled by Mrs Gertrude Hatton, of Birmingham. She is complaining about her next-door neighbour, Miss Betteena Vibark, a qualified therapeutic sadist with a well equipped Torture Chamber. This contains a cage, a rack, a pillory, numerous whips, belts, manacles and, as an extra luxury, a gas mask. It is here that she eases her clients' inner tensions by suspending them from the ceiling and beating them till the blood flows.

Mrs Hatton claims that many of Miss Vibark's patients knock on her door by mistake. Can't she see the advantage of this situation? Miss Vibark's clientele are undoubtedly a representative cross-section of society. Instead of spurning them abruptly, she should invite them in, inform them 'You are My SLAVE!' and order them to obey her every whim.

If the man turns out to be an accountant, his first task would be to make out her VAT returns, lawyers could pen threatening letters about her defective cooker, grocers could run down the road to supply her with essential foodstuffs, and so on. Even unskilled workers could tidy up the house and weed the garden. Only when they have made themselves useful in some way, should she claim her £10 'Introduction Fee' and refer them next door to Miss Vibark.

THIS IS MY PRESENT WIFE

SCHMIDTBIT

'Slidie' Jim Callaghan[4] told Herr Schmidt[5] that television's endless reshowings of old war films should in no way be interpreted as being 'anti-German'. It was only, he assured the Chancellor, that young people today are keenly interested in 'History' (for an impartial account of World War Two, may I recommend 'How We Bashed the Boche' by Professor John Mills). His visitor was too polite to reply that, with 'Slidie' in charge of the present and near future, it was small wonder that we looked back with affection to the relative euphoria of wartime.

HAIR APPARENT

Since nobody else has noticed it, I would like to send my belated congratulations to Reginald Bosanquet[6] for his touching tribute to Lord Avon on 'News at Ten'. It was a moving and appropriate gesture to wear his wig at half-mast. I only question his apparent decision to take part in a private wake before the broadcast, but I am sure he knows best.

EQUITABLE LIFE

My own union, Equity, are an odd lot. My first contact with them was in 1959 when they asked me to change my name to avoid confusion with Peter Coke, who played Paul Temple on the radio. I dutifully gave them two suggestions – Wardrobe Gruber and Sting Thundercok. They seemed to think I was being frivolous, and after rejecting the excellent stage name of Lord Hymie Poke they gave up and allowed me to retain my own rather boring title. I assured them that I would not go round boasting that I was Paul Temple.

Daily Mail, 31 January 1977

DECLARING WAUGH ON ALL OF US

I couldn't agree more with Auberon Waugh on the decline of British manners. I also subscribe to Sloan Wilson's advice that the best way to prevent your children drinking is to drink to excess yourself. I would take this theory further and suggest that one's offspring are almost certain to grow up to be complete opposites of oneself.

Auberon lends credence to this notion. His father was a drunken, boorish part-time pederast;[7] inevitably Auberon is an abstemious, courteous and devout heterosexual. This faces young Mr Waugh with an agonising choice. Should he, for the sake of his young ones, force himself into unwanted drinking bouts and simulated outburst of vile temper? Or would it be better to remain his natural, modest, gentlemanly self, knowing that his children are likely to develop into aggressive, loutish hooligans. I hope he choose the second option. The worst that could happen is that a new generation of Waughs would dominate Parliament, Industry or the TUC.

£5 SAYS HE CAN'T

I think most people know by now that Michael Parkinson hails from Barnsley. I will donate £5 to any charity (unconnected with Barnsley) for every 'Parkinson' programme that omits the word 'Barnsley'. I know it will be hard, Michael, but it CAN be done. Try it with your next guest, Mort Sahl. He's one of those rare people who have probably never heard of Barnsley.

Daily Mail, 7 February 1977

LEGAL LOTTERY

I won £500 last week on a bet I would have been pleased to lose. It was over the outcome of the latest round in the litigation between *Private*

Eye and Sir James Goldsmith.[8] I correctly forecast that two judges would come down against the *Eye*, while one would support it.

My wager was based on observing the behaviour of the three judges during the hearing. In my inexpert view Lord Denning's[9] intervention seemed generally favourable to the *Eye*'s case, while Scarman's[10] and Bridges' did not. Ladbrokes have quoted odds on the eventual result of the criminal libel action brought by Sir James against *Private Eye*. Now judges are as fallible as any other profession and subject to the same temptations. This could lead to some bizarre, hypothetical conversations.

'Ladbrokes?'

'Yes, sir?'

'I'd like £50 on Villa for the Cup.'

'Is that all, sir?'

'What are the odds on the Strangler Muldoon murder case?'

'Acquittal is five million to one.'

'And how do they bet on Justice Quistnargling burning his wig, juggling with six hardboiled eggs and directing the jury to find themselves guilty of treason?'

'I'll have to get through to the Special Bets Department on that, sir. Can you hold on?'

'Yes, I thought I might have a little fun money on that . . .'

I was wondering last week where Sir James pays his taxes. I am informed that if he spends more than ninety days a year in the UK he must be liable here. Unless, that is, he has some special dispensation from the Inland Revenue.

DUD OR ALIVE

When our LP *Derek & Clive (Live)* was released, my minute seaweed-eating partner had one irrational fear. Because of one track that involved the late Jayne Mansfield,[11] her bum and lobsters, he was terrified of being duffed up by Mickey Hargitay, Jayne's muscular ex husband. I talked to Dudley yesterday. He has just rented a house in Los Angeles for six months. Only after he had moved in did he discover the identity of his next-door neighbour. Yep. Mickey Hargitay.

AH'M IN CHARGE

I have the solution to the Government's dilemma over President Amin's[12] visit to Britain for the Commonwealth Conference. For a token payment (say a peerage), I will arrange for Idi to be picked up at Heathrow and treated with the respect such a 'Third World' leader deserves.

My personal chauffeur Brigadier Moses (Rtd) will collect the President from the airport and take him on a sightseeing tour of famous cemeteries. The brigadier has assured me that he will make certain that his trusty 12-bore rifle does not go off accidentally. Furthermore, if God forbid, any mishap did occur, he has an arrangement with a Chinese Takeaway Crematorium with instant autopsy facilities and a variety of suitable urns.

Daily Mail, 28 February 1977

IF HYPNOSIS CAN'T CURE ME, WHAT CHANCE DOES PREACHING STAND?

According to Christian Barnard, the type of man least likely to suffer a heart attack is 'an effeminate municipal worker who is completely lacking in physical and mental alertness and is without drive, ambition or competitive spirit.' Is this a fair description of our Minister of Health David Ennals?

If it is, and Barnard is correct, this ghastly man is likely to be with us for a long time, especially if he follows another of the doctor's recommendations, namely 'prophylactic castration'. His latest priggish initiative against smoking is a transparent ploy to divert attention from his failure to do anything to prevent the imminent collapse of the National Health Service.

I and nineteen million other addicts will doubtless continue to cough up further billions of pounds in revenue when the tax on cigarettes is raised again. At the moment we only pay for about one third of the cost of the Health Service. I have tried many 'cures', including hypnosis, strange filtering devices and good, old-fashioned will power. All, alas, have failed except for brief periods.

One way of dissuading me that I know won't work is PREACHING at me. So please save the tax payers' money and scrap those costly anti-smoking commercials. If I ever do manage to quit I'll keep lots of ashtrays in the house and were I to become teetotal there'd still be plenty of booze for the visitors. Self-righteousness is one of the many things I can't stand.

Daily Mail, 14 March 1977

SEPARATE TAX TABLES

With the cost of an armchair divorce coming down to 15 quid, I have been mulling over an old idea. I got married at about the same time as Healey[13] became Chancellor. Since then, Judy and I have been wondering about the financial benefits of divorce or separation. The advantage, of course, being that our incomes would be taxed individually. But would we have to live separately?

I read that John Cleese was 'separated' from his wife Connie Booth but was staying in the same house. I don't know how this works. Does the Inland Revenue make random spot checks to see that they are genuinely 'separated'? If they are caught passing each other in a corridor, does that make them 'married' again?

The whole idea has a certain appeal. We could arrange clandestine romantic meetings in various parts of the house, always aware that an Inland Revenue detector van might be lurking outside to monitor illicit 'togetherness'. If we were caught in bed I would argue that we were lying there for the sole purpose of discussing the division of property. In this case, which part of the bed was mine.

WHAT A MAN
DOES IN PRIVATE
IS HIS OWN AFFAIR
BUT THAT'S THE BIT
THAT INTERESTS ME

PC

I don't think we shall go ahead with this plan. I have no wish to place an extra burden on the tax collectors. These dedicated men and women are grossly overworked and underpaid. I fear that their only effective recourse is immediate STRIKE ACTION. It might be a long struggle lasting months, maybe years. But their cause is just and they would have the nation united behind them.

POOLS LOSER

I told you some weeks ago about my minute partner's fear of meeting his next-door neighbour Mickey Hargitay. He has so far avoided it and there has been no confrontation about the late Jayne Mansfield, lobsters and her bum. There is however a bizarre new development. Dudley has discovered that the muscular young man who cleans his pool is Hargitay's son. The immaculate pool gleams invitingly but Dudley daren't use it. I think I'll send Mickey a copy of *Derek & Clive*. I reckon he'll like it. If he doesn't the man has no sense of humour and I'll have no partner.

Daily Mail, 4 April 1977

SAINTS ALIVE

I'm intrigued by the plan to beatify the reformed Irish drunk Matt Talbot. People who preach to me about the evils of drink tend to drive me to it. I also have a vague mistrust of chaps who wrap chains around their bodies as a sign of repentance; but I dare say he was a worthy fellow and deserves to be canonised. I wonder if there's any chance of my being made a saint if I give up smoking. It would certainly be an inducement, but only if I was to get the award during my lifetime. I have no wish for a sainthood when I'm six feet under.

The Church would do well to institute an order of Life Saints along the lines of the House of Lords. Since Harold Wilson's[14] Honours List most of us have lost any interest in being seen in that company. A House of Saints would boost churchgoing enormously. I'm quite willing to design it for no fee at all. The magnificent building would include a brothel, a casino and several bars none of which would be open to members. These facilities would be solely for the use of visiting politicians, businessmen, journalists and tourists. We Saints would sit quietly on Spartan wooden chairs reading Lord Longford's[15] *Humility*.

DIVINELY DRUNK

One explanation of the Universe that has been little probed by theologians is that God is a benign drunk and that the world is His Hangover. If we were to regard the Creation as the result of a cosmic binge everything would fall neatly into place. I believe He meant very well and still does. When He wakes up and surveys the mess He resolves to straighten it out at once.

The trouble is that He always has 'a little nip' to steady Himself and so the chaos continues. I know this is blasphemy and please don't send me pamphlets. The God I'm in touch with has a sense of humour and even tolerates bad jokes. When I die I hope to go like WC Fields, reading the Bible and 'looking for loopholes'.

NINE MONTH WONDER

How sensible of Princess Anne to decide on having a Scorpio. I've only met the lady once. It was at a charity TV do a few months back. She passed gracefully down the line and paused briefly in front of me looking understandably baffled. After a few moments silence I decided to break the ice and said: 'My name is Stewart Granger and this is Mickey Rooney.' She smiled and quipped 'you're not.'

As you know, I am an expert 'teeth reader.' (Feb 28) One glimpse was enough to foresee her destiny. I should have plucked up the courage there and then and told her that she would produce an heir on the 17th of November. The happy child will share its birthday with me and Auberon Waugh.

My daughters heard the news on the car radio. Lucy (12) asked me if I thought it would be a boy or a girl, to which I replied wittily: 'Yes, I don't think it will be a rotary lawn mower although she has been seen out with one.' Daisy (11) immediately composed a brief but suitable poem:

The happy event saw
The birth of a centaur.

Eat your heart out Sir John Betjeman.[16]

Daily Mail, 11 April 1977

RICHARD NIXON

A gentleman from *Time* magazine rang me last Friday to get some quotes about David Frost. I imagine they'll print the mildly knocking and unoriginal remarks I made such as : 'As a comedian, he's a good interviewer.' I fear they will omit my main reason for thinking that Frostie is on occasions too 'soft' with his subjects. 'This 'softness' comes from David's unassailable 'niceness'. He really LIKES most of his guests, and Nixon[17] will be no exception.

To ask David to be 'tougher' is like asking Val Doonican to be more biting and satirical. The Frosticle and Nixon have a lot in common. They both refuse to go away and be written off (this, incidentally, is meant as a compliment to David, as I remain a firm admirer of the President in exile). Something went out of my life when Nixon dramatically told the Press that they would not have Richard Nixon to kick around any more. Luckily he changed his mind and duly returned to be kicked around in the prescribed manner.

Something tells me that Richard Nixon will be back in some form of public life unless he is granted God's merciful gift of death. Even then, there will be no guarantee that a knowledgeable apparition will not haunt the White House, possibly in the guise of an angel bearing prophecies to the God-struck Jimmy Carter. If Thursday's first instalment reveals absolutely nothing we don't know already, I shall be delighted. Nixon and Frostie should remain exactly as they are: great mates in approximately the same field of endeavour – politics and show business.

Daily Mail, 2 May 1977

COMEBACK

My prediction that Richard Nixon would be back in some form of public office looks like coming true: the news came from his own mouth. He told David Frost and the viewing millions that there was absolutely no possibility of him ever serving his country again (implying that at some time he had actually served his country).

This is just Nixon's way of saying he will return and I notice that Carter[18] has already hinted that he might consult the former President over such matters as China. The pre-fight publicity had promised the sight of a beaten, stuttering, humiliated Nixon destroyed before our very eyes by the ruthless questioning of the Frosticle. In fact at the end of a lot of the Same Old Nixon looking a bit younger, it was David who was left looking pale and drawn. I hope not overdrawn as I read that Sir James Goldsmith invested in this dubious endeavour.

BOTTOMS UP

Not unsurprisingly, Barbara Windsor's bottom crept into Russell Harty's show. She had, after all, won the 'Bottom of the Year' award. What must have baffled millions of viewers was Russell asking her if she had ever seen her own bottom. There followed a discussion in which Russell seemed most evasive about whether he'd ever seen his own bottom at all.

This must be cleared up at once. If he hasn't seen his own bottom it's high time he did. How can he expect to be networked when there are doubts about his bottom? The public have the right to know.

Daily Mail, 9 May 1977

HOW I AVOIDED SUCCESS

I do feel for Peter Jay.[19] It is very difficult to be the most beautiful, brilliant, able, gifted, tall and huggable figure of your generation. I have been through the whole thing myself. Revered and adored by all at Cambridge, I popped over once to check the opposition at Oxford. There I found dear Peter, President of the Union, surrounded by gorgeous men, women and animals destined for unavoidable 'Success'.

He compared favourably, I thought, with our own President of the Union, Christopher Tugendhat, widely believed at the time to be the most boring man in the world and similarly doomed to public prominence. As you know, he is currently earning £40,000 a year in Brussels as Britain's resident Butter Mountain. I resolved there and then to avoid 'Success' if humanly possible. This glittering generation which includes myself, Dr Owen,[20] Peter Jay, Melvyn Bragg,[21] David Frost and Jeffrey Archer[22] is now supposed to provide a 'refreshing new image' for Britain. This is a little hard on us as we are far more 'fuddy duddy' than the vivacious Sir Peter Ramsbotham who entertained me so magnificently two years ago on my wedding anniversary.

I fear Jay is far too old for the job in Washington. I refuse to believe that President Carter is 52 as has been put about by the media. He is not a day over 19 and is from a different planet. His arrival on Earth was predicted in John Wyndham's novel *The Midwich Cuckoos* in which smiling humanoids from outer space took over a village.

Regrettable though it is, Peter's posting was inevitable. It was written in his teeth. Compare his smile to Jimmy Carter's and you will see that they were destined for one another. As for myself, I shall try and remain 'unsuccessful'. I could be fighting a losing battle.

Daily Mail, 16 May 1977

SQUARE ONE

To no one's astonishment, inflation is back to 17½%, exactly where it was a year ago. There are encouraging signs that the good men and women from the Inland Revenue may take strike action. Perhaps with Peter Jay safely in Washington, his father-in-law[23] will adopt the policies that Jay has put forward over the years in *The Times*,[24] namely that governments, like individuals, should not spend more than they have. But this is a complicated thought and may take several years to filter through the agile mind of Wily Jim. Mrs Thatcher will have to do something extremely foolish – for example, assault the Queen Mother – to lose the next election.

DUD LIVES

My minute partner, Dudley Moore, made a rare public appearance last night at a 'Benefit'. He is living a Garbo like existence these days. Arriving in London, he hid himself in a white Rolls-Royce and then sought further solitude at Tramp.

OVER MANNING

For some obscure reason, possibly his wife, that fat heap of lard Bernard Manning made a misguided attempt to become an 'all round entertainer' on ITV last week. He is extremely good at being nasty and should abandon all hopes of becoming lovable. He is far more successful as himself.

Daily Mail, 23 May 1977

IN HIS DEPTH

Meanwhile, America's first Martian President has spent nine hours under water in a submarine, presumably looking for Atlantis in the Bermuda Triangle. Unlike mere Earthlings, Carter realises that the sea is also his constituency. I look forward to hearing his views on the morality or immorality of sharks. Is he for or against them or does he want to meet them halfway? Isn't it time that our own Prime Minister went sub aquatic? A year under water for Jim would be a tremendous boost for Britain's image.

BUM RAP

Not unnaturally, Russell Harty devised an enormous conspiracy to prevent the truth about his bottom coming out. To disconcert me, the car that was to pick me up from Hampstead at 4pm was sent to Acton.

When I finally arrived half an hour late, I was whisked straight on camera without make-up (Russell had obviously spent hours on his). When grilled about whether he had ever seen his own bottom he produced a blatantly fraudulent photograph. All this proves is that now Russell has seen a photograph of somebody else's bottom. As this was his last show, we may have to wait until September to get anywhere near the truth.

As expected, he inflicted massive cuts (I took the precaution of recording the entire interview). Among other things, viewers were deprived of my tips on how to get Raquel Welch[25] out to dinner and why she won't appear on his show, namely, 'She is a very shy, vulnerable girl, Russell, and she hates your guts.' Never mind. I'm used to censorship.

I should warn any one-legged people who might be invited to Russell's show that the lavatory is ill equipped for them. It can be flushed only by standing on one leg and pressing a pedal on the floor with the other. This is quite hard for two-legged people and is all part of Russell's determination to keep his guests off balance.

WISE MEN

When something controversial occurs, it is often suggested that things be looked into by one, two, three or five 'wise men' or experts. Experts are the last people to come up with the solution to anything. It would be far better to set up a team of five old idiots to probe matters.

It heartens me, therefore, that Sir Harold Wilson is looking into what's wrong with the British film industry. What's wrong is that it is scarcely financially worthwhile to make films in this country, because of our tax laws.

Talking about his new role, Sir Harold said he had scarcely seen a film for 30 years but had remained awake during *The Omen*, the movie about devilish Damien, the male counterpart of Amy Carter. Sir Harold also told us he had an ability to go to sleep at any given moment. At last the Wilson years are explained.

For readers who do not share his happy knack, I have found that a very good way of nodding off is to listen to tape recordings of Sir Harold's speeches. They have a strange rhythmic, repetitive quality and recurring themes which will lull the most confirmed insomniac into a deep slumber.

BLAME THE BEEB

Dear Mrs Whitehouse[26] says: 'If anyone were to ask who above all was responsible for the moral collapse which characterises the 60s and 70s I would unhesitatingly name Sir Hugh Carleton Green[27] (late of the BBC).' Her new book holds the media responsible for our present state. Quite right too. Has Mary seen the Muppets? The sensible Finns think they are too violent. The sight of Fozzie Bear being beaten over the head with a mallet while singing 'Lady of Spain' drove Judy and me to acts of mindless destruction.

ROYAL TV

Critics complain about the quality of television's numerous Royal Galas. The truth is that many performers are reluctant to appear for nothing and do new material. Unless you are terribly anxious to meet the Queen there is really no point in them at all. This is unfair on the Queen, unfair on the performers and also on the viewers. Much more entertaining would be a Royal Gala Performance in which we the viewers saw the Queen playing Scrabble at home.

Daily Mail, 30 May 1977

GORBALS AND BANGLES

I am glad in a way that Scotland beat England at Wembley.[28] For three days London had been overrun by drunken Bay City Rollers. If they had lost I fear little of this city would have remained standing. As it is, they seem to be content with a few goal posts and some turf.

I know their feelings exactly. It is very difficult to come to London and not be envious. Like New York in America, it sends every other part of the country into paroxysms of resentment. But on their overhung journey home they should remember that they are ruled by a commodity far more valuable than North Sea Oil. The Queen has been running for 25 years, and she and her family must provide the biggest 'invisible export' that we have. When the oil runs dry in ten years, let's hope that there is still a Royal Family to make up for the loss of revenue.

PETER PANNED

My less talented comtemporary, Peter Jaybotham (our Ambassador in Washington), has put it about that he will not accept the traditional knighthood. He described it to friends as 'totally inappropriate'.

I too would have put it about that it would be totally inappropriate for me, but mainly on the grounds of the company into which I would be thrust. So let me now spare the Queen any needless paperwork. Showing enormous taste, she has mentioned Dudley, myself and Kojak as being her favourite television performers. But this is no reason to waste her time offering me an honour which I would not accept.

NETWORK

ABC Television News, who pay their lady newscaster Barbara Walters a million dollars a year, are over here to cover the Jubilee. Understandably, they approached Dudley and myself to represent Britain at its finest.

It was great fun working with network censorship. For example, it was all right to say that you could buy inflatable life-size Queens who wave their left arms when you let air out of their legs. It was also fine to talk about souvenir tights with the Queen on one leg, Prince Philip on the other, and a corgi somewhere else. But they drew the line at our joke allegation that in his pre-photographic days, Tony Armstrong-Jones[29] was an all-in wrestler known as Tony Strongarm-Jones, 'The Man in the Iron Mask'.

I marvel at the way these decisions are made. In the course of filming at Madam Tussaud's, we established that Dudley is slightly shorter than Princess Margaret's waxen effigy. Look at their respective teeth and you will see that they were made for each other. But alas, Dudley is already happily married.

Daily Mail, 6 June 1977

SHOULD THIS COLUMN BE BANNED
FOR EXPORTS' SAKE?

I am a little concerned by the effect this column is having on the nation every morning. Judging by my letters, the majority forsake all thought of work, throw instant street parties and light fireworks in a spontaneous turmoil of joy; pensioners link arms with soccer hooligans and there is widespread dancing. Factories and offices are deserted.

How will this unofficial holiday affect the balance of payments? I'd like to think the lost workday will attract enough invisible earnings in the shape of tourists eager to see these celebrations to make up for any loss of productivity.

GAY GALS

Two young lesbian ladies, Shauna McDonald Brown and Suzanne Khanbatt, have been telling us about their life. Shauna says: 'Neither Suzanne nor I are the dominant partner in our relationship. When one of us needs support we lean on the other. Neither of us takes the initiative in anything, whether it's doing the laundry, cooking, working, or love making.'

Judy and I tried this method for a week and found at the end that we were very hungry, short of money and with a pile of dirty laundry. We tried leaning on each other for support but fell down through general weakness.

HAIR APPARENT

There has been vulgar speculation that Prince Charles may be going slightly bald. This should not worry him in any way. As a future King he will be adored, especially if he takes to a long blond curly wig like his Regency predecessors. Nor should he be dismayed by the teenyboppers in the crowds who root for his younger brother, Randy Andy.

True, Andy is prettier, but think back to the days when the Queen was overshadowed by Princess Margaret. Charles is being groomed for the Throne – part of the procedure being to subject him to severe tests such as keeping a bearskin on in a gusty wind whilst controlling a by no means predictable horse. While he is King, all eyes will be on him. Andy will probably run off with some unsuitable older woman like Margaret Trudeau.[30]

RANDHI GANDHI

At the age of 76, Gandhi used to take young naked girls to bed to test his celibacy. I hope to follow his saintly example in my twilight years. I'm sure my devotees will understand.

Daily Mail, 13 June 1977

ROYAL WAVE

I ran into Johnny Rotten, lead singer of the Sex Pickles,[31] the group named after the Queen's corgis: he told me of the film they are to make written by the cockney rebel with a Rolls, Johnny Speight.[32] Johnny R seemed contemptuous of the idea of getting up every morning at six. I see no problem for director Russ (*Super Vixens*) Meyer.[33] All he has to do is to film the group going to bed at that hour. It can't miss. Johnny was a little irreverent about Mr Speight's tasteful house: 'It was like some museum in Eastbourne,' said Britain's new youth leader.

Daily Mail, 20 June 1977

IF GOD IS A WOMAN,
SHE REALLY LET HER SIDE DOWN

Good news from a group of Jesuits. According to their pamphlet God may well be a Woman. I hope and pray She is. I shall have stern words with Her about Her appalling mismanagement in creating the female reproductive system. It seems totally unfair that there should be so many things to go wrong gynaecologically.

Man can look forward at worst to a prostate operation and (if he is promiscuous) the occasional but easily curable 'dose'. But the female system is geared to achieve maximum pain during birth and a high punishment rate for so called 'social diseases' and abortions. If God has any intention of returning me to this Earth after my demise I ask her to send me back male. If She insists on my being female, I want to belong to that little tribe in Africa, where the men go out into the forest and experience their wives' labour pains while the good ladies, I'm told, lie back reading comics and smoking cigarettes.

LIFE QUEER

I am sorry Tom Driberg,[34] or Lord Bradwell as the old snob became, has left out all the really juicy bits from his autobiography 'Ruling Passions'. the highly enjoyable story of a poof with a sense of humour who spent a great deal of time picking up working-class lads in public lavatories. He tells us almost nothing of his infinitely more interesting activities with his colleagues in the Labour Party, not to mention his dealings with certain prominent Tories. Being a man of wide-ranging interests it would not surprise me if he'd been on more than nodding terms with members of the Liberal Party.

As a matter of fact, a predilection for working-class youths is probably as good a reason as any for joining the labour movement. Alas, I was too middle-class for Tom and he never made the remotest pass at me – apart from one rather lingering handshake when he delivered his excellent crossword to *Private Eye*. At his burial, there was a very dignified Mass. When the body had been sprinkled with Holy Water and the black cloth removed from the coffin, the Red Flag was revealed. I don't think this joke was up to Tom's real standards. I had been hoping for a naked working-class lad to spring from under the shroud and shout some slogan for Gay Lib.

DOG DAYS

I am rehearsing these days with my minute partner Dudley Moore who has just jetted in from Durango, Mexico. We start shooting

The Hound of the Baskervilles on July 11 with the best cast ever assembled. Dudley is still not quite sure how to play Watson. I tell him that Dr Watson is basically a small, bumbling, ineffective fool, but Dudley has some objection to playing himself.

DON'T LOOK BACK

The lunatic bore John Osborne[35] has gone into a fit about George Bernard Shaw who he says 'writes like a Pakistani'. This is very rude to Pakistanis, most of whom write far better than John Osborne. Try sitting up one night with strong black coffee and lots of glucose to read 'Look Back In Anger'. Believe it or not, it's even duller now than it was then. I think Mr Osborne should open an all-night delicatessen or at least do something useful like most of the Pakistanis I know. His former wife, Jill Bennett, tells us she has gone completely off sex. I'm not at all surprised. Perhaps I can introduce her to a Pakistani who would keep her amused.

Daily Mail, 27 June 1977

CAN I STILL WIN THE LADIES' SINGLES?

Like the rest of the country, I ground to a halt last week as Wimbledon took over. It was inevitable that Ginny[36] would win – it's written in her teeth, and what's more the Queen popped over, which always means that you get the right result. Another part of the secret is, of course, her mentor, the 60-year-old Mr Jerry Teeguarden, who says, 'She can win Wimbledon for the next three years, she can be the greatest.'

I think I could benefit from Mr Teeguarden's advice. My game is very much like Nastase's[37] without the shots. When I win the toss, I always ask my opponent to serve as I know that my mental attitude is not correct for getting the ball over the net. I'm also a very contentious player and will assert that the balls are the wrong shape, that base lines have been repainted while my back is turned, and will shout and jeer at any crowd that may have gathered.

I've given up hope of becoming the men's singles victor at 40, but I think that with the right coach the women's title might be within my grasp. The operation is costly and may have some effect on my marriage, but I feel that with Mr Teeguarden behind me, my natural talent would begin to flow. In 1978 – provided, of course, the Queen comes – Wimbledon will echo with cries of 'For she's a jolly good fellow'.

KING PONG

The only game of which I am undisputed world champion is indoor candle-lit ping-pong, played with six foot planks and tennis balls. The championship match took place in my garage and was between myself and world number two, Spike Milligan.

Spike is not a good loser and still queries the legality of my match-winning smash which also destroyed the table. If there are willing sponsors, Spike and I will have a rematch. The only conditions are that we both be allowed a choice of planks, a mutually agreed degree of darkness, and luminous balls. All proceeds would go to us.

Daily Mail, 4 July 1977

HICK UP

Professor John Hick, one of the seven authors of the 'controversial' new book about the divinity of Christ, tells us 'Jesus was possibly the most wonderful human being who ever lived.' Another of the authors puts Gandhi, Mao and Martin Luther King in the same category as Jesus.

Unlike Gandhi, Jesus did not choose to test his celibacy by going to bed with countless naked young girls, nor did He, as far as I know, encourage his followers to have unnecessary enemas. Unlike Mao, He never presided over a ruthless totalitarian state responsible for the deaths of millions. Unlike Dr Martin Luther King, Jesus was not a philanderer. For the time being I shall regard Jesus as an even more 'wonderful human being' than these three.

HAM 'N' SEXBURGER

I am delighted to learn more of two much neglected 7th-century feminist saints. They were the lovable sisters the virgin St Ethelreda (the ever unready) and her tiny sister St Sexburga. Ethelreda was the more flamboyant: she married two kings and refused to sleep with them for 20 years.

Fed up with her husband's unreasonable demands she fled to a sanctuary in a swamp at Ely where flocks of wives, widows and virgins rushed to join her. There is a lesson here for present feminists. Instead of moaning about their state, why don't all disgruntled wives, virgins and widows do something positive and dash to a similar spot?

They should follow the example of Ethelreda, who took no money with her. She did not believe in alimony either. To finance the operation I suggest they set up a chain of Sexburger stands where we could buy delicious Biburgers (half beef/half onion), not to mention the deliciously appealing Gayburger, with a militant lesbian.

Daily Mail, 11 July 1977

NO SMOKE

My favourite line of the week came from our First Assistant helping us with our filming and recently back from New York. A man stopped him in the street and asked him for a light. 'I'm sorry, I don't smoke,' Ian replied. 'I asked you for a light, not your [fucking] life story,' said the terse New Yorker.

I SCREAM

The new EEC agreements about the labelling of ice cream are rather alarming. I have always suspected that my ice cream is in fact made out of frozen glops of pig fat, soya beans and fish oil, but it is not a truth that I wish to have shoved down my throat. The whole labelling craze is going too far.

Next our milk bottles will be covered with stickers informing us of the exact method whereby it is brought about. I have no wish to know about those hideous contraptions which are attached to the udders of defenceless cows to provide me with my nourishing pint. At a very early age I was informed by my Nanny that butter was made by shaking a cow violently. This made me scream with distress. It took me years to overcome an instinctive distaste for the product. As far as I know butter is made out of milk. If it's not, I hope the EEC keep quiet about it. I don't want to dollop a mixture of pig fat and fish oil on my toast.

Three Appeal Court judges ruled on Friday that it was illegal for Stork SB margarine to advertise 'that it tasted like butter'. The court ruled that it would NOT be illegal to put out an advertisement saying 'Why waste money on Butter? Buy Stork,' but it WOULD be illegal to say 'Buy Stork – it's better value for money than butter.' I'm glad this has been cleared up. I trust no one will insist on informing me of the true components of Stork margarine.

SHRINKS EXPAND

A group of 100 psychologists have been meeting in Cardiff to discuss the difference between men and women. It is called The International Conference on Sex Role Stereotyping. I trust they had no difficulty sorting out which of them were men and which of them were women. I just hope that when they made this startling discovery they didn't do anything commonplace like go to bed with each other. I would hate to think of a Cardiff Psychologist Birth Explosion. Their madness could well be hereditary.

Daily Mail, 18 July 1977

PICKLED PINK

I was delighted that the Queen's cousin, Lord Harewood, was acquitted of 'failing to report an accident' in Covent Garden. He had backed his Jaguar XJ12 into a parked sports car last September, setting off the car's burglar alarm horn. My neighbour the earl said that he hadn't noticed the incident as the burglar alarm horn sounded to him like a Mozart wind serenade. When asked what sort of wind instrument sounded like a car horn, Lord Harewood replied: 'Jack Brymer's clarinet, I suppose. He's a very, very good clarinettist.' I can confirm this: Jack sounds even BETTER than a car horn.

The decision has helped my marriage. When I ran over Judy Sexburga Cook last week outside the house in my pink Mini, I claimed not to have noticed the incident because her screams sounded very much to me like the cassette of the new Sox Pickles hit Pretty Vacant that I was playing. The Bow Street Court decision reinforced my argument and I now have limited access to parts of the house.

DENIS MENACE

To nobody's surprise, dreadful old Mrs Sirimavo Bandaranaike was beaten in the Sri Lankan General Election which was won by Mr Junius Jaywardene (no relation, I trust). Like Indira Gandhi in India, one of the issues was nepotism, but this good lady at least did not forcibly sterilise people against their will. Mrs Thatcher must beware falling into the same trap when she assumes the helm. However nice her husband Denis is, she must not make him head of British Rail, neither should her children become Ambassadors. She should resist a natural temptation to sterilise union leaders. Many of them are impotent already and the rest are too busy trying to run the country to pay much attention to breeding.

Daily Mail, 25 July 1977

WHAT'S IT ALL ABOUT, BERTIE?

Kenneth Williams, who is playing the part of Sir Henry Baskerville in the epic production starring myself and Dudley Moore, tells me of a cabby who recognised him and went on about how he had had Bertrand Russell[38] in the back of his cab. The brilliant philosopher was quite surprised when the cabby turned around and said, 'Hello, Bertie, I've read a lot of your books. What's life all about then?' Apparently the aged sage was speechless. 'Would you believe it?' the cabby said to Kenneth. 'I asked the world's greatest philosopher a simple question, and he didn't know the [fucking] answer.'

Daily Mail, 1 August 1977

IF YOU'RE A BIT OF A CELT, DON'T PICK ON A PICT

It was strangely calming to return to the stately tranquillity of the Metropolis after another week with the Celts in Cornwall. Life in the remote village roars on at a dizzying rate. In addition to the nightly coven meetings, I was persuaded to take up the booming sport of 'grass boarding'.

This perilous pursuit involves hurtling down an almost vertical hill at speeds of well over 90mph. My first attempt was something of a failure. Lying on an ordinary Georgian silver tray, I lost control of the 'board' and wound up on the twelfth green of the local golf course. Luckily it was midnight and despite the full moon I do not think there were any witnesses.

My friend, the GP, is still up to his medically dubious fishing endeavours. I spent the Bank Holiday travelling by lugger to his now notorious lobster pots. This time it was crabs he was after – and crabs he got. Twenty seven giant crustacea were hauled about and hypnotised into calm before being placed in large plastic bags. I asked the good doctor why he had let one crab remain in each pot.

'They baint be crabs, m'dear,' he beamed. 'They be models.' It turned out that he had persuaded his children to make lifelike Plasticine effigies of his intended victims. These he had daubed with pheromones, which as you all know are hormones carried outside the body, and make that body intensely sexually attractive. The turbulence I noted in the water was probably caused by sex-mad crabs racing to their bogus mates.

I watched the doctor's victims being thrown into vast pans of boiling water. There were no screams, but I would not say that death was absolutely instantaneous. Some of them were wiggling about, albeit feebly, after one minute's immersion. I pointed this out to the doctor who sagely replied: 'If we took them out now and returned them to the sea they would not be at all well.' My moral doubts vanished when we devoured a delicious meal of crab on the rocks. Later that night I was rapaciously attacked by Judy Sexburga Cook. Only the next day did I learn that the GP had sprinkled pheromones on my T shirt.

Whilst in Cornwall I argued with the locals about how they had treated my race, the Picts. We Picts used to have a very nice civilisation in parts of northern England. Our music and art were superb, but most of the time was spent building walls. These beautiful walls were persistently overrun by uncivilised people called Celts. In those days the rudest thing a Pict could say was 'You're a Celt.'

No matter how many walls we built the dreadful Celts kept climbing over them. We used to paint ourselves quite a bit, thus pre-dating Veruschka by centuries. Our tattooed bodies were also the talk of the nation. At the moment I'm the self-appointed leader of the Independence for Picts Movement. All we ask is that our stolen lands be returned. We Picts laugh bitterly when we hear the ludicrous phrase 'North Sea Oil.' It's 'Pict Sea Oil' and if pushed we'll build a wall around it to prove it.

MIND THE DORS

I used to be a great admirer of Diana Dors,[39] the well-known film artiste. Locked away in a vault at my bank is a first edition of 'Diana Dors in 3D'. This priceless publication showed a nude mini Dors in elegant postures on bits of fur. More recently I have enjoyed her as Mrs Bott in *Just William* (though I do feel she should not wear so much artificial padding). But now Diana, at whom I used to peer through my red and green plastic spectacles, has told the world about her so-called affair with the late Elvis Presley. She calls it the 'best-kept secret in show business'.

I have no reason to doubt this, but wouldn't be surprised if Elvis had not been let into the secret either. It is quite possible that the King gave our Diana a Cadillac. He did that for many people for whom he felt sorry. I imagine that he pitied 'the poor man's Mansfield' for being married to the repulsive Dennis Hamilton, who died in my sleep several years ago. Far too many women are screaming about affairs they may have had with dead men. I should not be surprised to read an account of Ms Dors's shenanigans with the late Groucho Marx.

GOON BUT NOT FORGOTTEN

As a youth at school it was my practice to fall ill on Friday night in order to listen to the *Goon Show* in the Sanatorium. The genial Matron seemed unaware of this weekly pattern of 'feeling a bit under the weather' on a Friday evening. On one occasion, weak with laughter after a particularly hilarious episode, I said I felt 'strangely feeble'. The good lady carried me to the bathroom, took off my pyjamas and gave me a bath. During the course of this she soaped my back with her bare hands. This innocent action caused me severe pleasure and embarrassment which I disguised with a large sponge. Later I exaggerated the incident to my friends and intimated that rather more had gone on. Thus an impeccable Matron's name became sullied by the school's rumour mills.

Daily Mail, 5 September 1977

A CORNISH CELT GP AND
PARANORMAL PARKING OFFENCES

I am a Pict and therefore extremely courteous. I wrote to my Cornish GP to thank him for the sailing trips and the jar of natural clotted Cornish pheromones that he gave me. It must have been almost a year's supply. I only have to dab a suspicion of this highly erotic powder on my lapel and gorgeous women come flocking.

I fear the good doctor may have mixed in some deviant strains. I have no wish to be enormously sexually attractive to rats and wasps. Twice I have been forced to call in the Pest Control Authority, and it was distressing to be simultaneously assaulted by Judy Sexburga Cook and a large white mouse. Judy was naturally jealous, especially as the mouse got in the first kiss. I think I managed to get the mouse out of the house without hurting its feelings, but my wife remains glum about the affair.

The dubious Doctor wrote back to tell me that he was researching a paper on 'paranormal parking offences'. Apparently on numerous occasions he has parked his car in the designated car park prior to sailing in his lugger, only to discover on his return that it has moved 300 yards by supernatural means to a double yellow line. Cornish traffic wardens are doubtful about his explanation.

He asked me if I had ever experienced anything similar. Of course it has happened to me often but I feared that people in authority would deem me mad. All my parking tickets have been caused by paranormal forces. There has been an alarming increase in these incidents since the election of Martian president Jimmy Carter.

Isn't it time that the Government set up an inquiry into this eerie phenomenon with the support of the Society for Psychical Research? I would welcome readers' own experiences of psychic parking tickets, and related matters. I should tell you that only yesterday, with Uranus very much in charge of my star sign, I saw a strange glowing cigar-shaped object hovering in front of me. For five minutes it hovered, gradually getting smaller and glowing continuously. Suddenly it disappeared. My cigar had dropped out of my mouth. In this case there was a rational explanation, but these things can be alarming.

LANCE THE BOIL

Thanks to the influence of a Martian Presidency there is a new rage in the State for a ten-legged three-inch-wide pet. Predictably, these creatures eat peanut butter and jelly. One Florida firm expects to sell at least 750,000 of them this year. These remarkable pets, which cost a mere two pounds, are long-lived, docile and sociable. They do not have to be licensed, neutered, or inoculated. They are quiet and don't bite. It is of course the Coenobita Clypeatus, or 'CC' as Martian Jimmy refers to his.

They are tropical hermit crabs which many experts believe came from Space millions of years ago with Erich von Daeniken[40] and Uri Geller.[41] It is significant that this breed of crab flourishes in the Bermuda Triangle where the President goes fishing and plays tennis on the water. Snobbish owners buy costly shells to serve as little crab houses. They also lash out good money for coral trees for

CCs to play in, and the real socialites buy tiny leashes. This could be the reason for President Carter going on network television and saying 'I am proud of you Bert,' about his budget director Bert Lance, after a report had shown Mr Lance to be guilty of 54 illegalities in his banking transactions.

Healey may get his figures wrong about our money but at least he runs a tight ship personally. I much admire and envy his lucrative property transactions. Mr Lance, who is in no way related to Mr Vance, or for that matter Butch Cassidy and Sundance, the well-known Georgian law firm, made a practice of securing himself enormous bank overdrafts in somewhat dubious circumstances.

It is hard to believe that virtuous President Carter would defend anybody in the least bit morally tainted. Mr Lance is obviously innocent and in the Senate hearings I expect him to explain to his inquisitors that he is a crab, and by nature inclined to grab hold of green things and hold on to them very tight. Either Lance (or 'The Boil' as he's known by his Georgian chums) owns up to being a Martian crustacean or else he'll have to resign. I have nothing against crabs in high office, but we have a right to know who they are.

HIRE AND HIGHER

Mr Edward Richards was found guilty last week of 'persistently refusing to maintain himself, his wife and six children, who are eight to sixteen.' Mr Richards has refused to register for work on the grounds of conscience.

After the hearing Mr Richards said that he would rather go to prison than accept paid employment. The only paid job he would consider was lecturing on his belief and philosophy. He should be hired at once. Millions, like me, share his view, but are unable to put it over as coherent philosophy.

With one million six hundred thousand unemployed at the moment he would have a ready audience. They would all like to hear about unemployment being 'man's highest estate'.

Daily Mail, 12 September 1977

TULIP LIQUEUR AND FLABBIGO
SPOIL MY DUTCH TREAT

My sympathy goes out to Fergus Montgomery, MP, who was fined £60 for theft, plus £70 costs. In a 'trance like' state he had inadvertently put Selwyn Lloyd's autobiography and Viv Nicholson's *Spend, Spend, Spend*[42] into his hold-all. He did, however, pay for another book.

As might be expected, a Labour MP was largely to blame. Dr Dickson Mabon, our Minister of State for Energy, had given Fergus some Ponderax slimming pills. From my experience of Ponderax they do induce an artificial state of energy but I'm sure Mr Mabon is not dependent upon them. Poor Mr Montgomery had also taken several whiskys and a sleeping pill.

Dr Julian Silverstone, a psychiatrist at St Bartholomew's Hospital, said in court that the combination of drugs and alcohol would probably leave whoever took them in rather a daze, the equivalent of a chemical bonk on the head. How very true. Only last weekend I was in Amsterdam to attend the launching of the triple LP, *Consequences*, by Lol Creme and Kevin Godley. Lady Judy Sexburga Cook, Sarah Vaughan and myself are guests on this work.

At the party I consumed a few glasses of a Dutch liqueur made out of tulips. I suddenly became aware that I was 8oz overweight and asked a Japanese journalist if he knew a good doctor. He replied that he was himself a doctor. His doctorate had been obtained in Tokyo, where he took first class honours in witchcraft and hang gliding. Rashly I accepted two Flabbigo tablets which he proffered with the quip, 'in Japan we know how to make people small.' Almost immediately I went into a 'trancelike' state and wandered into a nearby museum.

There, according to Dutch authorities, I seized five three-foot antique wooden carvings of windmills and a bust of the Dutch Prime Minister Joop den Uyl, made of Edam cheese. These I put into a dustbin liner. I did stop to purchase a postcard. I was apprehended by the Dutch police who had been watching the whole episode on closed-circuit television. I was taken to a very clean police station and questioned.

My first thought was to get in touch with a solicitor. Accordingly I rang the manager of the hotel, who for some reason misunderstood me and sent down the wine waiter, who remarked that it was unusual to provide room service in police cells. I explained my dilemma. This inventive man said 'don't worry. I have studied a little law.' He explained to the police that I was 'artistic' and therefore prone to steal things for no apparent reason. I was released on bail, which I raised by selling my trousers to one of the arresting officers.

When I got back to the hotel the manager refused me entry because I was trouserless. I then sold my jacket to the wine waiter and bought a pair of trousers with the proceeds. An hour later when he had left for home I discovered that I had left my plane ticket in the jacket. I was seen later persuading a bewildered American to wrap me in brown paper and carry me on board as his hand luggage.

I do not know what the extradition laws are but I imagine that now we are in Europe the Dutch will be able to whisk me over to Holland for the same sort of trial that Mr Montgomery had to endure. It will be a sad day for justice if a British citizen who was in the grip of Flabbigo can be convicted of theft. Mr Montgomery is quite rightly appealing. The lesson for us all is to never accept slimming pills from Labour politicians – or Japanese journalists.

WISE WORDS

We can all learn from John Vernon 'Black Jack' Bouvier the Third, who passed on many wise words to his daughter, Jacqueline Onassis.[43] Among Black Jack's pearls were 'Be hard to get. Don't accept everything. Never be too available. To be tantalising you must always be exasperating. When you refuse a date the man will hate it (but love you more) if you say you're staying at home to wash your hair and you're not.' And perhaps most important, 'by all means never grow up.'

I tried to follow Black Jack's rule book when courting Judy

Sexburga Cook. When I met her I played hard to get. As a result I didn't see her for 12 years. On our first meeting she suggested that we meet in a year's time, but I looked in my diary and lied, saying that I was staying at home to wash my hair. I attempted never to grow up but found that nature had a nasty way of intervening. Only years later did I discover that La Sexburga had been following the same set of rules.

If everybody followed Black Jack's advice it would solve the problem of population control. We could all stay at home pretending to wash our hair and never contact anybody. Judy tried to arrange a marriage contract similar to Jackie's with Aristotle Onassis. I agreed that 'separate bedrooms were to be provided whenever we were together', but cunningly inserted my own clause which said a double bedroom must be provided whenever we were apart. I went along with the clause that said that Judy's personal expenses, her hairdresser, cosmeticians, etc, would be paid for by me with an upper limit of £4,000 a month. I balked at the suggestion that in the event of my prior demise the sum of sixty million should be settled on her. As a compromise we agreed that she should inherit my overdraft.

BAN U MAN U

It will be a little bit ridiculous if Manchester United are banned from Europe as a result of some of their fans' overzealous behaviour at St Etienne. When I was beaten up by a Manchester United supporter I didn't blame it on the club or the players. If this ban is upheld, surely victims of razor attacks could sue Wilkinson Sword and if someone was run down by a drunken driver he could collect vast damages from the distillers. Can I sue the producers of *Emmerdale Farm* for provoking me to acts of mindless violence, including shooting a perfectly good Japanese television set? If not, why not?

Daily Mail, 26 September 1977

THE SUN ALSO ERASES

Part of my job is the read the daily newspapers, however rubbishy. Last week I was thrown into utter confusion by identical pictures of Jackie Onassis that appeared in the *Sun* and the *Daily Mirror*. For the first time in my long study of official pictures of Jackie Money In The Box, did I see her pert, not to mention aggressive, nipples outlined under a close-fitting strapless dress. This picture appeared in the *Mirror* and showed Jackie with two attendant figures behind her. In the *Sun* was an identical picture but with no people and no nipples.

The big question, of course, is whether the page three *Sun* airbrushed Jackie's nipples out along with the people, or did, even more unscrupulously, the *Mirror* paint them in. My own view is that the *Mirror* retouched nothing. The *Sun* editor can expect a sharp rap on the knuckles from Rupert Murdoch for implicitly suggesting that his newspaper doesn't believe in people or nipples. Murdoch's empire is founded on people's nipples.

MORRIS DANCING

I'm a little worried about body language. So far I have received conflicting advice about what my various body movements mean. Now I see that Dr Desmond Morris[44] is to tell us about 'man watching' in today's *Mail*. I have studied various ladies' magazines in an attempt to discover what my various gestures mean. Similarly, I have sought to be enlightened about what ladies' movements indicate. The results of my investigation so far are disconcerting. Scratching my knee can mean either:

1) Intense sexual excitement
2) The statement that I'm intensely shy, or
3) My knee is itching.

Similarly, a lady who crosses her legs from left to right is:

1) A widow
2) A nymphomaniac, or

3) Somebody who wishes to dance.

But body language is undoubtedly an important subject. I just hope I never get to learn it. I saw Desmond Morris on 'Parkinson' inadvertently stroking his knee. Was he really asking Parkinson to arrange a candle-lit evening with music by Ambrose and his orchestra? Or was he merely scratching his knee? Perhaps only Parkinson can tell.

MALE PILLS

A new statistical analysis has shown that more people who were born are likely to be divorced than those who were never conceived. This alarming report confirms what many experts thought – namely, that a living person is far more likely to become married and therefore divorced than somebody who has never existed. Meanwhile, a similar shock survey showed that men on the so-called 'Pill' were far less likely to develop fatal diseases than their female counterparts. This is thought, tentatively, to be a result of men failing to invent a contraceptive pill that is in any way effective for them. This shows that men are more than willing to experiment on women, over a period of 30 years, and then alarm them with statistics.

Daily Mail, 10 October 1977

THORN FREE

The Thorn Lighting Company, in Merthyr Tydfil, have come up with a brilliant productivity deal for their workers. In addition to their normal wages, lucky Thorn employees will be given a £5 a week bonus for what is known in the industry as 'turning up'. A spokesman for the firm said 'If more people come to work, then obviously more work will be done and productivity will go up.'

While this is not necessarily true – they might well get in each other's way and distract one another if too many 'turned up' – it is definitely a positive step. Provisional statistics show that workers who 'turn up', or to put it another way, 'arrive' at their factory, tend to produce more than those who stay at home knitting.

There is a chance, however, that this deal may breach the Government's pay policy. The Department of Employment commented 'If you are asking me whether this is a self-financing productivity deal, the answer is . . . I don't know.' While the issue is in doubt, we should all ask our employers for a 'turning up' bonus.

HAIRY LACQUER

An appalling example of the British double standard occurred last week when an innocent spider was sprayed to death with hair lacquer and underarm deodorant. Angelo, believed erroneously to be a deadly Mexican Red Knee spider, had been at large in Basildon. He had been nestling in a box of heavy goods vehicle licence application forms which Mrs Blanche Miles was carrying. He fell to the floor and nervous Mrs Miles screamed.

Mr 'Chuck' Beck, the driving school owner, rushed to her aid and imprisoned Angelo under a large bowl and sprayed every available can of aerosol under it and left the spider to suffocate. Andrew Gardner on *Thames At Six* showed us the pathetic hairy corpse and revealed that the innocent victim was not a Red Knee spider at all. A genuine Red Knee spider was then placed on his hand, where it crouched in an endearing and cuddly way.

Meanwhile, the real 'Beast of Basildon' is still at large. I trust that when he is found there will be no hasty hair lacquer spraying. He will only bite if bitten and is far less dangerous when cornered than the average giraffe. The nation is still in mourning for Victor, but few seem to care about the late Angelo.

263

ASIAN FLOW

There was surprise in diplomatic circles when Mr Morarji Desai, the Indian Prime Minister, did not receive the traditional Soviet bearhug when he arrived in Moscow. Mr Brezhnev[45] and Mr Kosygin[46] merely shook his hand. This on first sight would indicate a lack of warmth, but then the Soviet leaders may well have read, as I did, that it is Mr Desai's habit to have himself massaged all over in his own urine in addition to drinking two glasses of the same daily.

Daily Mail, 24 October 1977

BUNNY HOP

It was very rude of reporters to ask Jeremy Thorpe why he wrote in a letter to Norman Scott the words 'Bunnies can and will go to France.'[47] Mr Thorpe could think of no reason why he should have written these words. To most right-thinking people it just reads as an interesting statement of fact. A fact about which, until now, I have been woefully ignorant – and who else but the Liberal Party would concern themselves with the important but overlooked issue of the fact that bunnies not only CAN go to France, but bloody well WILL?

It remains unclear whether Mr Thorpe was addressing himself to the trade in frozen rabbit meat to the Continent or the rare occasions when rabbits take to the sea and swim the Channel. Only Mr Thorpe seems to be alert to one of the key issues in North Devon: Where does Mr Callaghan stand on French bunnies?

So far we only have Mr Thorpe's dramatic prophecy. Reporters who probe such irrelevancies as a possible homosexual past should have asked the key question: 'Mr Thorpe, in view of the fact that bunnies can and will go to France, what steps would the Liberal party take to bring them back?'

DUKE'S TREAT

Prince Philip has been controversial again. For those who have not read the speech in full, here is an easily understood précis of the Prince's provocative message to the country. 'Things may well get pretty ghastly in the future, but on the other hand, there is a good chance they won't.'

The Duke, characteristically, is not afraid to be ruthlessly outspoken. It appears that he prefers love to hate, and thinks freedom is a good idea. Perhaps the Duke should stick to mild statements of obvious fact, such as 'Bunnies can and will go to France.'

TOILETS SPOIL IT

Going through my filing cabinet, I discovered a letter from a friend. One sentence stood out as a piece of cogent thinking: 'Modern lavatory seats can and will fall down at the worst possible moment.' My friend is a Liberal, though not in any way connected with the current furore which is, alas, obscuring important prospects, such as the Liberal voice in the forthcoming Queen's speech.

The letter was written 15 years ago, since when lavatory seats have been crashing down all over Britain with embarrassing results. British lavatories used to be the pride of the world. There is no reason why a lavatory seat should not remain in an upright position for long periods of time. The Americans have solved the problem of unfortunate incidents by building their lavatory seats with a gap in the front, but this is an admission of failure.

If there are any of the old lavatory craftsmen left I challenge them to fix me a reliable lavatory seat in my home. No magnets or screws, please – just an ordinary seat which stays up when it's up and goes down without a major physical exertion by the user. No wonder Prince Philip has doubts about the future. Rabbits are fleeing the country, and lavatory seats are falling with depressing regularity.

MAKE UP THE DIFFERENCE

In a week where chorus girls successfully applied for the same wages as male dancers, Ray Rennie, a waiter at the Playboy Club, in Manchester, is asking for the same wages as the Bunny Girls. In addition to higher wages the girls get a £300 a year tax allowance for make-up and tights, while their male counterparts get nothing.

A spokesman for the Equal Opportunities Commission said: 'This seems to be a unique case. We have had waitresses successfully apply for equal pay with waiters, but this is the first time we've had the problem the other way about.' Ray has justice on his side. Not only do the ladies get more money and perks – it is a well-known fact that bunnies can and will go to France.

Daily Mail, 31 October 1977

KEEP YOUR POWDER WET

There has been confusing information in the media about what to do during the firemen's strike. Most of the information is devoted to ways of not starting fires. I have learnt that fires become more likely when you set light to things, that beds burn slowly, and plugs should be removed firmly from their sockets. And don't throw water on a fire – it only excites it.

Here are some additional tips. Don't brush your hair too fast – it causes electrical sparks. Keep all matches away from children – or leave the country. This I did yesterday in order to avoid having to answer questions about an LP that will be issued on November 18, *Derek & Clive Come Again*, which was apparently recorded by me and my minute partner Dudley Moore in a trancelike state. It is my belief that I was drugged by an employee of the notorious Virgin Record Company, who, as you know, are responsible for the Sox Pickles. Dudley claims to have no memory of having made the record at all. The last thing he remembers is that somebody handed him a walnut whirl.

I have listened to this disgusting record with genuine shock and horror. It is nothing but a stream of obscenities about unpleasant subjects. A learned Australian journalist who had heard the tapes had counted that there were 144 [Fucks] and 89 [Cunts] in the space of 60 minutes. I urge you not to buy it, unless perhaps as a cheap form of Breathalyzer. If you laugh at *Derek & Clive Come Again* you definitely shouldn't drive.

Daily Mail, 14 November 1977

Chapter Ten
Not Also But Only

After Peter's partnership with Dudley ended, he never made another classic TV series, like *Not Only But Also*, or appeared in another long-running West End or Broadway stage show, like *Behind the Fridge*. He acted in some good to middling television dramas, and some bad to middling movies. But although his acting was usually adequate, and occasionally rather good, he was never going to be remembered for reciting other people's lines, however well – or badly – he recited them. Yet it's one of the riddles of Cook's work that in this era of listless inactivity he actually created several of his finest sketches. Admittedly, his humour was now spread pretty thin – in public, at any rate. But although during his last fifteen years he only performed his own material in a handful of stage and small screen appearances, these occasional curtain calls still comprised some of the funniest sketches of his life.

The first two were both from *The Secret Policeman's Ball*, a fundraising show for Amnesty International, at Her Majesty's Theatre, London, in June 1979, in which Peter appeared alongside Rowan Atkinson, Eleanor Bron, John Cleese, Billy Connolly,

Terry Jones and Michael Palin. Cook teamed up with Cleese to reprise 'Interesting Facts', his old Footlights encore – reproduced here, since a lot of its facts had altered during the intervening twenty years. He also paired off with Bron in 'Balloon', a bizarre duet about a phantom pregnancy (too visual to really work in print) and dusted down 'The End of the World', his finale from *Beyond the Fringe*, with Atkinson, Cleese, Jones and Palin filling in for Bennett, Miller and Moore.

It was a pleasant enough way for a few charitable celebs to raise some cash for a good cause, and some comedy fans prefer seeing old routines to new ones – but critics usually expect comics to come up with something new, and some of them complained that this show was rather tame. Nowadays, most benefit gigs are one-night stands, but *The Secret Policeman's Ball* ran for four nights, and for once, the 'crickets' spurred Peter into action, rather than inaction. The next night, he performed a new monologue he'd written that afternoon, a send up of the Judge's summing up in the trial of Jeremy Thorpe – until 1976 the leader of the Liberal Party, and MP for North Devon until the month before.

A week earlier, Thorpe and three others had been acquitted of charges that they'd conspired to murder Norman Scott, a former male model who claimed to have had a homosexual relationship with Thorpe – a claim Thorpe denied. In his summing up, the Honourable Mr Justice (Sir Joseph) Cantley called Scott 'a hysterical, warped personality, accomplished sponger and very skilful at exciting and exploiting sympathy'. He called Andrew Newton, who alleged he'd been hired to murder Scott, 'a chump'. He called the chief prosecution witness, Peter Bessell, formerly a Liberal MP and close colleague of Thorpe's, 'a humbug'. 'The judge took it upon himself to destroy the good character of these three key witnesses,'[1] claimed Cook's *Private Eye* colleague, Auberon Waugh, who'd stood against Thorpe in the General Election earlier that year 'to protest about the behaviour of the Liberal Party generally and the North Devon Constituency Liberal Association in particular'.[2] (Waugh lost his deposit, but Thorpe lost his seat.) Cook's deadly spoof of the trial judge's summing up still stands as one of the greatest satirical speeches ever made.

Incredibly, ITV cut it from their televised version of the show, but it was included in a cinema version, and even released on record.

The next year, Cook made it onto ITV, alongside Atkinson, Cleese and Jones, in *Peter Cook & Co* – a one-off, hour-long special, filmed by London Weekend Television. For once, he'd made a TV show that was more visual than verbal, which is why, despite several fine sketches, only one, 'Ants', is included here. Of the others, the most revealing sketch was one in which Beryl Reid played a giant bee. Usually, 'don't tell me – show me' is the golden rule of television comedy – but unusually, you get the feeling that this sketch would actually have been funnier as a monologue. Cook was far better at describing his flights of fancy than actually enacting them. With its low budgets, last-minute preparation and improvisation, *Not Only But Also* was a very theatrical TV show. Conversely, *Peter Cook & Co*, like his screenplay for the movie *Bedazzled*, was another instance of Cook's conversational stage skills pulling against a picture-led medium. Nevertheless, this tug-of-war merely made *Peter Cook & Co* a good programme, rather than a great one. Critically acclaimed (for the most part) in Britain, it won prizes in America, and LWT wanted to make a series. However Peter opted instead to star in an American sitcom called *The Two of Us*, about an American woman and her English butler. The original British version, *Two's Company*, starring Donald Sinden, had been a hit in Britain – but after a strong start, Cook's US version faded badly.

Another benefit gig, *An Evening At Court*, provided the forum for Cook's next virtuoso turn. Again, it involved a court case and a Liberal politician, but this time the defendant – and beneficiary – was Cook's old Footlights friend, Adrian Slade. After Cambridge, Slade had gone into advertising and got involved in Liberal politics. In 1981, he was elected onto the Greater London Council, but the Conservatives accused him of election overspending. Slade won, but a technicality saddled him with the bulk of the court costs. He asked his showbiz chums to help him raise some cash. Cook was the first to say yes. Cook was joined by his Footlights contemporaries Eleanor Bron and David Frost, plus Rowan Atkinson, Graham

Chapman and John Cleese. The cast also included Barry Took, French & Saunders, and Tim Brooke-Taylor, Graeme Garden and Bill Oddie (aka The Goodies).

Aptly, Cook revived Mr Grole, the alter ego that Slade had urged him to perform for the first time at a Footlights Smoker, all those years ago. However this time, with John Cleese perfectly cast as his uptight, put-upon straight man, Cook came up with a completely new sketch. His court costs paid, Slade continued to serve as a councillor for the GLC until 1985, when Mrs Thatcher abolished it. As the last president of the Liberal party, and first president (with Shirley Williams) of the Liberal Democrats, he almost persuaded Cook to stand as a Liberal Democrat in his local Hampstead constituency, against Glenda Jackson, during the 1992 General Election.

In 1986, Cook was invited to host an edition of *Saturday Live*, the TV flagship of the Alternative Comedy boom. Peter was revered by many of these new-wave comedians, who'd been weaned on Pete & Dud and Derek & Clive, and Peter also enjoyed much of their humour – especially Harry Enfield, *Saturday Live*'s brightest rising star. However, the press depicted Alternative Comedy as a revolt of radical yoof against old age, and even though Cook's work was more radical than most of the knee-jerk anti-Thatcher rants that had replaced it on prime time telly, his age marked him out as one of the old guard, so this gig was a significant endorsement from a younger generation of comedians. In fact, Alternative Comedy was a revolution of form rather than content. When he wanted to, Peter could be far more vicious and shocking than anyone half his age on *Saturday Live*. What was out of fashion was the sketch formula he'd grown up with, and duly revolutionised. Peter had honed his satirical instincts from the Fifties to the Seventies – an era of woolly political consensus, when what was comical about Britain's main two parties was how little they differed, not how much. The oblique humour of Cook's sketches suited this foggy consensual climate, but in the Eighties, Thatcherism had created a huge rift between Left and Right, a polemical age which suited a far more polemical format – stand up.

Cook's subtle, discursive talents were ill suited to this direct, aggressive style, so wisely, he stuck to what he knew – and although playing characters made it rather difficult to introduce the other acts, his actual sketches were sublime. Again, he wrote a new sketch for an old character, Mr Grole, pestering his old Cambridge friend, John Fortune. He also teamed up with John Bird, another friend from Cambridge, for a timeless skit about a pair of cowboy builders knocking up The Pleasure Dome of Kubla Khan. Ingenuously, Cook also revised his Harold Macmillan impersonation that had caused such a stir in *Beyond the Fringe*, but updated him to his new role, as the nonagenarian Lord Stockton.

Fittingly, Cook's last substantial TV performance was also one of his very best – a Christmas special on Clive Anderson's chat show, barely a year before his death. Cook played four different characters, each interviewed by Anderson, as if they were real people. And despite his broad comic brush-strokes, that was how they seemed. 'The virtuosity and variety of the invention might be taken for granted but compared with the early style which made him famous and which is associated with his name, there is something new here,' argued Bird, 'an insight and even a sympathy in the way in which Cook approaches his characters.'[3] Indeed, all four were so rounded that they could quite easily have been interviewed more than once – or, at the very least, for twice as long. Moreover, Cook had an infinite supply of other characters, whom he could adopt at will – as he often did in private, with only his wife, Lin, to hear them. 'I wish we had done some more now,'[4] regrets Anderson. The ones they did do are wonderful, but like the rest of Cook's work in the Eighties and early Nineties, they merely hint at what might have been.

～

PETER COOK

MORE INTERESTING FACTS
(*The Secret Policeman's Ball,* Her Majesty's Theatre,
London, 1979)

(John Cleese is sitting on a park bench, reading a newspaper. Enter Peter Cook as Arthur Grole. Cook sits beside Cleese.)

ARTHUR GROLE: Good day.

JOHN CLEESE: Good day.

ARTHUR GROLE: Good day again.

JOHN CLEESE: Good day.

ARTHUR GROLE: Did you know that you've got four miles of tubing in your stomach?

JOHN CLEESE: I beg your pardon?

ARTHUR GROLE: I said did you know that you've got four miles of tubing in your stomach?

JOHN CLEESE: No. No, I didn't know that.

ARTHUR GROLE: A good thing I'm here then. Aren't you interested in your intestine?

JOHN CLEESE: Not particularly.

ARTHUR GROLE: Well you should be, because if you didn't have your intestines, you wouldn't be able to digest, and then you'd look a bit of a fool. You'd look a fool without your intestines wouldn't you? Shall I show you a diagram of your intestines? See how far the food has to travel. Four miles at one mile an hour! This means that none of the food in your stomach is ever really fresh. It's always at least four hours old.

JOHN CLEESE: Fancy that.

ARTHUR GROLE: No I don't fancy that, thank you very much indeed. I do not fancy that in the least, thank you very much. I wish my intestines were shorter. Don't you wish your intestines were shorter?

JOHN CLEESE: Look, let's just forget about my intestines shall we?

ARTHUR GROLE: All right. On your own head be it. But I'll tell you an interesting fact. I'll tell you a really interesting fact. It's about the whale. Do you know the whale is not really a fish? It's an insect. And it lives on bananas.

JOHN CLEESE: The whale is an insect? I've never heard such rubbish.

ARTHUR GROLE: I know. That was a joke. I made it up. It wasn't a fact. It was a joke. But I'll tell you what is a very interesting fact, it's about the grasshopper. The interesting fact about the grasshopper is its disproportionate leaping ability, due to its powerful hind legs. Hop, hop, hop it goes, all over arable land. That is land what is actually tilled by Arabs. And the interesting fact about your Arab is that he can live for a whole year on one grain of rice. Imagine that! A dirty big Arab, living for a whole year on one grain of rice. It's incredible.

JOHN CLEESE: A whole year on one grain of rice?

ARTHUR GROLE: No, it's the mosquito that can live for a whole year on one grain of rice. You wouldn't get a filthy dirty, great six foot Arab living for a whole year on one grain of rice. For heaven's sake, your Arab needs four square meals a day. No I get those two muddled up because they're next to each other in the dictionary.

JOHN CLEESE: What are?

ARTHUR GROLE: Mosquitoes and mosques. And I'll tell you the really interesting fact about the grasshopper. Do you want to hear a really interesting fact about the grasshopper?

JOHN CLEESE: No.

ARTHUR GROLE: Well if the giraffe could leap, pound for pound, as high as the grasshopper, they'd avoid a lot of trouble.

JOHN CLEESE: Shall I tell you something? You are one of the most boring, tedious, uninteresting, monotonous, flatulent, flat-headed, cloth-eared, swivel-eyed, fornicating little gits I ever met in my life.

ARTHUR GROLE: Is that a fact? How very interesting.

ENTIRELY A MATTER FOR YOU
(*The Secret Policeman's Ball*, Her Majesty's Theatre,
London 1979)

Ladies and gentlemen of the jury, it is now my duty to advise you
on how you should vote when you retire from this court. In the last
few weeks we have all heard some pretty extraordinary allegations
being made about one of the prettiest, about one of the most
distinguished politicians ever to rise to high office in this country –
or not, as you may think.

We have heard, for example, from Mr Bex Bissell – a man who
by his own admission is a liar, a humbug, a hypocrite, a vagabond,
a loathsome spotted reptile and a self-confessed chicken strangler.
You may choose, if you wish, to believe the transparent tissue of
odious lies which streamed on and on from his disgusting, reedy,
slavering lips. That is entirely a matter for you.

Then we have been forced to listen to the pitiful whining of Mr
Norma St John Scott – a scrounger, parasite, pervert, a worm, a
self-confessed player of the pink oboe, a man or woman who by his
or her own admission chews pillows. It would be hard to imagine,
ladies and gentlemen of the jury, a more discredited and embittered
man, a more unreliable witness upon whose testimony to convict a
man who you may rightly think should have become Prime
Minister of his country or President of the world. You may on the
other hand choose to believe the evidence of Mrs Scott – in which
case I can only say you need psychiatric help of the type provided
by the excellent Dr Gleadle.

On the evidence of the so-called hit man, Mr Nolivia Newton-
John, I would prefer to draw a discreet veil. He is, as we know, a
man with a criminal past but I like to think no criminal future. He
is a piece of slimy refuse, unable to carry out the simplest murder
plot without cocking it up, to the distress of many. On the other
hand, you may think Mr Newton-John is one of the most
intelligent, profound, sensitive and saintly personalities of our
time. That is entirely a matter for you.

I now turn to the evidence about the money and Mr Jack
Haywire and Mr Nadir Rickshaw, neither of whom, as far as I can

make out, are complete and utter crooks, though the latter is incontestably foreign and, you may well think, the very type to boil up foul-smelling biryanis at all hours of the night and keep you awake with his pagan limbo dancing.

It is not contested by the defence that enormous sums of money flowed towards them in unusual ways. What happened to that money, we shall never know. But I put it to you, ladies and gentlemen of the jury, that there are a number of totally innocent ways in which that £20,000 could have been spent – on two tickets for *Evita*, a Centre Court seat at Wimbledon, or Mr Thorpe may have decided simply to blow it all on a flutter on the Derby. That is his affair and it is not for us to pry. It will be a sad day for this country when a leading politician cannot spend his election expenses in any way he sees fit.

One further point – you will probably have noticed that three of the defendants have very wisely chosen to exercise their inalienable right not to go into the witness box to answer a lot of impertinent questions. I will merely say that you are not to infer from this anything other than that they consider the evidence against them so flimsy that it was scarcely worth their while to rise from their seats and waste their breath denying these ludicrous charges.

In closing, I would like to pay a personal tribute to Mr Thorpe's husband, Miriam, who has stood by him throughout this long and unnecessary ordeal. I know you will join me in wishing them well for a long and happy future. And now, being mindful of the fact that the Prudential Cup begins on Saturday, putting all such thoughts from your mind, you are now to retire – as indeed should I – you are now to retire, carefully to consider your verdict of Not Guilty.

THE WORLD OF ANTS
(*Peter Cook & Co*, ITV, 1980. *Written with Bernard McKenna.*)

ROWAN ATKINSON: Tonight I'm talking with Professor Heinrich Globnik, arguably the world's leading authority on ants and ant-related behaviour.

PETER COOK

HEINRICH GLOBNIK: Now when you say 'arguably', there is no
doubt, not a scintilla of doubt in the world that I am numero
uno in the ant racket. There is no one in the world who knows
more about ants than yours truly. The ant is my speciality.

ROWAN ATKINSON: So what led you into this particular field?

HEINRICH GLOBNIK: Well, I first got interest in the ant at school.
I was a curious child. And I remember asking the teachers
questions such as 'what is the function of the ant in a capitalist
society?' And basically, I was given the brush-off. I get no real
answers so I tell myself 'no one knows the answers to this
question about the ants,' and this caused me to drift into the
field of ants and learning about the ants and what we have
learned from the ants and so I have studied the ants for the last
fifty-one years.

ROWAN ATKINSON: Excellent. Tell me, are there many different
categories of ants?

HEINRICH GLOBNIK: Yes, there are three main categories of ants,
loosely divided into the big ant, the small ant, and then, perhaps
the most interesting of all, the medium-sized ant.

ROWAN ATKINSON: What do ants do?

HEINRICH GLOBNIK: Very simply, the ant wanders around. A
typical ant will wander around for a while, and then he will find
some rubbish, some piece of twig or something like that. Then
he will grab hold of it with his mouth, get hold of the twig or the
rubbish, wander back to the ant hill, drop it, then wander out
again and go scurrying around for some more rubbish, pick it
up, take it back to the ant hill, go wandering out again, find
some piece of rubbish, pick it up, go wandering back to the ant
hill. And after a bit of wandering for hours and hours he get a bit
sleepy and sometimes the ant will lie down, fall asleep for a few
minutes. And then, as likely as not, some other stupid ant will
come along and drag him away back to the nest, mistaking him
for rubbish.

ROWAN ATKINSON: You make it all sound very random, but isn't
an ant hill a very organised society?

HEINRICH GLOBNIK: If your view of an organised society is
thousands of ants milling around in corridors, bumping into

each other with bits of twig and other rubbish in their mouth, then I understand why you elected that woman. In my view, the ant society is a shambles – a complete and utter shambles!

ROWAN ATKINSON: So how do ants reproduce?

HEINRICH GLOBNIK: I thought you get round to this. Anywhere in the world I go always sex it rears its head. You want to know about the sex life of the ant? Alright, I tell you about the sex life of the ant. Basically, it is a shambles! One ant will see another ant and then, for no apparent reason, he will jump on the other ant. Then, having jumped onto the other ant, they will roll around for a little while, jump off each other without so much as a hello, goodbye or anything. Sometimes they jump on a twig and they seem to have as good a time as they do with the other ant. The sex life of the ants is a shambles in my view.

ROWAN ATKINSON: Have you done any behavioural experiments with ants?

HEINRICH GLOBNIK: Yes, of course. I have done much research and behavioural experiments with ants. I have found, for example, if you put an ant in a locked metal box with no light and no food, after several weeks, this is interesting, after several weeks the ant will die. Also, if you feed the ant the equivalent of a bottle of vodka, one bottle of vodka, an ant is incapable of operating heavy machinery. This is what I have learned about the ant.

ROWAN ATKINSON: Well, Professor, I'm sure we could go on all night talking about ants.

HEINRICH GLOBNIK: No we couldn't! We have hammered the subject into the ground! I have said everything there is to know about the ant and that is it. Kaputt! We could not talk one moment longer.

ROWAN ATKINSON: OK. So, er, how would you sum up your career, Professor?

HEINRICH GLOBNIK: An utter waste of time.

ROWAN ATKINSON: Professor Globnik, thank you very much.

INALIENABLE RIGHTS

(*An Evening At Court,* Theatre Royal, Drury Lane,
London, 1983. *Written with Bernard McKenna.*)

(*John Cleese is sitting on a park bench, reading a newspaper. Enter
Peter Cook as Arthur Grole. Cook sits beside Cleese.*)

ARTHUR GROLE: Hello.

JOHN CLEESE: Hello.

ARTHUR GROLE: Hello again. I see you're reading *The Times.*

JOHN CLEESE: Yes. Yes, I am.

ARTHUR GROLE: As you're fully entitled to do. That is one of your
inalienable rights. Aren't we lucky in this country to have
inalienable rights?

JOHN CLEESE: I suppose so.

ARTHUR GROLE: You suppose so? You only suppose so. Aren't you
certain that we're very lucky to have inalienable rights?

JOHN CLEESE: Yes I am.

ARTHUR GROLE: Yes you are because, of course, you would be
perfectly entitled to disagree with me. That is one of your
inalienable rights. You have the inalienable right in this country
to disagree with anyone you like. Or, for that matter, with
anyone you don't like.

JOHN CLEESE: Yes, I see what you mean.

ARTHUR GROLE: Yes, you see what I mean, don't you. I mean, in
Russia you wouldn't be allowed to sit in the park reading *The
Times.* You wouldn't have that inalienable right in Russia. You
would have to sit in the park reading *Pravda.*

JOHN CLEESE: Or *Izvestia.*

ARTHUR GROLE: Or *Izvestia,* and they are both pretty dull reads.
Unless you speak Russian. Do you speak Russian?

JOHN CLEESE: No, I don't.

ARTHUR GROLE: No you don't, you poor sod. And you have an
inalienable right not to speak Russian in this country. In Russia
you have to speak Russian. But in this country we have an
inalienable right not to speak Russian. I've got a smattering.
Well, not really a smattering – just the one word.

JOHN CLEESE: Just the one?

ARTHUR GROLE: Just the one, yes. Nyet. Do you know what that means?

JOHN CLEESE: No.

ARTHUR GROLE: Neither do I, no. I don't know what Nyet means – not that it worries me. I am just happy to be in this country with my basic freedoms and my inalienable rights. Have you ever wanted to eat a swan?

JOHN CLEESE: Well, now that you mention it, no.

ARTHUR GROLE: What a mercy. My heart goes out to all those people who crave the flesh of the swan. You see, that is not one of our inalienable rights. Only the Queen and her direct relatives are allowed to cram huge wadges of roast swan down their gobs. It is not one of our inalienable rights. It's one of hers, you see, because all the swans belong to the Queen and vice versa. I reckon that was what that Carl Sagan was after.

JOHN CLEESE: What?

ARTHUR GROLE: You know – the bloke who exercised his inalienable right to wander into the Queen's bedroom to see if she was tucking into a bit of swan.

JOHN CLEESE: The name is Fagan – Michael Fagan.

ARTHUR GROLE: Nice to meet you, Michael. My name is Xavier Blancmange the Third.

JOHN CLEESE: I beg your pardon?

ARTHUR GROLE: My name is Xavier Blancmange the Third.

JOHN CLEESE: Really?

ARTHUR GROLE: No, not really. Not Xavier Blancmange the Third. I was born Arthur Grole, but I found that too difficult to pronounce so I changed it by deed poll as was my inalienable right. Am I boring you?

JOHN CLEESE: Yes.

ARTHUR GROLE: Yes, I thought I was. I have an instinct about this sort of thing. I'm almost psychic on occasions. I would say you're irritated as well.

JOHN CLEESE: Yes I am.

ARTHUR GROLE: Bored and irritated – as you have every right to be. I mean, here you were, sitting quietly in the park reading *The*

Times, and some total stranger wanders up and starts talking to you about your inalienable rights.

JOHN CLEESE: Perhaps you'll shut up then?

ARTHUR GROLE: Perhaps I will, and then again perhaps I won't. Why don't we have a wager? I'm willing to bet you ten whole p that I won't shut up.

JOHN CLEESE: You're on.

ARTHUR GROLE: Hello.

JOHN CLEESE: Well, I certainly fell for that one, didn't I?

ARTHUR GROLE: Hook, line and sinker.

JOHN CLEESE: Well, I've got a little bet for you now.

ARTHUR GROLE: A little bet? Yes, it always interests me, a little bet.

JOHN CLEESE: My 10p says that I bet you can't come up with a good punchline for this sketch.

Silence.

JOHN CLEESE: Thank you very much.

GROLE'S LAST STAND

(*Saturday Live*, Channel 4, 1986. *Written with Bernard McKenna.*)

(*John Fortune is sitting on a park bench, reading a newspaper. Enter Peter Cook, as Arthur Grole. Cook sits beside Fortune.*)

ARTHUR GROLE: Hello.

JOHN FORTUNE: Hello.

ARTHUR GROLE: Hello again.

JOHN FORTUNE: Yes.

ARTHUR GROLE: Hello again and again and again. Fancy you being here.

JOHN FORTUNE: Yes.

ARTHUR GROLE: Yes. I reckon this was meant to happen. I think this was doomed to occur. It's all written down in the great book of fate, in horrible pink squidgy writing. I was meant to be here, you were meant to be here, and here you are.

JOHN FORTUNE: Yes, here we are.

ARTHUR GROLE: Here we are, as you so rightly point out. Well, now you're here, what are you going to do about it?

JOHN FORTUNE: Nothing. I'd just like to sit and read the newspaper.

ARTHUR GROLE: Oh, you'd just like to sit and read the newspaper.

JOHN FORTUNE: Yes.

ARTHUR GROLE: Is there anything interesting in it?

JOHN FORTUNE: I don't know. I haven't read it yet.

ARTHUR GROLE: Oh well, you wouldn't know if there was anything interesting in it, would you? If you haven't even read it yet, you wouldn't have a clue what's in it, interesting or not. I read quite an interesting thing in a newspaper a few days ago. Apparently, Anita Ekberg has set up this hamburger stand in Rome. That's quite interesting, isn't it?

JOHN FORTUNE: Not really.

ARTHUR GROLE: I found it very interesting indeed, thank you very much. I mean, one minute she's up on the silver screen, fifty yards wide – the next moment, she's peddling Big Macs on the Via Veneto. Are you an Ekberg fan?

JOHN FORTUNE: No.

ARTHUR GROLE: No, you're not an Ekberg fan. You're more the type to enjoy Audrey Hepburn.

JOHN FORTUNE: Yes, I do like Audrey Hepburn.

ARTHUR GROLE: Of course you do. You're the type – I can tell it in your eyes – who goes for elfin beauties. I prefer huge, mountainous women who wobble when they breathe.

JOHN FORTUNE: Well I don't.

ARTHUR GROLE: Well that's a good thing, isn't it? We won't start bickering about our womenfolk. You can have the thin, elfin ones and I'll go for the huge, mountainous, wobbly ones.

JOHN FORTUNE: It's a deal.

ARTHUR GROLE: Yes, it is a deal. What about Shelley Winters?

JOHN FORTUNE: What about Shelley Winters.

ARTHUR GROLE: Well, is she mine or yours? I mean, she's a bit too slim for me but she's probably too plump for you. We could toss for her.

JOHN FORTUNE: You can have her.

ARTHUR GROLE: That's very kind of you indeed. Of course, Liz Taylor is going to be a bit of a dilemma, isn't she? She's very up and down. One moment she's elfin, the next second she's ballooned up to 103 stone. But she's elfin at the moment so you can have Liz.

JOHN FORTUNE: Alright, I've got Liz and Audrey. You've got Shelley and Anita. OK?

ARTHUR GROLE: Perfectly alright.

JOHN FORTUNE: I'd just like to read my newspaper.

ARTHUR GROLE: Of course you would. Of course, Shelley looked enormous in *The Poseidon Adventure* when she was all underwater with her clothes billowing around her. I think what would be fair would be if I had Shelley underwater and you took care of her on dry land.

JOHN FORTUNE: Very well.

ARTHUR GROLE: Am I boring you?

JOHN FORTUNE: Yes, as a matter of fact, you are.

ARTHUR GROLE: I thought I was. I'm very perceptive that way, you know. It's almost a psychic gift. I've got this uncanny knack of knowing what's going to happen.

JOHN FORTUNE: Then I daresay you'll know what's in the offing.

ARTHUR GROLE: Oh, yes. I just have to shut my eyes and I'll be able to see it all.

(*Arthur Grole shuts his eyes – John Fortune stands up.*)

ARTHUR GROLE: Furling newspaper with a tetchy look on his face, he begins to beat man relentlessly about the head.

(*Furling his newspaper with a tetchy look on his face, John Fortune begins to beat Arthur Grole relentlessly about the head.*)

ARTHUR GROLE: I didn't foresee it being quite as hard as that.

(*Exit John Fortune.*)

ARTHUR GROLE: Oh dear. Well, thank you very much for the paper. Give my love to Audrey! Let's see. Good grief! 'Awful Man In Mac And Trilby Sought by Swedish Police.' I didn't see that coming.

BUILDERS OF XANADU

(*Saturday Live*, Channel 4, 1986. *Written with Bernard McKenna.*)

PETER COOK: Traffic was terrible. Took me about three hours to get out of downtown Xanadu.

JOHN BIRD: How did it go with Kubla?

PETER COOK: Kubla Khan, as he likes to call himself these days – toffee-nosed git. Well, it went alright.

JOHN BIRD: Got the job then?

PETER COOK: Yes, got the job.

JOHN BIRD: Big one?

PETER COOK: Well, fairly big. He's got very grandiose in his old age, Kubla has.

JOHN BIRD: Well what does he want? An extension?

PETER COOK: No, no. More than that. He wants a pleasure dome.

JOHN BIRD: Nice. What sort of pleasure dome did he have in mind?

PETER COOK: Well, he was a bit vague about it. He rambled on a bit. The only adjective I got from him was 'stately'. In fact, that's what he decreed.

JOHN BIRD: Oh, he's decreeing things now then, is he?

PETER COOK: Certainly. No pissing about with planning permission for Kubla. If he wants a stately pleasure dome, wallop! He decrees it.

JOHN BIRD: Yes, well why not?

PETER COOK: Why not, at his age?

JOHN BIRD: Did you bung him an estimate, then?

PETER COOK: No, it's a bit tricky, you see.

JOHN BIRD: What's the problem? A pleasure dome's straightforward enough. I don't know about this 'stately' though. What's this 'stately'? That's new to me. What's that? Plants? Hammocks? Not structural, is it?

PETER COOK: No, it's not structural, 'stately'. It's more of an ambience sort of area.

JOHN BIRD: Well then, we'll just budget for a regular pleasure dome, and see if we can pick up some stately trimmings down the market.

PETER COOK: Well it's not the stately bit that bothers me.

JOHN BIRD: Oh. What's the snag, Alf?

PETER COOK: That's the snag. Alph.

JOHN BIRD: Alf's the snag?

PETER COOK: Alph is the snag, yes.

JOHN BIRD: But you're Alf.

PETER COOK: Yes, but I'm not a sacred river, am I?

JOHN BIRD: No, of course you're not. I never suggested it.

PETER COOK: Well, this is my point, you see? Part of his decree, vis-à-vis the stately pleasure dome, is he has this bloody sacred river Alph running through the structure.

JOHN BIRD: A sacred river?

PETER COOK: Running right through the structure. He specified that.

JOHN BIRD: We'll need a plumber then. I can have Ronnie bodge up a river for you and we can bung up a sign saying 'Sacred River of Alph'. Something along those lines.

PETER COOK: Yes, but we've still got a problem with his specifications.

JOHN BIRD: What's that, then?

PETER COOK: These caverns he wants.

JOHN BIRD: Caverns are a doddle! How big does he want them?

PETER COOK: Well, this is the big crunch that we come to.

JOHN BIRD: Oh no, he doesn't want another river, does he? He doesn't want a sacred river Crunch, does he?

PETER COOK: No, he doesn't want a sacred river Crunch, but with these caverns, you see, he's specified, here, on the docket there, 'measureless to man'.

JOHN BIRD: Measureless? He wants caverns you can't measure?

PETER COOK: Yes.

JOHN BIRD: But how does he know they'll fit? I mean, he knows caverns come by the yard, doesn't he?

PETER COOK: I told him. I said 'Kubla, for goodness sake! Caverns come by the yard! You can't have caves measureless to man! I mean, where the bloody hell are you going to go next? Where's this bloody river going to go?'

JOHN BIRD: Exactly!

PETER COOK: Down to a sea that is measureless to man? With lots of boats bobbing about that are measureless to man?

JOHN BIRD: Jellyfish measureless to man?

PETER COOK: Jellyfish measureless to man? No.

JOHN BIRD: Where does he want it, then?

PETER COOK: He wants it to exit in a sunless sea.

JOHN BIRD: Margate.

PETER COOK: Yes, that'll do.

JOHN BIRD: Well, alright then. So leaving aside the caverns for a moment, what we have to provide is your standard pleasure dome.

PETER COOK: With stately trappings.

JOHN BIRD: Stately trappings, and I'll speak to Ronnie about the river aspect of the job. That's Sacred River, exit in Margate. And we'll deal with the 'measureless to man' bit when we get to it, that's all.

PETER COOK: Yes, I think that's what we should do. When I'm next in Xanadu, I'll tell him we're on.

JOHN BIRD: Right. As soon as we've finished the pyramid job.

PETER COOK: How is the pyramid job going?

JOHN BIRD: I don't know. I tried to stick to the specifications you gave me, but really, you know, from a design point of view, I still think it'd be better – make more sense – to have the pointy bit at the top.

LORD STOCKTON
(*Saturday Live*, Channel 4, 1986)

JOHN BIRD: Lord Stockton, as the Conservative Party prepares for the Fulham by-election . . .

LORD STOCKTON: It's remarkable, this chair, isn't it? You can't control the bloody thing! Like the Space Shuttle, I suppose. Yes, sorry – the Conservative Party?

JOHN BIRD: Yes, as they prepare for the Fulham by-election, what do you think their priorities should be?

LORD STOCKTON: Well, whenever I look around this great country of ours, I really have to weep. Big girls don't cry. That's what it says in the Bible. But I'm not ashamed. I see around me four million people unemployed. Millions of others out of work. And what does that ghastly woman do? Bugger all.

JOHN BIRD: So you blame Mrs Thatcher?

LORD STOCKTON: Hold on a moment. Don't start putting words into my mouth. When I said 'that ghastly woman,' I don't call her ghastly just because she's a woman, and I don't call her a woman just because she's ghastly. But she is a woman and she is ghastly. So I call her That Ghastly Woman.

JOHN BIRD: That ghastly woman, yes.

LORD STOCKTON: Mind you, she has many, many, many qualities. In some ways she reminds me of Winston Churchill. Slimmer, of course.

JOHN BIRD: Yes. You mentioned her qualities. What qualities do you admire in Mrs Thatcher?

LORD STOCKTON: Well, I suppose if I had to single out a single quality, I'd have to plump for her hair.

JOHN BIRD: Her hair?

LORD STOCKTON: She has outstanding hair, which has moved with the times. But the trouble is, the rest of her has remained completely static. But Jack Kennedy had wonderful hair.

JOHN BIRD: Did he?

LORD STOCKTON: President Kennedy, wonderful hair, yes. I remember once sitting with him in the Oval Office. This was before he was assassinated.

JOHN BIRD: I see. Yes.

LORD STOCKTON: And he leant over to me and he said 'Prime Minister! Who cuts your hair?' So I told him and, of course, a year later he was dead. And Martin Luther King, he had wonderful hair.

JOHN BIRD: Yes.

LORD STOCKTON: Different, of course. It was more wiry. I remember sitting with Dr King and his lovely wife, Billie Jean. And I didn't hear a word he said. I was transfixed. By his hair. Lovely hair.

JOHN BIRD: Tell me, do you see yourself as the voice of moderation, Lord Stockton?

LORD STOCKTON: Well, for many years and in countless publications, all of which, incidentally, have been published by Macmillan and are still in print, I've advocated moderation.

JOHN BIRD: Yes.

LORD STOCKTON: But in moderation you have to draw the line somewhere. I mean, take South Africa. Nobody could abhor the system of Apartheid more than myself, except perhaps the blacks who live in South Africa. But what do you do about it? I remember my wife, God bless her. She refused to have any South African produce in the house. And one day a footman brought in some Outspan orange segments in a tin. Dorothy, God bless her, seized the can from him, threw it out the window. Unfortunately, it landed on a passing African and killed him. Beautiful hair, but completely dead.

JOHN BIRD: Lord Stockton, you're now in the autumn of your years.

LORD STOCKTON: Nearly dead, yes.

JOHN BIRD: Nearly dead is right. What brings you the most pleasure now?

LORD STOCKTON: I think the thing that gives me the greatest single pleasure is being an absolute bloody nuisance. It's such fun. I mean, take that Sunday trading business. I'm completely for it! But when Earl Attlee, the drug addict, when he whispered to me that one vote would kill the whole thing off and the whole bloody caboodle would go back to those ghastly estate agents in the House of Commons, of course 'no' I said. Great fun.

JOHN BIRD: Great fun. And finally, Lord Stockton, if I may ask, do you have any further ambitions in your life?

LORD STOCKTON: Well, I've had a very full life. Yes, I've fought in two world wars, I've governed the country, and been on Desert Island Discs. Roy Plomley, wonderful man. Completely bald. And, of course, dead.

JOHN BIRD: Dead, yes.

LORD STOCKTON: But I regard the House of Lords as a stepping stone. A stepping stone to Vegas.

JOHN BIRD: Is that Las Vegas?

LORD STOCKTON: Las Vegas. I don't see myself carrying the whole show. On the other hand, I'm not going to open for Tony Bennett.

NORMAN HOUSE*
(*Clive Anderson Talks Back*, Channel 4, 1993)

CLIVE ANDERSON: Now it's my pleasure to welcome a man who in 1993 shot from obscurity to being very much one of the men of the year, following his extraordinary claims to have been abducted by aliens to another planet. So, for another out-of-body experience, please welcome Mr Norman House.

(*Enter Peter Cook as Norman House.*)

CLIVE ANDERSON: Obviously I'm going to ask you about the alien experience but first of all I'd like to establish who you are and where you're from. What do you do for a living?

NORMAN HOUSE: I am a quality controller in a leading biscuit factory. It is my job to test biscuits for comestibility and I do this by biting into them, tasting them for flavour and texture, and if the biscuit is satisfactory I allow another four million to go by.

CLIVE ANDERSON: Now where do you do this biscuit testing?

NORMAN HOUSE: Ipswich. Ipswich area. Environs of Ipswich. It's very quiet. It nestles in a little valley where we live. We're surrounded by countryside and we have a small garage. It's a fascinating area, because the Romans first put down their Roman baths in Ipswich.

CLIVE ANDERSON: Alright, I don't really want to ask you about the history of Ipswich. It's more to do with your astonishing experience of being abducted by aliens. Now where were you when this happened?

NORMAN HOUSE: I was out with my wife Wendy, who also lives in the Ipswich area. Just above the garage we have a little flatlet, and we were out of an evening. I was out metal detecting.

CLIVE ANDERSON: Is that a hobby?

NORMAN HOUSE: Yes. Actually, I found this metal detector years ago. I was very lucky because I'd borrowed a friend's metal detector, and I was out detecting, and suddenly I felt a strong feeling that there was something metallic under the ground and, sure enough, I dug away and, lo and behold, a metal detector – almost as brand-new.

CLIVE ANDERSON: Right, that's true, because metal detectors are made of metal, aren't they?

NORMAN HOUSE: They are made of metal. One of the problems with a bad metal detector is that if it's poorly made it'll start detecting itself. A friend of mine had a detector which detected itself and it started just curling up and trying to eat the handle.

CLIVE ANDERSON: But this is a good one.

NORMAN HOUSE: This is a good one. We were out in the car and then I got out of the car and started detecting. And suddenly I saw this strange glowing object hovering about one and a half feet above the ground?

CLIVE ANDERSON: It wasn't headlamps, was it, or anything like that?

NORMAN HOUSE: No, no. It was an unearthly, unearthly object. Non-metallic, otherwise the detector would have . . .

CLIVE ANDERSON: Immediately . . .

NORMAN HOUSE: Detected it. And I felt strangely calm but at the same time horribly terrified. And I didn't know what to do and it just stayed there, glowing eerily. It was just hovering there and I felt something beckoning me – a mental beckoning more than a physical beckoning – and I suddenly saw a creature get out of the orb and begin to slowly suck me into its orbit, mentally.

CLIVE ANDERSON: Mentally suck you?

NORMAN HOUSE: Mentally suck me into the orbit, and I fell into a trance and the next thing I knew, I was elsewhere.

CLIVE ANDERSON: I know we've got some pictures here. Did you take these pictures?

NORMAN HOUSE: No. These snaps were taken by my wife Wendy.

CLIVE ANDERSON: Right. What did these creatures look like?

NORMAN HOUSE: Well, they're rather otter-like, otter-like in shape.

CLIVE ANDERSON: And how long did you spend on this planet?

NORMAN HOUSE: I was there for approximately four years – or seemed to be about four years but in fact it was only three minutes of our time.

CLIVE ANDERSON: What planet were you on? Was it Mars or Venus?

NORMAN HOUSE: Ikea. They were people who arrived millions of years ago in cardboard boxes and were forced to assemble themselves.

CLIVE ANDERSON: Which accounts for the strange shape, I suppose.

NORMAN HOUSE: Yes. They had no instructions.

CLIVE ANDERSON: And why would they be interested in you? Was it you in particular?

NORMAN HOUSE: I think they shared my love of metal, but it was mainly because they have a museum up there devoted to Rock & Roll.

CLIVE ANDERSON: Our Rock & Roll?

NORMAN HOUSE: Our Rock & Roll. And the only Rock & Roll they've ever heard was Manfred Mann. And they were unsure about the lyrics of one of his hits which was 'There I was walking down the street, going Doo Wah Diddy Diddy, Dum Diddy . . .' and that bit of the lyric was missing. So they only got up to 'Doo Wah Diddy Diddy, Dum Diddy,' and they wanted to know what came after.

CLIVE ANDERSON: And you were able to tell them?

NORMAN HOUSE: No, I didn't know that lyric at all, so they were most dissatisfied with me, and they are dissatisfied with everything really, up there on Ikea.

CLIVE ANDERSON: How did they communicate with you? Did they speak English?

NORMAN HOUSE: No, they think they can speak and they communicate through thought waves, through vibrations, timeless aeon vibrations.

CLIVE ANDERSON: And you could pick this up, could you?

NORMAN HOUSE: I could tell they didn't like what they got.

CLIVE ANDERSON: Yes. What's the atmosphere like on the planet?

NORMAN HOUSE: It's very thin. Very, very thin atmosphere. If I hadn't had some air in my jumper and in my socks with me I would surely have been stifled. It's just what I imagine being in Mexico City is like.

CLIVE ANDERSON: What do they do for food? Do they eat?

NORMAN HOUSE: No, they've been on a diet for two million years. They don't eat. They have no stomachs or mouths, they just have two slit eyes. So it's a good thing they don't eat because there's really nowhere for them to put the food.

CLIVE ANDERSON: Has this experience changed you in any way?

NORMAN HOUSE: Yes. An experience like that – in fact, that experience – made me realise how insignificant they were.

CLIVE ANDERSON: Thank you very much, Mr Norman House.

SIR JAMES BEAUCHAMP*
(*Clive Anderson Talks Back*, Channel 4, 1993)

CLIVE ANDERSON: In the dusty world of the courts of law, one judge has recently had the courage to open his mouth and blow away some of the cobwebs of tradition and hypocrisy which sometimes cloud the pure waters of justice. He's arguably Britain's best-known, and indeed most notorious, judicial figure. Ladies and gentlemen, please welcome Sir James Beauchamp.

(*Enter Peter Cook as Sir James Beauchamp.*)

CLIVE ANDERSON: Sir James, it's good to see you, judge. Well, I say judge but you're actually suspended at the moment, aren't you?

SIR JAMES BEAUCHAMP: Yes, I'm temporarily suspended for some judicial mistake, apparently, I was deemed to have made.

CLIVE ANDERSON: Yes, being considered by an inquiry.

SIR JAMES BEAUCHAMP: Being considered by my peers, and we should get a result very soon. It was an incident arising from a defendant being shot.

CLIVE ANDERSON: Yes.

SIR JAMES BEAUCHAMP: In court.

CLIVE ANDERSON: By you.

SIR JAMES BEAUCHAMP: By myself, yes. It was a deeply unpleasant young woman with specs who was up on a charge of shoplifting and I really became extremely irritated with her because her testimony was obviously full of holes and completely untrue. And momentarily losing patience I just vaulted over the dock and got her straight through the heart with a little Derringer I always carry with me.

CLIVE ANDERSON: But capital punishment's been abolished for some time now.

SIR JAMES BEAUCHAMP: Yes it has, except in my neck of the woods. It's very much an individual choice, I think, whether one executes. And it is a deterrent, I think.

CLIVE ANDERSON: Well, I suppose so. But for a judge to take the law into his own hands . . .

SIR JAMES BEAUCHAMP: Who better to take the law into their own hands than a judge?

CLIVE ANDERSON: You come from a long line of judges, don't you? You father was a judge before you.

SIR JAMES BEAUCHAMP: My father was a judge before me, yes, and his grandfather was a judge before him. Long before him, actually. We go back in sequence as far as one can remember.

CLIVE ANDERSON: I've no doubt you've always had a strong sense of right and wrong, even at school.

SIR JAMES BEAUCHAMP: I hanged a boy at school, yes, for dumb insolence. He was looking at me in that particular way. Irritating look. I hung him, or is it hanged? I never know which. Well, I strung him up.

CLIVE ANDERSON: Was he your fag?

SIR JAMES BEAUCHAMP: He was my best friend.

CLIVE ANDERSON: Until the hanging incident, obviously.

SIR JAMES BEAUCHAMP: We cut him down in time. I mean, he didn't pass away, thank God. Otherwise I would have been in terrible trouble.

CLIVE ANDERSON: Yes. You've been involved in some notorious cases. The Tiverton Twelve. That was one of yours, wasn't it?

SIR JAMES BEAUCHAMP: There was a great deal of press comment about my gaoling twelve people for life for stealing some toffees. But it was not so much the crime that I gaoled them for. It was the intent beyond the crime. Having stolen the toffees – in my view, though it was never proved – having stolen the toffees, they then got into a first class carriage between Bristol and Plymouth and started smoking.

CLIVE ANDERSON: But they then spent, I think, twenty years in custody, and it was later proved it wasn't them at all.

SIR JAMES BEAUCHAMP: It was another twelve from the same area.

CLIVE ANDERSON: British justice has come in for quite a few knocks recently – mainly your cases, it has to be said. But do you think British justice is still the best in the world?

SIR JAMES BEAUCHAMP: I think if you've committed a crime this is not a particularly good country to live in. But if you are wholly innocent and have never been arrested, this is as good a place as any to stay indoors and thank your lucky stars.

CLIVE ANDERSON: A lot of people say there's one law for the rich, another for the poor.

SIR JAMES BEAUCHAMP: Well, this is all written down. Of course there is. There's one law for the rich – there's several laws for the rich – and very few for the poor. Lots of laws for the rich, most of them pretty good, very lenient, very lenient to the rich. Because there is a difference between the rich and the poor.

CLIVE ANDERSON: Money.

SIR JAMES BEAUCHAMP: The amount of money, yes, and honestly you can afford more law if you're rich than if you're poor.

CLIVE ANDERSON: Because there's lots of laws for the rich.

SIR JAMES BEAUCHAMP: Lots of laws for the rich. They can pick and choose whichever one would suit them and the poor have to make do with, er, the National Health, or whatever it's called.

CLIVE ANDERSON: Legal Aid.

SIR JAMES BEAUCHAMP: Yes.

CLIVE ANDERSON: A lot of people say that the judges, people like you – well, they don't like you, they rather dislike you – but they say judges are out of touch. Are you in touch with real people?

SIR JAMES BEAUCHAMP: Of course I'm in touch with real people.

I do everyday things. I go to sleep in the evenings. I wake up. I have breakfast.

CLIVE ANDERSON: But are you in touch with the television programmes that people watch?

SIR JAMES BEAUCHAMP: Yes, I watch a great deal of television. I enjoy a lot of it. That Gladiators stuff – very, very good. That's about it, really. I just watch that of a Saturday.

CLIVE ANDERSON: And do you think that gives you a feeling for, er . . .

SIR JAMES BEAUCHAMP: That gives me a feeling of what it's like out there.

CLIVE ANDERSON: Has any of this damaged your relationship with your wife at all?

SIR JAMES BEAUCHAMP: Not really. My wife, as you know, is slightly physically impaired. She fell off a horse, or was pushed off a horse. Nobody really knows.

CLIVE ANDERSON: But you were there.

SIR JAMES BEAUCHAMP: Well, I thought she fell but it's very hard to tell at that speed. Over those particular hedges, with barbed wire. But she had a nasty fall and she's partially paralysed. One side is completely immobile. So she's very plucky, but it means she can serve the drinks but not peanuts at the same time. I think she'll pull through.

CLIVE ANDERSON: We wish her well. But we have to leave it there. Thank you very much, Sir James Beauchamp.

ALAN LATCHLEY*
(*Clive Anderson Talks Back*, Channel 4, 1993)

CLIVE ANDERSON: When it comes to football, one man has for many years been the most noticeable, the most controversial and occasionally the most successful manager this country has ever produced, his pithy words and abrasive style making him as famous off the pitch as he is on. Ladies and gentlemen, please welcome Alan Latchley.

(*Enter Peter Cook as Alan Latchley.*)

CLIVE ANDERSON: Now it's obviously very topical to get you since you're being tipped for the England job.

ALAN LATCHLEY: Oh, it's too early to talk about the England job.

CLIVE ANDERSON: OK, I'll come back to that in about five minutes, if I may, because I want to talk about your early career. You were one of the youngest managers in the football league, weren't you?

ALAN LATCHLEY: Yes, I was appointed manager when I was sixteen and a half, on the outskirts of Scunthorpe, which was close to where I was born.

CLIVE ANDERSON: You're very much from Scunthorpe . . .

ALAN LATCHLEY: I'm from Scunthorpe, yes. I'm a Scunny man through and through.

CLIVE ANDERSON: But football is very much your life.

ALAN LATCHLEY: It's in me blood, Clive, it's in me blood. I mean, without football I'd be nothing. I love football. She's a cruel mistress. She's more than a mistress. She's a wife, she's a daughter, she's an errant child. She can make you laugh, she can make you cry, she can bring tears to me ears, she can bring blood to me shoulder . . .

CLIVE ANDERSON: She can bring the kettle to the boil.

ALAN LATCHLEY: She can bring the kettle to the boil. Football! Football is about nothing unless it's about something and what it is about is football!

CLIVE ANDERSON: Now, Scunthorpe. You were manager there.

ALAN LATCHLEY: Scunthorpe, yes. I were manager there until sixteen and a half.

CLIVE ANDERSON: And what do you think you brought to Scunthorpe?

ALAN LATCHLEY: I brought heart and I brought defiance and I brought all those qualities that make this country what it is today. A certain feeling. A certain love. A certain toughness. Mental toughness! And physical toughness! And something so beautiful, I can scarcely express it. See, when I was a manager, briefly, when I was young, I didn't know much. I knew nothing. I come straight up from the moors and I was suddenly put in charge of a thriving club. So what did I do? I was just a lad! What did I do? I'll tell you what I did, Clive. I went home and read a book. 'How To Manage.'

CLIVE ANDERSON: Whose book was that?

ALAN LATCHLEY: That was my dad's book. 'How I Managed.' It was not about football but it was about life in general.

CLIVE ANDERSON: But what do you say you have to do to get a team going?

ALAN LATCHLEY: Belief. Motivation.

CLIVE ANDERSON: Motivation?

ALAN LATCHLEY: Motivation. Motivation. Motivation. The three M's. That's what football is all about. It's all about motivation. You've got to get those boys on the pitch motivated. It's no good saying 'go out and buy some ice cream, go to the pictures.' You've got to tell them what they're doing. You've got to motivate them onto the pitch. Push them out with forks if you need to, but get them out on to the pitch. And when the game's over, get them in again!

CLIVE ANDERSON: You went to Hartlepool where you had this system of getting them angry.

ALAN LATCHLEY: Well, rage is very much an adrenalin inducing factor in all sports. I mean, Linford Christie wasn't in a good mood when he won the hundred metres, was he?

CLIVE ANDERSON: Well, he was afterwards.

ALAN LATCHLEY: Yes, but you've got to be in a rage to bring out the best in yourself. What I'd do to my players – one of the tactics I used, an early tactic – was to kidnap their wives or girlfriends. Girlfriends or wives, I'd send them all on a bus up to Grimsby, with no ticket back, and the lads went mad! One game, against Rotherham, my whole team were sent off almost as soon as they got on.

CLIVE ANDERSON: Your father was something to do with the circus.

ALAN LATCHLEY: The Great Escapini, my father was. He used to do a vanishing act. He would lock himself up in a suitcase – usually in a hotel room, as soon as the bill arrived – and he would escape from the suitcase. And with that background I formed the

Escapini Defence, which consisted of a ten-man defensive unit. I had them stood on each other's shoulders in the goal mouth, with their backs to the opposing team, and they would sit there and we'd rely on rebounds.

CLIVE ANDERSON: You only lasted a couple of weeks at Hartlepool.

ALAN LATCHLEY: Two weeks. You see, I'm a Scunny man and they don't like Scunny people at Hartlepool.

CLIVE ANDERSON: And along with many other managers, you went to Manchester City.

ALAN LATCHLEY: Man City, yes. That's where I introduced the concept of equal playing facilities. Namely, if you had skilful people on your team, that was no excuse for them playing better than the others. That would make the other ones feel inferior which – let's face it, I wouldn't say this if I had a team with me now – but some of them are worse than the others. And my tactic was to get them all down to exactly the same level.

CLIVE ANDERSON: What do you think you could bring to the England manager's job? I mean, you're a friend of Graham Taylor's, I know.

ALAN LATCHLEY: I'm a friend of Graham and I won't speak ill of the man. He did a cracking job. When you look at the potential that he had there and his ability to transform them into those results, you have to realise you are dealing with someone unusual.

CLIVE ANDERSON: Yes. You say you won't speak ill of him, but you have spoken ill of him on TV programmes – and, indeed, of every other football manager. So what is it, do you think, that you could bring to the England job that your rivals couldn't?

ALAN LATCHLEY: I would bring heart and motivation. Let us work our way up from the bottom and stay there if we can.

CLIVE ANDERSON: Now I know that, apart from your football activities, you have management seminars that you run to apply your methods to other industries.

ALAN LATCHLEY: Yes. I have a course called Dare To Fail, in which people who are ambitious, people who have had some degree of success in life, can come along and see what it's like to be at the bottom of the pile, and learn how to get there with pride and dignity intact. It's with a slide presentation and it's a very nice week spent in the country – locked up. You're not allowed to smoke, drink or sleep. It's just teaching people.

CLIVE ANDERSON: So Dare To Fail is the slogan?

ALAN LATCHLEY: The other side of failure, Clive, is success.

CLIVE ANDERSON: I follow that. Would you say that your career has largely been a failure?

ALAN LATCHLEY: Or a success. Depends on how you look at the coin. Toss it in the air, let it fall you know not where. But I can look at myself in the mirror in the morning and say 'there is a man.'

CLIVE ANDERSON: Thank you very much, Alan Latchley.

ERIC DALEY*
(Clive Anderson Talks Back, Channel 4, 1993)

CLIVE ANDERSON: There are only a few great rock stars, and even fewer mega-stars, perhaps only a handful of rock legends, so it gives me great pleasure to introduce one of the only mega legendary star rockers, the great – not late – Eric Daley!

(Enter Peter Cook as Eric Daley.)

CLIVE ANDERSON: It's marvellous to have one of the great rock stars of all time, but let's go back to your early career, perhaps for the younger viewers.

ERIC DALEY: Well, as you know, I started very, very young, at school, with Reg and Jez. We were just sort of mucking around with skiffle – Ya Ha, a bit of Lee Ha, a lot of that old Ethiopian sound, which we had in before it got fashionable.

CLIVE ANDERSON: That was The Corduroys, of course.

ERIC DALEY: The Corduroys, yes – that was our first group, God rest them.

CLIVE ANDERSON: Jez was the motivating force.

ERIC DALEY: Well, Jez – God rest him – some would say he was the creative one of the three. I mean, without Jez we would have just been a duo. With Jez, there was three of us there. We all had our little battles. And he wrote the songs that were immediately available.

CLIVE ANDERSON: The successful songs?

ERIC DALEY: Er, yes.

CLIVE ANDERSON: Whereas your ones didn't really . . .

ERIC DALEY: Ours were more the sort of early white noise type – the sort of sound that you can't get into at once. It's the sort of sound you can only get into years later.

CLIVE ANDERSON: If then.

ERIC DALEY: Well, it's avant garde. But Jez was the one with the, er . . .

CLIVE ANDERSON: Talent?

ERIC DALEY: Tunes. Melodically, he had the tunes. But looking back on those records – or listening to them, even – you get a feeling of the times. You get a feeling of anything was possible.

CLIVE ANDERSON: It was the Sixties.

ERIC DALEY: It was a time of rejoicing, a feeling of you could do anything if you just tried. And Jez tried, and died. We tried, and lived.

CLIVE ANDERSON: In the Seventies, of course, you went on to form one of the first supergroups.

ERIC DALEY: Yeah, Ye Gods. It was, I suppose, one of the first great all-white supergroups – just me and some other people that I brought into the group, who were very good in their own right. There was a little boy who we found in Pittsburgh – Blind Tony Tin Tin. Just a little kid about eight years old, and he played like a dream.

(*Daley mimes drum solo.*)

CLIVE ANDERSON: He was the drummer, was he?

ERIC DALEY: No, that's vocals. Oh, he was a dream. But we never toured because we could never find the venues. Because those were the days – I say it myself – I mean, it's on the public record – I've done a lot of drugs. I've done a lot of drugs and I've slept with a lot of women. And, boys and girls at home – don't! If you think that by sleeping with thousands of women and taking thousands of drugs, you're going to have a good time, let me just

PETER COOK

say this – don't! Because I'm telling you, I've just got out of the Henry Ford clinic.

CLIVE ANDERSON: The Henry Ford Clinic?

ERIC DALEY: Yes.

CLIVE ANDERSON: Not the Betty Ford Clinic?

ERIC DALEY: No, the Henry one is a much tougher regime. You have to build a car before you're allowed out – seriously. Scrub your own toilets, and read your own newspapers, and everything like that. And I think God, just for today, I'm clean and sober – and I would not like it to be any other way. So don't! Whatever you do, don't!

CLIVE ANDERSON: That's your message?

ERIC DALEY: Just say 'Mmm . . . Maybe.' No – just kidding.

CLIVE ANDERSON: Now, Ye Gods' big hit was . . .

ERIC DALEY: I Love It. Yes, it's such a simple lyric. It's silly to be proud of it, but I am. The lyric is 'I love it.' Simple as that, just with a little tune underneath:

I love it I love it I love it
I love it I love it I love it
I love it I love it I love it
I love it I love it
It it it it it it it it!

Of course, you need all the other people there at the same time. It's no good just doing it, er, Al Policello, or whatever it is.

CLIVE ANDERSON: Fair enough. Now, what about your film career? Because that's been a bit up and down, hasn't it?

ERIC DALEY: I think I made a mistake in accepting the parts I did. I should never have played Edward the Confessor, because I was at a loss. It wasn't my territory.

CLIVE ANDERSON: No, and you've become very interested in the environment.

ERIC DALEY: I love it, I love, I love it – the environment. Can't get too much of it. It is such a great thing to have, and we are the only species in the world, Clive, who systematically goes round destroying it. You won't get a whitebait saying, er, you won't find an anchovy going into the rainforest and saying 'Let's tear it all down!' Only man. And without the environment, we would not be able to live. That is my view. And that's why I think we should succour it, harbour it, look after it – as if it was our own child.

CLIVE ANDERSON: And of course you have your own . . .

ERIC DALEY: Oh yes, I have my own child.

CLIVE ANDERSON: No, you have your own anchovy farm, don't you?

ERIC DALEY: Yes, it's just a small contribution to the environment. It's an unnatural salt lake which I've built in Hertfordshire, where I've got anchovies, millions of them, swimming around and breeding. And it takes a bit of money to keep it going, but it's lovely to see them happy. And the swans, the black swans, fly over and swoop, and I go 'Don't you dare! Don't you dare! I'm saving these little creatures, and just because you're peckish, mate, doesn't mean I'm not going to blast you out of the sky!' There's irony there, isn't there?

CLIVE ANDERSON: You've now come a long way since those early rocking days, and now you've got your country house and everything.

ERIC DALEY: I love the country. We're lucky enough to have a place in the country, very near town – so we've got the best of everything, really. And Laura adores it, you know.

CLIVE ANDERSON: That's your?

ERIC DALEY: That's my wife.

CLIVE ANDERSON: Your fifth wife, isn't it?

ERIC DALEY: Yeah, she came after the fourth one. She's a beautiful woman. Very wise, very very wise – probably got more wisdom in her than I have.

CLIVE ANDERSON: If that's possible. Now I've got to ask you, because I won't be forgiven, is there any chance of Ye Gods reforming?

ERIC DALEY: Well, what can I say?

CLIVE ANDERSON: Well, Yes or No would be handy.

ERIC DALEY: It's on the cards.

CLIVE ANDERSON: It's on the cards?

ERIC DALEY: There's a big gig for the environment in 2004, and we're hoping to get everyone – Mulvin and Melgood – out and get them all in from all over the world, and get them all on the stage and just play that stuff again.

CLIVE ANDERSON: OK. I want to be there!

ERIC DALEY: Be there, Clive!

CLIVE ANDERSON: OK. Well, thank you much, Eric Daley.

*Reproduced by kind permission of Hat Trick Productions Ltd and Channel 4

Chapter Eleven

SIR ARTHUR STREEB-GREEBLING

From Harold Macmillan in *Beyond the Fringe* to Sir James Beauchamp in *Clive Anderson Talks Back*, patrician characters always came easily to Peter Cook, but his ultimate upper-class archetype was Sir Arthur Streeb-Greebling – the complacent aristocrat who'd wasted his whole life trying to teach ravens to fly underwater. Sir Arthur made several appearances in *Not Only But Also*, where he echoed Cook's own lifelong fascination with creepy crawlies. In England, he tried (and failed) to teach worms to talk. In Australia, he tried (and failed) to tame the ferocious funnel-web spider. But his most substantial broadcasts came twenty years later, during the last few years of Cook's life, in two series of retrospective interviews, broadcast on BBC2, and Radio Three.

The first of these was *A Life in Pieces*, directed by John Lloyd and produced by Peter Fincham, who'd suggested doing a show about The Twelve Days of Christmas. With some help from Rory McGrath and Peter Fincham, Peter Cook and John Lloyd put together twelve five-minute scripts, in which Sir Arthur Streeb-Greebling was interviewed by Ludovic Kennedy – in theory about the twelve improbable gifts in that repetitious Christmas Carol, but in practice about twelve improbable incidents in Sir Arthur's long and utterly pointless life.

A Life in Pieces was fun to make – usually the sign of a successful show. 'The meeting would start, and within ten minutes we'd all be weak with laughter,'[1] recalled Lloyd, fondly remembering their scriptwriting sessions, at Lin Cook's house in Hampstead. However five minute programmes are always difficult to schedule, and often struggle to find an audience. Unfortunately, *A Life in Pieces* confirmed this televisual rule of thumb. Transmitted every night at ten to ten during the last week of 1990 and the first week of 1991, it was enjoyed by those viewers who caught it, but passed by largely unnoticed. This was a shame, since this idiosyncratic series was, in part, an oblique poetic confessional – scattered with personal clues, like a particularly cryptic crossword.

Peter Fincham also helped prepare Sir Arthur's (and Cook's) last series – *Why Bother?* Recorded less than a year before his death, it's still one of the best things he ever did, largely thanks to Chris Morris – the iconoclastic, enigmatic satirist most notorious for his fearless lampoon of the media's moral panic over paedophilia. *Why Bother?* benefited from Morris's brilliant interrogation of Sir Arthur. Since Dudley's US departure, Cook's straight men had been far too deferential – bland and empty ciphers that gave him nothing to fight against. Even in character, Cook's colleagues looked up to him, and were reluctant to intrude on his limelight. Morris treated Cook with the respect his talent deserved, taking off the gloves and matching him punch for punch. Morris left Cook enough space to land his own punchlines, but Morris also created a proper character of his own – a variation on his pompous, self-important news and current affairs anchorman, already familiar to fans of *Brass Eye* and *The Day Today*. Cook responded to this backhanded compliment in kind, resulting in some memorable bouts. 'This is far from being the dregs of some washed-up has-been scratching around to recreate lost glories,' declared John Bird. 'Rather, it looks like the last work of a considerable creative artist.'[2] The show's success prompted a commission for another series of *A Life in Pieces*. He never made it.

A PARTRIDGE IN A PEAR TREE
(BBC2, 1990/91)

LUDOVIC KENNEDY: Tonight and for the next twelve nights I am the guest of Sir Arthur Streeb-Greebling, a man who needs no introduction from me and so – without further ado – Sir Arthur, good evening.

SIR ARTHUR STREEB-GREEBLING: Good evening. And season's greeblings.

LUDOVIC KENNEDY: Streeb-Greebling, Sir Arthur – that's a very unusual name.

SIR ARTHUR STREEB-GREEBLING: Yes, the Streebs originally hailed from Iceland – or Norway, as it was then, and what is now modern Denmark. Streeb is in fact a corruption of the original Norsk name Struwb.

LUDOVIC KENNEDY: Does that have any meaning in Norsk, in fact?

SIR ARTHUR STREEB-GREEBLING: It means Struwb in Norsk. It's almost impossible to translate, really. It basically means a sort of wooden bucket with two holes in it. Underwear, really – wooden underwear, which is the only sensible way to deal with the cold Norsk summer. You just take off your underwear, set it on fire and huddle round it for warmth.

LUDOVIC KENNEDY: Do you speak any Lap, yourself?

SIR ARTHUR STREEB-GREEBLING: I have a smattering – or a smeurtering, as they call it. They don't in fact call it Lap. They call it Leurp. But I do have a smeurtering of Leurp. A few words – Strerb, Stuwb, Luwp. I like to think if I found myself in fourth century Lapland I could get by – probably. Or preurbeurbly.

LUDOVIC KENNEDY: The Streebs then presumably migrated, did they?

SIR ARTHUR STREEB-GREEBLING: In their long proud underwear, yes. They migrated to Britain, which is where they first encountered the Greeblings. Now the Greeblings were Picts and they were quite unlike the Streebs, you see, for whereas the

Streebs were tall, blond, willowy people, the Greeblings were short, dark, shrublike folk who worshipped the ladder.

LUDOVIC KENNEDY: Why was that?

SIR ARTHUR STREEB-GREEBLING: Well, because they'd never actually seen one, so they couldn't prove it existed and, naturally, they believed in it. Question of faith, really. Various animals were sacred as well. The giraffe, for example. Legend had it that were a Pict to kill a giraffe, his family would be cursed for all eternity.

LUDOVIC KENNEDY: How did the Picts know about the giraffe?

SIR ARTHUR STREEB-GREEBLING: Well, they only knew the theoretical giraffe, which they revered because it didn't need a ladder. Naturally, a giraffe, of course – cave paintings show a cylindrical sausage-like animal, yellowish in colour, with one cylindrical leg and a two-hundred-foot long neck ending in, um, another leg. Or neck, it could be. It's not very well drawn. In fact, I think it might very well be upside down, the one I saw.

LUDOVIC KENNEDY: I see.

SIR ARTHUR STREEB-GREEBLING: They call it the two-hundred-foot-long dog.

LUDOVIC KENNEDY: What would that be in Norsk?

SIR ARTHUR STREEB-GREEBLING: Well, it wouldn't be in Norsk. These were Greeblings, remember, not Streebs or Struwbs.

LUDOVIC KENNEDY: Oh yes. Of course.

SIR ARTHUR STREEB-GREEBLING: But if it was in Norsk it would probably be something like The Too Hoondrood Fooot Loong Doog.

LUDOVIC KENNEDY: Yes. Now you say cave paintings?

SIR ARTHUR STREEB-GREEBLING: Yes, they lived in subterranean caves. Caves from which they kept up their underground resistance movement.

LUDOVIC KENNEDY: Against the Romans?

SIR ARTHUR STREEB-GREEBLING: Yes.

LUDOVIC KENNEDY: Was it effective?

SIR ARTHUR STREEB-GREEBLING: Very effective. The Romans

never got to the bottom of it. In fact, I don't think the Romans were aware of how much resistance was going on underground, since the Greeblings never surfaced and the Romans went back to Rome in 410 AD none the wiser.

LUDOVIC KENNEDY: What's your first gift, Sir Arthur?

SIR ARTHUR STREEB-GREEBLING: My first gift is a partridge in a pear tree.

LUDOVIC KENNEDY: Why that?

SIR ARTHUR STREEB-GREEBLING: For two reasons.

LUDOVIC KENNEDY: What's the first reason?

SIR ARTHUR STREEB-GREEBLING: Would you mind if I did my second reason first?

LUDOVIC KENNEDY: Of course.

SIR ARTHUR STREEB-GREEBLING: My second reason is that I am an enormous admirer of Marlon Brando.

LUDOVIC KENNEDY: What's the connection?

SIR ARTHUR STREEB-GREEBLING: Well, Marlon has a habit of dressing up as a partridge to avoid being bothered in restaurants. He'd go out to eat with his buddies. Walter Pidgeon, Howard Hawks, Gregory Peck, the usual crowd – and this is coming back to my first reason – in The Pear Tree. Which of course, was an exclusive restaurant in the Hollywood Hills, where you could only get in if you were disguised as a bird and you could only get out if you'd 'settled your bill,' which was a sort of in joke in Beverly Hills in those days.

LUDOVIC KENNEDY: Is a sense of humour important to you, Sir Arthur?

SIR ARTHUR STREEB-GREEBLING: Terribly important, yes. And of course it is the way to a woman's heart – soft music, a bottle of wine, candlelight, and then, just as the meal draws to a close, slip on an albatross costume and say 'Oh look! There's my bill!' Love will blossom. Or you could point to somebody called William, I suppose. Either would work, I imagine.

LUDOVIC KENNEDY: Sir Arthur, you have your partridge. You have your pear tree.

SIR ARTHUR STREEB-GREEBLING: Thank you.

LUDOVIC KENNEDY: We look forward very much to seeing you

tomorrow and finding out what your second gift is.

SIR ARTHUR STREEB-GREEBLING: Thank you very much.

TWO TURTLE DOVES
(BBC2, 1990/91)

LUDOVIC KENNEDY: Good evening once again, Sir Arthur.

SIR ARTHUR STREEB-GREEBLING: Good evening.

LUDOVIC KENNEDY: You spoke yesterday of the history of the Streeb-Greeblings. I'd like now, if I may, to move on to your immediate family.

SIR ARTHUR STREEB-GREEBLING: Yes.

LUDOVIC KENNEDY: Your father, now. What sort of relationship did you have with him?

SIR ARTHUR STREEB-GREEBLING: My father was a remote, icy man. Remoter, icier and indeed manlier than I was.

LUDOVIC KENNEDY: Were you close?

SIR ARTHUR STREEB-GREEBLING: Well, he was closer than me, but almost from the moment I was born he wanted no more to do with me. Not very paternal as a father. Instead, he preferred to have me reared by wolves. Fortunately for me, there were very few decent-sized wolves in the Aylesbury area at the time. In fact, the only thing that even remotely resembled a wolf was my Aunt Mary's Pekinese and my father, in his wisdom, drew the line at me being suckled by a Pekinese.

LUDOVIC KENNEDY: Really? Why?

SIR ARTHUR STREEB-GREEBLING: I don't know. I don't think it was a racial thing. He had a great respect for the Pekinese. They were the Chinese hunting dogs, you know.

LUDOVIC KENNEDY: Were they?

SIR ARTHUR STREEB-GREEBLING: Oh yes. Bred to track down the hippotami that infested the Fuzhou valley and drag them out of their warrens. Hence the huge, boggling eyes they developed.

LUDOVIC KENNEDY: Yes.

SIR ARTHUR STREEB-GREEBLING: Now a lot of people think the Pekinese developed their huge, boggling eyes in order for them to be able to see in the dark down the hippopotamus warrens, but not so, no, not so at all. The reason why the Pekinese developed such huge, boggling eyes is purely one of surprise that anyone should ask them to perform such a function. They're terribly small, the Pekinese, and the hippo by contrast is gigantic, and it'd take about five hundred Pekinese working as a team to drag the hippo out of its lair. So my father decided to have me raised by goats.

LUDOVIC KENNEDY: As a child you ran free with the goats?

SIR ARTHUR STREEB-GREEBLING: No, I wasn't free. Not free at all – far from it. I was shackled to a post – my father's way of getting me to stand on my own two feet.

LUDOVIC KENNEDY: Two feet, Sir Arthur, and your second gift – two turtle doves. Is there a sentimental reason for that?

SIR ARTHUR STREEB-GREEBLING: No, I'm afraid I can't be too sentimental about a bird that attacks helpless turtles. No, I eat them without compunction. I must say they're delicious. Lovely, lovely turtle flavour.

LUDOVIC KENNEDY: As well as a taste for turtle doves you've retained, I imagine, a lifelong fondness for the world of the goat – goat's cheese, goat's milk, and son on?

SIR ARTHUR STREEB-GREEBLING: No. Oddly enough, I went off goats somewhat after being raised by them. Never taken to goats' cheese. Got a few goat waistcoats, hats, shoes, underwear, things like that, but that's normal – everybody's got those. Kid gloves? I quite like them, but the actual cheese I've never had much time for.

LUDOVIC KENNEDY: What about your mother?

SIR ARTHUR STREEB-GREEBLING: My mother, by contrast, was a saint. Whenever I think of my dear mother, I have an abiding image of a small, kindly, plump, grey-haired lady pottering at the sink. 'Get away from the bloody sink!' my mother would yell at her. 'And get out of my kitchen, you awful plump kindly woman!' We never found out who she was. But she drove us all – and I mean absolutely all of us – stark raving mad.

LUDOVIC KENNEDY: Are you hinting there, Sir Arthur, at your father's breakdown?

SIR ARTHUR STREEB-GREEBLING: Yes indeed. One day, quite without warning, he became utterly convinced that he was a bat. Made a pathetic sight, standing there in the middle of the village green, asking the locals to throw cricket balls at him.

LUDOVIC KENNEDY: And did they?

SIR ARTHUR STREEB-GREEBLING: Oh yes, we all did. We all joined in. He was a deeply unpleasant and very unpopular man. But tough as teak – you have to give him that. He hung on in there for, oh, about six hours, until about four o'clock. But during the tea interval, they brought on the heavy roller and that did the trick. I think he had a pretty good innings.

LUDOVIC KENNEDY: Given the opportunity, Sir Arthur, is there any one thing that you wish you could say to your father now?

SIR ARTHUR STREEB-GREEBLING: On reflection, I think very much what I ought to have said to him at the time.

LUDOVIC KENNEDY: What was that?

SIR ARTHUR STREEB-GREEBLING: Well, something along the lines of 'Watch out, Papa, there's a heavy roller behind you.'

LUDOVIC KENNEDY: Thank you, Sir Arthur.

THREE FRENCH HENS
(BBC2, 1990/91)

LUDOVIC KENNEDY: Sir Arthur, what have you chosen for your gift this evening?

SIR ARTHUR STREEB-GREEBLING: I've chosen three French hens.

LUDOVIC KENNEDY: Three French hens? Why's that?

SIR ARTHUR STREEB-GREEBLING: Well, I chose three French hens because three is about the ideal number. I certainly don't want to have more than that, and a single French hen on its own tends to be rather self-centred – a huge eggo.

LUDOVIC KENNEDY: What about two French hens?

SIR ARTHUR STREEB-GREEBLING: Well, they'd be twice as self-centred and you don't want that.

LUDOVIC KENNEDY: And why French hens?

SIR ARTHUR STREEB-GREEBLING: I chose French hens because they're rather more sophisticated than the English hens – la poule anglaise – which is a rather dull creature. As Winston Churchill said, 'if the hen should ever leave the Tower of London, it wouldn't really matter very much.'

LUDOVIC KENNEDY: You certainly seem to know your hens, Sir Arthur.

SIR ARTHUR STREEB-GREEBLING: Yes, I do. I spent a great deal of time with hens in the Seventies working for the EHC.

LUDOVIC KENNEDY: The European Hen Commission.

SIR ARTHUR STREEB-GREEBLING: That's right, yes, in Brussels. It was our task to arrive at the Single European Hen – a hen combining all the good features of the individual national hens. The Italian hen, for example, has a lot to contribute.

LUDOVIC KENNEDY: What, in particular?

SIR ARTHUR STREEB-GREEBLING: The Italian hen? Its swagger, its braggadocio. One wants to keep that strain of the Italian hen in the Single European Hen but one could do without the exuberance, the unpleasant strutting and – dare one say it – the cowardice.

LUDOVIC KENNEDY: Cowardice?

SIR ARTHUR STREEB-GREEBLING: Yes. If a hen is unwilling to get into the oven then how on earth are we going to eat it? The SEH is one that is self-defeathering, one that comes without a great song and dance, moults neatly into the nearest bowl and jumps into the microwave.

LUDOVIC KENNEDY: With a swagger?

SIR ARTHUR STREEB-GREEBLING: No, no, no! We don't want it swaggering in, for heaven's sake! Nor do we want it entering so meekly, so despondently, that we feel sorry for it.

LUDOVIC KENNEDY: What are your main memories of Brussels during the 1970s?

SIR ARTHUR STREEB-GREEBLING: A lot of hard work involved, of course. Committee meetings, committee meetings, endless committee meetings. For example, it took seven years of committee meetings before they could decide on a venue for the committee meetings. The only thing we all agreed on was it shouldn't be Brussels. So, naturally, Brussels became the compromise choice.

LUDOVIC KENNEDY: Did you like Brussels?

SIR ARTHUR STREEB-GREEBLING: My attitude was very much 'when in Brussels, do as the Belgians do – leave as soon as possible.' Brussels can be a lonely place if you're completely on your own.

LUDOVIC KENNEDY: Does Brussels have much nightlife?

SIR ARTHUR STREEB-GREEBLING: The nightlife in Brussels is very similar to the daylife, but a bit darker and nothing's open. A sort of less hectic Luton.

LUDOVIC KENNEDY: A little dull?

SIR ARTHUR STREEB-GREEBLING: Yes, but there is another side to Brussels. If you get to know the right people you can get to see the pulsating underbelly of the city – the seedy bars, garish strip joints, sumptuous brothels and, of course, the National Railway Museum.

LUDOVIC KENNEDY: Very much Graham Greene territory.

SIR ARTHUR STREEB-GREEBLING: Very much, yes. A twilight world of drugs and prostitution to which I was introduced by a Norwegian seed tycoon.

LUDOVIC KENNEDY: Were you tempted by these secret delights?

SIR ARTHUR STREEB-GREEBLING: Not really. I'm a straightforward geranium man, myself – and a few busy lizzies scattered here and there.

LUDOVIC KENNEDY: No, I mean the 'bulging underbelly', the 'teeming nightlife'.

SIR ARTHUR STREEB-GREEBLING: Well, naturally, as a single man in a foreign country I was subject to the normal temptations and, I'm ashamed to say, that on two occasions, I weakened – those chocolates are irresistible. But most of all I missed female companionship.

LUDOVIC KENNEDY: Did you find it?

SIR ARTHUR STREEB-GREEBLING: Yes. I met the love of my life in

Brussels. A Tuesday evening. The committee had just broken up in disarray. The French had walked out and the Germans had walked in, which, as you know, is a pretty fatal combination. I was at a loose end, and it was after nine o'clock, so there weren't any taxis and I decided to walk home through the Swiss Quarter.

LUDOVIC KENNEDY: The Swiss Quarter?

SIR ARTHUR STREEB-GREEBLING: Yes. Not a safe place for the casual visitor after dark. I was feeling rather restless and, as I was passing by the notorious Toblerone Complex, I saw a girl huddled in the doorway. She seemed to be sobbing and there was something about this frail little creature that drew me to her.

LUDOVIC KENNEDY: And this was to be the love of your life?

SIR ARTHUR STREEB-GREEBLING: She was to become that as time went by. Her name was Rochelle. She'd come to Brussels in search of the bright lights. A simple farm girl from Ghent, a girl who felt trapped by the sheep and the chickens and wanted to find herself, and, in so doing, she found me. I just took her back to my hotel.

LUDOVIC KENNEDY: Love at first sight?

SIR ARTHUR STREEB-GREEBLING: Yes. When we got to the room, I could see that she was a little overawed by the surroundings. I expect it was the first time she had seen furniture. So, to put her at her ease, I boiled up some Nesquik and started to tell her a little about myself. I brought her up to date about all the latest fracas with the Dutch, and the infighting between the Spanish farmers and the Fins, and I was just explaining the ramifications of the Community Potato Policy when I saw that her cup was empty. I went to the kitchenette and prepared another Nesquik and when I returned, she was gone.

LUDOVIC KENNEDY: So you never saw her again?

SIR ARTHUR STREEB-GREEBLING: Not as such.

LUDOVIC KENNEDY: Thank you, Sir Arthur. A very moving story.

SIR ARTHUR STREEB-GREEBLING: Yes, Rochelle. Or was it Michelle? No, Rochelle, that's the chap. Brussels, Brussels, Brussels. What's past is past and what's to come, with a bit of luck, won't happen.

FOUR CALLING BIRDS
(BBC2, 1990/91)

LUDOVIC KENNEDY: Sir Arthur, you have travelled widely.

SIR ARTHUR STREEB-GREEBLING: Yes, I've travelled widely but not well. I think it's better to travel widely than to arrive, if you understand me. Travel widens the world, as they say in the Sahara. Arrive arrive-o, arrive arrive-o, as they say in Dublin's fair city. But the short answer to your question is 'yes thank you, I will.'

LUDOVIC KENNEDY: What's your favourite place in the world?

SIR ARTHUR STREEB-GREEBLING: I think I'd have to say the Galapagos Islands. Extraordinary creatures live there in the Galapagos. Beautiful little two-footed millipede, to name but one. What particularly lodges in my mind is the armadillos. Luminous armadillos which are extraordinary to see. They swim in formation off the coast there – absolutely dazzling.

LUDOVIC KENNEDY: What is the cause of their luminosity? Phosphorescence?

SIR ARTHUR STREEB-GREEBLING: Paint.

LUDOVIC KENNEDY: Paint?

SIR ARTHUR STREEB-GREEBLING: Yes, luminous paint that's put on them.

LUDOVIC KENNEDY: By whom?

SIR ARTHUR STREEB-GREEBLING: By the painter bird. These are birds which once a year fly over to Latin America, dive into huge vats of luminous paint and then fly all the way back and wipe themselves off on armadillos.

LUDOVIC KENNEDY: That does sound a little unlikely, Sir Arthur, if I may say so.

SIR ARTHUR STREEB-GREEBLING: It is. Well, a lot of things in nature are unlikely. I mean, who could imagine an animal called the prottle, entirely made of curtain rings?

LUDOVIC KENNEDY: Does such an animal exist?

SIR ARTHUR STREEB-GREEBLING: No. I said who can imagine it?

LUDOVIC KENNEDY: Let me ask you now for your fourth gift.

SIR ARTHUR STREEB-GREEBLING: Certainly, yes. I would like four enormous larks, please.

LUDOVIC KENNEDY: Well I'm very sorry to tell you, Sir Arthur, that that has proved impossible at such short notice. We have in fact got you four calling birds.

SIR ARTHUR STREEB-GREEBLING: Four calling birds? That's no bloody use to anybody. I ordered four enormous larks and you come up with calling birds? I mean, calling birds are nothing like enormous larks. I mean, I was all geared up to reminisce about various things and, frankly, I insisted on four enormous larks for a very good reason – because four enormous larks would trigger off memories. Memories of, well, I don't know what. I mean, if there were four enormous larks out here on the lawn, well that would trigger off a memory. But there aren't four enormous larks here on the lawn. There's absolutely bugger all on the lawn apart from grass and the only thing it triggers off is a sort of memory of just looking out the window now and seeing the lawn completely denuded of larks, which is not the sort of thing I want to talk about at all. Actually, these calling birds don't remind me of anything. I mean, all they remind me of is how we should have had these four enormous larks there. We just seem to have reached a complete impasse.

LUDOVIC KENNEDY: You were, I believe, in the Twenties, in Montparnasse.

SIR ARTHUR STREEB-GREEBLING: What?

LUDOVIC KENNEDY: In Paris in the Twenties.

SIR ARTHUR STREEB-GREEBLING: Oh yes, in the Twenties in Paris, with all the larks in Montparnasse – which was a bit like London in the Sixties, actually, only in black and white and without subtitles. I was very poor, had a pathetically weedy little moustache and I was absolutely homeless. But I was young and I desperately wanted to paint.

LUDOVIC KENNEDY: You knocked on the first door you came to?

SIR ARTHUR STREEB-GREEBLING: Yes, and I painted it. There was no answer, but the door swung open and there, in the centre of the room, was this most peculiar melting bed, draped over an ironing board – I had stumbled into the garret of Salvador Dali.

LUDOVIC KENNEDY: Fascinating.

SIR ARTHUR STREEB-GREEBLING: Yes. What looked like a melting mattress over an ironing board was in fact his landlady, Madame Chevignon. Dali himself had had to leave in a hurry due to an accident with a burning giraffe. Silly fool, he could never look after them.

LUDOVIC KENNEDY: And later you met Edith Piaf.

SIR ARTHUR STREEB-GREEBLING: Yes, in that very room. I remember I was talking to her on this particular occasion and she said to me 'Je ne regrette rien.' I said 'Oh come on Edith – there must be something.' She said 'Absolutely not, apart from possibly I suppose agreeing to come to this room this very evening.' Do you know I admired her? I admired her for her honesty.

LUDOVIC KENNEDY: You lived with Piaf in Paris for some years, I think?

SIR ARTHUR STREEB-GREEBLING: No, I sat with Piaf in Paris for some seconds.

LUDOVIC KENNEDY: But you did know the Surrealists well.

SIR ARTHUR STREEB-GREEBLING: Oh yes, I loved the Surrealists. Very nice folk, beautifully well behaved people in a bizarre kind of a way. Magritte was a pain in the arse though, with his boiled eggs on lamp posts. And Dali was a little bit unreliable, never showed up of course – but the rest of them were a great bunch of mates. I was very much part of the Ploppy Ploppy Noink Noink that they moved in.

LUDOVIC KENNEDY: What?

SIR ARTHUR STREEB-GREEBLING: I was very much part of the Ploppy Ploppy Noink Noink that they moved in.

LUDOVIC KENNEDY: Of the circle they moved in?

SIR ARTHUR STREEB-GREEBLING: No, no, no! They didn't move in a circle. Good grief no. The Surrealists move in a circle? The idea of all the Surrealists moving round and round in a circle is ludicrous! It conjures up a picture which is completely surreal. No, they didn't move in a circle – they moved in a hot water bottle.

LUDOVIC KENNEDY: A hot water bottle?

SIR ARTHUR STREEB-GREEBLING: Bibble! They despised hot water bottles, wouldn't have them in the house. 'Bourgeois!' they said

– apart from Magritte. Magritte had a hot water bottle. He used to boil his eggs in it whenever he needed one for a lamp post or whatever. We all disliked him instensely.

LUDOVIC KENNEDY: Why?

SIR ARTHUR STREEB-GREEBLING: Frankly, we thought he was a bit mad. Frightful little man and that stupid little waxed moustache on his bottom.

LUDOVIC KENNEDY: Thank you Sir Arthur.

SIR ARTHUR STREEB-GREEBLING: Thank you, but if you'd just had the larks here then I could have remembered something. All I can remember is you didn't bring the larks, so – frightfully disappointing.

FIVE GOLD RINGS
(BBC2, 1990/91)

LUDOVIC KENNEDY: Good evening, Sir Arthur.

SIR ARTHUR STREEB-GREEBLING: Good evening, good evening, good evening.

LUDOVIC KENNEDY: By the way, Sir Arthur, I'm very sorry about the mix-up yesterday with the four enormous larks. The man responsible has been dismissed.

SIR ARTHUR STREEB-GREEBLING: Don't be silly. Not at all. I mean, it's all water under the bridge – all forgotten now. You've destroyed his career, I imagine.

LUDOVIC KENNEDY: Yes.

SIR ARTHUR STREEB-GREEBLING: Good, good, good! Everything alright today?

LUDOVIC KENNEDY: Yes, five gold rings.

SIR ARTHUR STREEB-GREEBLING: Five gold rings. Lovely, lovely, lovely.

LUDOVIC KENNEDY: So, five gold rings, Sir Arthur. Is there some connection with the Olympics there, perhaps?

SIR ARTHUR STREEB-GREEBLING: Yes indeed – the Olympic symbol. I have extremely fond memories of the Olympic Games.

PETER COOK

LUDOVIC KENNEDY: Were you an athlete as a young man?

SIR ARTHUR STREEB-GREEBLING: What? Me, an athlete? Good
Lord, no! I was absolutely hopeless. Completely feeble. Asthma,
flat feet, huge wobbly bum, the lot. I always came last in
everything.

LUDOVIC KENNEDY: So your memories of the Olympics are as a
spectator?

SIR ARTHUR STREEB-GREEBLING: No, as a sprinter.

LUDOVIC KENNEDY: You competed in the Olympics?

SIR ARTHUR STREEB-GREEBLING: Yes indeed. Berlin. Thirty-Six.

LUDOVIC KENNEDY: You ran for Britain in the 1936 Olympics?

SIR ARTHUR STREEB-GREEBLING: No, for Barbados.

LUDOVIC KENNEDY: Why?

SIR ARTHUR STREEB-GREEBLING: Because Hitler asked me to.

LUDOVIC KENNEDY: Hitler?

SIR ARTHUR STREEB-GREEBLING: Yes. He asked me and obviously
I was terribly flattered.

LUDOVIC KENNEDY: Why did he ask you to run for Barbados?

SIR ARTHUR STREEB-GREEBLING: Well, he said he didn't want the
Germans to win everything because it'd get a bit monotonous.

LUDOVIC KENNEDY: I get the feeling you didn't know Hitler
terribly well.

SIR ARTHUR STREEB-GREEBLING: Not terribly well, no. In fact I
only met him once.

LUDOVIC KENNEDY: Where?

SIR ARTHUR STREEB-GREEBLING: A wine and cheese party at his
place at Berchtesgaden. Just a few friends. Leni Riefenstahl, the
Mitfords, who dragged me along as usual, and the normal
crowd, basically. Drinks, not dinner, but it was a fairly formal
affair.

LUDOVIC KENNEDY: Black tie?

SIR ARTHUR STREEB-GREEBLING: Black tie, black shirt, black
underwear, black boots, black everything. Come to think of it, it
was a very formal affair indeed. Anyway, I was chatting to a
couple of blondes when Hitler drifted over with the sausage rolls
and casually asked me if I'd care to run in the Olympics.

LUDOVIC KENNEDY: What did you do?

319

SIR ARTHUR STREEB-GREEBLING: Well, I'm ashamed to say I totally ignored him at first. Tiny little man in a uniform. I thought he was the waiter. But after the blondes had gently explained my gaffe, Hitler and I went over to a quiet corner and he repeated the offer.

LUDOVIC KENNEDY: Why did he choose you?

SIR ARTHUR STREEB-GREEBLING: He said that the black chaps were absolutely hopelessly inferior and only a white man could win a race. He was banging on about that for quite a while actually, and I'm afraid I nodded off. I didn't get all the details but the gist was that I disguise myself as a black man for form's sake.

LUDOVIC KENNEDY: Why did you go along with it?

SIR ARTHUR STREEB-GREEBLING: Well, he had been terribly sweet about the sausage roll thing, but I also got a fairly strong hint from the note nailed to my hotel room door when I got back that he'd have me shot if I refused.

LUDOVIC KENNEDY: What happened on the day of the race?

SIR ARTHUR STREEB-GREEBLING: It was fantastic. Hundred yards. Climax of the whole games. Ninety thousand people waiting for the great German sprinter Laughingberg Tobreastthetape-victorious. I lined up with the rest of them, fully expecting to trail in last. But then the bloody pistol went off. I got such a scare, I ran like the clappers and won. The crowd went absolutely wild.

LUDOVIC KENNEDY: And Hitler too, I should think.

SIR ARTHUR STREEB-GREEBLING: I don't know. He rushed out straight after the race. But during the ceremony, when Goering hung the medal round my neck, he told me I was definitely for the high jump. I was very willing to give it a go, but unfortunately I had to nip straight back to London for something or other so I never got the chance.

LUDOVIC KENNEDY: What were your impressions of Hitler?

SIR ARTHUR STREEB-GREEBLING: Well, as we all know, he later acquired the reputation of an absolute sod, but in those days he was all charm. One could have had no inkling that he would go on to blot his copybook in such a spectacular way.

LUDOVIC KENNEDY: You didn't suspect that he chose you to run because he wanted a black man to come last?

SIR ARTHUR STREEB-GREEBLING: What? Good Lord no. He wasn't the practical joking type at all.

LUDOVIC KENNEDY: You can't have struck him, though, as exactly the athletic type.

SIR ARTHUR STREEB-GREEBLING: I was holding my tummy in.

LUDOVIC KENNEDY: And you didn't notice any hint of evil about Hitler?

SIR ARTHUR STREEB-GREEBLING: No, no, far from it. Although now you mention it, there was one thing I found a little peculiar.

LUDOVIC KENNEDY: What was that?

SIR ARTHUR STREEB-GREEBLING: He absolutely hated dogs. I always thought that a bit odd. Quite honestly, that was the only sign of instability that I detected.

LUDOVIC KENNEDY: Well, thank you, Sir Arthur.

SIR ARTHUR STREEB-GREEBLING: Thank you. I enjoyed that one very much. Care for a glass of sherry?

SIX GEESE A-LAYING
(BBC2, 1990/91)

LUDOVIC KENNEDY: Towards the end of the War, Sir Arthur, you managed to escape from a Japanese prisoner of war camp.

SIR ARTHUR STREEB-GREEBLING: Yes, that's right – on a trawler bound for Kuala Lumpur.

LUDOVIC KENNEDY: Though the trawler never in fact reached Kuala Lumpur, did it?

SIR ARTHUR STREEB-GREEBLING: No, never made it, no. The Sargasso sea reared its ugly head and we became becalmed. After a few days, we were weak from lack of food and we decided the only thing to do was for one of us to be killed and eaten by the others.

LUDOVIC KENNEDY: How did you decide who to kill?

SIR ARTHUR STREEB-GREEBLING: What?

LUDOVIC KENNEDY: Did you draw lots?

SIR ARTHUR STREEB-GREEBLING: Lots? Oh yes, I drew a great deal. I still do. Not particularly good at it, but it's relaxing – more of a hobby than anything else.

LUDOVIC KENNEDY: No, I meant . . .

SIR ARTHUR STREEB-GREEBLING: Just little sketches – sketches, little things like that.

LUDOVIC KENNEDY: But the situation on the trawler, where you had to kill these men – did you draw lots?

SIR ARTHUR STREEB-GREEBLING: Yes, I've just said – I drew all the time.

LUDOVIC KENNEDY: I mean did you draw straws?

SIR ARTHUR STREEB-GREEBLING: No, I've never drawn a straw. May be easy to draw, I suppose, if you come to think about it, but not very attractive. And quite honestly, when you're sitting around, on the point of murdering a fellow passenger, I don't think it'd be really tactful to do that. And I can't really see the point in producing a drawing of a straw, however lifelike. I can't see it selling very well. I mean, it's hardly a gypsy woman with a tear, is it? No, no, no. Andy Warhol might have exhibited a straw, in a can of Coke. I don't know, but he might have done that.

LUDOVIC KENNEDY: Sir Arthur, how did you decide which man to kill?

SIR ARTHUR STREEB-GREEBLING: Well, not by sitting around doodling, I can tell you that! Oh, I see! Oh yes. Well a group of us got together in the stern and decided to gang up on Davidson. One of us – Pickering, I think it was – said he'd prefer it to be done fairly.

LUDOVIC KENNEDY: Done fairly?

SIR ARTHUR STREEB-GREEBLING: Yes, Jimmy Dunn-Fairley – he was the quarter master, great buddies with Penrose.

LUDOVIC KENNEDY: That would be Chief Petty Officer Penrose?

SIR ARTHUR STREEB-GREEBLING: Yes. Jimmy Dunn-Fairley and Chalkie Penrose.

LUDOVIC KENNEDY: How were the men killed, incidentally?

SIR ARTHUR STREEB-GREEBLING: They weren't. No, at the last minute it was decided that, rather than one of us being discussed and then eaten, why didn't we all chip in a toe? I for one was tremendously relieved at that idea.

LUDOVIC KENNEDY: Yes, I can imagine.

SIR ARTHUR STREEB-GREEBLING: You see, because the Streeb-Greeblings for some genetic reasons have been blessed with fourteen toes, so obviously a couple missing here or there don't make a blind bit of difference. In fact, it would probably have saved me a fortune in later years not having it done cosmetically on the National Health. So really a heaven-sent opportunity to get rid of some toes and have a jolly nice meal into the bargain.

LUDOVIC KENNEDY: How are they cooked, the toes?

SIR ARTHUR STREEB-GREEBLING: Well, we toyed with the idea of kebabbing them, but eventually we settled on a stew. It seemed to be the best way because, aesthetically speaking, a load of toes on a stick is enough to put you off your food.

LUDOVIC KENNEDY: It was discovered later, wasn't it – by Penrose, I think, who went to your locker – that you'd been eating sandwiches that you'd kept to yourself.

SIR ARTHUR STREEB-GREEBLING: Yes. I kept a whole stock of food in my locker. Penrose was furious but luckily I was a lot quicker than him because he didn't have enough toes to balance properly and he could scarcely move, poor sod. So I trapped him and ate as much of him as I could on the spot and then made the rest of him into sandwiches which I put back in the locker. Now let me say right away, I'm not in favour of cannibalism – I've got nothing against it, mind you, I just take no position on cannibalism – but when you're stuck in the Sargasso sea with nothing to eat apart from a cupboard full of food, the mind plays strange tricks.

LUDOVIC KENNEDY: When you got back to England, did you ever see any of these people again?

SIR ARTHUR STREEB-GREEBLING: Yes, I saw Fairley at the Inn On The Park at a convention for petty officers.

LUDOVIC KENNEDY: Did he say anything to you at that time?

SIR ARTHUR STREEB-GREEBLING: No. I asked about his foot and I thought he looked at me in a rather stony way.

LUDOVIC KENNEDY: Have you ever worried that one of the men from your past might catch up with you?

SIR ARTHUR STREEB-GREEBLING: The man who has no enemies has no friends. That's always been my view.

LUDOVIC KENNEDY: But you have no friends either, do you?

SIR ARTHUR STREEB-GREEBLING: I don't mix easily. I don't know – it's a Streeb-Greebling trait. A combination of shyness and violence which makes it difficult for us to form lasting attachments.

LUDOVIC KENNEDY: Sir Arthur, the gift you have chosen tonight is six geese a-laying. Now why's that?

SIR ARTHUR STREEB-GREEBLING: Well, I don't know about you, but I'm absolutely starving!

LUDOVIC KENNEDY: Thank you, Sir Arthur.

SIR ARTHUR STREEB-GREEBLING: Thank you.

SEVEN SWANS A-SWIMMING
(BBC2, 1990/91)

LUDOVIC KENNEDY: Sir Arthur, we meet again!

SIR ARTHUR STREEB-GREEBLING: Yes, indeed.

LUDOVIC KENNEDY: And you've settled on this occasion for a swan motif.

SIR ARTHUR STREEB-GREEBLING: Yes, I've always been fond of swans. Very graceful beasts. Especially the young swans, known as singlets, due to their vest-like appearance. And this is why, in the winter of 1954, I started Greebling Mail Order.

LUDOVIC KENNEDY: With virtually nothing?

SIR ARTHUR STREEB-GREEBLING: Virtually nothing. My entire stock consisted of two extra small army surplus long-necked singlets which I'd got on the cheap because they had no arm holes, and half a dozen boxes of matches. I advertised the singlets as Swan Vests and anyone who replied was sent a box of matches.

LUDOVIC KENNEDY: Did anybody reply?

SIR ARTHUR STREEB-GREEBLING: Not really reply as such, to be perfectly candid with you, no.

LUDOVIC KENNEDY: But from these modest beginnings you were able to diversify?

SIR ARTHUR STREEB-GREEBLING: Yes. Fortunately, due to a mix-up with the matches, both vests were burnt to the ground one night and I therefore claimed on the insurance – they were very noble about it – and I moved on to personalised light bulbs. I had a hunch that a light bulb with your Christian name on it – or any name you care to specify – would be both a talking point and lend a certain amount of kudos for business and leisure activities.

LUDOVIC KENNEDY: And was your hunch correct?

SIR ARTHUR STREEB-GREEBLING: Let me put it this way – before I'd even begun trading, demand was such that there were only two names left available.

LUDOVIC KENNEDY: And what were they?

SIR ARTHUR STREEB-GREEBLING: They were, if I remember correctly, Philips and Osram.

LUDOVIC KENNEDY: Did you have many enquiries?

SIR ARTHUR STREEB-GREEBLING: Not from anyone called Osram. I suppose the Osrams of the world tend to feel a bit shy, a bit shrinking violety in their behaviour, for obvious reasons. We had a number of enquiries from people called Philip, but they were not willing to tackle the DIY element of the bargain.

LUDOVIC KENNEDY: The DIY element?

SIR ARTHUR STREEB-GREEBLING: Yes, crossing off the S with a Magic Marker or whatever. My best lead was from a chap I ran into in a pub called Watts who said he was toying with the idea of christening his daughter Sixty. It turned out he was lying – you can't trust anyone in this business – so I abandoned the light bulbs. But then, luckily, along came the Balinese fighting fish.

LUDOVIC KENNEDY: The what?

SIR ARTHUR STREEB-GREEBLING: Balinese fighting fish! It's a tiny creature about a quarter of an inch long but, pound for pound, the most savage animal in the world.

LUDOVIC KENNEDY: I've never heard of it.

SIR ARTHUR STREEB-GREEBLING: Haven't you? We sold millions of the little blighters. The only trouble with Balinese fighting fish – nineteen pounds a pair, by the way – is that, such is the savagery of these tiny Oriental animals, they very often devour each other in the post, even first class mail. A day in the post and when you've opened your package – no sign of the fish whatsoever.

LUDOVIC KENNEDY: Did you consider separating the fish and sending them individually?

SIR ARTHUR STREEB-GREEBLING: Of course not! To separate a Balinese fighting fish from his mate is an awful thing to do.

LUDOVIC KENNEDY: They pine?

SIR ARTHUR STREEB-GREEBLING: A – they pine, and B – it's bloody dangerous. Try to separate two Balinese fighting fish and you could lose an arm. And even if you manage it – using tweezers or a spade or a cattle prod or whatever – you actually get one of the little horrors into the envelope, the chances are the consignment will never arrive.

LUDOVIC KENNEDY: Because the fish will eat the envelope?

SIR ARTHUR STREEB-GREEBLING: The fish will eat the envelope, turn upon itself in a feeding frenzy and take its own life. The whole caboodle disappears en route and the customer gets bugger all, and that's a teensy weensy bit dishonest, I think.

LUDOVIC KENNEDY: Sir Arthur, were you ever accused of fraudulent trading?

SIR ARTHUR STREEB-GREEBLING: No, no, no, no, no, no, no, no, no, no, no, no. Well let me put it another way. Yes. From time to time there were complaints – frequently. We had to install a whole hot line for the complaints, but fraud is very much in the eye of the receiver, isn't it? What I was doing was not so much fraud as teaching people a valuable lesson. Many famous figures in history have made mistakes and have been taught a severe lesson from them. And one of the lessons I like to think I have taught people is do not write away for mail order fighting fish. The whole notion is bloody ludicrous. I mean, if you're stupid enough to do that, far better you should learn your lesson for a very reasonable nineteen pounds plus twenty-eight days for delivery, rather than by, say, losing a million in the snows of Russia. I mean, that is idiotic.

LUDOVIC KENNEDY: So, Sir Arthur, seven swans a-swimming – a line from Yeats of course.

SIR ARTHUR STREEB-GREEBLING: What?

LUDOVIC KENNEDY: Was he a friend of yours?

SIR ARTHUR STREEB-GREEBLING: Who?

LUDOVIC KENNEDY: Yeats.

SIR ARTHUR STREEB-GREEBLING: What?

LUDOVIC KENNEDY: WB Yeats.

SIR ARTHUR STREEB-GREEBLING: W?

LUDOVIC KENNEDY: B Yeats.

SIR ARTHUR STREEB-GREEBLING: Never head of him. D Yeats, yes. D Yeats Lawrence. I knew Lady Chatterbox and her whatnot.

LUDOVIC KENNEDY: Well, at any rate, Sir Arthur, seven swans a-swimming – your seventh choice.

SIR ARTHUR STREEB-GREEBLING: No it wasn't.

LUDOVIC KENNEDY: Thank you, Sir Arthur.

SIR ARTHUR STREEB-GREEBLING: I distinctly remember ordering seven pairs of ex-army binoculars, those x-ray things. I've always hankered after those. Bloody inefficient – you order binoculars and you get swans.

EIGHT MAIDS A-MILKING
(BBC2, 1990/91)

LUDOVIC KENNEDY: Sir Arthur, after the War, I think you went into the City where you briefly worked for a commodity broker in Threadneedle Street.

SIR ARTHUR STREEB-GREEBLING: Yes, a broker by the name, oddly enough, of Fred Needle. Charming chap. I worked in the futures market.

LUDOVIC KENNEDY: How does that work?

SIR ARTHUR STREEB-GREEBLING: Well, basically, you have to get hold of a number of clients with lots of money and they give it to you to speculate with. If, for example, you came to me and told me you thought the price of lichen was going to go up, I'd pocket the money and hope it went down and say 'Sorry, old chap, you've lost your money.' If it went up, I'd change my name and start all over again. That's basically how it works.

LUDOVIC KENNEDY: Did you do well?

SIR ARTHUR STREEB-GREEBLING: Initially, yes. I did very well, but along came the Korean War, and I took the view that liniment would probably go up during the war because obviously there'd be a lot of injuries and people would need to rub liniment into their legs. But, unbeknownst to me, Korea is absolutely littered with liniment wells which could produce about fifteen million barrels a day. So I had a liniment glut on my hands which was thoroughly unpleasant, as you can imagine.

LUDOVIC KENNEDY: Is that when you moved back to Greebling Manor?

SIR ARTHUR STREEB-GREEBLING: Yes. As you know, my father and I were never particularly close but he was in the autumn of his years and one day I received a particularly upsetting telegram from him which really meant I had no alternative but to return home.

LUDOVIC KENNEDY: Was it his last wish?

SIR ARTHUR STREEB-GREEBLING: Well, 'the last thing he wanted' was the way he phrased it, but I knew what he meant. In those days Greebling Manor was surrounded by 28,000 acres of wonderful farmland, none of which, unfortunately, belonged to us. My father didn't see why that should stop us farming it – secretly.

LUDOVIC KENNEDY: How do you mean, 'farm it secretly'?

SIR ARTHUR STREEB-GREEBLING: Well, I'd rise at 2am, preferably on a night when there was no moon, and we'd go out into the adjacent fields and till them, do the weeding, hose down the neighbour's Land Rover, that sort of thing. Very much the sort of thing a normal farmer does, except done secretly and not on one's own land. Ploughing, harrowing, blocking the local roads with sheep, yelling at people to get off the property, that sort of thing.

LUDOVIC KENNEDY: What was the idea?

SIR ARTHUR STREEB-GREEBLING: I haven't the foggiest. It was absolute madness. My father was working all night long basically for the benefit of the bloody next-door neighbours. They woke up each morning – farm, which had been an utter tip the night before, looking absolutely tickety-boo. He'd even stacked the cow pats in immaculate little piles.

LUDOVIC KENNEDY: But your own concept of secret farming was different.

SIR ARTHUR STREEB-GREEBLING: Yes, entirely different. To me, secret farming meant going into the fields by night and planting very quick-growing crops which one can then harvest by dawn. The secret is to find a product that grows very, very quickly indeed.

LUDOVIC KENNEDY: What? Mustard and cress, or something like that?

SIR ARTHUR STREEB-GREEBLING: Oh heavens no. Mustard and cress is far too slow. Mushrooms, they're the chaps. You've heard of the button mushroom? Well, we cultivated pin-point mushrooms – very, very small indeed, because they'd often been growing for as little as twenty minutes before pucking.

LUDOVIC KENNEDY: Some might say that was rather sharp practice.

SIR ARTHUR STREEB-GREEBLING: Best eaten raw with a bit of fresh lemon and a spot of pepper. Next question?

LUDOVIC KENNEDY: Secret dairy farming?

SIR ARTHUR STREEB-GREEBLING: Yes, secret dairy farming. Now that really made a great deal more sense.

LUDOVIC KENNEDY: Hence your eighth gift.

SIR ARTHUR STREEB-GREEBLING: Eight maids a-milking, yes. We always used maids – Filipino maids – working in teams of eight. Seven on each team were employed by me – secretly milking up to a hundred cows a night – and the other one worked for my father, doing any secret washing up, secret hoovering and so on, as he felt needed doing.

LUDOVIC KENNEDY: A very sensible arrangement. Sir Arthur, thank you.

SIR ARTHUR STREEB-GREEBLING: Thank you.

NINE DRUMMERS DRUMMING
(BBC2, 1990/91)

LUDOVIC KENNEDY: In 1932, Sir Arthur, you went up to Cambridge. Were you a scholar?

SIR ARTHUR STREEB-GREEBLING: Oh good lord, no. When I entered Cambridge, the only qualification one needed was the Russian for 'homosexual'.

LUDOVIC KENNEDY: You studied under Professor Hilary, I think?

SIR ARTHUR STREEB-GREEBLING: Hilary, yes.

LUDOVIC KENNEDY: Who used to recruit for MI6.

SIR ARTHUR STREEB-GREEBLING: Yes, Hilary was a spymaster. He was always looking out for recruits, people who could work secretly for or against the Government.

LUDOVIC KENNEDY: He wasn't bothered which?

SIR ARTHUR STREEB-GREEBLING: Not his job. He merely recruited and then melted away into the background.

LUDOVIC KENNEDY: So, you became a deep-level mole at that time?

SIR ARTHUR STREEB-GREEBLING: It sounds overly dramatic, doesn't it, a 'deep-level mole', but you know, much of the business of spying is just routine, really. Not really important stuff. It's simply paperwork, you know, reading through transcripts of conversations – transcripts of telephone conversations, conversations over garden walls, conversations on aeroplanes, conversations in bathrooms, conversations in potting sheds – all sorts of conversations transcripted and then built up to form a picture.

LUDOVIC KENNEDY: A picture of what?

SIR ARTHUR STREEB-GREEBLING: A picture of everybody in the world, really. You see, MI6's view is that if you know what every single person in the world is going to do at any given time, we'd be able to anticipate what they'd do next. Well, as you can imagine, the paperwork is absolutely monstrous.

LUDOVIC KENNEDY: Yes, I can imagine.

SIR ARTHUR STREEB-GREEBLING: For example, we've been so busy collating all the relevant information that it was only in

March this year, I think – far, far too late – that we predicted that war was inevitable.

LUDOVIC KENNEDY: When?

SIR ARTHUR STREEB-GREEBLING: 1914 I think it was. We're dreadfully behind at the moment, dreadfully behind with all this paperwork, but a lot of us are popping into the office at the weekend to try and catch up. We're doing our best.

LUDOVIC KENNEDY: Was it Professor Hilary who first introduced you to The Aphids?

SIR ARTHUR STREEB-GREEBLING: The Aphids, yes. That was a secret society in Cambridge. Very, very exclusive and aristo-cratic. One dressed up in 14th-century costumes with frilly collars and gigantic flowing wigs and met in the crypt under St Bartholomew's every Tuesday evening.

LUDOVIC KENNEDY: How did you become a member?

SIR ARTHUR STREEB-GREEBLING: One was approached.

LUDOVIC KENNEDY: Covertly?

SIR ARTHUR STREEB-GREEBLING: Yes, they were very, very discreet. I was actually told later that I had been approached thirty or forty times before my successful luring.

LUDOVIC KENNEDY: What was the vetting procedure?

SIR ARTHUR STREEB-GREEBLING: You had to swallow four bottles of vintage port from a silver bucket and you were then expertly probed by the Master Aphid, whose name I forget.

LUDOVIC KENNEDY: Aphid?

SIR ARTHUR STREEB-GREEBLING: Aphid, that was the fellow. Wherever I went in life after that, if ever I got the secret sign I knew I was amongst friends and colleagues.

LUDOVIC KENNEDY: The secret sign?

SIR ARTHUR STREEB-GREEBLING: Yes, chap in a red wig and a pair of lacy pantaloons waving a silver bucket at you, that was the giveaway.

LUDOVIC KENNEDY: In 1934, The Aphids went on a coach trip to Barcelona.

SIR ARTHUR STREEB-GREEBLING: Yes. Our ostensible purpose was to view the cathedral.

LUDOVIC KENNEDY: Your actual purpose was what?

SIR ARTHUR STREEB-GREEBLING: Exactly the same. This is one of the secrets of good espionage – to be pretending to be doing exactly what you are doing.

LUDOVIC KENNEDY: But you were the only one who wasn't pretending.

SIR ARTHUR STREEB-GREEBLING: No, I was pretending to pretend. There were twelve of us on the bus and only one returned. I don't think it takes a genius to work out who that was – Barlow. I slipped away by submarine.

LUDOVIC KENNEDY: So, only Barlow knew of the incident at the cathedral when ten Aphids fell to their deaths because their gargoyle snapped off at the root?

SIR ARTHUR STREEB-GREEBLING: Yes. You see, the reason why ten Aphids had to go was that they had been penetrated.

LUDOVIC KENNEDY: By Hilary?

SIR ARTHUR STREEB-GREEBLING: By Professor Hilary, who'd introduced me to them in the first place and knew of their existence due to his copious files.

LUDOVIC KENNEDY: Of course, you later found that Hilary had been penetrating Barlow, didn't you?

SIR ARTHUR STREEB-GREEBLING: Yes, and once Hilary had penetrated him the Aphids were no more.

LUDOVIC KENNEDY: Is Hilary still alive?

SIR ARTHUR STREEB-GREEBLING: Inasmuch as he ever was. Yes, he must be in his eighties now, but his mind is still as sharp as a . . . as sharp as a . . .

LUDOVIC KENNEDY: A razor?

SIR ARTHUR STREEB-GREEBLING: Sharp as an eraser, yes. That's about the size of it.

LUDOVIC KENNEDY: What became of Barlow?

SIR ARTHUR STREEB-GREEBLING: Barlow confessed to the Government that he was working for them and got forty years. This pleased our masters in Moscow, so honour was satisfied.

LUDOVIC KENNEDY: And finally, what is your ninth gift, Sir Arthur.

SIR ARTHUR STREEB-GREEBLING: I think you know me better than to ask me a question like that.

LUDOVIC KENNEDY: It's nine drummers drumming, isn't it?

SIR ARTHUR STREEB-GREEBLING: I'm afraid you won't catch me that easily. My lips are sealed.

LUDOVIC KENNEDY: Thank you Sir Arthur.

SIR ARTHUR STREEB-GREEBLING: Come back in 2075. I might have something for you then. Enough said, you devil.

TEN PIPERS PIPING
(BBC2, 1990/91)

LUDOVIC KENNEDY: Sir Arthur, good evening.

SIR ARTHUR STREEB-GREEBLING: Good evening. Sorry I was a bit odd yesterday.

LUDOVIC KENNEDY: That's alright. We come now to your tenth gift and you've chosen ten pipers piping. Why is that?

SIR ARTHUR STREEB-GREEBLING: Well, some years ago I became friendly with a chap called Peter Piper who at that time was Britain's leading pipe mogul, making industrial piping. Riveting stuff. Well, not all that riveting, actually. There was some welding as well, I gather. Anyway, he did pretty well on the business side but he had one absolute passion in life. He was a cricket lover. I thought it was jolly peculiar and so did his wife.

LUDOVIC KENNEDY: Why?

SIR ARTHUR STREEB-GREEBLING: Well, are you a cricket lover?

LUDOVIC KENNEDY: Well, yes I am rather, as a matter of fact.

SIR ARTHUR STREEB-GREEBLING: Really? There's a lot of you about, aren't there? Well, this will fascinate you, then. Peter had a small cricket team sponsored by Peter's Piping.

LUDOVIC KENNEDY: A small team of cricketers?

SIR ARTHUR STREEB-GREEBLING: No, a team of small crickets.

LUDOVIC KENNEDY: Oh, I see.

SIR ARTHUR STREEB-GREEBLING: Ten of them. You know the wonderful sound of the cicada and the limegrove, rubbing their legs together, producing this absolutely haunting, melodic racket. You are doubtless familiar with the haunting cricket racket?

LUDOVIC KENNEDY: Oh yes. Yes indeed.

SIR ARTHUR STREEB-GREEBLING: Yes, you would be. Well, Peter absolutely loved this noise. He used to spend hours listening to these ten crickets of his. He felt they deserved a wider audience and he wanted to take them on a national tour. I thought he was mad, personally, but out of friendship I went into partnership with him. And also out of sympathy for his poor wife. I think he offered me a fairly reasonable retainer. Fifty grand, I think it was. I can't remember. I'm absolutely hopeless with figures.

LUDOVIC KENNEDY: And did you take the crickets on tour?

SIR ARTHUR STREEB-GREEBLING: Oh yes indeed.

LUDOVIC KENNEDY: What did they do?

SIR ARTHUR STREEB-GREEBLING: Crickets, as you know, of course, are very tricky to train. Almost untrainable. Very individual creatures with precious little discipline. So, in practice, all they did was a lot of leg rubbing as and when they felt inclined. Temperamental little sods. An Evening With Cricket Noises we called it.

LUDOVIC KENNEDY: Was the show a hit?

SIR ARTHUR STREEB-GREEBLING: Well, it was a tremendously good idea in principle. But, as we discovered on the opening night, there was one crucial flaw. We'd turn up at the venue, set up stage, install crickets – and the crickets would all be there on their podia, rubbing legs together like nobody's business, but as soon as anyone got within ten yards they would fall into a deathly silence.

LUDOVIC KENNEDY: Oh dear.

SIR ARTHUR STREEB-GREEBLING: We were stymied.

LUDOVIC KENNEDY: What did you do?

SIR ARTHUR STREEB-GREEBLING: Well, while Peter tried to get them going again, I went onto the stage and tried to explain it away by saying they were miming. I don't think they believed me for a second. Then Peter came up – practically in tears – and begged the audience to rub their legs together to try and encourage the artistes.

LUDOVIC KENNEDY: What sort of a noise did that make?

SIR ARTHUR STREEB-GREEBLING: Basically, the sound of twill on twill, really. Nylon on tweed. Nothing terribly inspiring, quite honestly. So to liven things up, I suggested that the men in the audience might like to rub their legs against the ladies in the audience to see if that produced a better sound. And indeed, a number of rather interesting noises ensued. I think the audience got value for money. It became something of a bacchanal, so we kept the format and became something of a success d'estime.

LUDOVIC KENNEDY: Do you still see Peter Piper?

SIR ARTHUR STREEB-GREEBLING: We rather lost touch after the Wembley concert. His wife and I still have ... lunch occasionally.

LUDOVIC KENNEDY: You say the Wembley concert?

SIR ARTHUR STREEB-GREEBLING: Yes, I suggested to Peter that the crickets would be more likely to perform at their best in an outdoor setting. I took charge of the publicity, promotion, lighting, sound system, merchandising and so on, and Peter basically provided the financial backing as well as liaising with the crickets.

LUDOVIC KENNEDY: Ten crickets? In Wembley Stadium?

SIR ARTHUR STREEB-GREEBLING: Yes. A huge venue. Of course, staging a concert like this is very, very expensive. Our pre-production costs were close on a quarter of a million pounds. And I took the view that this money would be better spent on, er, myself.

LUDOVIC KENNEDY: So the concert never took place?

SIR ARTHUR STREEB-GREEBLING: Oh yes it did! But, due to a silly oversight, I'd booked the stadium the same night as Led Zeppelin, and, as I explained later to Peter on the phone from Bogota, where I was staying with a girlfriend at the time, ten crickets could never hope to drown out Led Zeppelin, however adept their leg-rubbing skills. But Peter, silly fool, insisted on going ahead. Perhaps I was wrong, in a way, because if you listen to Led Zeppelin II on compact disc you can just about make out the sound of Jimmy Page treading on them during one of his riffs. Squawk! It sounds something like that. I can't do it exactly, but it's a sort of squawk, but softer.

LUDOVIC KENNEDY: That was their last performance?

SIR ARTHUR STREEB-GREEBLING: Alas, yes. The final gig, as I believe it's called. The final gig of Peter Piper's PipingTen.

LUDOVIC KENNEDY: What's Peter Piper doing today?

SIR ARTHUR STREEB-GREEBLING: He's retired from the biz – showbusiness – disillusioned by the Wembley tragedy and the gigantic financial losses. And, of course, the divorce from Clare. He's thrown himself back into the piping, which is where he really belongs.

LUDOVIC KENNEDY: Thank you Sir Arthur.

SIR ARTHUR STREEB-GREEBLING: I wasn't ever really very, very close to Peter. Frankly, he was a bit of a shit.

ELEVEN LADIES DANCING
(BBC2, 1990/91)

SIR ARTHUR STREEB-GREEBLING: You got my ladies?

LUDOVIC KENNEDY: Yes.

SIR ARTHUR STREEB-GREEBLING: All eleven of them?

LUDOVIC KENNEDY: Yes.

SIR ARTHUR STREEB-GREEBLING: But are they dancing? That's more to the point.

LUDOVIC KENNEDY: Yes.

SIR ARTHUR STREEB-GREEBLING: Don't trust you BBC people an inch. Let's get on with it.

LUDOVIC KENNEDY: Well, Sir Arthur – your son.

SIR ARTHUR STREEB-GREEBLING: Good grief, Roger. Yes, what about it?

LUDOVIC KENNEDY: He had a somewhat unconventional upbringing.

SIR ARTHUR STREEB-GREEBLING: I had him educated privately, if that's what you mean.

LUDOVIC KENNEDY: But not by governesses.

SIR ARTHUR STREEB-GREEBLING: No, by goats. Not governesses. Goats.

LUDOVIC KENNEDY: Despite your own childhood experiences with goats?

SIR ARTHUR STREEB-GREEBLING: Well it was either that or King's College, Canterbury. I'm not entirely heartless, you know.

LUDOVIC KENNEDY: How did you provide for the goats to bring up your son? Did they have a stipend or an annuity?

SIR ARTHUR STREEB-GREEBLING: Yes, that's right. A stipend or an annuity. We left that very much up to them. I mean, once you start trying to boss a goat about, you find they tend to take against you. Bob Helsome of Coutts, he dealt with all the technicalities of the thing. He was delighted to have the goats pop in at any time.

LUDOVIC KENNEDY: Did that happen often?

SIR ARTHUR STREEB-GREEBLING: Never. Never once. Rather rude of them, I thought, after all the trouble we'd been to.

LUDOVIC KENNEDY: So how did they survive?

SIR ARTHUR STREEB-GREEBLING: The goats? Well, they survive very well in their usual way. They have a goat house which is quite large – it's about a mile from the main house – and surrounded by asphalt through which weeds grow up, and the goats live on the weeds and, obviously, Roger learnt to live off the goats which lived off the weeds. That's how it's done, really.

LUDOVIC KENNEDY: Did he have any formal education?

SIR ARTHUR STREEB-GREEBLING: Yes, we arranged for him and the goats, who he believed to be his parents, to go down to a very good prep school near Lymington in Hampshire, and they duly travelled down en famille, as it were.

LUDOVIC KENNEDY: By train?

SIR ARTHUR STREEB-GREEBLING: No, his mother – his real mother that is, not his goat mother – drove them.

LUDOVIC KENNEDY: By car?

SIR ARTHUR STREEB-GREEBLING: No, no, no! With a twig! A switch, a stick – that's how you get goats from one place to another. You bang them on the backside with a twig. No, I don't want goats in my wife's car, thank you very much. The smell is absolutely frightful! She wears this awful scent – Murielle by Paco Rabanne. Absolutely ghastly. Tried to cover it up by keeping a pot pourri in the glove compartment, but you can't disguise it. You can't.

LUDOVIC KENNEDY: How did the interview with the headmaster go?

SIR ARTHUR STREEB-GREEBLING: Frankly, it was a bit of a disappointment. The goats managed to get in by sheer force of personality, I suppose, but Roger was rejected.

LUDOVIC KENNEDY: How did you feel?

SIR ARTHUR STREEB-GREEBLING: I was elated. I'm very much a self-made man myself. After I'd outgrown my goats, my father kept me locked in a broom cupboard until I was fifteen with a pair of encyclopaedias. I always found that quite enough in life. Flags of the world, semaphore, deciduous trees, the difference between a mammal and a snake.

LUDOVIC KENNEDY: What is the difference between a mammal and a snake?

SIR ARTHUR STREEB-GREEBLING: Well, snakes are long thin scaly things and mammals are, of course, big fat hairy things. That's the difference between them. And insects are neither one thing or the other. No one knows whether they're mammals or snakes and, frankly, I don't care.

LUDOVIC KENNEDY: Like whales.

SIR ARTHUR STREEB-GREEBLING: Yes, I do like whales as a matter of fact, but I wouldn't want a son of mine to be suckled by one.

LUDOVIC KENNEDY: You left it very much up to the goats then, his education?

SIR ARTHUR STREEB-GREEBLING: Well, I think once I had made the decision to let him be reared by goats it would have been unfair to interfere with his way of life. You see, looking back in history at people who had been suckled by animals – wolves, for instance – you find that they often go on to achieve considerable distinction in later life. You only have to think of Romulus and Remus, who went on to found the Roman Empire. As you know, Romulus built Rome and Remus, er, built Reems.

LUDOVIC KENNEDY: Romanus.

SIR ARTHUR STREEB-GREEBLING: No, no, no! That was Rameses. Rameses the Second – suckled by tapirs.

LUDOVIC KENNEDY: Has anything similar been achieved by children suckled by goats?

SIR ARTHUR STREEB-GREEBLING: Er, Gothenburg possibly. I don't know.

LUDOVIC KENNEDY: Thank you, Sir Arthur. No more questions.

SIR ARTHUR STREEB-GREEBLING: Now where are these bloody ladies? I tell you, if they're not dancing there'll be hell to pay.

TWELVE LORDS A-LEAPING
(BBC2, 1990/91)

LUDOVIC KENNEDY: Well, Sir Arthur, I've very much enjoyed our talks.

SIR ARTHUR STREEB-GREEBLING: They've been fun, haven't they? Yes.

LUDOVIC KENNEDY: Now we come to your final gift. What's that?

SIR ARTHUR STREEB-GREEBLING: My last gift – I'm sure you've guessed it – is twelve lords a leaping.

LUDOVIC KENNEDY: Why have you chosen that?

SIR ARTHUR STREEB-GREEBLING: Well, it's a Christmassy thing, really, to remind us all in this season of goodwill of the twelve wise lords who came leaping into the stable at Bethlehem at the birth of our saviour.

LUDOVIC KENNEDY: I don't think they did, Sir Arthur.

SIR ARTHUR STREEB-GREEBLING: Oh yes! Boing, boing, boing! As in the carol.

LUDOVIC KENNEDY: No, I'm afraid you're mistaken.

SIR ARTHUR STREEB-GREEBLING: You sure?

LUDOVIC KENNEDY: Quite certain.

SIR ARTHUR STREEB-GREEBLING: Blast. Oh dear. Very confusing. Now, I never remember who was in the stable. Must have been three hens. No? Was it three goats in the stable? Partridges? Pear tree, two turtle dogs, three French lords, four enormous larks, twelve leaping lizards – um, I'm in a bit of a muddle. Not much of a Bible buff myself, I'm afraid. Don't take much interest in

Christmas. Used to be great fun in the old days when it was simply an orgy of commercial excess, but now I find that people are tainting the whole thing with a lot of religious mumbo jumbo. Thank the Lord it's over for another year.

LUDOVIC KENNEDY: Yes, I was going to ask you, Sir Arthur – how will you spend the rest of your year?

SIR ARTHUR STREEB-GREEBLING: The rest of the year? That goes completely into preparation for the Greebling Fete. I'll be going around putting up signs on all the trees saying 'August 4th – Fete' to get the villagers interested. I always put these up good and early on about August the 5th generally, as soon as the previous fete has lumbered to a close. I like to give plenty of notice.

LUDOVIC KENNEDY: Do you have stalls for the produce or is it more 'pick your own'?

SIR ARTHUR STREEB-GREEBLING: We find that people get more pleasure in picking their own, and in pursuing the worm. Particularly on their own – that is a lonely sort of hunt. 'Pick your own nettles' is quite popular, I suppose largely because the sign says 'mint'. As a result, we sell an awful amount of dock leaves. My own favourite is the 'bring and buy' aspect. The villagers bring a lot of their stuff and then they buy it back from us at a small percentage – a hundred, I think it is. Yes, a hundred per cent. They enjoy that. And, of course, we do have peg dancing.

LUDOVIC KENNEDY: Is that like Morris Dancing?

SIR ARTHUR STREEB-GREEBLING: Yes, very like Morris Dancing, really. A woman called Peg comes in and dances.

LUDOVIC KENNEDY: You're very fond of the gardens here at Greebling Manor, Sir Arthur.

SIR ARTHUR STREEB-GREEBLING: Oh yes, I'm tremendously fond of the gardens because we keep them right outside here, you see, and they're absolutely beautiful. That's why I was so completely devastated by these storms we've been having recently. They played havoc with the grounds. Had an enormous number of beautiful trees blown over – blown over from the neighbouring properties which landed here and took root. Absolutely ruined the putting green.

LUDOVIC KENNEDY: Nevertheless, the garden is open again now and is very popular with the public. Why do you think that is?

SIR ARTHUR STREEB-GREEBLING: Well, I think probably people are attracted by the enormous sign outside on the A34 saying 'miniature railway, farm, zoo, vintage car museum, tropical aquarium, jousting exhibitions, bonsai gardens and licensed restaurant'.

LUDOVIC KENNEDY: It is very impressive.

SIR ARTHUR STREEB-GREEBLING: Yes it is, isn't it? One of our neighbours, the Duke of Bedford, very kindly allowed us to steal it from him. But Greebling isn't a large garden. It's nothing like Woburn and Blenheim or any of those places. It's a compact garden. We have vines, of course. Well, no – we don't have vines, actually. We don't have any vines at all – not even a hint of vine. Well, we have cacti.

LUDOVIC KENNEDY: Why do you think people keep coming? Because you don't have many cacti, do you?

SIR ARTHUR STREEB-GREEBLING: Just the one. Well, I have a hunch that the sign may have something to do with it. It is a lovely sign. We just keep it outside – well, we keep all the outside outside. But more than that, it's a garden you can get around in a day, isn't it? Well, you can get around it in a minute, actually. You don't have to waste a whole day trailing around the garden. And the time is your own.

LUDOVIC KENNEDY: And entry is free, is it?

SIR ARTHUR STREEB-GREEBLING: Entry, yes, is free – but exit is very, very expensive. It costs absolutely nothing to get in and a hundred pounds to get out. It's a walled garden.

LUDOVIC KENNEDY: Apart from the cactus?

SIR ARTHUR STREEB-GREEBLING: That's it.

LUDOVIC KENNEDY: Well, finally, Sir Arthur, I feel I've got to know you a lot better over these twelve days, but I'm still curious as to one thing – what is it, in the end, that you really believe in?

SIR ARTHUR STREEB-GREEBLING: Well, I'd like to say I believed in God, of course, but I'm afraid that, as a thinking person who cares about the world around him, there are two very good reasons why I simply can't.

LUDOVIC KENNEDY: What are they?

SIR ARTHUR STREEB-GREEBLING: Well, A – Wasps. Can't see the point of a wasp, can you? Absolutely pointless. And B – caviar. I mean, really, what is the point of having caviar locked away inside sturgeon? So inaccessible. I'm sure that if there were a real God he'd have arranged for caviar to just sort of toddle over to your house on a pair of little legs in a self-opening jar.

LUDOVIC KENNEDY: Sir Arthur – thank you.

SIR ARTHUR STREEB-GREEBLING: Thank you, and season's greeblings to you all.

Why Bother?
(BBC Radio Three, 1994) Part One

CHRIS MORRIS: Right, we're almost ready. Have you done this kind of thing before?

SIR ARTHUR STREEB-GREEBLING: A long, long time ago in the Sixties, with John Freeman and the *Face to Face* thing. But he was a hopeless amateur – broke down and wept halfway through the interview.

CHRIS MORRIS: How did it resolve, that particular encounter?

SIR ARTHUR STREEB-GREEBLING: I gave him a hanky and told him to pull himself together. I did a bit of an appearance on *The Tube* with Paula Yates and Jools Holland – played a bit of boogie on that, but not radio. I've only done television, so this is all a new world to me.

CHRIS MORRIS: Sorry, I wasn't listening to that. Are you ready to go?

SIR ARTHUR STREEB-GREEBLING: Yes, I'm off any minute.

CHRIS MORRIS: Sir Arthur, your work with eels is very well documented, it's perhaps less well known that during one experiment you came very close to death. How did that happen?

SIR ARTHUR STREEB-GREEBLING: I was trying to test the strength of the eel, and whether the strength of the eel was enhanced by an injection of Thybizalin, which, as you probably know, is a steroid, much used by Betty Grable in the early days of Hollywood, which gave her those wonderful legs, because she was born with legs only three inches long, and her parents were determined to have a world-class film star style daughter. But through administration of this drug, and what is called 'tugging', namely pulling by the ankles, they managed to get Grable's legs up to the required film star length.

CHRIS MORRIS: Wasn't there also a functional problem in this process – sometimes things got horribly out of hand?

SIR ARTHUR STREEB-GREEBLING: Yes. Well, there was one occasion. I don't know if you've ever seen the sequence, but there are out-takes in the British War Museum, which show Grable starting off her dance routine with these very long legs, and winding up basically looking like a tea cosy. And the effects of the drug and the tugging were variable. There were many days she couldn't shoot, because her legs got, frankly, too long for comfort.

CHRIS MORRIS: They weren't just long were they? They flexed backwards.

SIR ARTHUR STREEB-GREEBLING: She could walk both ways, yes, which was an effect which startled Louis B Mayer. Once I remember Louis B Mayer was on his casting couch, casting himself, and suddenly he thought he saw Betty Grable walking in. In fact she was walking out, and that got up his nose. He was easily slighted.

CHRIS MORRIS: Let's get back to you fighting the eel on the table. I believe during the course of that encounter you did very nearly die. Did you ever think during the struggle, 'I don't care if it kills me'?

SIR ARTHUR STREEB-GREEBLING: Well, there were moments, there were moments when I thought, 'Well, I've had a long life, I've had a varied life and I've had just about enough of it really' – all these bloody eels. Bloody, bloody, bloody eels. I mean, as soon as you get hold of one they start slithering all over the table. You ask them what's the secret of their jaw movement – the same bloody thing, so I was tempted. But there was work to be done, and it will be done, and I will be done.

CHRIS MORRIS: It makes one sorry to hear you talk like this. Many would say that before the eels, you were a different man.

SIR ARTHUR STREEB-GREEBLING: Well before the eels, of course, I was caught up in my love life.

CHRIS MORRIS: Caught up?

SIR ARTHUR STREEB-GREEBLING: Caught up, yes. I don't know if you remember the cha cha boogies of Edmundo Ros, but Lita Rosa, who was a magnificent singer. And we had – not an affair, more of a correspondence. I sent her a postcard from, I think it was Tibet, and never got a reply because she was a married woman, and so it all petered out.

CHRIS MORRIS: But you still haven't recovered. There's something unresolved about that relationship?

SIR ARTHUR STREEB-GREEBLING: I'm not easily given to tears, but, not hearing back from Lisa was a bit of a body blow.

CHRIS MORRIS: What was it about her that really moved you?

SIR ARTHUR STREEB-GREEBLING: Her name, I think. Lita. Lita, Lita, Lita, Lita – Rosa, Rosa, Rosa.

CHRIS MORRIS: And as a result of this great disappointment, I believe you dived headlong into a life of ill-advised abandon.

SIR ARTHUR STREEB-GREEBLING: Yes, well to try and forget her I embarked on a series of meaningless affairs. They weren't even flings – they were nightcaps.

CHRIS MORRIS: Did you ever meet Eric Clapton when you were there?

SIR ARTHUR STREEB-GREEBLING: Several times. He was frightfully nice – a great comfort to me, Eric. Because he'd been through so much, hasn't he? I mean, having to play the guitar all the time – must be absolutely awful for him. But Eric is a pathetic individual really. Give me Ginger Rogers, or Ginger Baker, whatever the other one is. The one who went to Africa and taught the natives how to play the drums.

CHRIS MORRIS: You were arrested with a gun in the vicinity of Eric Clapton's apartment in LA.

SIR ARTHUR STREEB-GREEBLING: Not arrested, I was taking part in the racial violence in Los Angeles after the Rodney King incident.

CHRIS MORRIS: Which side were you on?

SIR ARTHUR STREEB-GREEBLING: I was trying to mediate, between the police and Rodders. I got to know him very well. He's a very nice chap. And we were having a Big Mac together and the police blundered in to finish off a job they hadn't, you know, completed. So I tried to mediate by saying 'There he is officer,' to try and calm the whole thing down, because one hates to see Los Angeles go up in flames unless one's got a camera running.

CHRIS MORRIS: That was reported in one of the Sunday papers of the time, as the dark soul of Sir Arthur Streeb-Greebling. That night was a trail of wanton destruction, which many ascribed to your near-death experience, leaving you bereft of any hope.

SIR ARTHUR STREEB-GREEBLING: I like to think I mowed down as many whites as I did blacks. The Koreans did very badly out of the whole deal.

CHRIS MORRIS: Do you feel any pride now, about that?

SIR ARTHUR STREEB-GREEBLING: I feel nothing but pride. That's all I do feel. An empty pride, a hopeless vanity, a dreadful arrogance, stupefyingly futile conceit – but at least it's something to hang onto.

CHRIS MORRIS: And the fact that you got away.

SIR ARTHUR STREEB-GREEBLING: With murder, yes. Let's not mince words.

CHRIS MORRIS: And had to pay a menial fine.

SIR ARTHUR STREEB-GREEBLING: Well, I don't know what you call a menial fine. I had to do community work. I had to go and teach Tatum O'Neal to play tennis.

CHRIS MORRIS: Is there anything left for you to do once you've finished with the eels?

SIR ARTHUR STREEB-GREEBLING: Well, I've still got to work on her backhand.

CHRIS MORRIS: Sir Arthur, it does interest me. Why did you agree to these interviews?

SIR ARTHUR STREEB-GREEBLING: The reason is really very, very simple. I've lived a long time. I've been distorted, I've been misrepresented and I've been quoted accurately, which is perhaps the most appalling, and I thought in simple conversation with another human being I would get some things off my chest and on to other people's.

CHRIS MORRIS: What question would you ask yourself?

SIR ARTHUR STREEB-GREEBLING: The most fascinating question of all is that one which you didn't ask last time.

CHRIS MORRIS: And that's the one you would ask yourself?

SIR ARTHUR STREEB-GREEBLING: That's the one I would ask myself. I'm not sure if I have the reply yet.

CHRIS MORRIS: Well let's see. Ask yourself that question and then see if you have an answer.

SIR ARTHUR STREEB-GREEBLING: Not at the moment.

CHRIS MORRIS: You didn't ask the question though.

SIR ARTHUR STREEB-GREEBLING: I internalised it.

CHRIS MORRIS: Perhaps you need to get quite firm with yourself.

SIR ARTHUR STREEB-GREEBLING: No, I don't have the answer.

CHRIS MORRIS: Perhaps we'll come back to that.

SIR ARTHUR STREEB-GREEBLING: I'm sure we will.

Why Bother?
(BBC Radio Three, 1994) Part Two

CHRIS MORRIS: Sorry to hear about the stroke incidentally.

SIR ARTHUR STREEB-GREEBLING: Yes, suddenly the whole side of her body went. She can, she can still make signals.

CHRIS MORRIS: Obviously we ought to talk about the end of your life really. In later life one often follows very quickly on the heels of the other.

SIR ARTHUR STREEB-GREEBLING: Whatever you like really, but I really should give her a call. She can't pick up a phone now, of course, so they have to put it through loudspeakers into the ward.

CHRIS MORRIS: Sir Arthur, you are quite clearly to anyone who could see you nearing the end of your life. Who will receive the greater part of your fortune?

SIR ARTHUR STREEB-GREEBLING: I've made it very clear that all my assets go to a trust. I've often thought of giving all my money away, but then I've often thought again.

CHRIS MORRIS: I've just had a rather entertaining thought of you dying, your last breath coming out of your mouth. How would you like that to happen? Would you sort of collapse on the floor somewhere in public?

SIR ARTHUR STREEB-GREEBLING: You find, you find the prospect of my dying very amusing do you?

CHRIS MORRIS: Yes I do.

SIR ARTHUR STREEB-GREEBLING: Yes you do, yes. What about, what about your own death? How do you view that? With equal good humour?

CHRIS MORRIS: No, I wouldn't look as good lying on my back like a tortoise, sort of burbling fluids of some kind. Well let's talk about prisons. Your report on prisons is published tomorrow. What's it going to say?

SIR ARTHUR STREEB-GREEBLING: I think the key finding is that criminals are people who should not be treated with kid gloves. They are the dregs. And dregs should be kept at the bottom of the barrel, otherwise the wine will never get to the surface.

CHRIS MORRIS: Is this in any way linked with your experience of your own father who, as we know, was a profound criminal?

SIR ARTHUR STREEB-GREEBLING: My father had criminal tendencies which he exercised to the full. It was a, a learning experience to be a child in my father's household. Or whichever household he put me in. He was a very firm man, and he felt that the best education I could possibly have was to be put in prison and raised by hardened murderers. We were woken at dawn by the sound of hanging, we had to sleep naked because the warders feared that we might do ourselves injuries, stabbing ourselves with buttons, and things like that. And we used to draw straws about which clothes we got into because there were only fifty pairs of trousers and there were four hundred inmates.

CHRIS MORRIS: How did you as a four-year-old fare amongst grown men in this scrabble for clothes?

SIR ARTHUR STREEB-GREEBLING: I tended not to get any clothes.

All four-year-olds are not as big as twenty-year-olds. So if I was lucky I used to be put into somebody's pocket or stuffed down somebody's waistband. There was one particularly thin prisoner, who I got to know as Uncle Edward. And he used to stuff me down his trousers every now and then and take me down to the turnip fields and jiggle me up and down.

CHRIS MORRIS: Did you keep in touch with him after you left?

SIR ARTHUR STREEB-GREEBLING: No, he died in the field. And I was left there for several days because the policy in those days was if people died at work it was taken to be dumb insolence and so they were left as an example to the other prisoners.

CHRIS MORRIS: Did you hold this against your father, at all?

SIR ARTHUR STREEB-GREEBLING: We never spoke about it. I must say that at the time I resented being in prison for crimes I had not committed and forced into the company of, at best, rough diamonds, to be frank, because I became prematurely old as a four-year-old. I had the body of a four-year-old, and the mind of an eighty-year-old.

CHRIS MORRIS: You became a heavy smoker at the age of four?

SIR ARTHUR STREEB-GREEBLING: Yes, and this led to me falling out with Uncle Edward because at four I was getting through twenty cigarettes a day in his trousers.

CHRIS MORRIS: What contacts did you have with the outside world when you were in prison?

SIR ARTHUR STREEB-GREEBLING: I used to see planes going over sometimes.

CHRIS MORRIS: What did you think?

SIR ARTHUR STREEB-GREEBLING: I thought 'I'd like to be in one of those, I really would.' Anything in the air, I just longed for that. The war came as big relief.

CHRIS MORRIS: Well yes, you were conscripted weren't you? At the age of?

SIR ARTHUR STREEB-GREEBLING: Six. I joined the Foreign Legion and I was stationed just outside of Tunis with a bunch of Belgians.

CHRIS MORRIS: Now you were fighting alongside Rex Harrison at one point.

SIR ARTHUR STREEB-GREEBLING: Yes, Rex was awfully brave. He could have been an actor, you know. But he preferred the army. He preferred to be side by side with legionnaires, singing in French.

CHRIS MORRIS: Could he sing?

SIR ARTHUR STREEB-GREEBLING: Rex could never sing, and it's another sign of his courage that later in life, when most people would have considered themselves past it, let alone able to sing, he started to sing – and got money for it.

CHRIS MORRIS: When did you re-establish contact with your father then?

SIR ARTHUR STREEB-GREEBLING: When my father learnt that I had become buddies with Rex Harrison, he wrote me a letter asking if he could meet Rex. And I, of course, said I would try and arrange it. And I did. He met Rex. I wasn't there of course, he didn't want to meet me. He said he'd already met me, and hadn't liked what he'd seen.

CHRIS MORRIS: Now when he met your father, they fought.

SIR ARTHUR STREEB-GREEBLING: They had a skirmish. My father suggested to Rex that they collaborate on a musical for Esther Williams. My father thought if he could get her and Sonja Henie together they could combine underwater and ice so Esther would be under the ice and Sonja on top of the ice. So he'd have this combination of a woman frozen underwater looking up through the ice, up Sonja Henie's little skirt, and Rex thought it was a wonderful idea and took it to Louis B Mayer, and that's the last my father heard of it.

CHRIS MORRIS: Is this in any way associated with the episode in which you were forced to stand on a frozen lake by your father?

SIR ARTHUR STREEB-GREEBLING: He suggested I stand in the middle of Lake Ontario during a particularly bleak winter in Canada and I stood there, and I was waiting for a whistle or something. Some sort of signal that I could go, go to the shore, and the whistle never came.

CHRIS MORRIS: How long were you there for?

SIR ARTHUR STREEB-GREEBLING: About a year and a quarter. But anyway, I really don't like talking about this sort of thing, because it was all a long time ago and my memory of it is, is very detailed. I can remember every single pine needle on the trudge through the forest towards Toronto.

CHRIS MORRIS: I hope you won't mind if I hold you to it, because the next time we want to interview you, you'll probably be dead. Apart from the perilous cold, what other dangers did you have to fight off?

SIR ARTHUR STREEB-GREEBLING: Possibly the most dangerous element of the stay, as I call it, were the bears, because strictly speaking they're not vegetarians. And it was hard at times to fob them off.

CHRIS MORRIS: But you succeeded and furthermore in time became respected by them.

SIR ARTHUR STREEB-GREEBLING: I became loved by the bears, yes. It was when an old granny bear had come round one evening. She was on her last legs and wheezing and bits of fur were falling out. She was really in a very bad way. And I nestled up to her and gave her, I think it was a fish finger I had in my hamper, and she gasped with pleasure and fell to the ice and expired. And it was then that I skinned her and put her fur on me, and basically masqueraded as a bear for nine months.

CHRIS MORRIS: And how did you end up leaving the ice?

SIR ARTHUR STREEB-GREEBLING: I decided to walk off.

CHRIS MORRIS: Had you, do you think, during that time, fallen in love with frozen water?

SIR ARTHUR STREEB-GREEBLING: There was a certain bleak beauty about the place which appealed to me. And even now, years and years later, in the middle of the night I'll get up and go to the fridge, get out an ice cube and just perch on it, just to bring back those memories. Like that Proust used to dip his biscuits in his tea.

CHRIS MORRIS: Right, sorry it took a bit longer this evening.

SIR ARTHUR STREEB-GREEBLING: No that's, that's all right. I must say you're fairly persistent in that particular line of questioning. I really feel I was being grilled.

CHRIS MORRIS: Really? I'm sorry about that.

SIR ARTHUR STREEB-GREEBLING: No, no, no. I like to meet somebody who treats me really badly.

Why Bother?
(BBC Radio Three, 1994) Part Three

CHRIS MORRIS: Good evening, Sir Arthur. I'm sorry I'm late. I've got rather a tough schedule at the moment.

SIR ARTHUR STREEB-GREEBLING: Yes well I've made myself at home here.

CHRIS MORRIS: Well that's good. You've got lots of time, and I haven't because I'm quite busy, and I've got quite a lot of important things to do. It must be rather nice not having important things to do, and generally having a lot of time to fritter away. Sorry. You were saying?

SIR ARTHUR STREEB-GREEBLING: I was just saying that today we could start on, on the subject which we mentioned last week but didn't get around to, which was the bee keeping. I've got quite a few anecdotes because I started off with just one bee and used it to attract another bee, and eventually got a swarm going, and it's quite an interesting anecdote.

CHRIS MORRIS: It sounds dull to me actually.

SIR ARTHUR STREEB-GREEBLING: Well it's very lifelike.

CHRIS MORRIS: Well perhaps you'd like to start it off then.

SIR ARTHUR STREEB-GREEBLING: Yes, well if you ask me a question, a simple introduction, like tell us about bee keeping or something.

CHRIS MORRIS: Alright, I'm not really very interested, but hello, Sir Arthur, how are you?

SIR ARTHUR STREEB-GREEBLING: Fine. I had some bees in my youth and put them to work making honey.

CHRIS MORRIS: Now in your address to the Royal Society tomorrow, you intend to reveal the fossilised remains of the infant Christ. How do you feel that will go down?

SIR ARTHUR STREEB-GREEBLING: Well, it is a remarkable discovery. A group of us were up in the promised land, as I believe it was called. We were just rooting around for some sticks to start a fire with, and by some accident this tiny little form had been preserved perfectly. So I picked it up, put in my knapsack and brought it home and had it scientifically examined at my institute. It's Christ at the age of about nine months. Just beginning to walk – more crawling than walking. Crawling across the desert in search of followers, really, and then of course he died.

CHRIS MORRIS: So what are the implications then, if Christ was fossilised when he was that small?

SIR ARTHUR STREEB-GREEBLING: He was practising resurrection. Because if you're going to resurrect yourself in front of thousands of people, and found the whole religion on it, you don't want to make a cock-up, do you? So from a very early age he was dropping dead and resurrecting himself. There's probably thousands and thousands of bodies of Jesus and this is just the youngest one.

CHRIS MORRIS: A series of larvae?

SIR ARTHUR STREEB-GREEBLING: Almost, yes. Pupae. In fact he never really got it right at the end. I mean, not as if he was pronounced dead on the cross and then flew up and flapped his wings and said 'hello boys.' He did it in rather a complicated way, had to be put in a cave, a boulder put in front of it. I mean, Paul Daniels could do that. So I think he never really quite got the hang of it.

CHRIS MORRIS: Could you tell how quickly these practice resurrections happened?

SIR ARTHUR STREEB-GREEBLING: It took about six months. He died, as planned. Then, just as he was passing away, he suddenly forgot how to do it, but instincts carried him through, and gradually he resurrected himself, by which time, he was under the sand because of the wind, and he not only had to resurrect himself, he had to fight his way to the surface. He would of course have died while doing that.

CHRIS MORRIS: Suffocation?

SIR ARTHUR STREEB-GREEBLING: Suffocation, smothered by sand, so he died again. And there's some controversy about whether my tiny Christ is in fact the nine-month-old teetee or the nine and a half month.

CHRIS MORRIS: This fits in with your theory that as Christ practised resurrection throughout his life, he didn't do it flawlessly, did he? He produced several of himself at once.

SIR ARTHUR STREEB-GREEBLING: Well there was a time when he overdid it and reproduced eighteen other Christs, so he had to wipe out seventeen of them.

CHRIS MORRIS: But he had to stop them resurrecting themselves once they'd done it.

SIR ARTHUR STREEB-GREEBLING: Yes, he had to keep them under order. I think Saint Paul mentions it in passing.

CHRIS MORRIS: Now have you spoken to the Vatican about this?

SIR ARTHUR STREEB-GREEBLING: I've had words with their envoy over here, the special enunciate, and he's absolutely thrilled to bits, and has suggested a venue where we could put it up and have it start earning its keep.

CHRIS MORRIS: But does he know that you intend to clone from its tissue?

SIR ARTHUR STREEB-GREEBLING: I haven't gone into that with him, because frankly it's none of his business. And it is a business.

CHRIS MORRIS: Who's putting up the money for this?

SIR ARTHUR STREEB-GREEBLING: Honda.

CHRIS MORRIS: Now when or if this is successful, what do you feel the result of it will be?

SIR ARTHUR STREEB-GREEBLING: Well, I am very much hoping to be the first to shake Jesus by the hand and say 'well done.'

CHRIS MORRIS: How far are you prepared to take this? Say the experiment is four-fifths successful, and you end up with some animated tissue, which is not particularly man-like, would you allow that to carry on living?

SIR ARTHUR STREEB-GREEBLING: Well I think one would go on gut reaction. I think if one had three quarters of Jesus, you would know that it was Jesus, and I would settle for that.

CHRIS MORRIS: What diagnostic signs are you going to go for that make it Jesus?

SIR ARTHUR STREEB-GREEBLING: Just breathing.

CHRIS MORRIS: A voice?

SIR ARTHUR STREEB-GREEBLING: A voice, yes, maybe. But he could sign his message. He could wave his hands around like they do on Channel 4.

CHRIS MORRIS: Who will provide the words in that case?

SIR ARTHUR STREEB-GREEBLING: Well then we'd prerecord something, with Martin Jarvis or John Hurt or somebody suitable to do the voice under.

CHRIS MORRIS: Project a little sort of moving shape over his mouth?

SIR ARTHUR STREEB-GREEBLING: Probably just with an elastic band you could get some movement. Oprah Winfrey's interested. Oprah has lost a lot of weight hasn't she? And gained a lot of weight. One moment anorexic, the next moment bulimic – and in between regressing to child abuse.

CHRIS MORRIS: And where would the words come from?

SIR ARTHUR STREEB-GREEBLING: Oh we'd just do whatever he said in the Bible. The same stuff. Just recycle it a bit. What he said was perfectly good.

CHRIS MORRIS: I think you know what I'm getting at. I'm actually trying to find out whether you will be using him as some sort of conduit for your own warped ideas.

SIR ARTHUR STREEB-GREEBLING: No, no, no. It will be his warped ideas, not mine.

CHRIS MORRIS: And what role do BMW play?

SIR ARTHUR STREEB-GREEBLING: They're refurnishing the vehicles.

CHRIS MORRIS: Will he not be frightened by modern transport?

SIR ARTHUR STREEB-GREEBLING: Yes. The Sony Corporation are interested in a sort of hover donkey. They can move at about a hundred and ten miles an hour.

Chris Morris Now I'm told that the Japanese are more seriously involved than that.

SIR ARTHUR STREEB-GREEBLING: In the miniaturisation of Jesus, yes – given his consent, of course.

CHRIS MORRIS: And what will the Japanese do with these miniature Christs?

SIR ARTHUR STREEB-GREEBLING: They will market them in the normal way, because there's a lot of people out there, people who are yearning to find Christ, and who don't have the time to go out and look for him in person, who would like to have Christ through the letterbox.

CHRIS MORRIS: How will they eat?

SIR ARTHUR STREEB-GREEBLING: Who?

CHRIS MORRIS: These micro Christs.

SIR ARTHUR STREEB-GREEBLING: Conventionally, I think, through a tiny little tube, which will be supplied.

CHRIS MORRIS: And how will you guarantee their safety against . . .

SIR ARTHUR STREEB-GREEBLING: Theft?

CHRIS MORRIS: And dogs?

SIR ARTHUR STREEB-GREEBLING: Well, showing a tiny Christ to an Alsatian is like showing a red rag to a – whatever they're called, those big things with horns.

CHRIS MORRIS: Bishops.

SIR ARTHUR STREEB-GREEBLING: Bishops, yes. There are no guarantees. You've got a tiny Christ, he's six inches high, he's about three centimetres deep, and he has all the organs.

CHRIS MORRIS: Where do they come in?

SIR ARTHUR STREEB-GREEBLING: Look, I don't want to . . . You're rather pre-empting my address tomorrow.

CHRIS MORRIS: Alright, well let me put it to you like this. Don't you think that if you clone Christ, he will in some way want to remonstrate with you as soon as he can?

SIR ARTHUR STREEB-GREEBLING: Well that's up to him, but he'll be pretty lost without the batteries.

CHRIS MORRIS: Right, Sir Arthur, thank you. It took a while, didn't it? But I suppose we got it in the end.

SIR ARTHUR STREEB-GREEBLING: I think well worth it, yes. Do you think the stuff about the bee keeping went well?

CHRIS MORRIS: Yes . . . What are you doing this evening?

SIR ARTHUR STREEB-GREEBLING: Nothing written down, but I was thinking of going along to the YMCA and have a swim.

CHRIS MORRIS: Fancy a stroll first?

SIR ARTHUR STREEB-GREEBLING: Yes, that'd be nice.

CHRIS MORRIS: Where, do you think?

SIR ARTHUR STREEB-GREEBLING: Well, Tottenham Court Road's quite nice. You know, the swimming pool, the Oasis.

CHRIS MORRIS: I love walking up and down there.

Why Bother?
(BBC Radio Three, 1994) Part Four

CHRIS MORRIS: Well, I'll just introduce the reason you're here, Sir Arthur.

SIR ARTHUR STREEB-GREEBLING: Yes, there's just one thing. Would it be all right if Gavin came in and did my hair? He's a very nice young man from Camden Town. He's started his own particular salon. In case I didn't have time to have it done afterwards.

CHRIS MORRIS: Well, no.

SIR ARTHUR STREEB-GREEBLING: He's in now, and you might as well let him stand there.

CHRIS MORRIS: If you could just ask him to leave.

SIR ARTHUR STREEB-GREEBLING: I'll ask him to leave once we've finished the interview, yes.

CHRIS MORRIS: Or before would be better.

SIR ARTHUR STREEB-GREEBLING: Well that's rather tricky isn't it?

CHRIS MORRIS: Sir Arthur, I have to be clear – it will actually be very disruptive. It's really not done.

SIR ARTHUR STREEB-GREEBLING: Well, Gavin. I'm sorry I misled you. Go on the bus and get a receipt.

CHRIS MORRIS: Good. Now, Sir Arthur Streeb-Greebling, it's fifty years since you returned from Japan and your experience as a prisoner of war.

SIR ARTHUR STREEB-GREEBLING: Yes, fifty years to the day.

CHRIS MORRIS: You've seldom talked about this, but you've agreed to discuss it this evening. How were you captured?

SIR ARTHUR STREEB-GREEBLING: Well. I was in charge of a small unit of men, most of whom, alas, perished. I, seeing that there was nothing I could do to save them, since they were already dead, entered into what is called a concentration camp, under Japanese command, and was there throughout the war period.

CHRIS MORRIS: Now this is when you were the senior British officer in a prisoner of war camp which was building a railway line?

SIR ARTHUR STREEB-GREEBLING: That's right, and I think

anyone travelling on that line today will recognise the merits of the technology involved, because it's awfully difficult in that heat, carving through forests and deserts, mountains and valleys, to get a line going dead straight from Tokyo to the destination, which at that time was unknown.

CHRIS MORRIS: You talk with some feeling about the work that was involved in building this railway. You talk less about the fact that you didn't waste a single calorie of energy in making it yourself. You had nothing to do with the hard work.

SIR ARTHUR STREEB-GREEBLING: I don't quite understand the question.

CHRIS MORRIS: Well, you talk about the difficulties of building this railway.

SIR ARTHUR STREEB-GREEBLING: It was very difficult. I told you. It was very, very difficult, because there was nothing there. We had to import steel from Great Britain and the United States. Walt Disney, I believe, provided the last links.

CHRIS MORRIS: But you say 'We had to do it.'

SIR ARTHUR STREEB-GREEBLING: As you know full well, the seas were filled with enemy submarines, and just to get the steel and the iron there, that was work enough.

CHRIS MORRIS: But you keep saying 'We had to do this.' Isn't that a dishonest use of the word when you were perched on a mattress, watching your men sweat their guts out?

SIR ARTHUR STREEB-GREEBLING: Well as, as part of the arrangement, I was given accommodation slightly better than the other personnel, but not as good, I may say, as my boss, for want of a better word, General Nehow.

CHRIS MORRIS: You did get on rather well with your Japanese captors didn't you?

SIR ARTHUR STREEB-GREEBLING: Everybody is human, including my – your words – Japanese captors. I worked in the best interests of the British personnel under my command, and I attempted to organise an escape.

CHRIS MORRIS: Yes, and then you told the commandant twenty-four hours before it was put into operation.

SIR ARTHUR STREEB-GREEBLING: I informed my superior, but I'd already told my men to do it the day after, so they wouldn't get caught.

CHRIS MORRIS: And yet they all did get caught.

SIR ARTHUR STREEB-GREEBLING: They got caught. Well, they went on the wrong day.

CHRIS MORRIS: Many of them had been driven insane by the work they were doing, and those that could testify claimed that you had helped in that mental decaying process.

SIR ARTHUR STREEB-GREEBLING: I never physically beat anybody. You can see film footage showing me not beating anybody. You can see film footage of me sitting in my office, trying to get the air conditioning working.

CHRIS MORRIS: And four and a half seconds of film proves that you didn't hit them?

SIR ARTHUR STREEB-GREEBLING: Why would I hit my own men, unless they were shirking?

CHRIS MORRIS: Well, let's leave that aside.

SIR ARTHUR STREEB-GREEBLING: Leave that aside please.

CHRIS MORRIS: I put it to you that it's perfectly possible to drive a man out of his mind simply by using words and mental torture.

SIR ARTHUR STREEB-GREEBLING: Well, the fact that I may have said to a subaltern, I may have said 'get a move on' – if that is mental cruelty, well I'm a Dutchman.

CHRIS MORRIS: Is it or is it not mental cruelty to appear to that man as his wife in the middle of the night?

SIR ARTHUR STREEB-GREEBLING: I would call that a kindness in the conditions we were living in. Any man who got anybody coming to his cell posing as a man, woman or lizard was welcome.

CHRIS MORRIS: And then withhold favours?

SIR ARTHUR STREEB-GREEBLING: I did, yes.

CHRIS MORRIS: What I'm saying is that you persecuted this man until he went out of his mind, and he wasn't the only one.

SIR ARTHUR STREEB-GREEBLING: I played hard to get, and I may have talked about marriage but I mean, you know, we were both drunk. Or at least I was drunk, because that sake is remarkably powerful isn't it?

CHRIS MORRIS: And your men didn't even have enough water.

SIR ARTHUR STREEB-GREEBLING: Well, nor did I.

CHRIS MORRIS: You had something to drink.

SIR ARTHUR STREEB-GREEBLING: I had sake, and sake alone, because the water supply – this is one of the things I still correspond with General Nehow about, we have a long-standing joke about – incredibly efficient the Japanese may be, but in a prisoner of war camp can you get a cold drink? The answer I'm afraid was no. But that's neither here nor there.

CHRIS MORRIS: You needed severe coaxing to leave that camp?

SIR ARTHUR STREEB-GREEBLING: Well, I had acquired a leasehold interest in the property which covered two hundred and twelve acres of prime land. Rather too close to Hiroshima for my liking, but very verdant and with the opportunity to put in a hotel or leisure facilities, but negotiations broke down.

CHRIS MORRIS: And it was only that that made you return to this country?

SIR ARTHUR STREEB-GREEBLING: That and the ticket.

CHRIS MORRIS: Sir Arthur, sorry, I have to draw attention to something which people won't be able to see. You have during the past fifteen minutes been agitating so firmly at the sleeve of your jacket that it's now come off. Now, you're good at disguising it with the tone of your voice, but I read your body language as something akin to 'I'm telling lies.'

SIR ARTHUR STREEB-GREEBLING: Well it's a very old coat. I must say you have rather hit me below the belt there, because I had no idea that you were going to raise the subject of this herringbone being torn off.

CHRIS MORRIS: Well I must say I wouldn't have unless you had done it.

SIR ARTHUR STREEB-GREEBLING: Does the sight of flesh excite you?

CHRIS MORRIS: I can think of more attractive features on you.

SIR ARTHUR STREEB-GREEBLING: Well these speckles on my arm . . .

CHRIS MORRIS: That's candida though, isn't it?

SIR ARTHUR STREEB-GREEBLING: Candida?

CHRIS MORRIS: Isn't it an infection?

SIR ARTHUR STREEB-GREEBLING: I don't think it's an infection. It just spreads like wildfire once it starts. It starts up round about the shoulder and then gradually sort of speckles down towards the wrist and then it runs out. I dare say it will start on my hands very soon and then run out at the nails.

CHRIS MORRIS: Don't get me wrong, I didn't wish to be physically insulting. There are certain aspects of your appearance which . . .

SIR ARTHUR STREEB-GREEBLING: It's nerves. I'm not used to being in a room with a man.

CHRIS MORRIS: You see that's my lie detector test really. When a man pulls a sleeve off his jacket.

SIR ARTHUR STREEB-GREEBLING: He's fibbing? Yes, I thought you'd think that, yes.

CHRIS MORRIS: Will you just grant us the answer to one question, with an honest, straightforward answer?

SIR ARTHUR STREEB-GREEBLING: Yes, well it depends what the question is.

CHRIS MORRIS: Well, in many interviews . . .

SIR ARTHUR STREEB-GREEBLING: Yes, indeed, thank you very much.

CHRIS MORRIS: In many interviews the question that perhaps would extract the most valuable answer is the one which is never asked.

SIR ARTHUR STREEB-GREEBLING: Yes, well you haven't asked that one yet, so I haven't really been in a position to answer it.

CHRIS MORRIS: Right, well here we go. Obviously I can't ask the question which has never been asked otherwise it by definition stops being it, but you know that question. If you could keep it in your mind and give me the answer, then would get some value.

SIR ARTHUR STREEB-GREEBLING: The answer is no.

CHRIS MORRIS: And what do you mean by that?

SIR ARTHUR STREEB-GREEBLING: No is what I mean by that.

CHRIS MORRIS: Has the answer, for you, ever been anything other than no?

SIR ARTHUR STREEB-GREEBLING: No. The answer has always been no.

CHRIS MORRIS: So if I were to say to you, has the answer always
been no?
SIR ARTHUR STREEB-GREEBLING: I would say hold on a minute.

Why Bother?
(BBC Radio Three, 1994) Part Five

CHRIS MORRIS: Good evening Sir Arthur.
SIR ARTHUR STREEB-GREEBLING: Good evening.
CHRIS MORRIS: How's the voice? Have you lost it entirely, your
voice?
SIR ARTHUR STREEB-GREEBLING: Yes, it's almost completely
gone. Laryngitis. Talking too much.
SIR ARTHUR STREEB-GREEBLING: There is something we used to
do with Robin Day.
SIR ARTHUR STREEB-GREEBLING: Yes, a glass of water or
something like that.
CHRIS MORRIS: OK, if you could just sit quite still.
(*Thump*)
SIR ARTHUR STREEB-GREEBLING: Ah, that's much better, yes . . .
Right, yes I'm ready.
CHRIS MORRIS: Sir Arthur, before we come on to talk about the
orchestra, you were telling me how your life had been saved by a
puff adder.
SIR ARTHUR STREEB-GREEBLING: Yes, it was a stroke of luck
actually, because I was in Dorking, having lunch with an old
girlfriend, Rosetta, and she had a puff adder. It was a family
heirloom, and she was just pouring me a cup of tea, and the puff
adder jumped out of the little basket and I immediately
recognised it for what it was – a deadly snake – and rushed out
of the room. And moments later the whole house blew up. Poor
Rosetta was blown up in the air. There was no saving her, so I
didn't go back. I just left that to the emergency services, and her
house had been the subject of an attack by a former friend of
mine, an old business colleague who had got it into his head that

somehow or other, I had run away with funds which were due to him.

CHRIS MORRIS: It must have broken down pretty badly for you to have murdered him.

SIR ARTHUR STREEB-GREEBLING: Well, it was tit for tat – eye for eye, tooth for tooth, that type of thing – because he'd attempted to blow me up, and in so doing only destroyed the innocent life of a Guatemalan refugee. And I take against people who blow up people who I would like to go to bed with. So I wouldn't say I murdered him. I allowed him to die.

CHRIS MORRIS: Beneath your own hands and body?

SIR ARTHUR STREEB-GREEBLING: Yes, he was beneath I think. He started off on top. He was having some tea at Fortnum and Mason, and in those days they had those awful beaded tablecloths, and I positioned myself under the table and attacked him from below.

CHRIS MORRIS: In an unashamed way really?

SIR ARTHUR STREEB-GREEBLING: Yes, I was very blatant about it. I think if you're strangling somebody there's no point pretending that you're giving them a shave, you know.

CHRIS MORRIS: It caused considerable and long-lasting mental damage to many of the people who witnessed that attack.

SIR ARTHUR STREEB-GREEBLING: It was a horrifying attack. I mean, all the witnesses said that it was the most unpleasant episode they'd ever seen at Fortnum's – because people go in there and have a bit of seed cake and a cup of tea. They don't expect to see live strangling.

CHRIS MORRIS: But you became rather attached to this method of surprising business partners, didn't you?

SIR ARTHUR STREEB-GREEBLING: Yes, to the extent that it became predictable and I had to adopt another method, yes. Once I emerged from a huge vat of watercress soup.

CHRIS MORRIS: A one-off sort of thing?

SIR ARTHUR STREEB-GREEBLING: It was very much a one-off. I prefer to just lay on a trolley with a nice petit four and things like that, and then just jump off the trolley onto the victim.

CHRIS MORRIS: How did you feel when Leon Brittan & Co started mimicking your personal style?

SIR ARTHUR STREEB-GREEBLING: I was furious, because Leon is a naturally witty man and a gifted athlete, and if he'd continued high hurdling I think he could have been an Olympian. But Leon, for some reason, got attracted to imitating me, and he used to get on to trolleys and get himself pushed through restaurants for absolutely no reason, other than attention-seeking, I think. I don't think he was much loved as a child and this phase of his life has continued up to the present day. He's not much loved as an adult either.

CHRIS MORRIS: Where did it all go wrong between you and him?

SIR ARTHUR STREEB-GREEBLING: Well, I used to attend meetings as Leon Brittan, often making sure that I arrived ten seconds before he did, causing him trouble at the door, because once the doorman has admitted one Leon Brittan, it seems a little bit implausible that another one should turn up ten seconds later, so I caused a little bit of harmless fun for him. I think that's probably why he went to Europe, where they recognise him.

CHRIS MORRIS: But it was through Leon Brittan that you met and got to wrestle with Michael Heseltine.

SIR ARTHUR STREEB-GREEBLING: Well, Heseltine is an interesting man, because he's got many strings to his bow. He likes to relax with very violent physical exercise, and he employed Rudy the Giant Vacuum Cleaner, who was one of the World Wrestling Federation stars at that time, to do workouts in his barn. And they used to wrestle each other late into the night in an improvised ring made of bales of hay. And I used to go along, just, as a referee really and to fix the results, because Heseltine liked to win, and Rudy the Giant Vacuum Cleaner was also a man who didn't like to lose. The fights were often rather torrid.

CHRIS MORRIS: Now it's said that under this, some would describe it as guidance, he developed an over-enthusiasm for use of his physical prowess, at perhaps inappropriate moments?

SIR ARTHUR STREEB-GREEBLING: Yes, I always remember King Feisal being hurled to the floor at Heathrow by the Heseltine handy.

CHRIS MORRIS: Now, you've never mentioned these incidents in public before, and it does interest me why you've maintained such a rigorous media silence for the last ten years.

SIR ARTHUR STREEB-GREEBLING: Everything in life is, is about, about appearances, and I restrict my appearances as much as I can, and this is the only appearance per se that I am making this year.

CHRIS MORRIS: Well yes, it's not television here is it? And you haven't appeared on television for over ten years.

SIR ARTHUR STREEB-GREEBLING: No, this is not television. I prefer radio in many ways because the fact is that the radio is easier to look good on than television.

CHRIS MORRIS: Is it not true that the reason you won't appear on television is because a crack pipe can't be hidden?

SIR ARTHUR STREEB-GREEBLING: It can be hidden. I am willing to own up to the errors I have made and if there are any young people listening, for goodness sake don't spend one thousand pounds a day on crack, because you can get it a lot cheaper than that in Leicester Square.

CHRIS MORRIS: So on television you would not be able to last without resorting to one of the tools of your addiction?

SIR ARTHUR STREEB-GREEBLING: I would have to, after really one and a half minutes, to be realistic, and I think we are in the business of honesty here, after one and a half minutes I would have to leave the studio, unless the presenter was himself able to inject me, which I think the viewer would object to.

CHRIS MORRIS: Well, there was a failed experiment on a talk show when you appeared with an intravenous device which came from beneath the chair.

SIR ARTHUR STREEB-GREEBLING: No, I think you're confusing that with Joan Rivers, who did come from beneath the chair, and I sat next to her. But Joan is not a proscribed substance. She's just a pain in the arse.

CHRIS MORRIS: Can you describe what it feels like to wake up in the morning without . . .

SIR ARTHUR STREEB-GREEBLING: Not unless you've got something there with you, because I'm reaching the end of my tether. Thank you very much.

(*Sir Arthur lights up.*)

God. Now I tell you the downside of this is you feel awful, but the upside is you feel terrific. Where did you buy these?

CHRIS MORRIS: Kings Cross.

SIR ARTHUR STREEB-GREEBLING: It's alright, it's alright. Anyway I can talk for another minute.

CHRIS MORRIS: How did the drugs affect your writing of the Queen's speech?

SIR ARTHUR STREEB-GREEBLING: Improved it a great deal.

CHRIS MORRIS: Opium too helped Her Majesty to broadcast the speech, didn't it?

SIR ARTHUR STREEB-GREEBLING: Well, I'm talking out of school here, but it is well known in court circles that the Queen in particular is fond of dancing in the nude prior to speaking engagements. The routine is she puts on some Thin Lizzy, slips her clothes off and just throws herself onto the marble, which they have at the palace – it's part of the deal – and writhes around and then she is showered by footmen, composes herself, takes her shot, and looks serene.

CHRIS MORRIS: Why were you fired from the role of writing the Queen's speech?

SIR ARTHUR STREEB-GREEBLING: We left by mutual agreement.

CHRIS MORRIS: When was the last time you saw the Queen?

SIR ARTHUR STREEB-GREEBLING: Last night.

CHRIS MORRIS: What happened?

SIR ARTHUR STREEB-GREEBLING: I, as a favour, gave her some, I think it was opium, it could have been feminax.

CHRIS MORRIS: Now, Sir Arthur, I should point out that during that last answer you held up a legally threatening note.

SIR ARTHUR STREEB-GREEBLING: It's not a threat, it's just a statement of fact – something along the lines of if you pursue this line of questioning then we shall pursue you through the courts.

CHRIS MORRIS: I see, OK. Well, perhaps you could tell us about the occasion that you came to sing a song with the voice of Frank Sinatra to over a thousand paying punters.

SIR ARTHUR STREEB-GREEBLING: The episode where I borrowed

his larynx? Yes, well it was a whim, really. I just thought people would like to hear 'Strangers in the Night' sung by somebody other than Frank Sinatra, but with Frank Sinatra's voice.

CHRIS MORRIS: And he was sleeping, but did he agree to the exit . . .

SIR ARTHUR STREEB-GREEBLING: It was tacit – tacit consent. His, his bodyguards had no complaints.

CHRIS MORRIS: Were they conscious at the time?

SIR ARTHUR STREEB-GREEBLING: They were very, very helpful in getting the larynx out of the throat and into my briefcase. Luigi in particular, a charming man, he said 'Mr Sinatra will never miss it. He's having a dream now. You can tell by the way his elbows keep twitching. He's having one of the those exciting dreams of his homeland.' So we just went off into the night and I flew to Capri and Gracie Fields and I sang, 'The Biggest Aspidistra in the World, and closed on 'Strangers in the Night' and a 'My Way' medley.

CHRIS MORRIS: Now I have to ask you, did you not do this purely out of financial greed?

SIR ARTHUR STREEB-GREEBLING: I'm more than happy to answer that question, but I would prefer to do it without the tape spinning round. So if you'd just stop the tape, I'll give you the answer.

CHRIS MORRIS: Right, we've stopped the tapes.

SIR ARTHUR STREEB-GREEBLING: Thank you

CHRIS MORRIS: And what was the answer?

SIR ARTHUR STREEB-GREEBLING: What was the question?

CHRIS MORRIS: Well it was about money, and whether you made an awful lot of money.

SIR ARTHUR STREEB-GREEBLING: Yes, I made an awful lot of money out of that, yes. You can start the tape running again now.

CHRIS MORRIS: Even before I ask you how much money?

SIR ARTHUR STREEB-GREEBLING: No, have you started it up running?

CHRIS MORRIS: No, we haven't yet.

SIR ARTHUR STREEB-GREEBLING: Good. Well, four million pounds.

CHRIS MORRIS: And now I can start it again?

SIR ARTHUR STREEB-GREEBLING: You can start it running again, yes.

CHRIS MORRIS: So it was purely then for artistic reasons?

SIR ARTHUR STREEB-GREEBLING: Exactly.

Chapter Twelve

Sports Reporter

Sport was a subject about which Cook could be completely serious or completely frivolous, because it was a subject that never bored him. 'Men must amuse themselves,' Cook told Hunter Davies, who wrote a classic book about Tottenham Hotspur, Peter's (second) favourite football team. 'That's the prime purpose of sport, and of life.'[1] Sport certainly kept Cook amused. He cultivated an encyclopedic knowledge of every conceivable sport – even those few he claimed to loathe, like Rugby League.

Cook took a perverse pleasure in following obscure TV sports, screened only in the small hours – but football was a particular passion, and he was no armchair fan. Half a century before Nick Hornby popularised middle-class football fandom in *Fever Pitch*, his memoir about supporting Arsenal (Cook's least favourite team), Cook was hauling his grandmother's housekeeper along to Plainmoor, to support his local childhood team, Torquay United. At his prep school, St Bede's, he played inside left – a sort of left sided attacking midfielder – back in those daredevil days when football teams habitually lined up in audacious 2-3-5 formations, rather than today's defensive 4-4-2.

Like most public schools, Radley College was a rugger school – but Peter sparked a fashion for soccer by mounting bootleg football matches. For anyone who's unfamiliar with the English class barrier between Rugby Union (a game for ruffians played by gentlemen) and Association Football (a game for gentlemen played by ruffians), this may not sound terribly subversive, – but it was actually a bit more rebellious than it might seem. For most public (and even grammar) schools, unswerving allegiance to Rugby (Union, not League) is a fundamental symbol of their (self-) perceived superiority over common comprehensives (or secondary moderns, in Peter's schooldays).

At Cambridge, Peter spent his first year playing football, rather than acting in Footlights. After he became famous, he modestly mocked his student efforts. Actually, he wasn't all that bad, but the fact that he was never an outstanding sportsman (even by school or college standards) was precisely what made his lifelong love of sport so special. A lot of things came very easily to him, and he soon tired of most of those things that didn't – like learning lines. However, he never tired of sport.

When Peter arrived in London, he started following Tottenham Hotspur. He claimed this was because their name began with the same two letters as his first footballing love, Torquay, but their romantic reputation as an attractive attacking side probably had a lot to do with it. When Peter started supporting them, they'd recently become the first twentieth-century English team to win the double (League Championship and FA Cup in the same season, for the benefit of anyone with better things to study). However Spurs were smaller, less prosperous and historically less successful than their local rivals, Arsenal. When Spurs beat Arsenal, Peter would goad friends of his who were Arsenal fans, like Rory McGrath. One of his favourite tricks was to feign ignorance of the result, and ask them the score. Spurs never won the League again in Peter's lifetime, but they did win the FA Cup five times, as well as a couple of League Cups and several European trophies. Sadly, Cook didn't live to see Spurs lift their last League Cup, in 1999, but his death, in 1995, spared him the agony of watching Arsenal win a second League and Cup double in 1998 – and a third in 2002.

Peter was a season ticket holder at Tottenham's ground, White Hart Lane, where he was a vociferous supporter. He even attended away matches, and it was a vicious beating, administered by a gang of teenage Manchester United fans, which prompted his first piece of sports journalism, included here. 'A bloke had just come up to me to ask for my autograph and I had given it to him,' recalled Cook, nursing some bruises and a splitting headache. 'Then this other youth came up and I presumed he was going to ask for my autograph. Instead he just kicked me with his boot in my stomach – without saying a word. I picked myself up and a fair old fight got under way with about half a dozen of them. We both got bashed around quite badly.'[2] Peter was indeed quite badly bashed around – the encounter cost him his front teeth – but there was no mention that he'd watched the game from the Stretford End, a terrace favoured by diehard home supporters (or very brave and foolhardy away fans) and scarcely kept his own counsel.

Peter started playing golf at a very early age, and as a teenager, he already had a single handicap. In the Seventies, he became a regular guest on *Pro Celebrity Golf*, the long running series on BBC2. Surrounded by professional golfers, and celebrities trying to play like professionals, Peter often played for laughs – bringing along a pet goldfish to upstage the huge German Shepherd, Oscar, who always accompanied James Hunt, the racing driver, and dressing up as a transvestite World War One flying ace to distract England cricket captain Ted Dexter, who had caned Peter for drinking cider at the Henley Regatta when they were both schoolboys at Radley. Cook's assessment of his game was as self-deprecating as his televised match play. 'My driving hasn't been very good lately,' he warned his golf partner, the satirist John Clarke, in Australia, 'but my short game is among the shortest on earth.'[3]

In fact, Peter Cook the golfer suffered from the same modesty as Peter Cook the footballer. 'He played far more than many people realised and indeed, with a little more effort he could have become a low-handicap player,' claimed the great golfer turned commentator Peter Alliss. 'He had a sound swing, good rhythm and keen eye.'[4] Alliss reckoned he could have got his handicap down to single figures again, but Cook's sense of the absurd always overcame any desire to work on his game. One of his last ventures was a quartet of golfing archetypes, released on video as *Peter Cook Talks Golf Balls*. He also conducted a spoof campaign for his beloved Hampstead to host the Ryder Cup, and even designed the course, whose final four holes included an unusual range of hazards:

> The 15th: The North Circular. 701 yards, par five. Most professionals will play a one-iron off the tee to avoid Hendon and then take a taxi to Stanmore, which will afford them an interesting shot on to the green (Golders).
> The 16th: The Tomb, 154 yards, par three. From Karl Marx's grave in Highgate Cemetery, the green will be protected by bunkers and headstones. Anything short and you're definitely dead.
> The 17th: The Spaniards. 449 yards, par four. There will be a distinctly Pedrena feel to this hole, with its gorgeous scenery and lack of room service.
> The 18th: The Kenwood. 308 yards, par four. A glorious closing hole. The green will be within range of the big-hitters off the tee, but they will have to carry the lake, the orchestra and Edward Heath MP, who will be conducting.'[5]

However, Cook's passion for sport was mainly a friendly private affair. Throughout his life, any sport (but particularly golf and football) was an escape and a respite – a parallel universe with its own integral logic, which he could make fun of whenever he wanted to, but perhaps somewhere he didn't have to be funny. Its epitome is the game he invented on a Nile cruise as a guest of John Cleese and his wife to be, Alyce-Faye Eichelberger, along with about forty other guests, including Stephen Fry and Eric Idle. Ostensibly, The Royal & Not Noticeably Ancient Game of Abu Simbel merely consisted of trying to bowl a beach ball through the handrails of the steps that led into the swimming pool at the Royal Simbel Hotel near Abu Simbel, but Peter transformed it into a complete sport with its own arcane rules and vocabulary. By the end of the afternoon, all the hotel guests and staff were playing, and if a camera crew had been on hand, you'd probably be watching Pro-Celebrity Abu Simbel on BBC2 today.

∿

THE KICK I GET OUT OF FOOTBALL
(*Sunday People*, 4 February, 1968)

Yes, I confess, I'm hooked on Soccer and I have the marks to prove it, after being beaten up outside Old Trafford – but because I curled up like a hedgehog they are all in unshowable (penny-for-a-look) positions.

My friend and I hid behind a nearby gate and a man inside there said: 'You can't come in here.' I said: 'Well, we're being attacked.' He replied: 'It's more than my job's worth to let you in 'ere . . .' 'But we've got these people beating us up,' I said. 'Well, you must have said something provocative,' he insisted. I told him I had said nothing at all and they kicked me.

'Don't give me that,' he said. 'I could go out there now, walk up and down five times and they wouldn't touch me!' I said 'Try putting on this Spurs rosette, mate, and then see!' But I give notice here and now that I shall certainly continue to wear my Spurs rosette for away matches.

Mrs Brimacombe, my grandmother's housekeeper, first introduced me to football – in Torquay where I was born – when I was six years old. I became a complete fanatic. Torquay United – now pulsing at the head of the Third Division – wasn't then a difficulty ground to get into. But I used to queue up an hour and a half beforehand to get in the front row by the halfway line. By the time the players came out I had to rush off to the gents' so I always came back to find I'd lost my place.

Unfortunately, I went to a Rugger school where I had to play illicit Soccer at the end of a half-mile-long pitch, down by a forest. I played football at Cambridge but I was the worst kind of inside left – too flashy. I spent hours practising flicking the ball over my head. To me football is the best game in the world.

I sit in the old stand. I'm not a permanent season ticket holder because Spurs supporters rarely seem to die. When they do their seasons seem to fall into the touts' hands. I'm a shouter myself. I rise and boo heartily at the fouls that go on miles away from the play – while the ref isn't looking. I also enjoy hearing the sage remarks the crowd shouts at players, like 'go and get your handbag, dear.' The basic ignorance of the Soccer crowd of the rules of the game is extraordinary. Match after match people just refuse to believe in the offside rules.

Personally, I enjoy watching football so much that I don't need anything more. But most of the facilities are inadequate, aren't they? I mean, it's very strange, isn't it, that you can't really tell the difference between the bar and the gents' at most clubs? I don't suggest we need armchairs, infra-red heaters and cocktail lounges, but surely more clubs could heat the spectators.

As for half-time entertainment, well, I like the Dagenham Girl Pipers. Or a live band marching up and down, especially in the rain, although I prefer to hear songs of the last decade, not the music of the last century. I also enjoy someone having a big stick to throw in the air and drop, but not the English imitations of Drum Majorettes. Like most traditional fans, I don't think girls in mini skirts look right on a Soccer pitch.

My reaction to the report the other day that some Soccer fans get so excited that they beat up their wives when they get home is that I have no tendency to do this, but my wife has a tendency to beat me up when I get home. Actually, after a good match I return ashen-faced and emotionally drained.

We now come to crowd violence. Of course, I think a lot of kids go to a match to have an enjoyable fight on a Saturday afternoon. But I think wire netting as in South America would encourage hooliganism. If you are made to feel you are a wild animal on entering the ground, you start behaving like one – as some people seem to expect you to do. But it is idiotic of clubs to serve drinks in bottles or glasses, although I dislike paper cups.

I think it is essential to ban huge banners too, although one must remember that a fist is an offensive weapon and you can't insist that everyone who goes behind the goal should wear gloves. Unfortunately very often it is the boy who is provoked beyond endurance – sneered at and pushed – who lets fly and he's the one who gets arrested. The habitual troublemaker picks his fight when there is no policeman around. He puts the boot in and melts away. The only answer is for clubs to have as many policemen as they can afford in the crowd and outside the grounds.

I don't believe that violence on the field leads to violence on the terraces. There will always be violence on the field because Soccer is a very tough game now. But I am surprised in some ways at the lack of control some managers have over their teams. When you get Tommy Docherty[6] saying in print that he once assigned two players to scare the living daylights, by rough tackling, out of another player – that's a bit off, although to be fair to Tommy, he did repent afterwards. But, obviously, players do try to intimidate each other – and legitimately. When I see Dave Mackay[7] charging in for a tackle, every bit of him is extremely threatening, from the expression on his face to the speed he's going. I'd be scared out of my wits if he was charging me. At Wednesday's FA Cup replay, there were three occasions when a Manchester player just kicked the ball away when he saw Mackay charging up like a steam roller.

What about referees? Well, on Wednesday I just couldn't understand what he was doing from start to finish. The standard of refereeing is definitely going down . . . and the linesmen can often be booed into changing their minds. I think that refs and linesmen should be paid more and then, perhaps, we'd get better men.

Then there is the terrible snobbery. It is changing, but not quickly enough. This snobbery still separates the players and the people who run the clubs. The idea of players having a drink or even being allowed in the same room as the board still seems impossible to some pompous people . . . Thank God, good players are now less deferential to managements, and realise that the game is in their hands. They are still underpaid, compared with the entertainment they provide and the following they have plus the short career they enjoy. They should certainly be paid as much as the stars of show business.

As for hooliganism, of course, it is spoiling people's enjoyment and it must be stopped. I was lucky. I got away with only a few bruises. But the standard of English football at the moment is extraordinarily good. And if I ever become a millionaire I'd like to try to guide Torquay United's fortunes, although they are doing quite well now. It's just a coffee cup dream of mine.

I believe football is the best game to watch of them all. I mean you can't let off steam at a chess match, shrieking your head off. Make Chess A Spectator Sport! Thrilling Moves! It wouldn't work. Yes, Soccer has got everything – a fantastic degree of skill, also courage and toughness. It is beautiful to watch and even at its worst it is still exciting. That's why I'm a Soccer addict. What about Dudley Moore? He's not a fan. He doesn't know what he's missing!

GOD'S IN HIS HEAVEN – AND ALL'S WELL WITH LIVERPOOL
(*Daily Mail*, Monday 11 April, 1977)

At this time of the year my thoughts turn to Religion and Relegation and whether the two are intertwined. I fear that Easter for me has been inextricably tied up with the question of Tottenham rising again on the third day – or at least not going down.

When Spurs beat QPR on Saturday I regarded each Rangers defensive error as divine intervention. All of the reporters at the match overlooked the fact that the referee, Mr Dennis Turner, was the devil. What other explanation could there be for his persistent penalising of Tottenham players? It was obviously the blustery wind that was to blame for blowing them violently in the direction of their opponents' legs. Admittedly, in the last 20 minutes of the game he underwent a miraculous conversion and awarded a number of free kicks to the gallant men in white. By then it was three nil and I reckon the devilish Dennis had abandoned all hope of interfering with the Lord's wishes. This afternoon I'm going to Highbury. I'm sure that Terry Neill does not need to be reminded of St Paul's fine words. Spurs supporters will be arriving with two Christian necessities, Faith and Hope.

So far this season Arsenal have ignored Charity, widely believed to be the greatest virtue. Whenever they've been in a position to do us a favour by beating a lowly placed opponent they seem quite deliberately to have lost. Today they're at home, where Charity is supposed to begin. Let us pray that they do not fall victim to the sin of North London Pride.

My prayers at the moment are not exemplary. While I'm in favour of Peace on Earth and Goodwill to all men I do drift into asides such as 'if we get two points I'll definitely believe in You – a draw will leave me agnostic and defeat might tempt me to dabble in Black Magic.' Perhaps Liverpool fans have been praying this way for some time?

I realise, of course, that God is also being assailed by fans from Sunderland, West Ham and Bristol City. While I am in no way suggesting that these communities are latter-day versions of Sodom and Gomorrah and should be destroyed by fire and pestilence, I do feel that a spell in Division Two would do them no harm.

WE ARE THE CHAMPIONS
(*Daily Mail*, Monday 18 April, 1977)

Speaking of soccer, which I was last Monday, it's nice to know that God takes the *Mail*. His reaction has provided me with definite proof of His existence. I knew it was tempting fate when I suggested that West Ham, Sunderland and Bristol City would benefit from a spell in Division Two. Tottenham duly lost to Arsenal, while West Ham and Sunderland won. The next day the Almighty rubbed in His message by arranging for Spurs to lose at Bristol.

Hungover or not, He is certainly not lightly mocked. By Saturday I was resigned to relegation and explained to fellow supporters that it was entirely my fault for engaging in a futile skirmish with The Great Referee in The Sky with a Pernod in His

Hand. To lose would almost have been a relief. Instead we got the worst possible result, a draw. This merely prolongs the agony. I have resolved not to discuss Religion and Relegation again.

It was not an entertaining match, and during the desultory play I mused about soccer hooliganism. The answer came to me in a blinding flash in the gents at half time. In America sporting events are made more attractive by gorgeous, dancing cheer leaders and all kinds of showbiz razamataz. Over here we are lucky to get a dour band or a few police dogs jumping over fences.

I suggest we capture the undoubted energy of the hooligans for some useful purpose. Chelsea's lot are boasting that they are 'worse than Manchester United'. Let them put their money where their mouth is. Half an hour before the match, teams of opposing hooligans should line up on the pitch and beat the hell out of each other. This would entertain the shivering crowds and clearly establish which team's hooligans rule.

There are, of course, difficulties. How should we select the hooligans? Perhaps the fairest way would be for the hooligans to reach a 'democratically arrived at' team of eleven with one substitute. In other words, they should all gather in a selected pub the night before and the last twelve left standing would comprise the squad. Scoring is simple. One point for each hooligan on his feet after thirty minutes' 'play'.

There would, of course, be a League Table and I fear that Tottenham Hooligans might not do all that well. True, we managed to wreck Rotterdam a few years back, but since then it's been very middle of the table stuff. I'm willing to train a Spurs team of hooligans. They will be entertaining, skilful, and represent British thuggery at its best. As manager, I shall try to rely on local talent. If that fails, I shall obviously have to buy. I've been scouting one kid in Glasgow. He's big, brutal and as a midfield hooligan has the advantage of being a psychopath. He's good in the air, sound on the ground and lethal on the crotch.

THE GAME THAT ENGLAND HAVE TO WIN AND DARE NOT LOSE BUT WILL BE HAPPY TO DRAW
(*Evening Standard*, 8 September, 1993)

England's beleaguered national football team, struggling under their increasingly unpopular manager, Graham Taylor, were about to play Poland, in a crucial World Cup qualifying match at Wembley.

England starts at a severe disadvantage this first Wednesday in September. Under the vagaries of FIFA's labyrinth rules Graham Taylor is prohibited from selecting any Polish nationals for his squad. Needless to say, the Polish manager has the pick of any Pole he wants. Most of his team will have had experience of the Italian, French, Dutch or German leagues and will be thoroughly at home abroad, whereas Gascoigne, Platt and Walker will have had to travel all the way from Rome, Milan and Paris to the hostile environment of Heathrow.

The game will be won or lost or drawn in the midfield but ironically the goals (all-important under FIFA's crazy system) will in all likelihood be scored at the extremities of the pitch. England will be forced to kick the ball towards the ludicrously placed opposition goal man and then if they fail to score, run hundreds of yards in the opposite direction to defend their own net. Believe me, the Poles are ruthless and cunning enough to exploit this state of affairs. Not only will England be compelled to run vast distances on the notoriously strength-sapping Wembley turf, they will be subjected to a stream of unintelligible backchat from a Polish side who are notorious for the use of their own language as a deliberate ploy to unsettle their opponents.

It is too late for the England term to learn Polish. We shall have to stick to our own language. It is a difficult language as Graham Taylor will be the first to admit. There are over six hundred thousand separate words and it will be foolish to expect young men whose only wish is to don an England shirt with pride to be able to communicate fluently with each other. Let's stick to basics – 'our ball,' 'get rid of it,' 'knock him over' – that should suffice.

The referee will be neutral, i.e. from a foreign country, and probably bearing a deep-seated resentment towards a nation that once ruled three quarters of the world, and ruled it well.

Such are the injury problems facing Taylor that he has had to rejuggle the settled squad that has brought us all the way to the fabled twin towers stadium. England are playing a Seaman in goal in what will be an essentially land-based game. No one can doubt Seaman's courage, but is this the time to throw him in at the deep end?

Taylor has no choice. All his instincts and experience are terrestrial. He is essentially an earth-bound tactician, but never afraid to use the air, as he proved so emphatically at Watford. He is the proud possessor of over twenty-three recordings of the legendary pop superstars Earth, Wind & Fire. He good-humouredly bantered with reporters, saying 'I'm used to the earth, I can cope with the wind, and you boys have certainly put me through the fire.' Though delivered with a characteristic twinkle, there was a ring of steel in his voice. Even when joking, he is a deeply serious man. Under the rueful clown's face lives an intense, private man who is always struggling to get out, as indeed were many so called sports-writers from the gutter press who became impatient as the embattled England boss expanded on his, for want of a better word, philosophy. Some, disgracefully, actually left the room as he made his final and most devastatingly honest comment. Here are Taylor's words in full. This reporter respects the man, admires his candour and on this occasion was nowhere near the exits where these unseemly scenes occurred.

'I am the England manager. I did not ask for the job. I was given it. I do not pretend to be Bertrand Russell (the now almost forgotten wing half for Burnley), nor am I an intellectual like Beckenbauer or Nbane of Swaziland, but I can recognise a football when I see one. It's that round thing that used to be made of leather with great galumping stitches that, when wet, could cut open your forehead.

'Now don't get me wrong. I am not pining for leather through rose-tinted spectacles. Their time has come and gone. I am a realist. Football is bigger than the balls, no matter if you're kicking them or talking them. Football never changes and nor do I. When the whistle blows and the stadium empties I shall still be there. Wednesday night will be much the same as the others for me. Long after you boys have gone home, I will be in the business of planning the next game.

'England is just a microcosm of Watford – a small, safe place full of ordinary people doing ordinary jobs in an ordinary way. I am proud to be an ordinary man. They are the heart and soul of our nation. Just look at our Prime Minister. And please don't get me wrong. I'm not saying that Gary Lineker was an ordinary player. Given time and money, I, working together with the individual, can make any player ordinary. Even the greatest talents in the world can be moulded into a system. Take Watford as just one example. But at the end of the day, if the players don't deliver, the manager is powerless.'

By now he was inaudible, but his determination shone through like a laser. Graham Taylor, the quintessential Englishman, was making a telling point and this reporter at least took heed. He was preparing the ground for a really ordinary performance against the Poles. Two points would be excellent, one would be a bonus and none would be acceptable. The simplicity of the man is breathtaking and I salute it.

In spite of Cook's understandable pessimism, England beat Poland three nil. However Cook's general gloomy prognosis was more accurate. Despite defeating the Poles, England still failed to qualify for the 1994 World Cup Finals in the United States.

SWALLOW A SULTANA – IT'S TIME TO PLAY OUR WORLD CUP WAR GAME
(*Evening Standard,* 16 June, 1994)

Having actually qualified for the World Cup Finals in 1982, 1986 and 1990, when they reached the semi-finals, only going out on penalties to Germany, the eventual winners, the England football team returned to their traditional losing ways by failing to reach the 1994 Finals in the

USA. Yet unlike most sports fans, Cook simply refused to take this national humiliation lying down.

There has been a lot of defeatist talk about our so-called failure to qualify for the Finals in America. As Yogi Berra, the great American baseball coach, declared to anyone who would listen: 'It ain't over till it's over.'

Well, it isn't over; it hasn't even begun and the fat lady has yet to make her entrance. Not that Anne Shelton was ever fat. Robust, certainly, not a woman to be trifled with. 'Stand up and fight them, until you hear the bell'; that's the song she belted out long after the war had finished. Vera Lynn may have got us through the hostilities with 'We'll Meet Again' and 'The White Cliffs of Dover' but Shelton's power sustained the nation through the dark days of rationing. But what has this to do with World Cup 94?

I will tell you. We didn't qualify for World War One or Two. There was no arcane points system. We entered in our own good time when all seemed lost and our backs (and midfield) were truly up against the wall. We are never more dangerous than when we're cornered.

It is often said that we invented the game and gave it to the world; not strictly true. Remember we were once the world's greatest trading power and, prudently, patents were taken out to protect our product. From time to time, as the rules have been amended, new patents have been issued.

Strictly speaking, under International Law, we are entitled to 1p every time a ball is kicked anywhere in the world (with the exception of Bermuda, with whom we have a special arrangement). A further 2p is due whenever a player is kicked. Under Protocol 8 of The Treaty of Bruges 1954, we granted a secret waiver of royalties in return for a guarantee that England would take part in the final stages of the World Cup until 2024 irrespective of results. Until now we have not tried to enforce this ruling but if the World Cup goes ahead without us it will be a flagrant breach of a legally binding treaty and constitutes . . . an act of war!

I have it on the highest authority that, at the time of the Falklands, President Reagan tried to persuade Mrs Thatcher to renounce The Bruges Treaty in return for logistical assistance with the invasion. The Iron Lady stood firm, but did informally assure the President that the US could stage the World Cup provided her son Mark was employed as a consultant. The so-called 'Wyoming Compromise' was signed in a golf buggy on the Reagan ranch in the presence of Bob Hope. Alas, the vast organisational problems have put a strain on Mark's marriage and he was last seen driving around the Mojave Desert looking for the Silverdome where he was due to meet the Saudi Arabian squad.

President Bush continued to honour the Reagan-Thatcher Agreement, but all bets seemed to be off when Bill Clinton came to office. Still in a pique over the fact that he'd once smoked a dry sultana at Oxford under the impression that it was marijuana, he tore up the Agreement and told John Major to stick it 'where the sun don't shine' (American colloquialism for London).

Clinton's hypocrisy is staggering – here is a man who has declared a war on drugs but is happy to welcome Bolivia and Colombia to his shores; he is happy to celebrate D-Day with the Queen but unwilling to honour his obligation to the nation that made it all possible. But he had reckoned without the sagacity of our PM. Sensing that the President was not immune to flattery, he arranged for Oxford to present Clinton with an Honorary Degree.

During the long speech, in Latin by Lord Jenkins of Hillhead, Clinton smiled continuously and nodded agreement – never more so than during the passage that reads 'Semper Anglia victor Iudorum Cuppas Globalis sui erectum et cannabis orare inter-vectitest.' As the President donned the ceremonial orange cap he had agreed that England would be the only team in Group G.

Stop Press: a homeless former sultana vendor was arrested in Oxford this morning. He is due to be extradited to the US where he will face the death penalty.

Despite Cook's impassioned plea, England were not granted a wild card entry into the 1994 World Cup Finals, which were won by Brazil, who beat Italy on penalties after a nil nil draw.

CLIVE SPEAKS HIS MIND
(*Vox*, 1994)

As a lifelong Tottenham Hotspur supporter, Cook was duty-bound to loathe Spurs' local rivals, Arsenal, considered – by everyone apart from their own fans – to be Britain's most boring football team. Naturally, Cook's foul-mouthed alter ego, Clive, was also a Spurs fan, and so it was only natural that Derek should support the Gunners.

Derek supports Arsenal and you can see it in his face – that drugged zombie look that comes from substance abuse, genetic malfunction or even the occasional visit to Highbury. It started off innocently enough. His dad, Derek (no fucking imagination, these cunts), was an Arsenal fan and to placate his wife, Bo, took the then young Derek junior to watch an Arsenal Ipswich match as a punishment for wetting his bed. Fair enough, you might say, but Derek, being a cunt, became addicted to ninety minutes of boredom and began to watch the Gunners on a regular basis. He even interrupted his Saturday masturbation schedule on order to travel secretly to North London from Chadwell Heath. There he watched George Graham, Frank McLintock and nine other wankers stupefy thousands of otherwise ordinary decent folk.

Naturally friends became concerned, and when he started going to away games, and even reserve matches, a doctor was called in. Professor Groake saw at once that this was an almost hopeless case. The alternatives were powerful sedative medicines, the chemical equivalent of watching an Arsenal game live or regular attendance at AA (Arsenal Anonymous). These meetings are almost as dull as an Arsenal game, but it does keep the sufferer away from that first match which so often splits families, destroys careers, and leads to physical and spiritual bankruptcy.

Derek, alas, has yet to reach his rock bottom. Even the 1993 Cup Final and replay against Sheffield Wednesday did not convince him that he was powerless over Arsenal. He cannot get it into his head that Arsenal are responsible for all his troubles, and not only his. Since their foundation in 1886, this insidious force has been indirectly responsible for two world wars, famine, pestilence, countless acts of mindless violence, and, if anyone believes that the holes in the ozone layer are caused by aerosols, they should watch the Arsenal side as they hoof the ball into the air in the hope that it might bounce luckily to Ian Wright. Wright can actually play football and will obviously not feature in George Graham's long-term plans. When he goes, Derek will be watching an Arsenal team that will be in every way a match for the legendary double side of 1971. A team so paralysingly boring that they couldn't even arrange pre-season friendlies in South Africa or Japan.

Single, or rather mob handedly, they have almost killed off football. They will certainly kill Derek and serve him fucking right. I tell you, it will be the first fucking thing that Arsenal has done for the good of humanity. After that, who knows, they might blow themselves up and raze the stadium to the ground but I doubt it. Arsenal have never been known for entertainment.

MAJOR TITHERLY GLIBBLE
(*Peter Cook Talks Golf Balls*, 1994)

Up until a few minutes ago, this room was filled with jovial companionship – a selection of bankers, industrialists, market gardeners, accountants, people in various service industries and that type of thing. Now, of course, I'm the only one left. I'm just left here thinking about the day I've had today. I got up about eight o'clock in the morning for breakfast and that was bloody good. They do a very good breakfast here, actually – and all the old breakfast stuff. I have haddock, I have peas on sticks, they've got bits of bacon, poached eggs – just nice gentlemanly fare. They stop serving breakfast round about three o'clock in the afternoon, and that's the time, of course, one tends to think about popping out on the course to see if everything's in order, because one of the great difficulties with a golf club is keeping things all pleasant because the members like to come here and not be anywhere else. And we have a lot of trouble with golfers coming up with their clubs and their bags and stuff like that, and trying to get on the course and play golf, which doesn't really suit most of our members, who prefer to relax, to talk about the meaning of life, and to avoid getting mobile phone calls. But, every now and then, we do have the odd person who is a member – to become a member, one has to pay a lot of money – and they think they're entitled to go out on the course and start hitting these awful little balls about. It's all about stance and posture and breeding. Sir Francis Drake single-handedly held off the Armada by standing still. And standing still is still one of the most important parts of the game.

Golf in the old days was based on a very sound tradition – there should be somewhere in the world where one could just go to in the morning, have breakfast and stay until dinner. And then stay on after dinner, because it's too far away from home to get back. I happen to live about 18 inches from the clubhouse. It's a long, long, long walk at my age, so I tend to stay overnight and my wife can always be in touch with me by arranging a meeting sometime or other, which we can put in the diary, and then we can meet. Not here, of course. Not in the Antler Room of the club because it's, perversely, I suppose, in this day of PC, as they call it, this is an area which is women-free. I mean, I'm perfectly in favour of them bustling all over the place and doing jobs and things, but when they start leaving their balls and clubs around the course it gets on your nerves.

Not that we don't have women members. Every February the 2nd, there is a meeting to discuss the possibility of women existing, and I think they do. I'm fairly convincingly persuaded that I'm married to some such thing. But under the rules of golf you'll notice no mention of women as such – and far be it from me to interfere with the rules of golf. They're enormously long, as indeed is my wife. She's a huge, huge creature, towering up to about seven foot, and could make a very decent living as a basketball player. But we've been very lucky because we have a working arrangement – she works and I arrange things here, and we're very happy. She tried to take up the game but it didn't suit her at all. I think the Armed Response Unit at the club may have put her off. Apart from February the 2nd, when, of course, they're very, very welcome.

The trouble with the modern game of golf is it's all dominated by money and sponsorship, and slogans all over their knickers, and everything like that. I mean, when I was young we had the great players. We had Cotton, we had Varden, we had Silk, we had – armchairs, actually, in those days. We used to sit in those armchairs and just think how well people behaved on the course. None of this arrogant strutting around, surrounded by people saying 'yo, in the hole,' and all that stuff. If we ever watched golf, we watched it from the comfort of this particular window in the Antler Room where well behaved men of a certain age would wander up and hit the ball in a courteous manner. But nowadays you get these – well, I can't think of another word for it – hooligans. Hooligans on the courses, all jumping around – asking for quiet. Why should we be bloody well quiet? It's our bloody club, isn't it? Don't tell me to be quiet! The fact that it's the Open, as you so-called call it, doesn't mean I have to be quiet, because I'm a member here. I'm Chief Secretary of the Antler Room, thank you very much.

They've got no sense, these young players. They wear Bermuda shorts, Bermuda tights, covered in sort of spangles and things like that. Why can't they wear a tie? Nice long trousers, braces, belts, metal jackets, all the old stuff that we used to wear when we played golf in the Ryder Cup. It's never one I particularly enjoyed because it meant going out and losing to the Americans, until you get all these spivs in from the Continent who started winning it again, which made it all very disconcerting. Because in the old days, we'd just go and read the newspapers – 'we've lost the Ryder Cup' – and then suddenly we're winning it again, and who's 'we'? And is it the Swedes? Is it the Spanish? Is it the Dutch? Is it the English? Is it the Scots? Is it the Irish? Who gives a toss? The fact is that we play the Americans, we lose and then they bugger off home as far as I'm concerned. We do have Americans in the club as Recreational Artisan Members – provided they dress properly and call me 'Sir.'

At the end of it all, when you think about your arrangements, you have to consider yourself and I've never considered myself for a very, very, very long time – almost as long as I've existed. And I've come to certain conclusions but I'm not willing to share it with a camera. I mean, you might have Esther Rantzen round any moment telling me 'What were you doing in Morocco in 1948?'

'Well, it's none of your bloody business, Esther.' I was in Morocco – well, I'm not going to tell you – I was in Morocco looking at the beaches. The fact the beaches were covered with little boys in tiny bathing suits was nothing to do with my visit to Morocco. I was doing a brochure for the golf club because we wanted to see what kind of sand we were going to have in the bunker and, naturally, I went off to see what sort of sand they should have and, erm, I saw some sand and all these little boys lying down on it. I said 'Well, when we get back to the club we'll take this sort of sand as a sample, and just because we've gone to all this expense, why not take a few of the boys in the bag as well?' We still have the same sand and we still have the same boys. They're somewhat older now and they're very loyal. Nice chaps. Good blokes.

I find that if I stay here in the Antler Room a lot of people come up and ask me my views on women priests, and, on the whole, I think 'Good heavens, there's no particular reason why a woman shouldn't be a priest or why a woman shouldn't be a woman, but that's not the issue.' I mean, look at what happened to the Catholic Golf Circle when they started having women caddies, like Faldo had his, er, Fanny woman. I've got nothing against her – she's a strong, fine caddy. But do you want a woman distracting you from the, from the, from the, er, other bit of stuff which you do, which is, of course, the game of golf? I was talking to the Pope recently, just on the telephone, because he can't get here as often as he used to. And I asked him about the future of the game. And he's not a professional player – he's a professional Pope. But his view was that golf would eventually become the goal of all mankind. When he used the word goal, of course, he didn't mean it in the footballing sense – he meant the achievement of golf would be a beckoning to everybody. 'Tudo o mundo' he said – which was surprising since he's Polish with that bad hip injury.

But I see the future of golf this way – no particular sponsorship, just beautiful links courses with beautiful sunshine flooding down on them, onto which we can look out of the window from here in the Antler Room and see lissom young boys striding – naked if they wish – naked if I wish – all over the links, unencumbered by clubs or costume or all that – all that stupidity that surrounds the game.

Just young lads, in the nude, wandering around from bunker to bunker, from course to course, but all in view of the Antler Room here. I see the minimum age of the boys as being – one. And of course we'll have high handicappers as well. Up to sixteen. But, beyond that, I would be unable to form a judgement without meeting my committee of Moroccans who are waiting next door. As I said, young lads, running around, stark naked – that's the game of golf for me.

Chapter Thirteen
Small Hours Sven (LBC)

Almost as private as The Royal & Not Noticeably Ancient Game of Abu Simbel, Peter Cook's most unusual series was broadcast at antisocial hours, entirely unannounced, and with no advance publicity whatsoever. Yet for once, this obscure scheduling, minimal promotion and public indifference was nobody's doing but his own. For these sporadic ad hoc performances were transmitted in a phone-in show on local radio, in which Cook appeared completely incognito. And as far as the show's small band of nocturnal listeners, and even, initially, its presenter, was aware, these small-hours calls didn't come from Britain's greatest comic, but from an anonymous Norwegian insomniac called Sven.

Most people who phone programmes like the *Clive Bull Show* on LBC tend to be obsessed with a single subject. Sven was considerably more broad-minded. He was obsessed with two questions – the preponderance of fish in Norwegian daily life, and the disappearance of his estranged girlfriend, Jutta. Sven loathed the first of these subjects with the same passion that he loved the second – and his desperation to escape the fish that infested every avenue of

389

daily life in his native Norway was matched only by his desperation to find his dearly beloved, and recently departed, Jutta, again.

Inspired by a chance encounter with a Norwegian couple at a party, immediately followed, coincidentally, by a bizarre documentary about a remote Norwegian fishing village, Sven's plague of fish proved Peter hadn't lost his sense of humour. And despite their melancholy air, these calls revealed a remarkably resilient side to Peter Cook. Plenty of famous performers drone on about how important performing is to them, and how the resultant fame is a liability, rather than one of the perks of the job. Yet you won't find too many willing to perform without a fee, or even any hint of recognition. When Peter made these calls, he was still doing plenty of cameos and commercials, when he wanted to, and he was still famous enough to attract admiration everywhere he went. However, Sven proved that, for all his self-professed indolence, Peter actually preferred the performance to the fame. He was willing to forsake the superficial flattery of instant acknowledgement for the private satisfaction of a part well played. Of course, this was also a secret practical joke, played at other people's expense, but Sven was far too melancholic to qualify for *Candid Camera* or *Beadle's About.* John Bird called him 'a character of great sobriety and great subtlety, funny, poignant and technically extraordinary, the rhythm hesitant, the tone modest and unemphatic.'[1] Cook never played Sven for laughs, and even though the gags are as good as ever, they're almost incidental.

Clive Bull soon realised Sven wasn't who he said he was – the constant fish references were too surreal to be entirely believable, even with Sven's deadpan delivery, even at that time of night. However he didn't know that Sven was Peter Cook until George 'Rainbow' Weiss told him. Rainbow George was a friend and neighbour, and a prolific fringe politician, who frequently lobbied shows like Clive Bull's to spread the word about his movement, Captain Rainbow's Universal Party, and its various reincarnations. This revelation did dispel some of Sven's fishy magic. However George's main concern was to make sure Peter got past the switchboard. He also recorded Sven's conversations for posterity. Clive played along, and didn't spoil the fun. He didn't tell his listeners that he knew Sven was really Peter Cook, although Peter knew he knew.

∿

CLIVE BULL: Sven in Swiss Cottage.

SVEN: Oh, hello Mr Bull?

CLIVE BULL: Hello, Sven.

SVEN: Yes, I'm only a visitor here, from Norway – and I listen to the programme and think wonderful things because in Norway these phone-ins is mainly devoted to subjects like fish.

CLIVE BULL: Like fish?

SVEN: Yes, we have a phone-in.

CLIVE BULL: You have a fish phone-in?

SVEN: In Norway time, when people ring up, for one hour, and the gist of it is things about, is a carp very big, or is a tench very big, or how big is a guppy. It drags on and on all night, and it's so nice to come to this country and hear people talking about parliament and taking clothes off and singing. In Norway, all we get is this fish stuff going on and on.

CLIVE BULL: Yes, I imagine it would begin to drag after a while.

SVEN: Have you ever done a swap with Norway?

CLIVE BULL: A swap with Norway? Well, I'm not sure if I want to inflict the fish upon my listeners.

SVEN: Well no, we have other things. It's only eleven to twelve, the fish.

CLIVE BULL: You have the fish phone-in?

SVEN: Fish hour.

CLIVE BULL: We've been toying with the idea.

SVEN: And we are running out of fish.

CLIVE BULL: I mean, fishing is very popular over here as well.

SVEN: Well it's nice to go out and cast your flies on the water, but surely not listen to it every night – eleven to twelve.

CLIVE BULL: Well, I don't know. I mean, there has been a rumour about the place that LBC's going to start up a new fish watch service.

SVEN: Washing the fish? On the air?

CLIVE BULL: No, watch. Fish watch.

SVEN: Fish watch?

CLIVE BULL: Yes, it's going to be a bit like the Top Twenty share check. It's going to be regular fish updates through the day.

SVEN: Well, the carp is numero uno over there, but it gets so every week it is number one. And sometimes, not only you have the live fish phone-ins, but you also have a lot of conversation later in the night with experts talking about tinned fish and frozen fish. It is so nice to hear people talking about other things.

CLIVE BULL: Well, I'm afraid we were talking about gefilte fish.

SVEN: Flaking. We have a whole gefilte fish hour in the afternoon. It's a children's programme.

CLIVE BULL: I think it's a very good idea, Sven.

SVEN: But for one hour, all about gefilte, and how many times can you stand that? We have little quizzes and games like what is an anagram of gefilte, and nobody in Norway knows. We tried so hard. Do you know one of that? Gefilte? How does that swap around?

CLIVE BULL: Well, what's gefilte in Norwegian, anyway?

SVEN: In Norwegian, gefilte is gefilte. That's our translation of it.

CLIVE BULL: Oh, it's the same, is it? That's a lucky break, hey, Sven?

SVEN: I tell you once, it's probably silly of me to ask, but my wife Jutta fled to London a week ago.

CLIVE BULL: Fled to London?

SVEN: Yes, either to get away from the fish phone-ins, or otherwise to get away from me.

CLIVE BULL: Yes, or both.

SVEN: But she left a note saying 'the fish and you are all I can't bear.' And I wondered if you could, through your radio service, put out a message that if Jutta is fed up with the fish, well, that's fine. I'm a forgiving man, and if she's fed up with me, contact me through the – can I mention the name of the hotel?

CLIVE BULL: Well no, I'd rather you didn't. I think she'd better contact us and we'll put the two of you in touch, Sven.

SVEN: If you could, because she's very tall.

CLIVE BULL: Right, OK. We'll all look out for her. Look out for a tall Jutta from the Swiss Cottage area. Sven, thank you very much indeed for telling us about the Norwegian phone-in programmes, which do sound awfully dull. What do you think about having a fish hour?

(*Clive Bull is conducting a late-night competition, in which listeners have to phone in and guess the identity of a Mystery Sound.*)

SVEN: It's a fish.

CLIVE BULL: It's a fish?

SVEN: Well, I think fish.

CLIVE BULL: Sorry, our boiler is playing up terribly this morning. I'll just give it a knock.

SVEN: No, I can't hear very well, but I heard this sound and it reminded me of fish.

CLIVE BULL: I managed to switch it off anyway.

SVEN: It's possibly in combination with Jutta.

CLIVE BULL: Oh dear. Yes.

SVEN: This is not the right time to bring it all up, but . . .

CLIVE BULL: Your personal problems?

SVEN: Yes. I've been away a long time, and it sounded like Jutta and some fish.

CLIVE BULL: Well, I know that it's a big interest of yours, Sven. I don't want to pry, but is there any news of your love life?

SVEN: Well, I don't like to be disloyal to Jutta, of course, because, you know, for a man, you have to be a little bit loyal.

CLIVE BULL: That's very true.

SVEN: But Jutta went off with some fish, and the sound on the Mystery sounded like Jutta with some fish.

CLIVE BULL: So I was ringing a few bells for you. Probably a hurtful kind of sound.

SVEN: For me, but that's not important, because the point, surely, Clive, is that if the woman you love wants to go off with the fish, then why not? It's not for me to interfere.

CLIVE BULL: She's more interested in the fish than she is in you, Sven.

SVEN: Well, the fish she's with at the moment are a little bit more, in her view.

CLIVE BULL: Has she shown any interest in such things before?

SVEN: Well, she's always fish, fish, fish – all the time.

CLIVE BULL: But you're in fact not from this country, are you, Sven?

SVEN: No, I'm from Norway.

CLIVE BULL: From Norway, where you seem to be a bit obsessed by fish, if you don't mind me saying so.

SVEN: No, I don't mind, because I'm brought up in the school of hard knocks, and, you know, life is what you make it. I was just calling up to say I'm back in the country. I've been in Argentina.

CLIVE BULL: You've been in Argentina?

SVEN: Yes, because I met a nice woman in another launderette, who said 'Why not go to Argentina? It's a long way away.' And so I went with her. All kinds of problems, and now I'm back in Swiss Cottage.

CLIVE BULL: You go away to Argentina to forget? And there's no fish, really, in Argentina, are there?

SVEN: Not much.

CLIVE BULL: Not many.

SVEN: But is it a fish?

CLIVE BULL: I'm sorry to disappoint you.

SVEN: Was it a fish rubbing up against Jutta?

CLIVE BULL: No, it's not in fact a fish either, Sven. Tough luck on that one. You were very close, but not quite close enough. You do sound a bit down, Sven. If you want to have a chat about any of these things, you know, just feel free to give us a call.

SVEN: Well, I liked to get – who's in the afternoon? The man . . .

CLIVE BULL: Oh, Philip Hobson, yes.

SVEN: Does he deal with fish problems?

CLIVE BULL: I think he probably would be very interested, yes. He's always got a ready ear to listen to this kind of problem.

SVEN: Perhaps Philip would be the one. Just to thrash it out. Because I don't know what your life is like, Clive, and mine is, er . . . It's not really the time of night to talk of personal problems. I just hope to get lucky with, you know . . .

CLIVE BULL: With the Mystery Sound.

SVEN: With the Mystery Sound. But could I set a question?

CLIVE BULL: Yes, go on then.

SVEN: If it's not a fish with Jutta, what would a fish with Jutta sound like?

CLIVE BULL: OK. If anyone's got the answer to that one, then 891 8111. Thank you, Sven. It's one thirty. It's LBC.

CLIVE BULL: Sven in Swiss Cottage.

SVEN: Oh, hello Clive.

CLIVE BULL: Hello Sven.

SVEN: I'm sorry. I'm very tired. I just got in from Los Angeles.

CLIVE BULL: From Los Angeles?

SVEN: Yes, and a silly story. I am the biggest fool.

CLIVE BULL: You're not.

SVEN: No, I saw you know who on late-night TV. You see baseball at four o'clock in the morning. A week ago I saw Jutta in the crowd.

CLIVE BULL: You didn't!

SVEN: Well, I'm not sure. A woman very like Jutta was waving her pom-pom at some Dodgers game, and I thought that I'd better get over, you know, because she is my wife.

CLIVE BULL: You were getting the old feeling again, were you?

SVEN: Yes, and I arrive and – never go to Los Angeles, Clive, because it is very much they judge you on what you're like.

CLIVE BULL: Really?

SVEN: Yes, and at Customs, they ask me my purpose of visit to America, and I just said 'I'm Sven. I'm looking for my wife.'

CLIVE BULL: Seems reasonable to me.

SVEN: But they said 'Who isn't, Buster?' So depressing.

CLIVE BULL: Yes, I'm sorry. I shouldn't laugh.

SVEN: I went to some games, but Jutta wasn't there, and I came back. I should not have called, but it's so nice to be back here, where she isn't.

CLIVE BULL: So you didn't find her in Los Angeles?

SVEN: No, I find nothing there. I found only shallow values.

CLIVE BULL: Not like Norway at all.

SVEN: Well, just like Norway.

CLIVE BULL: Oh, really?

SVEN: I get back, I get back here, and first thing I read is a Mr Fishburn is in parliament in somewhere.

CLIVE BULL: That's right.

SVEN: And, oh God!

CLIVE BULL: Dudley Fishburn. You can't get away from it, can you?

SVEN: Dudley Fishburn, and where can I go?

CLIVE BULL: Yes, I've got some more bad news for you as well.

SVEN: What's this?

CLIVE BULL: We're launching the IRN Fishing Line. That's another one of those telephone services. And the 0898 number has got a rundown of all the fishing news.

SVEN: When do you get like Naughty Nancy?

CLIVE BULL: No, it's just fish on this occasion.

SVEN: Just fish. No way of getting anything interesting?

CLIVE BULL: Not a Naughty Nancy. How's your Naughty Nancy down at the launderette? Is that still going?

SVEN: Oh, no. Oh dear. It was so awful because at first sight she was a blossom of a woman and then, just as an icebreaker, I went up to her with some socks, and some underwear, and said 'this could be the start of something,' and she burnt them.

CLIVE BULL: Oh. And how did you take that?

SVEN: Well, I couldn't take it. I mean, she'd had all in front of my eyes. Petrol, lighter – up they went in flames.

CLIVE BULL: So you think she didn't really take it too well?

SVEN: No. Well, she doesn't understand Norwegian humour.

CLIVE BULL: No, clearly.

SVEN: I don't either.

CLIVE BULL: No, I can't see how she'd missed that, really. Sven, I think you'd better have a good bit of kip, actually.

SVEN: Yes, I spoke to the lady. I said I just got in from Los Angeles. I should have a big lie down and call tomorrow.

CLIVE BULL: Yes, well I'm sorry to hear that. No sign of Jutta at all?

SVEN: Only on TV and I saw Dukakis and everyone on the TV. And nowhere, nowhere over here in the newspapers is anything about the segment of the Dukakis speech, which he spoke for half an hour about fish.

CLIVE BULL: I missed that, actually. And I watched the whole of *Newsnight.* And they cut the fish, didn't they?

SVEN: Half an hour. Half of it in Greek, a bit in Spanish and all fish, fish, fish.

CLIVE BULL: You travel all the way from Norway, and what do you get?

SVEN: What do you get?

CLIVE BULL: Fish. Dukakis fish. There's no end to it.

SVEN: But nice to be back in this country, Clive.

CLIVE BULL: Welcome back, welcome back.

SVEN: Thank you, Clive.

CLIVE BULL: Thank you, Sven.

SVEN: Auf wiedersehen.

CLIVE BULL: Sven from Swiss Cottage. We'll have more calls after the latest news.

(*Clive Bull is talking with listeners about football hooliganism.*)

SVEN: Welcome, welcome back.

CLIVE BULL: Oh, thank you, Sven.

SVEN: I'm over here just a moment from Oslo, and I've stayed on because it's such exciting place here.

CLIVE BULL: Well, I'm glad.

SVEN: I've still not find Jutta.

CLIVE BULL: You've not found your wife yet?

SVEN: Not, no. She's gone, gone, gone. But I know it's very serious subject tonight, but in Norway we have no hooliganism because, I think, because of our so many fish programmes on.

CLIVE BULL: Yes.

SVEN: Every day we have programmes on fish. On TV and on radio. Phone-ins, everything – and at the football too. Before the match, people come on, expert fishermen showing how to catch chub and roach and everything like that.

CLIVE BULL: So it's more of a family occasion?

SVEN: It calms people down.

CLIVE BULL: But it might be a bit boring for you, though. I mean, if we introduced it here.

SVEN: Oh, it's very boring! This is what I'm saying. The more boring.

CLIVE BULL: So you're really boring hooligans to death?

SVEN: This is it. If a hooligan goes to football, knows he is going to see slides of fish on a big screen, slides of chub, roach, tench and so on.

CLIVE BULL: So there's more than one net at a football match.

SVEN: Yes, sometimes. Because they have tanks.

CLIVE BULL: They have tanks as well?

SVEN: Tanks of fish. Not tanks, armoured tanks. Tanks of fish.

CLIVE BULL: Oh, I see.

SVEN: And for one hour before the match, the experts come on and display how to net the fish. And is much the same every week.

CLIVE BULL: But wouldn't people get a little bit excited about that, though?

SVEN: Well, sometimes the fish struggle and the crowd get a little bit on the side of the fish, and they become a little restive.

CLIVE BULL: Bullfighting all over again.

SVEN: Well, yes. But the fish, when caught, is always thrown back.

CLIVE BULL: Yes, but I mean who wants to be thrown back after having a great hook in your mouth?

SVEN: No, never hooking.

CLIVE BULL: No?

SVEN: No, no. All fish in Norway are caught in a net, with a net, or with a very very soft hook.

CLIVE BULL: Well, we're still planning our LBC Fish Watch service.

SVEN: Is that going ahead?

CLIVE BULL: Well, we've been discussing it and there have been a couple of trial runs. We're looking for a sponsor, though. We'd really like LBC Fish Watch in association with a company, so if there's anyone listening at the moment who thinks . . .

SVEN: Would it be live description or would you have to prerecord, because of controversial things might happen? Like some fishermen might lose a fish and say 'oh drat' or something like that. You have to cut that out.

CLIVE BULL: We would, yes. We'd have to have a special button. That'd be alright. We'd probably do it live, although I'm a bit fearful of crowd trouble. The emotions . . .

SVEN: But in Norway we have no hooligans at all at football.

CLIVE BULL: No?

SVEN: We have no one at football. Because of this fishing that goes on before and at half time.

CLIVE BULL: Right. This probably would explain your Eurovision Song Contest entries as well.

SVEN: Nul fish.

CLIVE BULL: Exactly.

SVEN: Nul poisson. But I know it's serious.

CLIVE BULL: Where's your wife, Sven?

SVEN: Jutta? Well, Düsseldorf. She went off for a big match, the showdown.

CLIVE BULL: Yes? Was she the one with that rubber hammer in her hand?

SVEN: That one, yes. She was captured by the police. I saw her on TV. And she was beating up the Polizei like no man.

CLIVE BULL: Yes? She's not right for you though really, is she?

SVEN: No. Well, I rather like the policeman. He's a nice-looking young man with a firm hand, but he was no match for her.

CLIVE BULL: You don't want to get involved with the Düsseldorfians, though.

SVEN: But Düsseldorfians. I mean, what can one do when a woman like Jutta comes over and she was screaming like mad for Holland?

CLIVE BULL: Yes?

SVEN: Yes! All Holland, Holland, Holland! She has a very harsh voice and I think I better off with some little bit of English fluff. Where does one go to find them?

CLIVE BULL: Well, I should start in Swiss Cottage. I'd have a little wander round there. Have you met anyone so far?

SVEN: Well, I met some woman from, where was it? From Maida Vale.

CLIVE BULL: Maida Vale?

SVEN: Maida Vale. And she was working in the dry cleaners, and she said . . .

CLIVE BULL: Do you think you're going to be alright with her, then?

SVEN: I thought I might take some flowers and some clothes round to her.

CLIVE BULL: Yes?

SVEN: The flowers for romance and the clothes just to get something out of it.

CLIVE BULL: So even if the romance doesn't work . . .

SVEN: At least I've got my clothes done. She's called – may I say hello to her?

CLIVE BULL: Yes.

SVEN: Hello. Oh dear, this is a difficult name. Jenaker.

CLIVE BULL: Pardon?

SVEN: Jenaker.

CLIVE BULL: Jenaker?

SVEN: Jenaker. She's from Belgium, and has drifted into the dry-cleaning business.

CLIVE BULL: As you would.

SVEN: And she's a nice girl, firm-looking body, but, well, you know, coming from Norway I don't know what to talk to her about apart from fish.

CLIVE BULL: Well, I hope it goes alright. I mean, have you wooed her?

SVEN: No, I just said I'm from Norway and I have some money on me.

CLIVE BULL: And did her eyes light up when you mentioned the money?

SVEN: No, she just gave me that old look – I suppose it's blank amazement.

CLIVE BULL: Blank amazement?

SVEN: And got on a bus – 419, I think it was. But I thought if I go down to the shop with some old clothes and some flowers we might strike something up.

CLIVE BULL: I think you should. I'd forget Jutta, personally.

SVEN: I cannot forget her. She's on the TV screen in Düsseldorf.

CLIVE BULL: She sounds like a bad type to me. How did you get involved with her in the first place? I mean, honestly.

SVEN: Well, she's powerful. Powerful. Powerful family. Her family control the whole pilchard business in Oslo. And she picked me out at some disco.

CLIVE BULL: Yes? She said 'Hello, I'm big in pilchards'?

SVEN: Well, 'My father is very big in pilchards,' and then, you know, it was kiss kiss and then, you know, there it was.

CLIVE BULL: Are there any little pilchards?

SVEN: No, we've not got into that side of it at all.

CLIVE BULL: No? Maybe you and Jenaker . . .

SVEN: Jenaker? She is a nice girl. Big hips.

CLIVE BULL: Is she in fish?

SVEN: No, I don't think so, no. I can't stand that any more.

CLIVE BULL: Well, don't bore her with too much of the fish, will you?

SVEN: No, I think I talk about up-to-date music. Talk about Chubby Checker. Talk about, you know, Joey Dee and the Starlighters, and hip sounds.

CLIVE BULL: Yes, that'd be god. You're obviously a trendy old chap. No carping about the fish, though.

SVEN: Right.

CLIVE BULL: OK?

SVEN: OK Clive.

CLIVE BULL: I wish you well.

SVEN: Auf wiedersehen.

CLIVE BULL: Jenaker, isn't it?

SVEN: Jenaker.

CLIVE BULL: If you're listening, Jenaker, Sven – do you want to send a little night-time message?

SVEN: Just 'Sleep tight, Jenaker, but not too tight – get my meaning?' Bit saucy.

CLIVE BULL: It's eighteen minutes to four and we'll move on. Thank you, Sven in Swiss Cottage.

CLIVE BULL: Sven in Maida Vale.

SVEN: Clive, I just got back from Majorca.

CLIVE BULL: Oh, Majorca!

SVEN: You get my card?

CLIVE BULL: I got a postcard, yes.

SVEN: Well, oh dear, it was awful – it was dreadful.

CLIVE BULL: Oh dear. Why?

SVEN: Well, Jutta was there, you know. I don't want to bore everything, but Jutta was there with this man.

CLIVE BULL: She wasn't!

SVEN: Nice, nice man but everywhere was still fish. And I had tried to get to Oslo because this is where I live. My mother is still very ill, and I wind up in Palma and the Royal Family, all the security round there, and Jutta with this man. And I just got back tonight from Gatwick.

CLIVE BULL: You sound a bit depressed about it all, really, Sven.

SVEN: It was awful, and suddenly I tune in and I hear all this cheery talk and then it is almost worse because Ingaborg, in the dry cleaners . . .

CLIVE BULL: I think you're just going to have to forget about Jutta, quite honestly, Sven, aren't you?

SVEN: Well, I can't. She's part of my life.

CLIVE BULL: What was she doing in the same place? Where is this place? You sent me a postcard of – I can't quite make it out, actually.

SVEN: It's in Palma in Majorca.

CLIVE BULL: Right. It's a very pretty photograph. A lot of fish.

SVEN: But Jutta just was there. I was trying to get to Oslo, to speak to my mother. And when I get back, Ingaborg, who I meet in the dry cleaners, she says 'Oh, same time tonight as usual?' And I didn't know what she meant. And we met for coffee. And she seems to have been going out with someone who looks like me, and I don't know what to do.

CLIVE BULL: Oh dear.

SVEN: She was saying what I wonderful lover I am but I've never kissed her.

CLIVE BULL: No?

SVEN: No, so what on earth shall I do?

CLIVE BULL: Well, I don't know. I mean, at least you're away from the fish at the moment, though.

SVEN: Thank God. Everywhere in Majorca, so many fish.

CLIVE BULL: You went to the wrong place, you see. But you're obviously hooked on her as well, aren't you?

SVEN: On Ingaborg?

CLIVE BULL: Yes.

SVEN: Yes, well I just got back and got through Duty Free and everything, and I thought to give a call just to say I was home, and I'll call you another time when I'm feeling a bit more . . .

CLIVE BULL: Well, maybe somebody could call in and give you a little bit of advice, Sven.

SVEN: I thought that nice – what's he called? In the afternoon? That man?

CLIVE BULL: Philip Hobson. Maybe you should call him about it.

SVEN: Philip Hobson, yes. Because at least I've got a full head of hair so, you know, I've got an advantage there.

CLIVE BULL: Have you? What do you look like, in fact, Sven?

SVEN: Just like this man who is going out with Ingaborg. So should I break it to Ingaborg that I am not the man she has been seeing?

CLIVE BULL: I see what you mean. It's a bit of a dilemma.

SVEN: You think Philip might help?

CLIVE BULL: I think so. What do you feel inclined to do?

SVEN: Well, it's so hard because all my life has been always fish, fish, fish, when I was brought up in a little village just outside Oslo. Everyone's always saying – you know, to get hold of women – they all say 'Hello, Sven – how many fish you catch today?' And I say 'three' and he says 'Ha, ha, ha – I catch four.' And the one who catch four goes off discoing with the women. It's a bad, bad life. Is the YTS any good?

CLIVE BULL: Yes, there's the chance that employment training could be for you, I think. I tell you what, Sven, as you sound so miserable . . .

SVEN: Well, I confess gloomy.

CLIVE BULL: Yes, well maybe we'll play a little record to cheer you up later on.

SVEN: Nothing – not fish.

CLIVE BULL: No, no. No fish.

SVEN: No Marillion.

CLIVE BULL: No, no. No Marillion. We'll try and find something not too fishy for you. Something nice and jolly.

SVEN: Beach Boys.

CLIVE BULL: pardon?

SVEN: Beach Boys.

CLIVE BULL: Something like the Beach Boys maybe, yes. We'll find a nice song to cheer you up.

SVEN: I'm sorry I sound so depressed but I've had a bad time.

CLIVE BULL: It sounds like it. And a bit of jet lag, I should think. Well, you keep off the mackerel and we'll play you a little something later on.

SVEN: Thank you.

CLIVE BULL: Thank you, Sven.

SVEN: Bye bye.

CLIVE BULL: Bye bye.

CLIVE BULL: Sven in Maida Vale. Hello.

SVEN: Hello, Clive.

CLIVE BULL: Hello, Sven.

SVEN: Well, I've been back for about a year and sorry not to call back.

CLIVE BULL: Yes, we've been wondering about you and your fish.

SVEN: Well, I had several fish which Jutta ate, I think for a call for help. But I was ringing about the smoking.

CLIVE BULL: Yes

SVEN: Of cannabis.

CLIVE BULL: Oh yes?

SVEN: And my knowledge of the effect of cannabis on fish.

CLIVE BULL: Well, what's the verdict?

SVEN: Well, they swim around in circles much as before. But luckily a bit happier. I have never tried to give them tobacco.

CLIVE BULL: No.

SVEN: But they seem quite alright. But of course what a fish does cannot translate to the human being.

CLIVE BULL: No. And, presumably, does this have the effect of ready-smoking the fish?

SVEN: Well, from my experience, smoking fish is more harmful than cannabis.

CLIVE BULL: From what everyone's been saying, almost anything is more harmful than smoking cannabis.

SVEN: No, the facts speak for themselves.

CLIVE BULL: Really?

SVEN: Yes. I feel scarcely able to speak myself because if you smoke a fish you become giddy – especially if you're underwater.

CLIVE BULL: I don't know. I smoked a salmon quite recently.

SVEN: Was it a big one?

CLIVE BULL: It was. It was a fair size, yes, and it was a farmed one though, but I didn't feel any bad effects afterwards.

SVEN: With filter?

CLIVE BULL: No.

SVEN: Well, a lot of the death-dealing qualities of the fish come from mixing them up with tobacco.

CLIVE BULL: Yes, right. Sort of flaking.

SVEN: Flaking. Exactly.

CLIVE BULL: What about in pipes?

SVEN: Well, normally I am obviously smoking because I like to put a little sprat in a pipe and put it through the water in a hubble-bubble style. And so you get the effect of the scales without any of these other sides.

CLIVE BULL: Yes. Are there any particular types of fish?

SVEN: The gudgeon. The gudgeon produce a certain high. I don't know if you have Rolling Stones, in Hyde Park, many years ago. All the crowd with me, the in crowd from Norway . . .

CLIVE BULL: All on gudgeon, were they?

SVEN: All on gudgeon, and none of us can remember being there. It is a good thing that I wrote in my diary that I was there otherwise . . .

CLIVE BULL: You wouldn't have realised.

SVEN: But stay clear of the bass.

CLIVE BULL: So in many ways, fish ought to have some sort of government health warning on them?

SVEN: In my view a lot of people go to hospital and are suffering from fish-related illnesses, and I think armed guards should keep them away. Ordinary people who don't smoke, don't drink and don't do anything cannot get in because of the fish people.

CLIVE BULL: Well, I'm going to think twice before tucking into that smoked salmon now, Sven.

SVEN: That would be wise. Jutta sends her love.

CLIVE BULL: Just say no.

SVEN: Just say no for a moment.

CLIVE BULL: That's it. Thank you for the call.

SVEN: Danke Schön.

CLIVE BULL: Jenny in Hainault, hello?

CLIVE BULL: And Sven in Swiss Cottage is next. Hello, Sven.

SVEN: Hello, Clive. I'm in such an upbeat mood at the moment, because I was trying to get through on the voting, for the talent.

CLIVE BULL: Yes?

SVEN: But then my friend, who you may know, Jutta, came round and we had a little bit of a row so I went to next door. And now I am so happy to hear everything's working fine.

CLIVE BULL: Yes. How's Jutta, then?

SVEN: Jutta, usual stuff – saying fish should have won the Euro elections, all that stuff, she go on about them all the time and I said 'Well, Jutta, it is time of me to be a man.' And she just look at me and I think 'What the hell with it,' and just go next door and make a little call to say 'Well, everything is fine in the world.' The Greens, the fish, they all vote and we all a lot better because I give up in terms of personal things and I just like to be free and feel that the fish are winning because they can't be pushed out of the sea any more.

CLIVE BULL: I've got a quiz question for you, Sven. Can you have a listen to this?

SVEN: Yes. Is a fish song? Beach Boys?

CLIVE BULL: I think you might get this one, Sven. 'The Dutch eat these lightly salted, my family eat them schmaltzed, and the Scots eat them rolled and pickled, or they can be smoked to make an excellent breakfast dish. So what are these called?'

SVEN: This is a rottweiler?

CLIVE BULL: No, it's not a rottweiler, no.

SVEN: This is a rottweiler.

CLIVE BULL: No, no. You're close.

SVEN: Underwater dogs?

CLIVE BULL: Not underwater dogs, no. Do you want one more

guess?

SVEN: Well, Shlomo is – it must be fish.

CLIVE BULL: It's fish we're talking, yes.

SVEN: That little cod balls?

CLIVE BULL: Gefilte fish balls.

SVEN: Gefilte fish balls – well, close enough.

CLIVE BULL: Well, no. It's not gefilte fish balls, no. The answer is herrings.

SVEN: Herrings, they put in balls.

CLIVE BULL: Well, they can be if you really feel that way.

SVEN: There's no prize?

CLIVE BULL: Yes, there was a prize. It was five pounds worth of fish of our choice, but I'm afraid that goes back in the jackpot now.

SVEN: Oh dear. But I'm not depressed because I'm so pleased that Jutta is out of my life and now I can talk about things I care about.

CLIVE BULL: Yes. So Jutta's gone for good now?

SVEN: No, not gone for good, no. I'm here ringing in every night because I far prefer to be on the phone and not talking to this stupid woman with her fish problems and everything else. I was close with the balls?

CLIVE BULL: I think you were, yes, and you're obviously much chirpier than last time you spoke.

SVEN: You know, Clive, is always nice to think you make a decision in your life. You think, years and years you're involved with a woman or another woman – Ingaborg, whatever – and I went to Argentina and so on and all the bullfighters and so on, but just to get back to base is so pleasant. Just to think I have something to talk about and why not have fun with the idea?

CLIVE BULL: Are you going to look for a new companion?

SVEN: Yes, yes I am. Right now. How late is it?

CLIVE BULL: It's ten to four now.

SVEN: Ten to four. Where do you get companions at ten to four?

CLIVE BULL: You could go wandering round Swiss Cottage but I wouldn't recommend it.

SVEN: Not St Pancras? In my guide it said St Pancras for . . .

CLIVE BULL: For late-night meetings?

SVEN: Well, just for a cup of coffee and talk about what you feel like, and explore each other.

CLIVE BULL: You're going to give a wide berth to the launderette this time?

SVEN: Oh yes, I don't. I think is silly. I think go to swish places.

CLIVE BULL: Yes, I think you're wise. Well, the very best of luck, Sven.

SVEN: Thank you, Clive. I just wanted to say I have been so gloomy in the past, always talking about how miserable my life is and how these women are making me miserable, but it is up to me.

CLIVE BULL: It is, yes.

SVEN: It is up to me just to go out and say 'Look, I am alive, I am a man, I have a mackintosh and I have some money in my pocket, and why don't we have another cup of tea and talk about the misery of life?' And I feel a lot more upbeat.

CLIVE BULL: So you're going to go out there and grab life by . . .

SVEN: Grab life by the throat, wrestle it to the ground and kick it to death.

CLIVE BULL: Well, that's good to hear. It's a heartening story.

SVEN: It is. It is so much due to you because late at night one feels sometimes 'Where is the little woman in the bed just caressing my forehead?' And obviously the answer nowhere. But then you think, well there is the chance to just make it possible by popping out and wandering down the street. Who knows who might be there? Why not be upbeat? Don't want to get miserable. And I feel my mood switching at the moment. I could go to downbeat any moment.

CLIVE BULL: No, no, no. You hang on upbeat.

SVEN: You try to keep up my confidence, Clive.

CLIVE BULL: You hang on there upbeat. We're all rooting for you. And I hope you meet the companion of your choice.

SVEN: What do you think the lucky number for a woman is? What do you think a good lucky letter is?

CLIVE BULL: A lucky letter?

SVEN: Yes. Should it be S for Suzanne? Should it be L for Letitia?

CLIVE BULL: I think it should be F.

SVEN: F for Farina. I go out looking now.

CLIVE BULL: You go out looking for Farina?
SVEN: Farina in Swiss Cottage. Because I don't have enough money to get mini cabs all over the rest of London.
CLIVE BULL: Well, let us know how you get on, won't you?
SVEN: I will. Thank you.
CLIVE BULL: Thank you very much indeed, Sven in Swiss Cottage.

Chapter Fourteen
Goodbye-ee

Nearly ten years since his death, Peter Cook's life seems increasingly unreal, as the era he personified slips discreetly into history. Dudley Moore is dead too, after a half a lifetime lived half a world away, on the other side of the Atlantic. Some of the supporting players are still around. Alan Bennett, that mop-topped, bespectacled, baby-faced bookworm who started out sending up Church of England clergymen in *Beyond the Fringe*, has ended up as one of England's foremost men of letters. And Doctor Jonathan Miller has ended up as Sir Jonathan Miller, a knight of the realm.

Peter's old *Private Eye* editor, Richard Ingrams, is still going strong, as is his predecessor, Christopher Booker, though Ingrams edits *The Oldie* nowadays, while Booker writes about European red tape. However several of Cook's *Eye* colleagues have already followed him into comic folklore. Auberon Waugh is gone, as is John Wells – and so is Willie Rushton, *Private Eye*'s own Hogarth, who had caricatured Cook there as Jonathan Crake. Kenneth Williams and Peter Sellers both died before Cook. Yet ironically, he was outlived by Spike Milligan – his boyhood hero, creator of The Goons.

But though the cast of Peter's real life are passing on, the characters he created become more lively with each passing year – EL Wisty, Sir Arthur Streeb-Greebling, even Sven, the lonely Norwegian. They've never dated, and they never will, any more than Cook's Victorian soulmates, Edward Lear and Lewis Carroll.

New generations will discover Wisty & Co, on the printed page, or on video, even when the generation that first saw them onstage, in the flesh, has gone the way of all flesh, and the same way as Peter Cook. WH Auden said of WB Yeats that he became his admirers. You could say the same thing about Cook. Schoolboys young enough to be his grandchildren still perform his sketches every year at Eton. Grown men, growing older, but not too old to know better, still recite 'The Worst Job I Ever Had'. And somewhere, maybe a high court judge is muttering that he could have been a miner, if only he hadn't had the Latin. He was a funny bloke, that Peter Cook. He made a lot of people laugh. And he still does.

∿

LINES ON THE OCCASION OF THE QUEEN MOTHER'S EIGHTIETH BIRTHDAY
(*TV Times*, 1980)

Oh my goodness! Gosh and golly!
Writing verse for not much lolly.
Still, I'm sure it's good exposure.
Please excuse this short enclosure,
But my pen is out of Quink.
Will this do? What do you think?
Let me add, I'm very sorry that
I was made the Poet Laureate.

ROCK STARS IN THEIR UNDERPANTS
(1980)

A foreword to Paula Yates' (self-explanatory) book of photographs, published by Virgin.

As Shakespeare, or was it Cindy Breakespeare, put it, 'Some men are born in underwear and some have underwear thrust upon them.' This is as untrue today as it was when Will or Cindy said it. For far too long a veil of secrecy has been drawn over the knickers of our teen-idols and superstars. In this book Paula Yates courageously tears down the barriers and invites us to share the often dull experience of seeing rock stars as only their doctors, priests and managers have seen them before.

We in the West are free to choose our undies, and it is this freedom of choice that we see displayed in this volume. It is a measure of our liberty that such a work would not be allowed in the Soviet Union. When I showed the proofs to one prominent dissident gardener he gasped in amazement and said 'In Russia the author would be locked up in a psychiatric ward.' He was relieved to hear that the same thing will probably happen in this country.

One of the oldest of all natural laws is that 7/8ths of everything remains hidden. The same goes for rock stars. Nevertheless, much can be learned by a careful study of their undergarments. We are all born with certain propensities and endowments and the key to our future lies in our knickers. Pantie-reading is a skilled psychic art that has never gained the same respectability as astrology or palmistry. As a Matelot on the cusp I have never really been compatible with Dudley Moore, who is a typical Boxer with Y-fronts rising. You too can learn to read underwear. A close study of these photographs will show you why certain stars will never work together, why others are doomed to die young and, worst of all, how many will live to a ripe old age. Will Rod ever marry Elton? Will Leif Garrett form a supergroup with Phil Lynott? How long will McCartney keep it up? Is Chrissie Hynde going to record a Reggae version of 'Shrimp Boats Are A-Coming'? Why aren't the Troggs bigger in Japan? Was it 'artistic differences' or incompatible underwear that led to Godley and Creme splitting with 10cc? Why isn't it Creme and Godley? And who are they anyway? The answers lie hidden in the tell-tale creases of their knickers. As you learn to 'read' underwear you will learn more about yourself and your hidden potential to become a failure. Compare your own underwear with the rock stars' and discover your common bonds and differences.

This book does not pretend to provide all the answers – that will only happen when the Bishops open the Boxer Shorts (See Ezekiel – 3rd Book of Trousers) – but if you stick to the diet you should lose those unwanted inches.

There are those who will accuse Paula of 'Body Fascism' and I am amongst them. At a time when two million people are out of work it is sickening that this woman should get rich with this hastily assembled bunch of snaps. Before agreeing to do this foreword I insisted on 'reading' her underwear and saw at a glance that she had nicked the idea from a close friend. She did however assure me that all profits from this venture would go towards wiping out endangered species. I took this to be a reference to herself and agreed to put pen to paper.

A LIFE IN THE DAY
(*Sunday Times*, 5 August 1984)

Most of my current speculation is in the Yen, so I rise at 6.30am and call Tokyo. I then ring the manager of my jojoba farm in northern California. Of course, jojoba is the secret of Eternal Beauty, which a lot of people want, so I think it is a good long-term speculation. The jojoba needs no water; but there's been a lot of rain this year and from 5000 acres we've only produced 3oz of pure jojoba oil. So it's not been a good year for jojoba.

I always go to the bathroom to make my calls. I breakfast in the bathroom where I have a very nice statue of Dorothy Squires. She's always been my inspiration; she sets my mind at ease. Anyway, I had the statue made – I have a wonderful little man who lives around the corner who runs up statues. I'm very lucky to live in this large house. I bought it for the Gothic windows, which are now so filthy that you can't see out of them. Anyway, I can't give you the exact acreage of the loo. It is substantial. I don't want to make your readers envious, but a family of 12 could live in it. In fact are living in it. They are mainly dissidents who have been complaining lately about being out of fashion. They come over here expecting to be greeted with champagne and jobs at the BBC and in publishing, and now they're living in my bathroom.

I collect my thoughts while being shaved by my Personal Daintiness people. My beauty routine is a mixture of aerobics, isotonics, isometrics and a little bit of yoga. To the observer it would look as if I was merely lifting a cup of coffee to my lips and lighting a cigarette. But it's through mental control that you are in fact exercising every muscle in your body and also cleaning out the brain of all the toxins that can gather while asleep. I've been offered a lot of money to convert this method into one of those bestsellers, but I've preferred to retain the secret. However, I can and do supplement my income by appearing in movies: it's profitable and fun. In my latest one, *Supergirl*, I am a baddy called Nigel. The arch baddy – Faye Dunaway – causes me to age 80 years in an instant.

Round about eight, I've got Roxanne, who is my bodyguard and a qualified masseuse. She's very expert, and often it's all over in five minutes. Then I drink four cups of coffee and read all the papers from the *Star* to the *Financial Times*. On a typical day, I might get Lich-ed. Patrick [Lichfield] turns up with about 4000 umbrellas and takes a few shots. We're not really on first-name terms yet: I just call him 'Lich' and he calls me 'Sir.' About 11.30 Lich has gone, and I feed a few profitable ideas into the computer. I tend to sleep with a lot of spies (all female) and it often happens that during the lovemaking, or for that matter the sleeping, they blurt out the secrets of the country's defence stystem. And I sell them to the highest bidder. But I think I'm a fairly moral person. For example, in all my arms dealings I've always sold faulty equipment to the side that I wish to lose. I sold a huge consignment of those rockets that didn't work in the Falklands to Gadaffi. He said to me rather touchingly over the phone: 'My bodyguards are your bodyguards, Peter.' Of course, they're not much use to me, being in Libya, but it's a nice thought.

Quite a lot of famous people tend to drop by, like Jonathan Miller; but if no one does, I might rummage through a large cardboard box which is always something to do in solitude. I don't bother much with *Private Eye*, haven't been there for ages. In fact, I hardly ever leave Hampstead these days. When I do, weird things seem to happen to me. The other day a total stranger came up to me in the Tube and said: 'I'm just off to the British Museum. I always go there this time of day because they've got some very good tea they serve there. Have you ever had the tea at the British Museum?' 'No,' I said. 'Well, you really ought to try it. It's very good.' I asked if he ever went to see any of the exhibits. He said: 'No, I can't stand that part of the museum, with all those old things. No, I go there for the tea.' And recently, a taxi driver pointed out a factory which he said makes the best artificial limbs in the world. Douglas Bader got his from there. 'Of course there are advantages to being limbless,' he said. 'Put it this way. Sir Douglas Bader would not have been famous if he had had legs.' I get a lot of remarks like this from total strangers. John Cleese swears I attract them somehow.

I play a lot of golf – most afternoons, actually. I find it far more satisfying than business, which after all is not very involving, since you just sign a few papers occasionally, and the decisions are very time-consuming. I usually play at the Highgate Golf Club with my agent, who's a very good golfer, an airline pilot and a neighbour of mine. We only play for holes. I love tennis but find the organisation often gets in the way – you have to go to such a lot of trouble to arrange things. I prefer to throw my clubs spontaneously into the back of the car. I'm not famously good at golf, I haven't got the killer instinct for it, but I've done the pro-celebrity tournament at Gleneagles a few times and once partnered Lee Trevino. My handicap is about 14.

In the evening, I might have dinner with somebody, or go dancing, which I love to do. But I hate going to the theatre because you can't smoke and I like to keep up to my target of 40 a day. I also avoid dinner parties for which you have to dress. I have no interest in clothes at all except for T-shirts, although I rather like buying sunglasses and funny hats. I have amassed a substantial collection of sunglasses from all over the world. I don't keep them in a velvet cabinet, no; they're conveniently scattered all over the place so there's always a pair to hand. I've observed that a lot of them seem to be under the cushions at any one time.

All my friends are very casual. Last night they left the records in heaps all over the floor. That's the price you have to pay for hospitality. But someone seems to have made off with my favourite tape, a rough-cut of 'The Sloop John B' by as group called Baby Oil and the Seychelles. It's a group I'm very closely involved with – actually I made a vocal contribution. It would have been a big hit if it had got the exposure it deserved, but contractual problems resulted in the break-up of the group before the thing was released.

I never get to sleep before two or three in the morning, due to the way my metabolism works. So before bed I generally read a bit and drink a few cups of coffee as I unwind. I like the Simenon books, but the non-Maigret ones, Dick Francis, Graham Greene; if I can't sleep I read SJ Perelman, but then I laugh myself awake. If I really want to go to sleep I read one of Clive James's long boring poems. That's not anti-Clive. They're really very relaxing.

Written by Lesley Cunliffe. Reproduced from
the Sunday Times Magazine, 5 August 1984

PERHAPS AND MAYBE – A MODERN FABLE

Once upon a time in the city of Somewhere lived an old man called Maybe with his dear wife Perhaps. Maybe worked as a water drinker and Perhaps had a job as a sip counter. Whenever Maybe took a sip of water Perhaps threw a pebble in the well.

Just watching his wife throw the pebbles made Maybe thirsty, especially when she had to walk miles to collect a basketful of pebbles because she had already used up the ones near their house.

The days passed with Maybe drinking less and less because he had to wait for longer and longer whenever Perhaps had to go off to collect more pebbles. One day Perhaps got into a muddle with her counting and that made Maybe upset because that meant there was no accurate record of how many sips he had had. He worked himself into an agitated state and would not be calmed.

Perhaps did not know what to do. She leaned her weary self against the well upon which she had centred her life, and thrown in many a pebble. And suddenly, an idea came to her. She told Maybe she knew exactly how many sips of water he had taken over the years.

She said 'Maybe – you can count the number of pebbles I have thrown in the well.'

He answered 'Perhaps – you can do that too.'

Perhaps and Maybe – they settled to count together and when they finished Maybe decided to give up his drinking job and they lived happily ever after.

The moral of this tale is:

Never say die

All is not lost

There's always hope

Two heads are better than one

A problem shared is a problem solved

A man is as good as his wife

NEVILLE

Neville was just an ordinary newt. He had no particular ambitions, but every now and then he felt that perhaps he should be doing something more worthwhile than swimming round the pond and eating bits of stuff.

'For starters,' he thought, 'perhaps I might learn the name of the stuff I am eating.'

Obviously the people to ask were his parents, but to Neville, all the other newts looked the same. There was no one around with a sign round their neck saying Neville's Mum or Neville's Dad.

He did pluck up courage to ask one newt who had a particularly long tail if he was his father, to which the baffled stranger merely replied 'Not as far as I know. Are you mine? And by the way, what is the name of the stuff I am eating?'

Nevill was lost for an answer and out of embarrassment said the first thing that came into his head.

LIMERICKS

There was a young lady called Lin,
The nicest that ever has bin.
She wasted her life
Being Peter Cook's wife
But that isn't really a sin.

That atrabilious man from the west
Kept his cards very close to his chest
But a vodka and tonic
Made him oxymoronic
But his worst was also the best.

That atrabilious man from Torquay
Was affected by melancholy,
But his bile and his spleen
And the bits inbetween
Felt much better with wife number three.

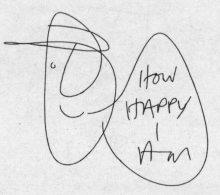

Notes

INTRODUCTION

1   *The Late Show*, BBC2, 1995
2   *Peter Cook: Bedazzled* by John Lahr, *The New Yorker* 23 January, 1995
3   *Person to Person*, BBC1, 1979
4   Roger Wilmut, *From Fringe to Flying Circus*, Methuen, 1980
5   *Something Like Fire – Peter Cook Remembered*, Methuen, 1996
6   *Peter Cook: Bedazzled* by John Lahr, *The New Yorker* 23 January, 1995
7   *Peter Cook: Bedazzled* by John Lahr, *The New Yorker* 23 January, 1995
8   *Person to Person*, BBC1, 1979
9   *Something Like Fire – Peter Cook Remembered*, Methuen, 1996
10   *Something Like Fire – Peter Cook Remembered*, Methuen, 1996
11   *Something Like Fire – Peter Cook Remembered*, Methuen, 1996
12   *Daily Express*, 1967
13   *Something Like Fire – Peter Cook Remembered*, Methuen, 1996
14   *Some Interesting Facts About Peter Cook*, Omnibus, BBC1, 1995
15   *Some Interesting Facts About Peter Cook*, Omnibus, BBC1, 1995
16   *Some Interesting Facts About Peter Cook*, Omnibus, BBC1, 1995
17   *Something Like Fire – Peter Cook Remembered*, Methuen, 1996

18 *Some Interesting Facts About Peter Cook*, Omnibus, BBC1, 1995
19 *Something Like Fire – Peter Cook Remembered*, Methuen, 1996
20 *Some Interesting Facts About Peter Cook*, Omnibus, BBC1, 1995
21 *Something Like Fire – Peter Cook Remembered*, Methuen, 1996
22 *Daily Mail*, 1994
23 *Something Like Fire – Peter Cook Remembered*, Methuen, 1996
24 *Something Like Fire – Peter Cook Remembered*, Methuen, 1996
25 *Something Like Fire – Peter Cook Remembered*, Methuen, 1996
26 *Something Like Fire – Peter Cook Remembered*, Methuen, 1996
27 *Something Like Fire – Peter Cook Remembered*, Methuen, 1996
28 *London Review of Books*, 1995
29 *Some Interesting Facts About Peter Cook*, Omnibus, BBC1, 1995
30 *Something Like Fire – Peter Cook Remembered*, Methuen, 1996
31 *Some Interesting Facts About Peter Cook*, Omnibus, BBC1, 1995
32 *Some Interesting Facts About Peter Cook*, Omnibus, BBC1, 1995
33 *Something Like Fire – Peter Cook Remembered*, Methuen, 1996
34 *Something Like Fire – Peter Cook Remembered*, Methuen, 1996
35 *Something Like Fire – Peter Cook Remembered*, Methuen, 1996
36 *Pebble Mill*, BBC1, 1994
37 *Some Interesting Facts About Peter Cook*, Omnibus, BBC1, 1995

Chapter One

1   *Something Like Fire – Peter Cook Remembered*, Methuen, 1996
2   *Something Like Fire – Peter Cook Remembered*, Methuen, 1996
3   *Something Like Fire – Peter Cook Remembered*, Methuen, 1996
4   *From Fringe to Flying Circus* by Roger Wilmut, Methuen, 1980
5   *From Fringe to Flying Circus* by Roger Wilmut, Methuen, 1980
6   *From Fringe to Flying Circus* by Roger Wilmut, Methuen, 1980
7   *From Fringe to Flying Circus* by Roger Wilmut, Methucn, 1980
8   *From Fringe to Flying Circus* by Roger Wilmut, Methuen, 1980
9   *From Fringe to Flying Circus* by Roger Wilmut, Methuen, 1980
10 *From Fringe to Flying Circus* by Roger Wilmut, Methuen, 1980
11 'Can English Satire Draw Blood?' Jonathan Miller, Observer, 1961
12 *From Fringe to Flying Circus* by Roger Wilmut, Methuen, 1980

Chapter Two

1   *That Was Satire That Was*, Humphrey Carpenter, Gollancz, 2000
2   *Something Like Fire – Peter Cook Remembered*, Methuen, 1996
3   Alan Bennett, *Writing Home*, Faber & Faber, 1997
4   *Some Interesting Facts About Peter Cook*, Omnibus, BBC1, 1995
5   *Some Interesting Facts About Peter Cook*, Omnibus, BBC1, 1995

6   *Something Like Fire – Peter Cook Remembered*, Methuen, 1996
7   *Something Like Fire – Peter Cook Remembered*, Methuen, 1996
8   *Blood From a Stone, The Complete Beyond the Fringe*, Methuen, 1987
9   Alan Bennett, *Writing Home*, Faber & Faber, 1997
10 Roger Wilmut, *From Fringe to Flying Circus*, Methuen, 1980
11 *Something Like Fire – Peter Cook Remembered*, Methuen, 1996

CHAPTER THREE

1   Roger Wilmut, *From Fringe to Flying Circus*, Methuen, 1980
2   *Daily Express*, 1967
3   *Daily Express*, 1967

CHAPTER FOUR

1   Roger Wilmut, *From Fringe To Flying Circus*, Methuen, 1980
2   Roger Wilmut, *From Fringe To Flying Circus*, Methuen, 1980

CHAPTER FIVE

1   Roger Wilmut, *From Fringe To Flying Circus*, Methuen, 1980
2   Roger Wilmut, *From Fringe To Flying Circus*, Methuen, 1980

CHAPTER SIX

1   *Something Like Fire – Peter Cook Remembered*, 1996
2   *Something Like Fire – Peter Cook Remembered*, 1996
3   *The Life and Times of Private Eye*, Richard Ingrams, Penguin, 1971
4   Auberon Waugh, *Will This Do?*, Century, 1991
5   Patrick Marnham, *The Private Eye Story*, Andre Deutsch, 1982
6   *Something Like Fire – Peter Cook Remembered*, 1996

CHAPTER SEVEN

1 Roger Wilmut, *From Fringe to Flying Circus*, Methuen, 1980
2 Roger Wilmut, *From Fringe to Flying Circus*, Methuen, 1980

CHAPTER EIGHT

1 *Some Interesting Facts About Peter Cook*, Omnibus, BBC1, 1995
2 *Something Like Fire – Peter Cook Remembered*, Methuen, 1996
3 *Some Interesting Facts About Peter Cook*, Omnibus, BBC1, 1995
4 *Today*, 1993
5 *Something Like Fire – Peter Cook Remembered*, Methuen, 1996

CHAPTER NINE

1 [Introduction] *Something Like Fire – Peter Cook Remembered*, 1996
1 Enoch Powell (1912–98) Conservative MP for Wolverhampton SW, 1950–74; Ulster Unionist MP for South Down, 1974–87.
2 Indira Gandhi (1917–84) Prime Minister of India, 1966–77 & 1980–84.
3 Bernard Levin (1928–) Journalist.
4 James Callaghan (1912–) Labour MP for Cardiff, 1945–87; Labour Prime Minister, 1976–9; Baron, 1987.
5 Helmut Schmidt (1918–) Chancellor of West Germany, 1974–83.
6 Reginald Bosanquet (1932–84) Newsreader.
7 Evelyn Waugh (1902–66) Novelist
8 James Goldsmith (1933–97) Businessman. Knight, 1976.
9 Alfred Denning (1899-1999) Master of the Rolls, 1962–82. Knight, 1944; Baron, 1957.
10 Leslie Scarman (1911–) Judge. Knight, 1961; Baron, 1977.

11   Jayne Mansfield (1933–67) American actress.

12   Idi Amin (1925–) President of Uganda, 1971–9.

13   Denis Healey (1917–) Labour MP for Leeds, 1952–92; Chancellor of the Exchequer, 1974–9. Baron, 1992.

14   Harold Wilson (1916–95) Labour MP for Ormskirk 1945–50; MP for Huyton, 1950–83; Prime Minister, 1964–70 & 1974–6. KG, 1976; Baron, 1983.

15   Francis Pakenham, Seventh Earl of Longford (1905–2001) Politician and social reformer.

16   John Betjeman (1906–84) Poet Laureate, 1972; Knight, 1969.

18   Jimmy Carter (1924–) Democratic President of the United States 1977–81.

19   Peter Jay (1937–) Economics Editor of *The Times*, 1967–77; Ambassador to the United States, 1977–9.

20   David Owen (1938–) MP for Plymouth, 1966–92; Foreign Secretary, 1977–9; left Labour Party in 1982, as one of the founders of the Social Democratic Party; leader of the SDP, 1983–90. Baron, 1992.

21   Melvyn Bragg (1939–) Novelist, author, broadcaster. Editor and presenter of *The South Bank Show* since 1978. Lord Bragg of Wigton, 1998.

22   Jeffrey Archer (1940–) Novelist. Conservative MP for Louth, 1969–74; Deputy Chairman of the Conservative Party, 1985–6. Baron, 1992.

23   Jay's father-in-law was the prime minister, James Callaghan.

24   Jay was Economics Editor of *The Times* from 1967–1977.

25   Raquel Welch (1940–) American actress. Appeared with Peter Cook and Dudley Moore in the feature film written by Peter, *Bedazzled* (1967).

26   Mary Whitehouse (1910–2001) Moral media campaigner. Launched the National Viewers & Listeners Association in 1965, and brought a private prosecution against *Gay News* in 1977.

27   As Director General of the BBC, Carleton Greene had sanctioned *That Was the Week That Was*, the short-lived but successful satirical show which made the name of David Frost.

28   The Scottish football team had beaten England 2-1. At the

end of the game, cheerful but unruly Scottish fans invaded the pitch, tore up turf and broke goalposts.

29 Antony Armstrong-Jones, Lord Snowdon (1930–). Photographer, married Princess Margaret in 1961, divorced 1978. Earl, 1961.

30 Margaret Trudeau (1948–) Wife of Pierre Trudeau (1919–2000), the Liberal Prime Minister of Canada, 1968–79 & 1980–4. They married in 1971 and were divorced in 1971.

31 The Sex Pistols, the group that epitomised Punk Rock.

32 Johnny Speight (1920–98) Comedy writer, most famous as the creator of Alf Garnett.

33 The Sex Pistols film, *The Great Rock & Roll Swindle* (1980), was actually written and directed by Julien Temple.

34 Tom Driberg, Lord Bradwell (1905–76) Journalist, politician.

35 John Osborne (1929–94) Playwright.

36 Virginia Wade (1946–) British tennis player, won the US Open (1968), Australian Championship (1972) and the Wimbledon women's singles (1977).

37 Ilie Nastase (1946–) Romanian tennis player, won the US Open (1972) and the French Open (1973).

38 Bertrand Russell (1872–1970) Philosopher and mathematician. Third Earl Russell, 1931.

39 Diana Dors (1931–84) British actress.

40 Erich von Daeniken (1935–) Swiss author. His most famous book is *Chariots of the Gods* (1968), which explores the hypothesis that our ancient civilisations may have been inspired by extraterrestrial visitors.

41 Uri Geller (1946–) Israeli celebrity psychic and paranormalist. Most famous for his uncanny ability to bend spoons.

42 British Pools winner, whose autobiography later became a musical.

43 Jacqueline Bouvier Kennedy Onassis (1929–94) Married Senator (later President) John F. Kennedy in 1953 and Aristotle Onassis, Greek shipowner, financier and founder of Olympic Airways, in 1968.

44 Desmond Morris (1928–) British zoologist, broadcaster and writer, whose books include *The Naked Ape* (1967).

45 Leonid Brezhnev (1906–82) Soviet politician. First Secretary of the Communist Party, 1964–82; President of the USSR, 1960–4 & 1977–82.

46 Alexei Kosygin (1904–80) Soviet politician. Prime Minister of the USSR, 1964–80.

47 See Introductions to Chapter Ten.

CHAPTER TEN

1 Auberon Waugh, The Last Word, Michael Joseph, 1980
2 Auberon Waugh, The Last Word, Michael Joseph, 1980
3 *Something Like Fire – Peter Cook Remembered*, Methuen, 1996
4 *Something Like Fire – Peter Cook Remembered*, Methuen, 1996

CHAPTER ELEVEN

1 *Something Like Fire – Peter Cook Remembered*, Methuen, 1996
2 *Something Like Fire – Peter Cook Remembered*, Methuen, 1996

CHAPTER TWELVE

1 *Independent*, 1993
2 *Daily Mail*, 1968
3 *Something Like Fire – Peter Cook Remembered*, Methuen, 1996
4 *Something Like Fire – Peter Cook Remembered*, Methuen, 1996
5 *Golf World*, 1993
6 Tommy Docherty (1928–) Footballer. Played for Scotland, Preston North End, Celtic and Arsenal. Managed Scotland, Chelsea, Man Utd, Aston Villa, Derby County and Queen's Park Rangers.

7   Dave Mackay (1934–) Footballer. Played for Scotland, Hearts, Spurs, Derby County and Swindon Town. Managed Swindon Town, Nottm Forest, Derby Country, Birmingham City and Walsall.

CHAPTER THIRTEEN

1   *Something Like Fire – Peter Cook Remembered,* Methuen, 1996

COMING SOON IN CENTURY HARDBACK

Goodbye Again

William Cook ed.

Peter Cook and Dudley Moore are still commonly regarded as the greatest comic double act that Great Britain has ever produced. Today it's impossible to imagine modern sketch shows without them. If you're a fan of *Monty Python*, *The Comic Strip* or *The Fast Show*, then you're a fan of Cook and Moore. This collection of their works is a comprehensive compilation of the finest sketches that Cook and Moore ever wrote together – from the beginning of their partnership, in the groundbreaking stage show, *Beyond The Fringe*, to the notorious taboo busting Derek and Clive LPs that captured the spirit of punk rock, and inspired the scantological anarchy of Alternative Comedy. Featuring transcripts of one night stands long since almost forgotten, such as their Royal Variety performance, as well as a wealth of virtually unknown material, including previously unpublished scripts for *Not Only But Also*, *Goodbye Again* promises to be a revelation, even for Cook and Moore's most informed fans.

Goodbye Again will chart the extraordinary friendship between the two men and it's almost telepathic intensity, which not only brought them together but also pulled them apart time after time, until their eventual reconciliation.

It's a book not only for confirmed Cook and Moore fans, old and new, but also for anyone who's interested in comedy, popular culture – and, above all, for anyone who loves to laugh.

CENTURY

Something Like Fire
Peter Cook Remembered

Lin Cook ed.

An intimate and entertaining portrait of one of comedy's greatest geniuses by those who knew Peter Cook best and can write about his rare talent. The contributors include Clive Anderson, Alan Bennett, John Cleese, Stephen Fry, William Goldman, Barry Humphries, Eric Idle, Dudley Moore and Michael Palin.

'Read it for yourself. No other biography will ever better tell the truth'
The Times

'One thing nearly all of the friends invited to contribute to this book have in common: by God they can write . . . The authors are a ministry of all the talents; the book is most enjoyable'
Spectato

'This book contains excellent contributions by comic writers. The gems are Peter Cook's'
Sunday Times

arrow books